CONTAINMENT:
DOCUMENTS ON AMERICAN POLICY
AND STRATEGY,
1945–1950

CONTAINMENT:
DOCUMENTS ON AMERICAN POLICY AND STRATEGY, 1945-1950

Thomas H. Etzold and John Lewis Gaddis

EDITORS

NEW   YORK   COLUMBIA   UNIVERSITY   PRESS   1978

Library of Congress Cataloging in Publication Data
Main entry under title:
Containment: documents on American policy and strategy, 1945–1950.
Includes bibliographical references and index.
1. United States—Foreign relations—1945–1953—Sources.
2. United States—National security—History—Sources.
3. United States—Foreign relations—Russia—Sources.
4. Russia—Foreign relations—United States—Sources.
I. Etzold, Thomas H.   II. Gaddis, John Lewis.
E813.C68   327.73   77-20024
ISBN 0-231-04398-8
ISBN 0-231-04399-6 pbk.

Columbia University Press
New York   Guildford, Surrey
Copyright © 1978   Columbia University Press
All rights reserved
Printed in the United States of America

CONTENTS

4 / IMPLEMENTATION: THE SOVIET UNION AND THE COMMUNIST WORLD, 1948–49   161

PREFACE

"ECRASEZ LES DOCUMENTS! Or, rather, the documents books." [1] Such was the possibly intemperate reaction of one of us to the recent publication of a new documentary collection on World War II diplomacy. After making this statement, collaboration on a similar collection dealing with the early Cold War might seem courageous, foolhardy, or merely inconsistent; we prefer to regard it as confirming the proposition that to every sweeping generalization there is at least one notable exception.

Our purpose in publishing this collection is to illustrate the first systematic attempt by the United States in peacetime to integrate political and military considerations in national security planning. The initial product of that effort—the strategy of containment—shaped United States foreign policy during the early stages of the Cold War. The institutions involved—the National Security Council, the Policy Planning Staff, and the Joint Chiefs of Staff—remain at or near the center of policy formulation to this day.

We believe that a collection of this type is needed for four reasons: (1) most of the documents printed here have only recently become available through the process of declassification; (2) although a substantial percentage of them have appeared in the Department of State's *Foreign Relations* series, that indispensable publication makes no attempt to single out documents for particular emphasis, or to make comparisons between them; (3) others of these documents have been published individually in various sources, but not in *Foreign Relations;* (4) finally, a considerable number of the documents appear in print here for the first time, notably Documents 10, 12, 22, and most of the documents on strategic planning included in Chapter 6.

No collection of this size can aspire to comprehensiveness, especially for a period in which documentation is so copious. We have tried, rather, to identify and publish in a single volume those documents most influential in

1. Thomas H. Etzold, "The Great Documents Deluge," Society for Historians of American Foreign Relations *Newsletter,* VII (March 1976), 14–21.

shaping United States foreign and military policy between the end of World War II and the onset of the Korean War. Not everyone will agree with our choices; nonetheless we have made what we believe to be a conscientious effort to select documents that represent positions held within the government at the time and demonstrate how policy evolved during the period in question.

Many individuals and several institutions have assisted us in this project. Vice Admiral Julien J. LeBourgeois, USN (Ret.), the former president of the Naval War College, encouraged us to undertake it. The Naval War College Center for Advanced Research supported copying and travel expenses. Jeanne W. Davis and Steven Skancke of the National Security Council, William Cunliffe and Milton Gustafson of the National Archives, Wilmer P. Sparrow of the Department of State, and Philip D. Lagerquist of the Harry S. Truman Library responded patiently and promptly to requests for information and documents. Jonathan Knight of the American Association of University Professors first suggested that we undertake this volume. David A. Rosenberg of the University of Wisconsin at Milwaukee shared generously with us the results of his own findings, and provided valuable suggestions regarding the selection of documents. Steven T. Ross of the Naval War College assisted us in the early stages of this project, and Samuel F. Wells, Jr., of the University of North Carolina, and James E. King of the Naval War College gave us the benefit of their comments at its conclusion. Our wives, Suzanne B. Etzold and Barbara Gaddis, provided both encouragement and suggestions for improved organization and presentation of these documents. As always, it has been a pleasure to work with Bernard Gronert and the Columbia University Press.

Nonetheless we alone are responsible for the final selection of documents (which appear here in their original punctuation, with only obvious typographical errors corrected), the headnotes, and the introductory essays. Although this was in every way a collaborative project, Gaddis assumed chief responsibility for chapters 1, 2, 4, and 7, Etzold for chapters 3, 5, and 6.

In appreciation for the institutional support provided by the Naval War College, we have designated the Naval War College Foundation, Inc., a nonprofit association, as the recipient of royalties from the sale of this volume.

Newport, Rhode Island   Thomas H. Etzold
July 1977   John Lewis Gaddis

ABBREVIATIONS AND ACRONYMS

AA	antiaircraft
ABC	atomic, biological, and chemical weapons
AEC	Atomic Energy Commission
ASW	antisubmarine warfare
AW	all weather
CFM	Council of Foreign Ministers
CIA	Central Intelligence Agency
CINCAL	Commander in Chief, Alaska
CINCEUR	Commander in Chief, Europe
CINCFE	Commander in Chief, Far East
CINCLANT	Commander in Chief, Atlantic
CINCNELM	Commander in Chief, U.S. Naval Forces, Eastern Atlantic and Mediterranean
CINCPAC	Commander in Chief, Pacific
CMEA	Council of Mutual Economic Assistance
DC	Defense Committee
ECA	Economic Cooperation Administration
ERP	European Recovery Program
EWP	Emergency War Plan
FBI	Federal Bureau of Investigation
FY	fiscal year
GATT	General Agreement on Tariffs and Trade
IBRD	International Bank for Reconstruction and Development
IMF	International Monetary Fund
ITO	International Trade Organization
JCS	Joint Chiefs of Staff
JSPC	Joint Strategic Plans Committee

LOC	lines of communication
MB	medium bomber
MDAP	Mutual Defense Assistance Program
MOC	Military Offensive Complex
MVD	Ministry of Internal Affairs (Soviet Union)
NAP	North Atlantic Pact
NATO	North Atlantic Treaty Organization
NME	National Military Establishment
NSC	National Security Council
NSRB	National Security Resources Board
OEEC	Organization for European Economic Cooperation
ORE	Office of Research and Evaluation
PICAO	Provisional International Civil Aviation Organization
POL	petroleum, oil, and lubricants
PPS	Policy Planning Staff
RAF	Royal Air Force
SAC	Strategic Air Command
SANACC	State-Army-Navy-Air Force Coordinating Committee
SC	Secretary's Committee (Department of State)
SCAP	Supreme Commander Allied Powers (Japan)
SWNCC	State-War-Navy Coordinating Committee
UNAEC	United Nations Atomic Energy Commission
UNESCO	United Nations Educational, Scientific, and Cultural Organization
UNO	United Nations Organization
UNRRA	United Nations Relief and Rehabilitation Administration
USIE	United States Information and Educational Exchange Program
VHB	very heavy bomber

CONTAINMENT:
DOCUMENTS ON AMERICAN POLICY
AND STRATEGY,
1945–1950

AMERICAN ORGANIZATION FOR NATIONAL SECURITY 1945–50

Thomas H. Etzold

WAR, IT HAS been said, is the great arbiter of institutions; so, one must add, is Cold War. In the Second World War, officials concerned with American organization for the employment of military force in the interests of state overcame the primitive inadequacy of prewar institutions and developed a politico-military bureaucracy unprecedented in size and complexity. Impressed by the lessons of war, American officials from about 1944 onward paid increasing attention to the problems of managing diplomacy and warfare in complementary ways, and directed much of their thought to organizational improvements that would outlast war's emergency. Indeed, the interest in reorganizing the government for foreign and military affairs took on such momentum that one may suspect certain officials of longing for war's end less in anticipation of the blessings of peace than in hope of a timely opportunity to institutionalize the improvised arrangements of the war years regarding defense and diplomacy. When growing Soviet-American tension reinforced the new linkage between foreign policy and military capability, organizational concerns were both confirmed in importance and accelerated in pace.

I

World War II revealed American lack of preparedness both in the military and political spheres. The Rainbow Plans—American war plans of the in-

This essay owes much to the information assembled in Robert D. Little's useful study, "Organizing for Strategic Planning, 1945–1950: The National System and the Air Force" (Washington: 1964), declassified with deletions on December 1, 1975).

terwar years, color-coded in the hues of a rainbow—had in effect no operational significance because of lack of logistic preparation and failure to integrate political with military considerations (military officers had considered these plans so "secret" that their contents were not revealed to the highest-ranking officers of the Department of State until the very eve of war in Europe). The war in Asia opened for the United States with a resounding failure of military intelligence and political analysis. It continued in Asia and in Europe with challenges in every dimension—geographic, matériel, manpower—and plagued by the difficulties of coalition warfare, which complicated definition of objectives, formulation of strategy, and conduct of operations.

The war's physical scope and political context—the necessity of working with the British—influenced the first attempts of American officers and officials to deal with weaknesses of government organization for war and policy. Combined planning with the British virtually required that the United States emulate the British system of joint staff work, and, in one of the first innovations of wartime organization, American officials formed a Joint Chiefs of Staff (JCS), with supporting committees analogous to those in the British staff. (See Figure 1.)

The Joint Chiefs of Staff constituted a genuine improvement in American organization for devising and executing military policy and strategy. In war, the Chiefs helped to formulate military policy in line with national policy as expressed by the President. The Chiefs also undertook to devise strategic concepts that, after presidential approval, would become the basis for outline war plans within a framework of defined national goals. In fulfilling wartime responsibilities, the Joint Chiefs of Staff worked via a committee system, with principal committees for strategic planning and for logistical planning. With representatives from each of the services, the committees supervised the efforts of working groups drawn from the staffs of the individual services; these groups actually translated strategic concepts into outline war plans.

Of course, the formation of a joint staff did not alleviate all the problems of organization in war. For one thing, many factors disturbed the orderly operation of the new American staff. In British-American planning, the Combined Chiefs of Staff, an interlocking British and American military staff, often interfered with the plans of the American Joint Chiefs of Staff. Further, the dispositions of Roosevelt, Churchill, and many high military leaders to make strategic decisions outside of channels also hindered the approach to order via organizational change. Finally, the United States

Figure 1

THE JOINT CHIEFS OF STAFF, 1942

Mirroring the British

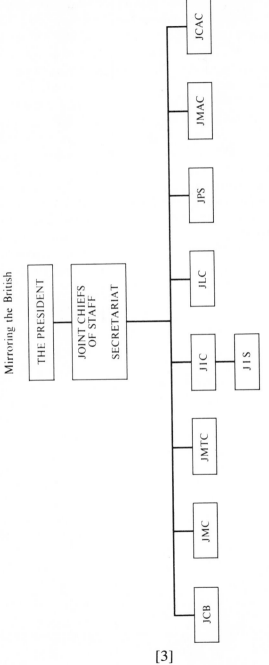

Note:

JCAC — Joint Civil Affairs Committee
JCB — Joint Communications Board
JIC — Joint Intelligence Committee
JIS — Joint Intelligence Staff
JLC — Joint Logistics Committee

JMAC — Joint Munitions Allocations Committee
JMC — Joint Meteorological Committee
JMTC — Joint Military Transportation Committee
JPS — Joint Staff Planners

Source: Little, "Organizing for Strategic Planning," p. 88.

[3]

Army and Navy continued to make plans and control military operations apart from the new joint staff, as did the Army Air Force.[1]

A second and more important reason for the continuation of wartime organizational problems was the failure to coordinate military and political affairs at any point below presidential level. Franklin D. Roosevelt's haphazard, highly personal approach to government organization is well known. (See Figure 2). Whatever success the President may have had in peacetime and in domestic affairs with his informal style, that style—it was scarcely a method—proved inadequate to the great issues of wartime. One man could not, finally, join either the disparate considerations of policy and strategy or the discrete concerns of various agencies in competition and in disagreement. The evolution of the Morgenthau Plan for dealing with a yet-to-be-conquered Germany illustrated the difficulty only too well. The Joint Chiefs of Staff, the Department of State, the Treasury Department, the Foreign Economic Administration, several influential individuals, and the British Government all besieged Roosevelt with their points of view. Policy made

Figure 2

THE PRESIDENT AS COORDINATOR-IN-CHIEF:
Military and Political Affairs, 1942-44

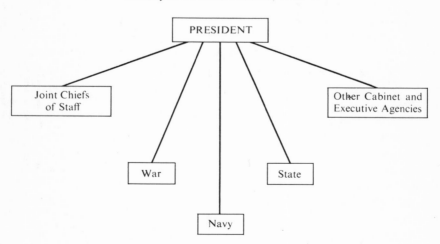

1. Little, "Organizing for Strategic Planning," pp. 1, 2. These difficulties can be followed in great detail in volumes of the official history, *The United States Army in World War II: The War Department*, IV, pts. 2, 3, 4 (Washington: various), by Mark S. Watson, Ray S. Cline, Maurice Matloff, Edwin M. Snell, Richard M. Leighton, and Robert W. Coakley. See also Michael S. Sherry, *Planning for the Next War: American Plans for Postwar Defense, 1941-46* (New Haven: Yale University Press, 1977).

one day was unmade the next, as the President refereed and announced the winners in successive bureaucratic contests over the issues.[2]

The experience of politicking over policy for a defeated Germany in the latter months of 1944 convinced a number of high government officials that the time had come to improve the coordination of political and military policy, especially given the anticipated problems of war's end and aftermath. The organizational result of this conviction was the establishment in December 1944, by an exchange of letters among the Secretaries of State, War, and Navy, of the State-War-Navy Coordinating Committee (SWNCC). Composed of assistant secretaries from the three departments, SWNCC almost immediately assumed considerable importance, drawing up plans for military government in occupied enemy areas, devising surrender terms, and considering such other questions as postwar aid to China. Representatives of the Joint Chiefs of Staff sat in on committee deliberations, with the result that differences in political and military perspectives often were discovered and assessed, if not always resolved, before matters went to the President for decision.[3] (Figure 3 illustrates the intermediary coordinating position of SWNCC.)

The end of the war naturally did not bring an end to the work either of the Joint Chiefs of Staff or of SWNCC. Both the responsibilities and the committee system of the JCS continued after the war; indeed, both soon expanded. In 1946, the Chiefs received the responsibility for strategic direction of American fighting forces, adding operational control to the previous burden of planning. The committee system, which had burgeoned to meet war's exigencies, remained vital, and in fact experienced growth as well as refinement. The Joint Strategic Survey Committee, a senior planning group, together with committees and working groups concerned with war plans and logistics, continued as the nucleus of the system, along with a much-strengthened intelligence group, a new committee on weapons development, a reorganized munitions and mobilization committee, and many other committees from the war years. (See Figure 4.) Like the Joint Chiefs of Staff, the State-War-Navy Coordinating Committee functioned from 1945 to 1947 pending the "ultima ratio" of the bureaucrat, namely, a statutory rationalization of a structure for coordinating political and military affairs.

The work of the JCS and SWNCC provided elements of continuity and di-

2. The most recent treatment of the Morgenthau Plan's complex evolution is Warren F. Kimball, *Swords or Ploughshares? The Morgenthau Plan for Defeated Nazi Germany, 1943–1946* (Philadelphia: Lippincott, 1976). For a brief and engaging treatment of the origin and functioning of SWNCC, see Ernest R. May, "The Development of Political-Military Consultation in the United States," *Political Science Quarterly,* LXX, No. 2 (June 1955), 161–80.
3. Little, "Organizing for Strategic Planning," p. 88.

Thomas H. Etzold

Figure 3

POLITICO-MILITARY COORDINATION 1944-47:
First Improvements

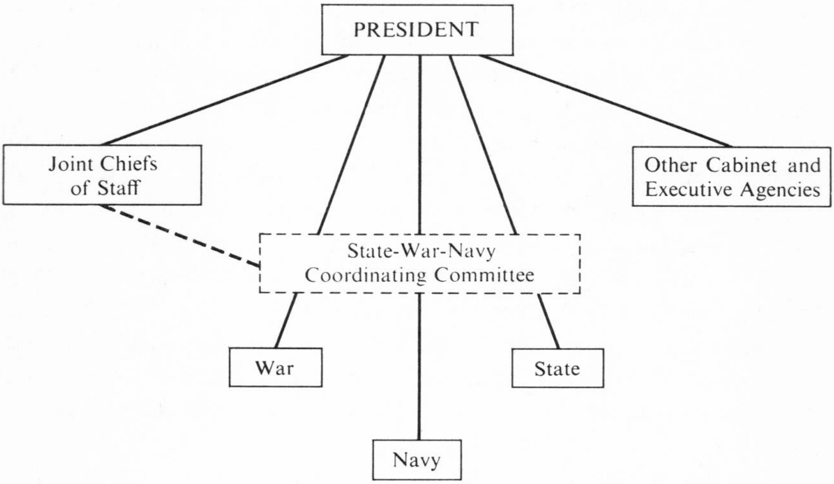

rection for national security concerns amid the organizational mania from 1945 to 1947. The war had indeed shown up weaknesses in American institutions, but it had not indicated appropriate solutions with any clarity. Great debates developed over such questions as whether to unify or diversify the military services, whether to expand or to circumscribe the powers of the presidency, how to reorganize the Department of State, the Foreign Service, and the forty-three other government agencies that in wartime had entered into overseas operation and representation. There was also considerable disagreement over how to organize and assign responsibility for collection and dissemination of intelligence, in view of the obvious prewar deficiencies of the military services in this regard. Out of war's experiences and improvisations in these contexts, only two premises met with widespread agreement among American officials responsible for formulating policy in defense and diplomacy: the value of joint staff planning and command was affirmed, and the need for integrated consideration of political and military factors bearing on U.S. security was recognized.

The many disagreements over government organization might never have been resolved had it not been for the circumstances of the Cold War, which made it essential to address national security concerns with a constancy un-

Figure 4

THE JOINT CHIEFS OF STAFF, 1946

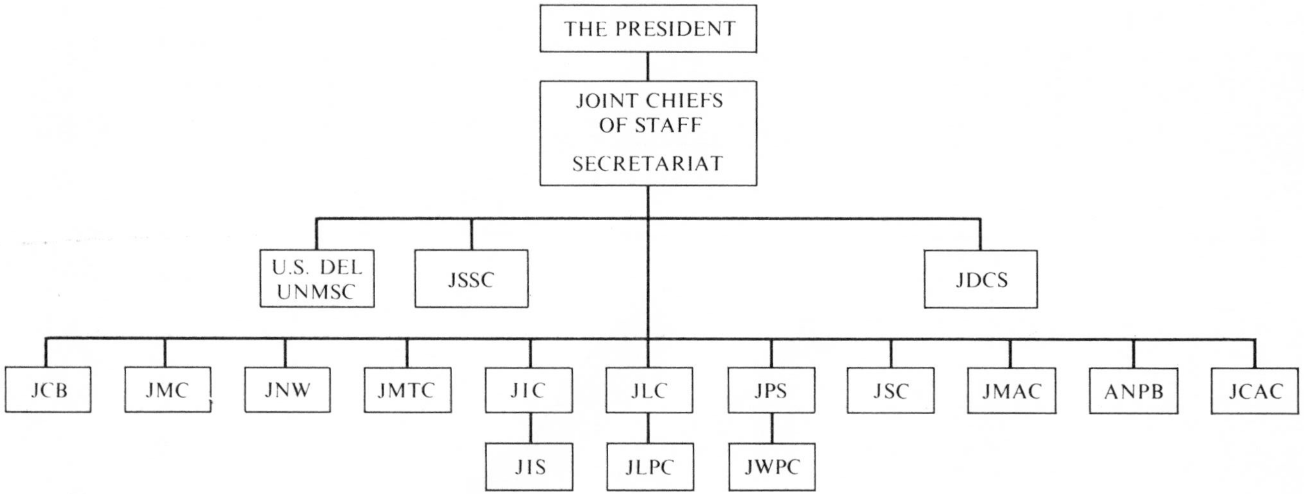

Note:

ANPB — Army-Navy Petroleum Board
JCAC — Joint Civil Affairs Committee
JCB — Joint Communications Board
JDCS — Joint Deputy Chiefs of Staff
JIC — Joint Intelligence Committee
JIS — Joint Intelligence Staff
JLC — Joint Logtstics Committee
JLPC — Joint Logistics Plans Committee

JMAC — Joint Munitions Allocations Committee
JMC — Joint Meteorological Committee
JMTC — Joint Military Transportation Committee
JNW — Joint Committee on New Weapons and Equipment
JPS — Joint Staff Planners
JSC — Joint Security Control
JSSC — Joint Strategic Survey Committee
JWPC — Joint War Plans Committee
UNMSC — UN Military Staff Committee

[7]

traditional for the United States in peacetime. In the Cold War as in world war, American policy makers faced the rigorous necessity of ordering policies and interests worldwide into a consistent and analytically helpful pattern.[4] Similarly, the wartime problem of allocating resources—whether financial, military, or merely the undervalued but extremely scarce resource of high-level attention—endured into the Cold War, and if anything became more acute. Many new postwar problems were as urgent as those of wartime. Some were associated with terminating the war and making the transition to peacetime political and economic relations with erstwhile enemies and friends; some were novel issues, such as the management of atomic power. Paradoxically, although none of these problems could await amelioration of Soviet-American antagonisms, few if any of them could be resolved while the antagonisms remained so intense.

II

The National Security Act of 1947 offered answers to many of the questions about government organization raised by the war and by the Cold War.[5] The provisions of this much-written-about act have become widely known, but to clarify the structure of national security affairs from 1947 to 1950, with special reference to agencies producing the documents printed in this book, it may be helpful to recapitulate the organizational results of the statute. In setting out a new framework for policy, decision, and operation in political and military affairs, the National Security Act dealt with three principal issues, each with a context in the experience of World War II: coordination of political and military policy; improved intelligence capability; and rationalization of the defense community, including the various services.

At the head of the new American organization for national security, the President of the United States directed an apparatus which, though complex, possessed greater coherence than either prewar or wartime institutions. (See Figure 5)

In addressing the first principal concern mentioned above, coordination of political and military matters, the National Security Act created two new agencies to assist the President: the National Security Council (NSC) and the

---

4. This point is discussed at greater length in Thomas H. Etzold, "The Far East in American Strategy, 1948–1951," in Etzold, editor, *Aspects of Sino-American Relations Since 1784: Hazy Principles for Changing Policies* (New York: Franklin Watts/New Viewpoints, 1978).

5. The National Security Act of 1947 appears in 61 Stat. 495.

Figure 5

ORGANIZATION FOR NATIONAL SECURITY, 1947

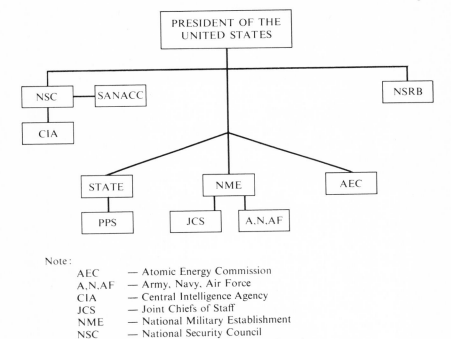

Note:

AEC	— Atomic Energy Commission
A,N,AF	— Army, Navy, Air Force
CIA	— Central Intelligence Agency
JCS	— Joint Chiefs of Staff
NME	— National Military Establishment
NSC	— National Security Council
NSRB	— National Security Resources Board
PPS	— Policy Planning Staff
SANACC	— State-Army-Navy-Air Force Coordinating Committee
STATE	— U.S. Department of State

National Security Resources Board (NSRB). The National Security Council was to advise the President "with respect to the integration of domestic, foreign, and military policies relating to the national security so as to enable the military services and the other departments and agencies of the government to cooperate more effectively in matters involving the national security." [6] In another important provision, the act directed the NSC to "assess and appraise the objectives, commitments, and risks of the United States in relation to our actual and potential military power," [7] and to make recommendations to the President in such matters. The law also fixed membership

6. 61 Stat. 496.
7. 61 Stat. 497.

on the NSC, naming the President, the Secretaries of State, Defense, Army, Navy, and Air Force, and the Chairman of the National Security Resources Board. (See Figure 6) The act further specified other officials whom the President had authority to include, such as the secretaries of the other executive departments and the chairmen of the new Munitions Board and the Research and Development Board, the functions of which are defined below. In 1949, in response to complaints that military representatives were dominating the NSC, Congress amended the membership, eliminating the three service secretaries from the Council.[8]

Subsequent to the creation of the NSC, the State-War-Navy Coordinating Committee in October 1947 received a change of name (or perhaps one should say of acronym). Reflecting both the establishment of the NSC and another of the National Security Act's innovations, an independent Air Force, SWNCC became SANACC—that is, the State-Army-Navy-Air Force Coordinating Committee—with its function altered to that of advising and aiding the NSC. Unanimous decisions of SANACC were to be considered in effect decisions of the Secretaries of State, Defense, Army, Navy, and Air Force. SANACC remained active for several years, producing important background papers and preliminary decisions for the NSC.[9] It is important to note that neither SANACC nor the NSC interfered with the right of direct access to the President enjoyed by cabinet-level executive departments and the Joint Chiefs of Staff (the latter via the Chief of Staff to the President).

The second new agency at the top of the national security structure of 1947, the National Security Resources Board, held only fleeting importance. Originally the Board, composed of a chairman and representatives from various executive departments or other agencies, was supposed to be nearly as important as the NSC, for the NSRB was responsible for coordinating all aspects of mobilization—military, industrial, and civilian. In 1947 the immensity of the task of mobilization in World War II, as well as the problems of resource supply and allocation, still loomed in the memories of many officials. However, the NSRB never achieved great importance in the overall scheme of national security policy after 1947, perhaps because much of the planning for mobilization and associated matters actually fell to agencies in the new Department of Defense, in particular to the Munitions Board and to the committees of the Joint Chiefs of Staff.

8. May, "Development of Political-Military Consultation," pp. 178, 179.
9. This statement is an inference drawn from declassified lists of NSC papers, which include references, by number only, to SANACC series, and which indicate that the subjects were highly classified.

Figure 6

ORGANIZATION FOR NATIONAL SECURITY, 1947:

Representation

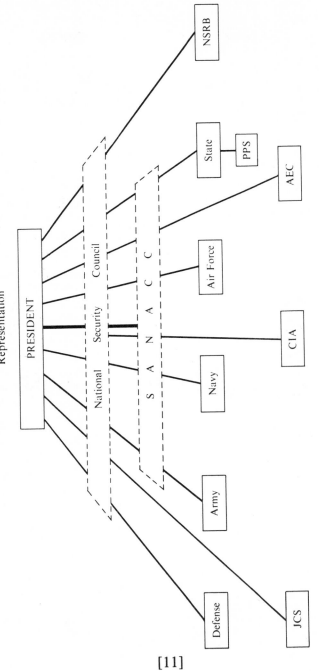

Note: The six agencies in the upper tier of the chart were statutory members of the National Security Council. The three agencies in the lower tier participated in the Council's deliberations either informally or at presidential request from the beginning of the system's operations.

In attending to a second principal concern, improvement of government intelligence functions, the National Security Act of 1947 established the Central Intelligence Agency (CIA) in a particularly interesting organizational context. Owing to security regulations and to bickering among the intelligence organizations of the military services and other executive departments, policy makers at high levels were receiving belated and inadequate intelligence in the years immediately after the war. In this sense, the Cold War experience reinforced the lesson of military intelligence failure at the outset of World War II and emphasized the continuing need for improvement in this function. The Congress's artful approach to this touchy issue showed itself in several features of the statute of 1947. The intelligence organizations of the services and of the Department of State, the Federal Bureau of Investigation (FBI), the Treasury Department, and the Department of Commerce were left intact. The CIA was specifically subordinated to the NSC, and directed to coordinate, not supervise, the intelligence activities of other government agencies "in the interest of national security." [10]

In addition to its function as coordinator of intelligence activities in government, the Central Intelligence Agency received other important assignments. The National Security Act of 1947 directed the CIA to advise the NSC in intelligence matters, to make recommendations to the NSC involving coordination of intelligence activities, to correlate, evaluate, and disseminate intelligence relating to national security, to perform for the benefit of existing intelligence agencies whatever "services of common concern" would be more efficient if centralized, and to "perform such other functions and duties related to intelligence affecting the national security as the National Security Council may from time to time direct." [11]

Despite the National Security Act's extensive phraseology concerning CIA duties, the principal mission of the agency derived more from bureaucratic continuity than from statute. From its wartime and postwar predecessor organizations, the CIA assumed the task of producing national intelligence estimates, that is, forecasts of likely developments bearing on United States national security, and especially regarding the capabilities and intentions of the Soviet Union. It is important to note that the new CIA also assumed other functions of its immediate predecessors, including both overt and clandestine collection of information. [12] As Document 12 in the present

10. 61 Stat. 498.   11. 61 Stat. 498.
12. Anne Karalekas, "History of the Central Intelligence Agency," in U.S. Congress, Senate (94th Cong., 2nd sess.), Select Committee to Study Government Operations with respect to Intelligence Activities, *Final Report: Supplementary Detailed Staff Reports on Foreign and Military Intelligence: Book IV* (Washington: 1976), p. 15.

volume demonstrates, the CIA's covert action capability came later, in 1948. It is also important to recall that in the first years after the war the Department of State was eager to see the military and intelligence professionals concentrate somewhere other than within the Department itself. A postwar influx into the Department of former Office of Strategic Services personnel had irritated the professional elite of the Foreign Service, so that both the Department and the Foreign Service favored, rather than objected to, legislation centralizing intelligence functions outside the Department of State.

By far the largest portion of the National Security Act of 1947 addressed the third principal organizational concern of the era, the rationalization of the American defense community. As in dealing with the problems of intelligence functions, the Congress compromised and provided for an organization with more central direction than previously, but with somewhat less than the unification that might have provided optimum organizational solutions to institutional weakness. The novelty was the creation of a National Military Establishment (NME), headed by a Secretary of Defense, with retention of the individual services as discrete entities with cabinet-level civilian heads. (See Figure 7)

The nature of congressional compromise in setting out the framework of the National Military Establishment showed in the assignment of duties to the Secretary of Defense, for his duties constituted a mandate to unite the planning, procurement, and policies of the services as a substitute for unifying their organizations. Thus the Secretary of Defense presided over a two-tiered military establishment, with an upper tier of agencies designed to coordinate issues, problems, and activities either insoluble at or arising out of the second tier, namely, the individual services.

The five agencies in the upper tier of the new National Military Establishment were not, of course, all equally significant. The Military Liaison Committee to the Atomic Energy Commission (AEC) worked on the difficult problems associated with the fact that, in postwar organization for national security, the AEC retained both administrative and physical control over all atomic weapons components, a possible obstacle to their timely deployment and potential combat use. In constituting a Research and Development Board, the National Security Act removed development in new weapons technology from the immediate responsibilities of the Joint Chiefs of Staff and raised the importance of the matter. With a civilian chairman and two representatives each from the Army, Navy, and Air Force, the Board assumed the duties of preparing a "complete and integrated" military research

Figure 7

THE NATIONAL MILITARY ESTABLISHMENT

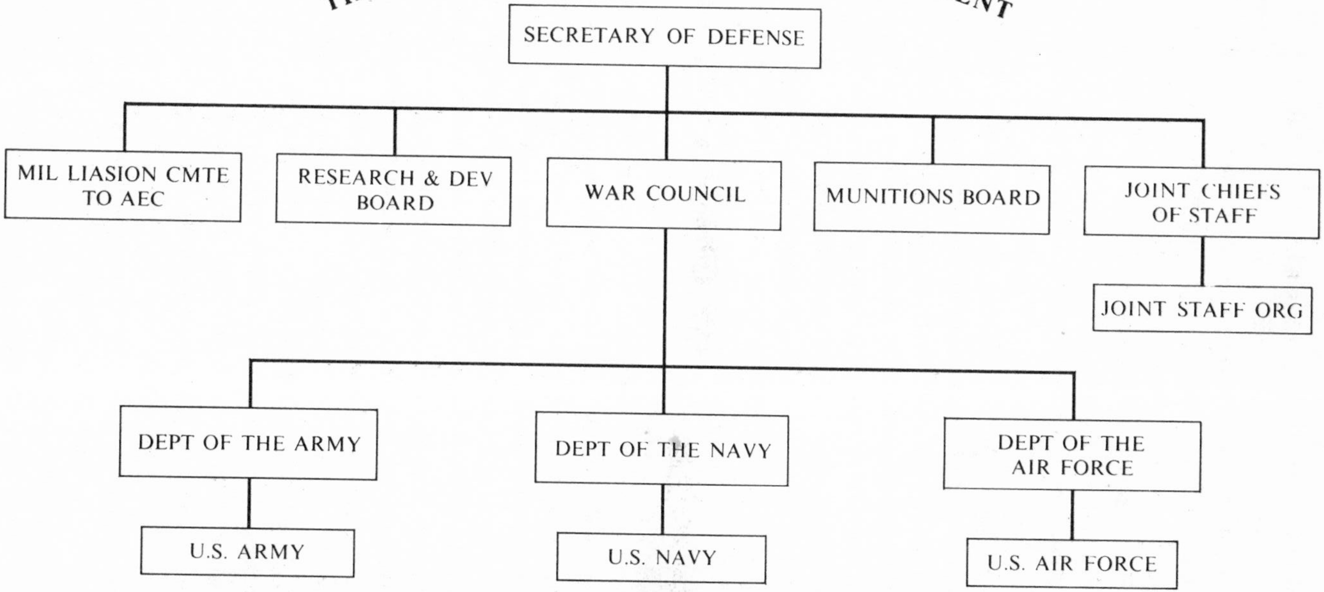

Source: Little, "Organizing for Strategic Planning," p. 89.

[14]

and development program, advising the Secretary of Defense on scientific research relevant to national security, recommending coordination and allocation of research tasks among the services, formulating policy on militarily significant research outside the National Military Establishment, and considering the "interaction of research and development and strategy" for the purpose of advising the Joint Chiefs of Staff.[13] The War Council, with the Secretary of Defense, the Secretaries of the Navy, Army, and Air Force, and the service chiefs as members, advised the Secretary of Defense on broad policy matters, and soon fell into relative disuse.

The Munitions Board, also in the upper tier of the National Military Establishment, was composed of a civilian chairman and undersecretary- or assistant-secretary-level representatives of each of the three military departments. It became responsible for coordinating military and industrial mobilization plans, as well as for making preparations in regard to procurement, production, and distribution of matériel, including the establishment of priorities in production and allocation. In one extremely important duty, the Board was to prepare estimates of potential production for use in logistic evaluation of strategic plans.[14] In policy, planning, and coordination for matériel, the Munitions Board became as authoritative as did the Joint Chiefs of Staff in strategy.[15]

The congressional compromise in organizing a National Military Establishment—united policies and plans rather than organizations—greatly raised the importance of the last upper-tier agency in the new structure, the Joint Chiefs of Staff. The Chiefs became the primary body for devising unified military policy and strategy. In the most important of its manifold duties, the Joint Chiefs of Staff continued to prepare strategic plans and provide strategic direction to the military forces; to formulate logistic plans and assign service responsibilities for logistics; and to review the matériel and personnel requirements of the military establishment as an essential part of correlating strategic and logistic plans with politico-military forecasts and budgetary processes. (Figure 8 shows the organization of the Chiefs.)

In the most important organizational alteration of the Joint Chiefs of Staff, the National Security Act added to the JCS its own working staff. As mentioned previously, during the war and immediately thereafter, the Joint Chiefs of Staff had depended on the individual service staffs for the members of working groups, an arrangement that limited the freedom of

13. 61 Stat. 504–7.
14. 61 Stat. 505, 506.
15. Little, "Organizing for Strategic Planning," pp. 10, 11.

Figure 8

THE JOINT CHIEFS OF STAFF, 1948

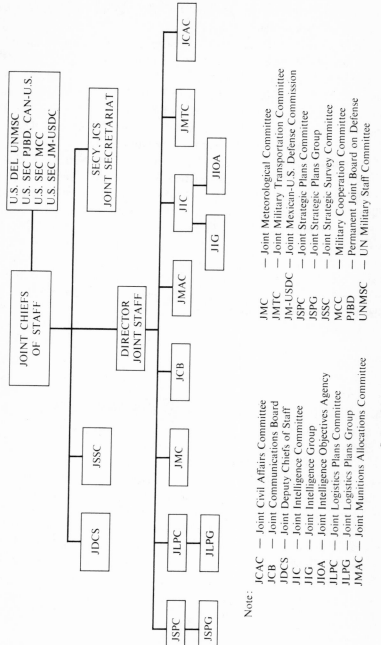

Note:

JCAC — Joint Civil Affairs Committee
JCB — Joint Communications Board
JDCS — Joint Deputy Chiefs of Staff
JIC — Joint Intelligence Committee
JIG — Joint Intelligence Group
JIOA — Joint Intelligence Objectives Agency
JLPC — Joint Logistics Plans Committee
JLPG — Joint Logistics Plans Group
JMAC — Joint Munitions Allocations Committee

JMC — Joint Meteorological Committee
JMTC — Joint Military Transportation Committee
JM-USDC — Joint Mexican-U.S. Defense Commission
JSPC — Joint Strategic Plans Committee
JSPG — Joint Strategic Plans Group
JSSC — Joint Strategic Survey Committee
MCC — Military Cooperation Committee
PJBD — Permanent Joint Board on Defense
UNMSC — UN Military Staff Committee

Source: Little, "Organizing for Strategic Planning," p. 90.

hand, unifying effect, and continuity of the JCS. The act authorized the Chiefs to create a staff of up to 100 officers, a number later legislatively increased to 400.[16] The staff continued to operate in the familiar committee system, with the Joint Strategic Planning Group, the Joint Logistic Planning Group, and the Joint Intelligence Group forming the core. As in the years prior to the act, the Joint Strategic Survey Committee, on which each of the services had full-time representation, functioned as the senior policy-planning committee.

One of the most important components of the structure for national security affairs after World War II depended not on the National Security Act but on an act of Congress approved July 27, 1789. The Department of State, originally called the Department of Foreign Affairs, retained principal responsibility for the political component to be integrated—or coordinated—with military factors in the dangerous era of great power for the United States. Indeed, high-ranking military officers recognized the importance of the political dimension, as well as the fact of the State Department's responsibility for it, from the very beginning of the new organizational relationship. In November 1947, only months after Congress passed the National Security Act, the Vice Chief of Staff of the Air Force, Hoyt S. Vandenberg, impatiently articulated his understanding of the point that defining national objectives was a function of the State Department; that the National Security Council would have to relate such objectives to military requirements; and that only then could the Joint Chiefs of Staff prepare the many plans urgently necessary for effective national security programs.[17]

Within the State Department, the Policy Planning Staff (PPS) possessed functions and responsibilities analogous to those of the Joint Chiefs of Staff in the military establishment. Founded by departmental order on May 5, 1947, the Policy Planning Staff received five assignments: (1) to formulate and develop long-term programs for the achievement of American objectives in foreign affairs; (2) to anticipate difficulties for the department; (3) to study and report on large problems in politico-military affairs; (4) to evaluate current policy in the context of developments in world affairs; and (5) to coordinate planning within the Department of State.[18] The first director of the Policy Planning Staff, George F. Kennan, more than any other individ-

16. Lawrence J. Korb, *The Joint Chiefs of Staff: The First Twenty-five Years* (Bloomington: Indiana University Press, 1976), p. 18. This volume constitutes the only book-length treatment of the JCS yet to appear in print.
17. Little, "Organizing for Strategic Planning," p. 23.
18. George F. Kennan, *Memoirs: 1925–1950* (Boston: Little, Brown, 1967), p. 327.

ual shaped the centerpiece of politico-military coordination from 1945 to 1950: the strategy of containment.

III

Organizations on paper are one thing; organizations in action are another. It is necessary, therefore, not only to set out the statutory form of the American apparatus for national security affairs, but to appraise that mechanism, at least to the modest extent that documentation now permits. One may well ask whether the organization worked the way it was supposed to, and whether for better or for worse in American politico-military affairs from 1945 to 1950.

Previous answers to the foregoing questions have stressed the negative aspects of national security organization and functioning, and not only for the first years of the Cold War.[19] In a curious retrospective test of organizational gamesmanship, Presidents Truman, Kennedy, and Johnson were criticized for not using the NSC machinery very frequently; apparently the critics felt that such a fine apparatus ought to be employed by any right-thinking leader of the republic. Paradoxically, President Eisenhower's constant use of the NSC has received approbation, while President Nixon's reliance on and expansion of the NSC structure has provoked not only suspicion but opprobrium. Perhaps this paradox derives from the premise that such institutions as the NSC need regular exercise to keep them from withering into vestigial appendages, but not too much exercise lest they mutate into antidemocratic monsters. In any case, the convolutions of national security affairs in the 1970s have obscured the earlier functioning of the NSC, and thus increased the difficulty of appraising it in its early years of operation.

The available record of national security organization in its first years leaves an impression not so much negative as mixed; admirable accomplishments and substantial shortcomings both abound. Because most of the minutes of National Security Council meetings, Policy Planning Staff meetings, and most records of the Joint Chiefs of Staff remain classified, as do nearly all records of the decisions and actions of those bodies, the present appraisal must remain preliminary, subject to revision as further documentation be-

19. Two recent examples of such negative evaluation are: Alfred D. Sander, "Truman and the National Security Council: 1945–1947," *Journal of American History,* LIX (September 1972), 369–88; and David S. McLellan, *Dean Acheson: The State Department Years* (New York: Dodd, Mead, 1976).

comes available. Still, it is not mere historian's caution that compels a middle-of-the road stance. The system worked; it worked well; it did not, and indeed by any reasonable assessment could not, do all that it was supposed to do, or in fact all that American national security required from 1945 to 1950.

Of all the agencies in the new structure for national security affairs, the National Security Council perhaps functioned most nearly as it should have, and to best effect. From 1947 to 1950, the NSC studied, discussed, and made recommendations to the President on some seventy topics pertaining to American national security.[20] A number of these topics received repeated attention; there are eleven major documents in the NSC series on Taiwan. Some topics received extremely lengthy treatment; NSC 48/1 and NSC 68 (Documents 33 and 52 in the present volume) testify to that fact. The NSC considered every crisis and virtually every major issue in American national security affairs during the interval from 1947 to 1950—from problems of communism in Western countries such as Italy and Greece to base rights in various regions of the world to the many facets of China's collapse, alliance with Western Europe, Japan's revival, fissures within the communist camp, the Berlin crisis, difficulties over Palestine, and programs for assuring the internal security of the United States.[21] President Truman accepted a great many of the recommendations of the NSC, and even when he did not, the studies and discussions of the organization weighed heavily in his foreign policy decisions.

Further, the documents produced in the NSC system show careful attention to the meshing of political objectives with military capabilities, as well as a measuring of the political effects of various military postures, deployments, and plans. Indeed, the coordination of political and military considerations was not, perhaps, as difficult at first as one might have expected, for as documents in this volume illustrate, both diplomats and military officers shared the conviction that American resources were severely limited; they disagreed, of course, on where and how those limited resources should be allocated and expended. In such disagreements, the NSC, and ultimately the President, forced analysis and made decisions, much as the system had been intended to work. Neither the NSC nor the NSRB were themselves capable of significantly altering the limitations on resources. By the time of NSC 68,

---

20. List of NSC papers 1 through 177, October 15, 1947, through December 30, 1953. Under a cover sheet dated April 16, 1976, this list is available in the Modern Military Records Branch, National Archives, Washington, D.C.

21. *Ibid.*

however, the Council was willing to call for more resources, and not only to discuss allocation of what was available. Still, it took the President, the Congress, and the North Koreans to obtain the additional resources.

Like the National Security Council system itself, the Central Intelligence Agency has come in for much contemporary criticism as a result of recent, and to some Americans reprehensible, activities. The fact of its founding and its acquisition in the latter 1940s of a covert-operations capability, are not, however, proper bases for evaluating its functioning in the first years of the Cold War. It is far more pertinent that, according to the history prepared for a Senate investigating committee, the agency failed in its foremost task of preparing the national intelligence estimates essential as a basis for medium- and long-range planning. The CIA's Office of Research and Evaluation (ORE) fell victim to "pressures of current events. . . .   As ORE attempted to satisfy the widespread demands of many clients, its intelligence became directed to a working-level audience rather than to senior policy makers. As such, it lost the influence it was intended to have. Gradually, the ORE built up a series of commitments which made it less likely and less able to direct its efforts to estimate production." The same account also noted another weakness of CIA functioning in the early years: the CIA received virtually all its current information from the State Department, a fact that does not speak well for the agency's information-collection capability in those years.[22]

The third great component of a revised national security apparatus in the late 1940s, the National Military Establishment, presents one of the most complex mixtures of achievement and failure. Some important objectives of the reorganization of the defense agencies never came close to realization. Other objectives took much longer to achieve than anyone had expected, despite praiseworthy efforts from the beginning.

One notable failure concerned the intention to subordinate, if not end, interservice rivalry while eliminating duplication, overlap, and inefficiency within a multiple-service defense establishment. As is well known, in both aspects this objective fell far short of attainment. The services competed for strategic missions, for responsibility in the delivery of atomic weapons, for manpower and equipment and budget dollars. Instead of challenging the services to seek new efficiency, the shortage of resources motivated them to seek bureaucratic victories. The results were considerable delay in allocation of strategic missions and resources, delay in development of assumptions ac-

---

22. Karalekas, "History of the Central Intelligence Agency," p. 15.

ceptable to all the service chiefs as a basis for strategic planning, and a long interval of interservice rivalry within the Joint Chiefs of Staff, where of all places a sense of common and pressing purpose was necessary for the effectiveness of the new system.[23] Ironically, the acrimonious Navy-Air Force feud over responsibility for delivering atomic weapons became so heated and publicized that Truman had Acheson reassure the Russians secretly, for fear that otherwise they might become convinced the United States was planning an atomic attack on the Soviet Union.[24]

An additional aspect of service ambition to control atomic weapons had an ambiguous, rather than clearly negative, consequence. Because of the persistent arguments of the services, and in particular the Air Force, that the military establishment and not the AEC should maintain physical custody of atomic weapons, the President decided soon after 1950 to make that change. From the point of view of military efficiency, this was surely good, for up to that time arrangements for the deployment and use of such weapons were time-consuming and cumbersome in the extreme. To opponents of nuclear war and people concerned about the accelerating pace and power of modern warfare, however, this improvement in military efficiency may seem both unwanted and unwise.

The focus of military planning and direction in the new system, the Joint Chiefs of Staff, functioned very much as it was supposed to; but, ironically, its magnitudinous endeavors brought only minuscule results between 1947 and 1950 if one measures by output and not by the refinement of operations that eventually would lead to more effective strategic planning and direction. In truth, the years 1947 to 1950 for the Joint Chiefs of Staff were a necessary "shakedown" period, a basis for later productive efforts. Yet some aspects of operation in the shakedown interval seem perverse. In the first postwar years the Chiefs proved capable of agreeing on war plans only for short-range or immediate contingencies, supposedly on the basis of forces available. Each of the four plans approved by 1950 was later declared infeasible on the basis of its logistic and force requirements. The Chiefs persistently planned on the basis of a somewhat larger military budget in peacetime than they had any right to expect under current political conditions.

23. Some aspects of these controversies appear in Vincent Davis, *The Admirals Lobby* (Chapel Hill: University of North Carolina Press, 1967). Professor David A. Rosenberg of the University of Wisconsin (Milwaukee) is doing substantial research into associated issues. His article, "The U.S. Navy and the Problem of Oil in a Future War: The Outline of a Strategic Dilemma, 1945–1950," *Naval War College Review*, XXIX, No. 1 (Summer 1976), 53–64, affords glimpses of such difficulties.

24. McLellan, *Dean Acheson*, p. 169.

Thomas H. Etzold

Early war plans included incomplete intelligence estimates, unrealistic assessments of the capabilities of new allies in the North Atlantic Treaty Organization (NATO), and inflated expectations about the areas the United States would be able to defend. Finally, planning could not keep up with the pace of events. By far the greatest proportion of plans and studies begun in the joint staff addressed current problems that, for good or ill, usually faded from view before the study or plan reached completion. The result: "At the end of 1950 a multitude of uncompleted plans and study projects stretched in every direction. Although the Korean War was perhaps not foreseeable, its planning had to proceed virtually from scratch, barely ahead of implementing actions and operations." It is both a negative and a positive assessment to say that by 1950 planning in the Joint Chiefs of Staff was procedure; the products came later.[25]

About the State Department as about the National Security Council, much has been written bearing on its performance in the years following World War II. These were years of drastic decline for the State Department as an institution, and concurrently, years of soaring prestige for the Secretaries of State and, for a time, the Policy Planning Staff. George C. Marshall and Dean G. Acheson both proved influential not only with the President but within the NSC system. Both used extensively the more than sixty papers of the Policy Planning Staff from 1947 to 1949. Many of these papers, by virtue of their political vision, logic, and felicity of expression, became the bases for drafts of NSC study memoranda and recommendations. The Department of State and the Policy Planning Staff promoted a long perspective on American interests in foreign affairs, vigorously contended with their military counterparts in the policy process, and compiled a very fair record in sustaining their views in the NSC system. The limitations of their success were two: (1) bitter and debilitating disagreements between Kennan and the rest of the Department, in particular Secretary Acheson, which show in the present volume in the documents on Germany and the evolution of NATO;[26] and (2) the press of events, which worked against proponents of a long view, and with the Korean War actually foreclosed real opportunity for patient and flexible, rather than militant and rigid, policy.

In sum, the Cold War proved as stern an arbiter of American institutions

25. These points are discussed in Little, "Organizing for Strategic Planning," *passim,* especially pp. 16, 43, 76. The quotation is from p. 76.

26. The developing controversy between Kennan and Acheson is both important and well known. See especially Kennan, *Memoirs: 1925–1950,* pp. 466–500; John Lewis Gaddis, "Was the Truman Doctrine a Real Turning Point?" *Foreign Affairs,* LII (January 1974), 386–402; McLellan, *Dean Acheson.*

as had World War II. For one thread ties together these assessments of the new national security structure from 1947 to 1950: a lack of readiness arising from inability to anticipate, to plan ahead, to prepare. This is no small matter. It is a reminder of the critical role of intelligence and of estimates, or forecasts. It also recalls Thucydides' writings on the Peloponnesian Wars, in which he calls *pronoia,* the ability to anticipate the course of events, one of the necessary qualities of a statesman. Despite the organizational improvements made during and after the war, many of which were intended to improve American anticipation of and readiness for a variety of threats, the crises of the Cold War from Europe through the Mediterranean to the Far East found the United States unprepared militarily, politically, and psychologically.

Of course, the circumstances early in the Cold War mitigate the extent to which either American leaders or American institutions should be condemned for lack of ability to anticipate. Neither as a people nor as a government were Americans in 1945 to 1950 accustomed to play at power politics in peacetime, to possess powerful and constant enemies, to bear responsibility for the security and well-being of other major nations, and to have vital interests constantly in question in many regions of the globe. It is understandable that the United States should have required some experience before its government acquired competence in dealing with conflicts of interest in such circumstances. Further, it seems fair to say that the new institutions of American national security coped with events better than they anticipated them, and very likely coped with problems much more effectively than any prewar organizations could have hoped to do. This in itself is a substantial achievement.

Thus the system worked, but it worked imperfectly. It is necessary to be reminded from time to time that one can neither organize away the problems of foreign affairs nor predict with complete confidence all that will be of significance for security and interests. So long as those two premises remain valid, the American people will have to expect from their institutions some successes, some shortcomings. They will have to guard against the unreasonable expectation of error-free foreign policy, or, for that matter, error-free government.

THE STRATEGY OF CONTAINMENT

John Lewis Gaddis

◇◇◇◇◇

ONE OF THE characteristics most firmly rooted in the human mind is the desire to render the complex simple. Intellectual lassitude, the inexorable pressures of time, the belief that simplicity facilitates communication—these and other considerations incline the policy maker toward reductionism, and the historian of policy as well. The recent past is littered with unsuccessful attempts to convey complicated ideas economically: "appeasement," "détente," "massive retaliation," "liberation," "pacification"; in each instance, the term employed obscured more than it illuminated. But none of these caused greater confusion than "containment," the word most often used to characterize United States foreign and military policy during the early years of the Cold War.

George F. Kennan, who coined the term, has acknowledged partial responsibility: he admits that his most visible explanation of "containment," the article on "The Sources of Soviet Conduct" which appeared in the July 1947 issue of *Foreign Affairs,* employed "careless and indiscriminate language" inconsistent with his own beliefs at the time.[1] But confusion also grew out of the tendency of others, both within and outside the government, to apply the label "containment" haphazardly, without reference to the ideas that lay behind it. This tendency led Kennan, twenty years later, "emphatically [to] deny the paternity of any efforts to invoke that doctrine . . . in situations to which it has, and can have, no proper relevance."[2]

Nevertheless, Kennan's was the most coherent single attempt made during the early Cold War to formulate a comprehensive strategy for dealing with

Portions of this essay appeared in slightly different form as John Lewis Gaddis, "Containment: A Reassessment," *Foreign Affairs,* LV (July, 1977), 873–887, and are included here by permission of the Council on Foreign Relations, Inc.

1. George F. Kennan, *Memoirs: 1925–1950* (Boston: Little, Brown, 1967), p. 360. Kennan's article appeared under the pseudonym "X," and is partially reprinted in this collection as Document 6.

2. *Ibid.,* p. 367.

the Soviet Union. As such, it merits careful examination. The following essay is an effort to reconstruct and present systematically Kennan's original concept of containment, on the basis of the documents printed in this volume. It will also attempt to explain how such a disparity came to exist between the recommendations Kennan made, as director of the State Department's Policy Planning Staff, and the measures actually implemented under the label he had invented.

I

The purpose of any nation's foreign policy, it seems clear, is to create an international environment conducive to the survival and prospering of that nation's domestic institutions. Arguments, when they develop, tend to focus on the choice of means to achieve the end, not on the desirability of the end itself.

Americans, in the course of their history, have approached this problem in two ways. One approach, which might be called "universalism," has sought congeniality through homogeneity: by working to make the world resemble the United States as much as possible, on the assumption that, once it did, nothing in it could pose a serious threat. The other approach, which might be characterized as "particularism," argues that what is important is to ensure that the world does not threaten the United States, whether it resembles it or not. Security, from this perspective, depends on diversity. The "universalist" tends to see harmony as an attainable state in international affairs, and thinks that security can come only through its achievement. The "particularist" tends to regard harmony as unlikely, but thinks that security can be obtained, nonetheless, through a careful balancing of power, interests, and antagonisms.

Kennan ranged himself firmly on the "particularist" side of this debate because he saw it as the only approach capable of achieving its objectives without disrupting the ends foreign policy was supposed to promote. Any attempt to seek security through uniformity would, he thought, outrun limited capabilities; it would also compromise American ideals, since there would be a disturbing incongruity in a system that sought freedom of choice at home while working to impose its institutions elsewhere in the world. "The greatest danger that can befall us in coping with this problem of Soviet communism," Kennan wrote in 1946, "is that we shall allow ourselves to become like those with whom we are coping." [3]

3. Kennan to James F. Byrnes, February 22, 1946, *Foreign Relations of the United States: 1946*, VI, 709 (Document 3). See also Kennan's distinction between universalism and particu-

It followed that American interests would best be served not by trying to control the world—the "universalist" solution—but by trying to maintain equilibrium in it, so that no one country, or group of countries, could endanger American security. "All in all," Kennan wrote late in 1947, "our policy must be directed toward restoring a balance of power in Europe and Asia."[4]

Two important corollaries proceeded logically from this argument. One was that not all parts of the world were equally vital to American security. Industrial capacity, together with the access to raw materials necessary to sustain it, was the key to power in the world, Kennan believed; the United States could tolerate the existence of unfriendly regimes in many areas provided they lacked the means of manifesting that hostility in ways that could threaten the United States. "Repeatedly, at that time and in ensuing years," Kennan wrote in his *Memoirs*, "I expressed in talks and lectures the view that there were only five regions of the world—the United States, the United Kingdom, the Rhine valley with adjacent industrial areas, the Soviet Union, and Japan—where the sinews of modern military strength could be produced in quantity; I pointed out that only one of these was under Communist control; and I defined the main task of containment, accordingly, as one of seeing to it that none of the remaining ones fell under such control."[5]

The second corollary was that the internal organization of other states was not, in and of itself, a proper matter of concern for American foreign policy. "It is a traditional principle of this Government," Kennan wrote in 1948, "to refrain from interference in the internal affairs of other countries. . . . Whoever proposes or urges such intervention should properly bear the burden of proof (a) that there is sufficiently powerful national interest to justify our departure . . . from a rule of international conduct which has been proven sound by centuries of experience, . . . and (b) that we have the means to conduct such intervention successfully and can afford the cost in terms of the national effort it involves."[6] The United States could coexist

---

larism in PPS 23, "Review of Current Trends, U.S. Foreign Policy," February 24, 1948, *Foreign Relations: 1948,* I, 526–27 (Document 8), and the discussion in George F. Kennan, *Realities of American Foreign Policy* (Princeton, N.J.: Princeton University Press, 1954), pp. 3–30.

4. PPS 13, "Resumé of World Situation," November 6, 1947, *Foreign Relations: 1947,* I, 771 (Document 7).

5. Kennan, *Memoirs: 1925–1950,* p. 359.

6. PPS 39/1, "U.S. Policy Toward China," November 23, 1948, *Foreign Relations: 1948* VIII, 208 (Document 32).

with, even benefit from, diversity, Kennan thought; what was dangerous was the combination of aggressive intent with the physical capacity to do something about it.

Such, then, was the definition of national interest upon which the strategy of containment was founded. Several things are noteworthy about it in retrospect. First, it defined the national interest in terms of ends, not means; what was at stake was the preservation of American society, not the fortunes of the administration in power, not American alliances, not American credibility, all of which were only means to a larger end. Second, it took into account the limits imposed by the nation's physical capabilities, recognizing that little is gained by projecting interests beyond the capacity to defend them. Third, it paid relatively little attention to ideologies: friends and enemies were to be distinguished by their ability to affect American interests, not by the internal structure of their governments. Fourth, it associated those interests, not with the erection of artificial structures for keeping peace in the world, but with "natural" or "organic" forces—nationalism, the balance of power, and, above all, diversity.

II

The only nation that met Kennan's test of combining hostility with the capability of doing something about it was, of course, the Soviet Union. World War II had produced a significant expansion of Soviet influence in both Europe and the Far East; this circumstance, together with the presence throughout much of the rest of the world of communist parties subservient to Moscow's will, gave the Russians the opportunity to shift the international balance of power in a manner detrimental to United States interests.

Soviet hostility toward the West, Kennan argued, stemmed from a deep-seated, brooding sense of insecurity on the part of Russian leaders. Partly this was the result of historical experience: lacking protective geographical barriers, subject, throughout its history, to recurrent invasion, the Russian state had never enjoyed a luxury Americans had taken for granted throughout most of their history—free security. Partly this uneasiness reflected also the conspiratorial habits formed by Bolshevik leaders during years in the underground: survival, for them, had come to depend on not trusting anyone. It was these two forms of paranoia—historical and organizational—which accounted for the peculiar and difficult behavior of the Soviet state under Josef Stalin.

Ideology of course did play a role in this. Marxism-Leninism served to legitimize an illegitimate regime: if one could not rule by the will of God, as had the Russian tsars, then ruling by the will of history in the form of dialectical materialism was the next best thing. Ideology also provided justification, in Kennan's view, for the repression without which unimaginative Soviet leaders did not know how to rule: as long as the rest of the world was capitalist, harsh measures could be justified as necessary to protect the world's leading communist state. Ideology was also important because it associated the Soviet government with the revolutionary aspirations of people in other countries, thus making the international communist movement an instrument with which to project influence beyond Russian borders.

But Kennan did not see the ideological writings of Marx and Lenin as a reliable guide with which to anticipate Soviet behavior. Communist doctrine was so amorphous that, like any ideology, it required an intermediary—in this case, the Soviet government—to apply it to the real world. This circumstance placed that intermediary in a position to say what ideology was at any given moment. "The leadership is at liberty," Kennan wrote, "to put forward for tactical purposes any particular thesis which it finds useful . . . and to require the faithful and unquestioning acceptance of that thesis by the members of the movement as a whole. This means that truth is not a constant but is actually created, for all intents and purposes, by the Soviet leaders themselves. . . . It is nothing absolute and immutable." [7]

Ideology, then, was not so much a guide to action as a justification for action already decided upon. Although Stalin might not feel secure until he had come to dominate the entire world, this would be because of his own unfathomable sense of insecurity, not out of any principled commitment to the goal of an international classless society. It followed that the object of containment should be Soviet expansionism, and that communism would be a threat only to the extent that it was an instrument of that expansion.

Kennan did not expect the Soviet Union to resort to war to gain its objectives, although he acknowledged that miscalculations could always occur. More likely, he thought, was the possibility of conquest by psychological means: the danger that the peoples of Western Europe and Japan, two of the five vital centers of industrial power in the world, might become so demoralized by the combined dislocations of war and reconstruction as to make themselves vulnerable, through sheer lack of self-confidence, to communist-led coups, or even communist victories in free elections. Since both European and Japanese communists were, at this time, reliable instruments of

7. "The Sources of Soviet Conduct," p. 573. This summary of Kennan's explanation of Soviet behavior is based on the analysis in this article.

Soviet foreign policy, such developments would have meant in effect the domination of Europe and much of Asia by a single hostile power—the very nightmare World War II had been fought to prevent. It was against this contingency that the strategy of containment was aimed—not Soviet military attack, not international communism, but rather the sense of psychological malaise in countries bordering on Russia which made them, and hence the overall balance of power, vulnerable to Soviet expansive tendencies. As Kennan later put it, "it had been the shadow, rather than the substance, of danger which we . . . had been concerned to dispel." [8]

III

Because Kennan saw the problems as psychological, his solution, too, was psychological in character: to produce in the minds of potential adversaries, as well as potential allies and the American people, attitudes which would facilitate evolution of a congenial international environment for the United States. Kennan saw three steps as necessary to accomplish this objective: (1) restoration of self-confidence in nations threatened by Soviet expansionism; (2) reduction of the Soviet Union's ability to project influence beyond its borders; and (3) modification, over time, of the Soviet concept of international relations, with a view to facilitating the negotiated settlement of outstanding differences.

The idea, in seeking a restoration of self-confidence, was to avoid a direct confrontation with Soviet power, but at the same time work to alleviate conditions that rendered neighboring states vulnerable to it. This end could most effectively be accomplished, Kennan thought, through economic means. For Western Europe, he strongly endorsed, and in part inspired, the Marshall Plan, an ambitious five-year program of economic assistance. For Japan, he proposed a reorientation of occupation policy away from the punitive approach of the early postwar period toward measures designed to encourage that country's emergence as an independent center of power in the western Pacific.

It is interesting to note the role Kennan assigned to military power in this process. He acknowledged the importance of maintaining strong armed forces, but evinced an extreme reluctance to commit them overseas. In part, this view reflected his fear of dispersing scarce resources; in part, too, it arose out of skepticism regarding the American military's ability to operate

---

8. Kennan, *Memoirs: 1925–1950*, p. 351.

overseas without alienating populations with which it came into contact.[9] Reinforcing this distrust of military solutions was Kennan's conviction that the most effective instrument the United States had for projecting influence in the world was its economic power—the capacity to affect, to varying degrees, the rate at which other countries reconstructed or modernized their economies. Thus, the Marshall Plan, in its original form, did not call for a permanent United States military commitment to Europe; its emphasis, rather, was on economic aid. Similarly, in the Far East, Kennan endorsed General Douglas MacArthur's concept of concentrating on the defense of islands—notably Okinawa and the Philippines—while avoiding commitments on the mainland.[10] There was in these arguments a harking back to the "arsenal of democracy" concept of the 1939–41 period: the idea that the strongest contribution the United States could make to the task of maintaining the balance of power was not its manpower but its technology.

It is also interesting to note that this concern for the balance of power did not imply a "zero-sum game" view of the world; not every "gain" for the Soviet Union necessarily represented a "loss" for the United States. The vital task was to keep major industrial and raw-material-producing areas out of hostile hands; as to the rest, although the United States would hardly welcome a communist takeover, neither would it expend significant amounts of energy to prevent such a development, given its own limited capabilities, given the vital interests at stake elsewhere in the world.

Finally, it should be noted that what Kennan was advocating was not an American sphere of influence in Europe and Asia, but rather the emergence of centers of power in these regions independent of both Soviet and American control. Russians and Americans could not indefinitely confront one another across World War II truce lines, Kennan argued; ultimately some kind of withdrawal from these artificial positions would have to take place.[11] To replace them, Kennan hoped for a world order based not on superpower hegemony but on the natural balance only diverse concentrations of authority, operating independently of one another, could provide.

Kennan's second major prescription for action involved reducing Russian

---

9. PPS 23, February 24, 1948, *Foreign Relations: 1948*, I, 516–17. See also Kennan, *Memoirs: 1925–1950*, pp. 129–30.

10. See Kennan to Marshall, March 14, 1948, *Foreign Relations: 1948*, I, 534; and PPS 28/2, "Conversation between General of the Army Douglas MacArthur and Mr. George F. Kennan," May 26, 1948, *ibid.*, IV, 700–2 (Document 26).

11. PPS 37, "Policy Questions Concerning a Possible German Settlement," August 12, 1948, *Foreign Relations: 1948*, II, 1288 (Document 15). See also the citations in the preceding footnote.

influence in the world by exploiting actual and potential splits between the Soviet leadership and the international communist movement. The Kremlin would not, he thought, indefinitely be able to maintain its authority over international communism, partly because of its own inability to tolerate diversity, partly because the very act of coming to power in foreign countries would tend to make communist leaders less dependent on Moscow. Soviet expansionism was nothing but an updated variety of colonialism, subject to all of the vulnerabilities of that earlier phenomenon. In time, Kennan believed, two opposed blocs might develop within the communist world—one dominated by the Soviet Union, the other made up of communists defiant of Moscow's leadership. Although a noncommunist government would obviously be preferable to a communist one from the American point of view, at the same time a communist government independent of Moscow would be preferable to one which was not.[12]

Between 1947 and 1949, several efforts were made to implement this strategy. At Kennan's recommendation, Marshall Plan aid was offered to the Soviet Union and its Eastern European satellites—not with any expectation that the Russians would accept it, or allow their neighbors to, but in the hope that a Soviet rejection would strain Moscow's relations with its satellites. Early in 1948, Kennan recommended relating the level of United States naval and air operations in the eastern Mediterranean to the intensity of communist activity in Italy and Greece. If the Russians came to realize that increased commuist militancy would produce an increased American military presence, then a conflict would develop, Kennan thought, between Soviet security interests and the interests of Greek and Italian communists.[13]

Such a conflict did develop, of course, in Yugoslavia in the summer of 1948. Kennan was quick to welcome Tito's heresy and to see in it a trend to be encouraged elsewhere. "A new factor of fundamental and profound significance has been introduced into the world communist movement," a June 1948 Policy Planning Staff study noted, "by the demonstration that the Kremlin can be successfully defied by one of its own minions."[14] The situation could be expected to recur elsewhere, another study predicted, "because the Kremlin leaders are so overbearing and so cynical in the discipline

12. See NSC 20/1, "U.S. Objectives with Respect to Russia," August 18, 1948, National Archives (Document 22); and NSC 58, "United States Policy Toward the Soviet Satellite States in Eastern Europe," September 14, 1949, National Archives (Document 24).

13. NSC 20/1, August 18, 1948; PPS 23, February 24, 1948, *Foreign Relations: 1948,* I, 518–19.

14. PPS 35, "The Attitude of This Government Toward Events in Yugoslavia," June 30, 1948, *Foreign Relations: 1948,* IV, 1080. (Document 21).

they impose on their followers that few can stand their authority for very long. . . . Conditions are therefore favorable to a concerted effort on our part designed to take advantage of Soviet mistakes and of the rifts that have appeared, and to promote the steady deterioration of the structure of moral influence by which the authority of the Kremlin has been carried to peoples far beyond the reach of Soviet police power.''[15]

To a degree not yet adequately recognized, then, the strategy of containment involved aligning the United States with the forces of nationalism to resist Soviet expansionism. The European Recovery Program (ERP) can be seen in this light, as can Washington's Yugoslav policy and its attempts, in 1949 and early 1950, to encourage dissension between the Soviet Union and the newly victorious Chinese Communists. Behind all these initiatives was the conviction that the object of containment was Soviet expansionism, not international communism, and that that goal could be best accomplished, not through direct confrontation, but through associating the United States with that most powerful of organic ideologies— nationalism.

Kennan's third prescription for action was to encourage, over an extended period of time, a fundamental change in the whole Soviet concept of international relations: to make the Russians see the futility of trying to achieve security through expansion, and to bring them around to what he considered a desirable goal for American policy as well—diversity, not homogeneity.

Such an approach was possible, he believed, because whatever its internal rigidities, the Soviet Union was not totally impervious to outside influences. It had no fixed timetable for expansion; it would retreat when confronted by determined resistance. "If, therefore, situations be created in which it is clearly not to the advantage of [Soviet] power to emphasize the elements of conflict in their relations with the outside world," a Policy Planning Staff study from 1948 argued, "then their actions, and even the tenor of their propaganda to their own people, *can* be modified.''[16] This statement reflected a basic assumption underlying the strategy of containment—that ideology in the Soviet Union was a manifestation of Soviet national interests, not their determinant, and that as Soviet national interests changed, so too would Soviet ideology.

Once the Russians had come to accept the notion that security could be obtained by tolerating diversity, then the way would be open for negotiations on the resolution of outstanding differences. These negotiations, together with a mutual pullback of Russian and American forces and the

15. NSC 20/1, August 18, 1948.
16. *Ibid*. See also the analysis in "The Sources of Soviet Conduct," pp. 574–75.

emergence of the Soviet Union as a satisfied member of the international order, were the ultimate objectives Kennan's concept of containment was designed to achieve.

IV

Such was the design; as always, though, there was a considerable gap between concept and implementation. Kennan's strategy left unresolved several problems which made it difficult to put into effect:

(1) One difficulty was the extent to which Kennan's strategy relied on psychology. He sought to deny key industrial and raw-material-producing areas to the Russians, but to do so primarily by instilling a sense of self-confidence in the minds of people who lived in those areas. That approach placed his program at the mercy of whatever fears, rational or irrational, those people might hold.

The prospect of Soviet military attack, and the possibility that the United States might not be able to do anything about it, constituted one such fear. Kennan thought it groundless, but in the end he was forced to acknowledge that self-confidence in Western Europe and Japan would not develop without security guarantees by the United States, however remote the likelihood of Soviet aggression. Another fear was the revival of German militarism; that prospect made the permanent division of Germany more palatable to many observers than its reunification, especially if such a reunified state risked falling under Soviet control. The problem with these measures was that they tended to perpetuate the division of the world into two hostile camps, thereby delaying the roll-back of Soviet and American influence which Kennan thought essential. Nor, once the process of forming alliances had been started, would it be easy to call a halt: "There is no logical stopping point in the development of a system of anti-Russian alliances," Kennan wrote late in 1948, "until that system has circled the globe and has embraced all the non-communist countries of Europe, Asia, and Africa."[17]

Another unanticipated difficulty was the psychological effect that communist victories in countries not considered vital to United States security could have on those which were. It is significant that Kennan supported aid to Greece and Turkey in 1947 primarily because of the psychological effect their collapse would have had on Western Europe. For similar reasons, he endorsed the decision to aid South Korea in 1950, even though three years

17. PPS 43, "Considerations Affecting the Conclusion of a North Atlantic Security Pact," November 24, 1948, *Foreign Relations: 1948*, III, 286 (Document 17).

earlier he had described the American position in that country as hopeless, and had advocated withdrawal as soon as possible.[18] It was not all that difficult, then, to slide from a belief that the balance of power required nothing more than a limited application of effort in a few key locations to a conviction that the balance could be maintained only by massive applications of force in peripheral areas.

(2) A second problem had to do with the difficulty of maintaining the distinction between Soviet expansionism and international communism. Confusion on this point stemmed partly from the Truman Administration's imprecise public rhetoric: in order to get its foreign aid programs through the Congress, the Administration had found it necessary to present the Soviet threat in global terms, an approach that did not encourage differentiation between varieties of communism. The heated political atmosphere of the period also caused problems: even before Senator Joseph R. McCarthy gave his name to the tendency, expressions of willingness to deal with communists risked accusations of disloyalty, even treason. Reinforcing these trends was an increasingly widespread habit of using ideology as a predictive instrument, of assuming that ideological affiliation took precedence over other influences in determining the behavior of states, and could be used as a basis on which to anticipate their behavior. It was an odd manifestation of the faith Americans have always had in the efficacy of the written word as a guide to actions;[19] its effect was to preclude further attempts to exploit differences within the international communist movement.

(3) Kennan's strategy also ran into difficulties because it based its analysis of Soviet behavior on intentions rather than capabilities; on what the Russians were likely to do, rather than on what they could do.[20] This was not an easy approach to sustain, because it ran up against the natural preference, in dealing with any adversary, in favor of being safe rather than sorry. It required accepting on faith the notion that the Russians did not want a war, when in fact many of their actions—Czechoslovakia, Berlin, Korea—appeared to indicate the opposite. Kennan's emphasis on intentions became even harder to maintain once it became clear that the Soviet Union had the capability, should war come, of doing a considerable amount of damage to the United States and its allies. News of the Russian atomic bomb made it

18. Kennan, *Memoirs: 1925–1950*, pp. 316–19, 484–86. See also PPS 13, November 6, 1947, *Foreign Relations: 1947*, I, 776.

19. See, on this point, Charles Burton Marshall, *The Limits of Foreign Policy* (Baltimore: Johns Hopkins University Press, 1968), p. 56.

20. See Kennan, *Memoirs: 1925–1950*, p. 497; and George F. Kennan, "The United States and the Soviet Union, 1917–1976," *Foreign Affairs*, LIV (July 1976), 681–82.

appear much less risky to base military planning on Soviet capabilities rather than intentions; the price, though, was a persistent overestimation of Soviet strength, and an equally persistent lack of enthusiasm for negotiations until perceived strategic inadequacies had been remedied.

(4) Kennan had emphasized the importance of negotiations with the Russians, but he could not deny the risks such talks might pose for American credibility—whether with the Soviets themselves, who might interpret willingness to negotiate as a sign of weakness; with American allies, who might view it as a sign of neglect; or with the American public, a substantial percentage of which would have regarded negotiations, after 1948, as a sign of appeasement. Given the absence of indications that negotiations would produce results, or that their benefits would outweigh their risks, the Truman Administration, influenced especially by Secretary of State Dean Acheson, simply found it easier not to negotiate.[21]

(5) Finally, a fundamental assumption underlying the strategy of containment had been an awareness that the United States lacked the resources to sustain worldwide commitments, and that, accordingly, hard choices would have to be made between what it could reasonably expect to change, and what it would have to accept. American officials never entirely lost sight of that fact, but the basic conclusions of NSC 68[22]—that military expenditures could be increased without adversely affecting the economy—did have strong appeal; there ensued, as a result, a certain loss of sensitivity to the relationship between costs and commitments which Kennan had so strongly stressed.

There was, in all of these problems, a common thread: all of them—preoccupation with building alliances, the use of ideology as a predictive instrument, concern with credibility, the emphasis on commitments and neglect of costs—reflect excessive attention to the *processes* of diplomacy, and a corresponding tendency to lose sight of objectives. They reflect an inclination to let strategy dictate policy, rather than the other way around. To the extent that the United States contributed to the perpetuation of the Cold War, it did so in large part as a result of this confusion of ends and means, of concentrating so much on the processes of containment as to lose sight of precisely what it was that strategy was supposed to contain.

But if Kennan's critics within the government preoccupied themselves ex-

---

21. David S. McLellan, *Dean Acheson: The State Department Years* (New York: Dodd, Mead, 1976), pp. 163–64.
22. NSC 68, "United States Objectives and Programs for National Security," April 14, 1950, *Foreign Relations: 1950,* I, 234–292 (Document 52).

cessively with processes, it must also be noted that he himself leaned too far in the other direction, by failing to devote sufficient attention to the problems of implementing containment. Skeptical of the efficacy of written policy statements as guides to action, Kennan simply relied on the continued presence of qualified experts to guide the hand of policy makers, much as he had done with Secretary of State George C. Marshall between 1947 and 1949. Nothing better illustrated this tendency than his recommendation, in May 1948, that the Central Intelligence Agency be given a capability for covert political action, the employment of which would be under the strict control of the Department of State, the Department of Defense, and the National Security Council. "It did not work out at all the way I had conceived it," he later admitted; [23] the advice of experts counted for little if policy makers, and the organizations they controlled, chose not to seek it.

V

The documents in this collection demonstrate that the strategy of containment differed substantially from the way in which it was publicly understood at the time, and has usually been subsequently interpreted. They show, further, that the fundamental outlines of that strategy received the endorsement of the highest authorities of the United States government between 1947 and 1949. Nonetheless, the Truman Administration failed to move, in practice, beyond the first stage of containment: restoration of a balance of power along the periphery of the Soviet Union. Not until the early 1970s would the United States begin sustained efforts to exploit fissures within the international communist movement, or to explore with the Russians opportunities for reducing tensions through negotiations. There is much irony in the fact that these initiatives occurred during the administration of a president who, in his early career, had vigorously condemned containment. The diplomacy of Richard M. Nixon and Henry A. Kissinger can with some justification be regarded, therefore, not as a new departure but as a return, whether intentional or not, to the unimplemented concept of containment George F. Kennan had put forward a quarter of a century before.

23. Quoted in Anne Karalekas, "History of the Central Intelligence Agency," in U.S. Congress, Senate (94th Cong., 2nd Sess.), Select Committee to Study Government Operations with Respect to Intelligence Activities, *Final Report: Supplementary Detailed Staff Reports on Foreign and Military Intelligence: Book IV* (Washington: Government Printing Office, 1976), p. 31. See also NSC 10/2, "National Security Council Directive on Office of Special Projects," June 18, 1948, National Security Council Secretariat, Washington, D.C. (Document 12), and George F. Kennan, *Memoirs: 1950–1963* (Boston: Little, Brown, 1972), pp. 202–3.

THE POSTWAR WORLD, 1945

IN THE MONTHS following World War II, Washington policy makers held divergent views regarding the nature of the postwar international environment, as the two documents printed in this section illustrate. SWNCC 282 (Document 1) reflects the position of the Joint Chiefs of Staff. It is noteworthy for its cautious anticipation of tension between former members of the Grand Alliance, its implied skepticism regarding the ability of the United Nations to maintain international order, and its advocacy, for the United States, of a peacetime military force sufficient to preserve a global balance of power. SC-169b (Document 2) is the State Department's response to this assessment. In it, the Department criticizes the Chiefs for neglecting the importance of enforcing peace terms on Germany and Japan, underrating the United Nations' potential as a peacekeeping mechanism, and exaggerating the likelihood of conflict between the United States, Great Britain, and the Soviet Union. Taken together, the documents suggest the absence of a consensus in Washington as late as the end of 1945 over what course postwar Soviet-American relations might take.

---

1 **TOP SECRET** *hardly an*
inf,
document

Basis for the Formulation of a U.S. Military Policy

SWNCC 282   September 19, 1945

[Source: *Foreign Relations of the United States: 1946,* I, 1160–65]

SWNCC 282 originated in the Joint Chiefs of Staff and was approved by that body on September 19, 1945. As the first comprehensive attempt to formulate a postwar military policy, it generated considerable discussion within the State-War-Navy Coordinating Committee, to which it was submitted on September 26, 1945. Never formally approved by that body, SWNCC 282 was finally removed from the agenda of SWNCC's successor organization, the State-Army-Navy-Air Force Coordinating Committee, in 1948.

1. The basic purpose for maintaining United States armed forces is to provide for our security and to uphold and advance our national policies, foreign and domestic. The essentials of our military policy are determined by our national policies.

2. The major national policies which determine our military policy are:

    a. Maintenance of the territorial integrity and security of the United States, its territories, possessions, leased areas and trust territories.

    b. Advancing the political, economic and social well-being of the United States.

    c. Maintenance of the territorial integrity and the sovereignty or political independence of other American states, and regional collaboration with them in the maintenance of international peace and security in the Western Hemisphere.

    d. Maintenance of the territorial integrity, security and, when it becomes effective, the political independence of the Philippine Islands.[1]

    e. Participation in and full support of the United Nations Organization.

    f. Enforcement, in collaboration with our Allies, of terms imposed upon the defeated enemy states.

    g. Maintenance of the United States in the best possible relative position with respect to potential enemy powers, ready when necessary to take military action abroad to maintain the security and integrity of the United States.

3. These policies in the aggregate are directed toward the maintenance of world peace, under conditions which insure the security, well-being and advancement of our country.

4. In the last analysis the maintenance of such a world peace will depend upon mutual cooperation among Britain, Russia and the United States. The possibility of a breakdown in the relation between these major powers and the resulting necessity to exercise individual or collective self-defense requires, for our own preservation, that we be so prepared that if necessary we can maintain our security without immediate or substantial assistance from other nations. Such an eventuality presents the maximum problem from the military point of view. A military policy that will maintain the security of the United States, standing alone, would meet all other military requirements. Any future conflict between major foreign powers will almost

---

1. The Philippines became an independent republic on July 4, 1946. [Ed. note]

certainly precipitate a third world war, in which we could not hope to escape being involved. Any nation, which in the future may attempt to dominate the world, may be expected to make her major effort against the United States and before we can mobilize our forces and productive capacity. The power, range and prospective development of modern weapons are such as to favor such an attack. As a result, there will be a marked reduction in the degree of invulnerability to ready attack that has been provided in the past by our geographical position.

5. It is to be borne in mind, however, that, in correspondingly equal degree, we will possess the means for retaliatory or punitive attack against other powers who may threaten the United States or the international peace structure in general. The means for preserving peace under the United Nations are both tacit and explicit. They are primarily tacit with regard to the major powers in that, whereas the existence of effective military power must be real, its implementation or assertion must be avoided, if possible. If the stability of the international structure is to be maintained, unbalanced power factors or stresses must be guarded against. From the point of view of the United States, this means that our country, if she is to play her proper part toward the maintenance of international peace, must have sufficient military power to make it unwise for any major aggressor nation to initiate a major war against the opposition of the United States. The relative military power required for fulfilling the potential role of this international sanction should not exceed that required for national security purposes, as set forth in the preceding paragraph. It would not be maintained for, nor used in any way as, an international threat, nor for purposes of asserting world domination.

6. More explicit is the maintenance of an international security force. The United Nations Charter provides for the use, if required, of certain armed forces made available to the Security Council, by previous agreement, to maintain international peace and security. Under its terms concerted military action by the United Nations can be taken only when all five of the permanent members of the Security Council, plus two non-permanent members, agree that other means are inadequate to maintain or restore international peace and security. It may therefore be assumed that the total requirement of the Security Council for armed forces will be small, and consequently, that the United States commitment will be only a small part of the military forces which will be required in any event for national security against the in no way remote possibility of a breakdown in the relation of major powers.

7. The other definite military commitment, and the one that is most immediate, is to provide the necessary forces for the occupation and demili-

tarization of Germany and Japan, and the prevention of their resurgence as aggressor nations.

8. It is recognized that the maintenance of overwhelmingly strong forces in time of peace is politically and economically unacceptable to the people of the United States. However, they should accept as requirements essential to their security:

    a. The maintenance of sufficient active forces to afford assurance of the security of the United States, its territories and possessions during the initial period of mobilization of national means—manpower, resources and industry.

    b. Readiness and determination to take prompt and effective military action abroad to anticipate and prevent attack.

    c. An intelligence system which would assure this government information concerning military, political, economic and technological developments abroad and hence provide the necessary forewarning of hostile intent and capability.

    d. A national organization which will promote and coordinate civilian and military activities in technical research and development.

    e. Maintenance of an adequate system of overseas bases.

9. It may be assumed that the United States, relative to other great powers, will maintain in peace time as armed forces only a minimum percentage of its war time potential. It is imperative therefore that these forces be the best trained in the world, and equipped with superior matériel and so disposed strategically that they can be brought to bear at the source of enemy military power, or in other critical areas in time to thwart attack by a potential aggressor. These forces must be supported by an adequate system of bases and machinery for the rapid mobilization of our national resources. Plans and preparations must be kept abreast of developments of new weapons and countermeasures against them and provide for exploitation of our superior mechanical and industrial capabilities. When it becomes evident that forces of aggression are being arrayed against us by a potential enemy, we cannot afford, through any misguided and perilous idea of avoiding an aggressive attitude to permit the first blow to be struck against us. Our government, under such conditions, should press the issue to a prompt political decision, while making all preparations to strike the first blow if necessary.

10. In view of the above, the United States military policy may be stated as follows:

Statement of United States Military Policy

11. *Basic Military Policy.* To insure the security of the United States and to uphold and advance its national interests by military readiness to support its national policies and international commitments.

12. *General Military Policy.* To be prepared to take prompt and effective military action wherever necessary with the armed forces of the United States:

a. To maintain the security of the United States, its territories, possessions, leased areas, trust territories and the Philippine Islands.

b. To secure and to maintain international peace within the Western Hemisphere, acting collectively with other American states, but if necessary acting alone.

c. To fulfill our military commitments in the maintenance of international peace and security as a member of the United Nations.

d. To fulfill our military commitments in the enforcement, in cooperation with our Allies, of the terms imposed upon defeated enemy states.

e. To maintain the United States in the best possible relative position with respect to potential enemy powers.

13. *Principal Supporting Military Policies:*

a. To maintain mobile striking forces in strength, composition and state of readiness for prompt and adequate action and to provide necessary fixed and mobile logistic support for such forces.

b. To maintain adequate forces required by our commitments for the enforcement of terms imposed on defeated enemy states.

c. To provide security for vital areas in the United States, its territories, possessions, leased areas and trust territories against possible enemy attacks, including attacks with newly developed weapons.

d. To maintain an adequate reserve of appropriate composition, both as to personnel and matériel, which is capable of rapid mobilization.

e. To develop and maintain an adequate system of supporting establishments within the continental United States for our operating forces, capable of rapid expansion.

f. To develop and maintain a system of outlying bases, adequately equipped and defended, for the support of our mobile forces, and capable of rapid expansion.

g. To develop and maintain an intelligence system which would assure adequate information concerning military, political, economic and technological developments abroad and provide the necessary warning of hostile intent and capability.

h. To promote research, development and provision of new weapons, processes, matériel and countermeasures, and in so far as possible and desirable to deny such knowledge and capacity to possible enemy states.

i. To provide for the rapid mobilization in an emergency, of national means—manpower, resources and industry—by supporting:

(1) Universal military training.

(2) Maintenance of a large United States Merchant Marine, both active and reserve.

(3) Development and maintenance of United States domestic and international commercial air transport systems.

(4) Plans and preparations for the mobilization of manpower, resources and industry.

(5) Maintenance of industries essential to the national war effort so designed and located as to give maximum insurance against destruction by enemy attack.

(6) Stockpiling of critical strategic materials.

j. To develop and maintain close coordination and mutual understanding between the State, War and Navy Departments, and those other agencies of government and industry which contribute to the national war effort.

k. To maintain liaison with and to support the development and training of the armed forces of the American republics, the Dominion of Canada, the Philippine Islands, and other nations which contribute to the security of the United States, its territories, possessions, leased areas, trust territories, and the Western Hemisphere.

l. In concert with political and economic measures taken by the other departments of the government, to maintain the United States in the best possible military position with respect to potential enemy powers.

~~~~~~

2 **T O P S E C R E T**

Action on Joint Chiefs of Staff Statement on United States Military Policy

SC-169b   November 16, 1946

[Source: *Foreign Relations of the United States: 1946,* I, 1125–28]

SC-169b, an excerpt from which is printed below, was prepared by the Secretary's Committee in the Department of State as a reply to SWNCC 282 (Document 1). It was intended not as an exhaustive commentary on that document but as an effort to bring the position of the Joint Chiefs of Staff more into line with national policy as expressed by the President. As such, it serves as a concise statement of the Department's expectations for the postwar world.

1. The Department of State recognizes its interest and concern in the Joint Chiefs of Staff statement on "United States Military Policy". Therein it is stated (paragraph 1) that "the basic purpose for maintaining United States armed forces is to provide for our security . . .". As the principal concern of statecraft is to obtain the maximum degree of security, it follows that the Department should scrutinize closely any formulation of military policy.

2. It is the view of the Department of State that the maximum degree of security can be obtained only if our foreign policy and our military policy are mutually helpful. Our foreign policy should not hamper our military policy. Neither should our military policy handicap the carrying out of our foreign policy. In fact, the demands placed upon our armed forces are based upon our foreign policy, as stated by President Truman in his address at New York on October 27, 1945. This relationship was stated in terms of the "four principal tasks" which, the President said, determined the kind of armed might we propose to maintain:

First, our Army, Navy and Air Force, in collaboration with our Allies, must enforce the terms of peace imposed upon our defeated enemies.

Second, we must fulfill the military obligations which we are undertaking as a member of the United Nations Organization—to support a lasting peace, by force, if necessary.

Third, we must cooperate with other American nations to preserve the territorial integrity and the political independence of the nations of the Western Hemisphere.

Fourth, in this troubled and uncertain world, our military forces must be adequate to discharge the fundamental mission laid upon them by the Constitution of the United States—to "provide for the common defense" of the United States.

These four military tasks are directed not toward war—not toward conquest—but toward peace.

We seek to use our military strength solely to preserve the peace of the world. For we now know that that is the only sure way to make our own freedom secure.

That is the basis of the foreign policy of the people of the United States.[2]

3. In the Joint Chiefs of Staff statement the place assigned the task of enforcing the terms of peace upon Germany and Japan seems to the Department of State to be less prominent than it should be. Hostilities with Germany came to an end a bare six months ago. Operations against Japan ceased less than three months ago. In neither case has the formal end of hostilities been proclaimed. Nor have treaties of peace been formulated, fixing among other things the period within which military forces of this country and of others of the United Nations will occupy German and Japanese territory. In the Joint Chiefs of Staff statement the significance of joint occupation and of joint enforcement of peace terms as parts of the job of securing the victory achieved through joint efforts has been largely overlooked. Politically, no aspect of our foreign policy carries greater potentialities for our future security than those relations with our allies involved in the enforcement of surrender and peace terms. It seems to the Department of State that a correspondingly important place should be given to this task in a statement of military policy.

4. Moreover, the responsibilities of the United States as a principal member of the United Nations should figure more prominently in making the estimate of our future military requirements. The political leadership we took in this venture was made possible primarily because of the military strength we mobilized during the war. It will continue in proportion to the relative military strength we maintain in the future. The United Nations is built upon the power relations existing among the United States, Great Britain, Russia, China, France, and the other members of the war-time coalition. Its future will depend upon power relations which will exist hereafter among the principal members. If the balance of this relationship in military potential were to be impaired or upset, the fabric of the United Nations would be weakened or at least would require reexamination. We do not wish this balance to be upset. Therefore, we should retain our military power in greater strength than that which would be needed merely to fulfill our strictly military obligations under the Charter. The question is: how much greater? This estimate can be made only on the basis of developing political factors. As our relations with other countries are conditioned by our duties and re-

2. *Public Papers of the Presidents: Harry S. Truman, 1945* (Washington: 1961), pp. 432–33. [Ed. note]

sponsibilities under the United Nations Charter, greater recognition should be given these factors as determinants of our military needs.

5. It is believed that the analysis of our military needs postulated on a breakdown in peaceful relations among Britain, Russia and the United States receives undue emphasis (paragraphs 4, 5, and 6). It is given more space than that based on the continuance of peaceful relations. This disproportion should be corrected. In this connection the last of the major national policies said by the Joint Chiefs of Staff to determine our military needs is overemphasized. This statement of policy is: "maintenance of the United States in the best possible relative position with respect to potential enemy powers, ready when necessary to take military action abroad to maintain the security and integrity of the United States" (paragraph 2g).

6. The hypothesis that our security may require extensive military operations overseas needs close examination for its possible effect on the relations with our principal allies in the recent war. This hypothesis runs through the entire statement (paragraphs 2g, 8b, 9, 13a). The need for examination is emphasized by the further hypothesis that such operations would be preventive in purpose (paragraphs 8b and c, 9). Despite our strength, our chances of survival in a future conflict would be increased were we to be assured of the help of allies. This political need must be a constant pre-occupation of our foreign policy. If a given hypothesis, such as the two just referred to, might handicap the Department of State in its conduct of foreign policy, a re-examination of this hypothesis should be made.

7. The Department of State believes that certain of the subsidiary policies listed in paragraph 13 of the Joint Chiefs of Staff statement also stand in need of examination before becoming part of our stated military policy. The examination should be undertaken from the point of view of our relations with other countries and particularly with our principal allies. As a matter of national policy "the maintenance of a large merchant marine, both active and reserve" (paragraph 13i (2)) might in time weaken the economic strength (hence the military potential) of certain of our potential future allies, and thus might defeat its purpose of contributing to our national security. The "maintenance of industries essential to the war effort" (paragraph 13i (5)) needs examination on economic as well as foreign policy grounds. The "stockpiling of critical strategic materials" (paragraph 13i (6)) likewise should be scrutinized from both economic and foreign policy angles. It is also questionable whether our policy should be to support the "development" of the armed forces of the other American republics, as stated in paragraph 13k.

8. In addition to studying most carefully the foreign policy implications

of the statement as it stands, the addition of certain new items seems to the Department of State to merit consideration. Respect for the territorial integrity and political independence of certain states, China, for example, might be considered for inclusion as a national policy determining our military needs (paragraph 2) since we are bound by treaty to accord this respect. Moreover, the United States as a member of the United Nations has agreed to refrain from the threat or use of force against the territorial integrity or political independence of any state (Article 2, 4). Consideration should be given to adding this principle as a national policy determining our military needs. Multilateral regulation of armaments in accordance with the Charter of the United Nations is also proposed as a policy determining our military needs which might be added to those already listed in the statement. Finally, consideration might well be given to including, as an additional policy determining our military needs, the political policy of maintaining friendly relations with other countries so as to prevent the actual outbreak of hostilities, or, in the event of such hostilities, to give us the maximum number of allies.

❧ 2 ❧

CONTAINMENT: THE DOCTRINE, 1946–48

By EARLY 1946, a consensus on the nature of the postwar world had begun to take shape in Washington. Of primary importance in influencing official attitudes was the famous "long telegram" of February 22, 1946, from George F. Kennan, *chargé d'affaires* at the American Embassy in Moscow (Document 3). Kennan's analysis of Soviet behavior quickly became the accepted wisdom in Washington, although agreement on this subject brought no firm conclusions as to what the American response should be.

One view, expressed most clearly by White House aide Clark M. Clifford in a September 1946 report to the President (Document 4), was that the United States should resist the expansion of Soviet influence wherever it occurred. This line of reasoning appeared in President Harry S. Truman's March 12, 1947, address to the Congress on aid to Greece and Turkey, in which the Chief Executive proclaimed, in what came to be known as the "Truman Doctrine," that "It must be the policy of the United States to support free peoples who are resisting attempted subjugation by armed minorities or by outside pressures." [1]

A different view, here reflected in JCS 1769/1 (Document 5), was that the United States lacked the capacity to act wherever Soviet expansion might occur, and that American policy makers would have to distinguish between areas of peripheral and vital interest. Although Kennan shared this position, he inadvertently contributed to confusion regarding administration policy with an article on "The Sources of Soviet Conduct," which appeared in the July 1947 issue of *Foreign Affairs* (Document 6).

Kennan later acknowledged that this article reflected only imperfectly his conception of what came to be known as the policy of "containment." To clarify Kennan's understanding of this term, two subsequent Policy Planning Staff memoranda, PPS 13 and PPS 23 (Documents 7 and 8), are also printed.

---

1. *Public Papers of the Presidents: Harry S. Truman, 1947* (Washington: 1963), p. 179.

3   **S E C R E T**

Moscow Embassy Telegram #511: "The Long Telegram"

February 22, 1946

[Source: *Foreign Relations of the United States: 1946*, VI, 696–709]

This 8,000-word telegram from George F. Kennan probably did more than any other single document to influence the evolution of early postwar United States foreign policy. As a member of the State Department's original corps of trained Russian experts, Kennan had earned repute for his insight into Soviet affairs, but his pessimistic assessments of prospects for postwar cooperation with Moscow evoked little sympathy during the war. By February 1946, however, official Washington had become sufficiently perplexed by rising Soviet-American tension to seek new explanations of Russian behavior. Kennan's "long telegram" did much to resolve that perplexity.

The "long telegram" was both an analysis of Soviet behavior and a prescription for action by the United States. In it, Kennan advanced an argument he was to make repeatedly in the future: that Soviet hostility sprang from nothing the West had done, but from the need Russian leaders felt for a hostile outside world as a means of justifying their own autocratic rule. In Kennan's view, communist ideology reinforced such tendencies but did not primarily motivate them. Soviet expansion could best be dealt with, he reasoned, not by direct confrontation but by building viable societies throughout the non-Soviet world which, through strength and self-confidence, would eventually become impervious to Moscow's influence.[2]

The "long telegram" is reprinted here as received in the Department of State.

511. Answer to Dept's 284, Feb 13[3] involves questions so intricate, so delicate, so strange to our form of thought, and so important to analysis of our international environment that I cannot compress answers into single brief message without yielding to what I feel would be dangerous degree of over-simplification. I hope, therefore, Dept will bear with me if I submit in answer to this question five parts, subjects of which will be roughly as follows:

1. Basic features of post-war Soviet outlook.
2. Background of this outlook.
3. Its projection in practical policy on official level.
4. Its projection on unofficial level.
5. Practical deductions from standpoint of US policy.

2. For further background on the "long telegram," see George F. Kennan, *Memoirs: 1925–1950* (Boston: Little, Brown, 1967), pp. 292–95.

3. This telegram had informed Kennan that the Department would welcome from him an interpretive analysis of what could be expected in future Soviet foreign policy. [Ed. note].

I apologize in advance for this burdening of telegraphic channel; but questions involved are of such urgent importance, particularly in view of recent events, that our answers to them, if they deserve attention at all, seem to me to deserve it at once. There follows

Part 1: Basic Features of Post War Soviet Outlook, as Put Forward by Official Propaganda Machine, Are as Follows:

a. USSR still lives in antagonistic "capitalist encirclement" with which in the long run there can be no permanent peaceful coexistence. As stated by Stalin in 1927 to a delegation of American workers:

> In course of further development of international revolution there will emerge two centers of world significance: a socialist center, drawing to itself the countries which tend toward socialism, and a capitalist center, drawing to itself the countries that incline toward capitalism. Battle between these two centers for command of world economy will decide fate of capitalism and of communism in entire world.

b. Capitalist world is beset with internal conflicts, inherent in nature of capitalist society. These conflicts are insoluble by means of peaceful compromise. Greatest of them is that between England and US.

c. Internal conflicts of capitalism inevitably generate wars. Wars thus generated may be of two kinds: intra-capitalist wars between two capitalist states, and wars of intervention against socialist world. Smart capitalists, vainly seeking escape from inner conflicts of capitalism, incline toward latter.

d. Intervention against USSR, while it would be disastrous to those who undertook it, would cause renewed delay in progress of Soviet socialism and must therefore be forestalled at all costs.

e. Conflicts between capitalist states, though likewise fraught with danger for USSR, nevertheless hold out great possibilities for advancement of socialist cause, particularly if USSR remains militarily powerful, ideologically monolithic and faithful to its present brilliant leadership.

f. It must be borne in mind that capitalist world is not all bad. In addition to hopelessly reactionary and bourgeois elements, it includes (1) certain wholly enlightened and positive elements united in acceptable communistic parties and (2) certain other elements (now described for tactical reasons as progressive or democratic) whose reactions, aspirations and activities happen to be "objectively" favorable to interests of USSR. These last must be encouraged and utilized for Soviet purposes.

g. Among negative elements of bourgeois-capitalist society, most dangerous of all are those whom Lenin called false friends of the people, namely moderate-socialist or social-democratic leaders (in other words, non-Communist left-wing). These are more dangerous than out-and-out reactionaries, for latter at least march under their true colors, whereas moderate left-wing leaders confuse people by employing devices of socialism to serve interests of reactionary capital.

So much for premises. To what deductions do they lead from standpoint of Soviet policy? To following:

a. Everything must be done to advance relative strength of USSR as factor in international society. Conversely, no opportunity must be missed to reduce strength and influence, collectively as well as individually, of capitalist powers.

b. Soviet efforts, and those of Russia's friends abroad, must be directed toward deepening and exploiting of differences and conflicts between capitalist powers. If these eventually deepen into an "imperialist" war, this war must be turned into revolutionary upheavals within the various capitalist countries.

c. "Democratic-progressive" elements abroad are to be utilized to maximum to bring pressure to bear on capitalist governments along lines agreeable to Soviet interests.

d. Relentless battle must be waged against socialist and social-democratic leaders abroad.

Part 2: Background of Outlook

Before examining ramifications of this party line in practice there are certain aspects of it to which I wish to draw attention.

First, it does not represent natural outlook of Russian people. Latter are, by and large, friendly to outside world, eager for experience of it, eager to measure against it talents they are conscious of possessing, eager above all to live in peace and enjoy fruits of their own labor. Party line only represents thesis which official propaganda machine puts forward with great skill and persistence to a public often remarkably resistant in the stronghold of its innermost thoughts. But party line is binding for outlook and conduct of people who make up apparatus of power—party, secret police and Government—and it is exclusively with these that we have to deal.

Second, please note that premises on which this party line is based are for most part simply not true. Experience has shown that peaceful and mutually profitable coexistence of capitalist and socialist states is entirely possible.

Basic internal conflicts in advanced countries are no longer primarily those arising out of capitalist ownership of means of production, but are ones arising from advanced urbanism and industrialism as such, which Russia has thus far been spared not by socialism but only by her own backwardness. Internal rivalries of capitalism do not always generate wars; and not all wars are attributable to this cause. To speak of possibility of intervention against USSR today, after elimination of Germany and Japan and after example of recent war, is sheerest nonsense. If not provoked by forces of intolerance and subversion "capitalist" world of today is quite capable of living at peace with itself and with Russia. Finally, no sane person has reason to doubt sincerity of moderate socialist leaders·in Western countries. Nor is it fair to deny success of their efforts to improve conditions for working population whenever, as in Scandinavia, they have been given chance to show what they could do.

Falseness of these premises, every one of which pre-dates recent war, was amply demonstrated by that conflict itself. Anglo-American differences did not turn out to be major differences of Western World. Capitalist countries, other than those of Axis, showed no disposition to solve their differences by joining in crusade against USSR. Instead of imperialist war turning into civil wars and revolution, USSR found itself obliged to fight side by side with capitalist powers for an avowed community of aims.

Nevertheless, all these theses, however baseless and disproven, are being boldly put forward again today. What does this indicate? It indicates that Soviet party line is not based on any objective analysis of situation beyond Russia's borders; that it has, indeed, little to do with conditions outside of Russia; that it arises mainly from basic inner-Russian necessities which existed before recent war and exist today.

At bottom of Kremlin's neurotic view of world affairs is traditional and instinctive Russian sense of insecurity. Originally, this was insecurity of a peaceful agricultural people trying to live on vast exposed plain in neighborhood of fierce nomadic peoples. To this was added, as Russia came into contact with economically advanced West, fear of more competent, more powerful, more highly organized societies in that area. But this latter type of insecurity was one which afflicted rather Russian rulers than Russian people; for Russian rulers have invariably sensed that their rule was relatively archaic in form, fragile and artificial in its psychological foundation, unable to stand comparison or contact with political systems of Western countries. For this reason they have always feared foreign penetration, feared direct contact between Western world and their own, feared what would happen if Russians learned truth about world without or if foreigners learned truth about world within. And they have learned to seek security only in patient but deadly struggle for total destruction of rival power, never in compacts and compromises with it.

It was no coincidence that Marxism, which had smouldered ineffectively for half a century in Western Europe, caught hold and blazed for first time in Russia. Only in this land which had never known a friendly neighbor or indeed any tolerant equilibrium of separate powers, either internal or international, could a doctrine thrive which viewed economic conflicts of society as insoluble by peaceful means. After establishment of Bolshevist regime, Marxist dogma, rendered even more truculent and intolerant by Lenin's interpretation, became a perfect vehicle for sense of insecurity with which Bolsheviks, even more than previous Russian rulers, were afficted. In this dogma, with its basic altruism of purpose, they found justification for their instinctive fear of outside world, for the dictatorship without which they did not know how to rule, for cruelties they did not dare not to inflict, for sacrifices they felt bound to demand. In the name of Marxism they sacrificed every single ethical value in their methods and tactics. Today they cannot dispense with it. It is fig leaf of their moral and intellectual respectability. Without it they would stand before history, at best, as only the last of that long succession of cruel and wasteful Russian rulers who have relentlessly forced country on to ever new heights of military power in order to guarantee external security of their internally weak regimes. This is why Soviet purposes must always be solemnly clothed in trappings of Marxism, and why no one should underrate importance of dogma in Soviet affairs. Thus Soviet leaders are driven [by] necessities of their own past and present position to put forward a dogma which [apparent omission] outside world as evil, hostile and menacing, but as bearing within itself germs of creeping disease and destined to be wracked with growing internal convulsions until it is given final *coup de grace* by rising power of socialism and yields to new and better world. This thesis provides justification for that increase of military and police power of Russian state, for that isolation of Russian population from outside world, and for that fluid and constant pressure to extend limits of Russian police power which are together the natural and instinctive urges of Russian rulers. Basically this is only the steady advance of uneasy Russian nationalism, a centuries old movement in which conceptions of offense and defense are inextricably confused. But in new guise of international Marxism, with its honeyed promises to a desperate and war torn outside world, it is more dangerous and insidious than ever before.

It should not be thought from above that Soviet party line is necessarily disingenuous and insincere on part of all those who put it forward. Many of them are too ignorant of outside world and mentally too dependent to question [apparent omission] self-hypnotism, and who have no difficulty making themselves believe what they find it comforting and convenient to believe. Finally we have the unsolved mystery as to who, if anyone, in this great land actually receives accurate and unbiased information about outside world. In atmosphere of oriental secretiveness and conspiracy which pervades this Government, possibilities for distorting or poisoning sources and currents of information are infinite. The very disrespect of Russians for objective truth—indeed, their disbelief in its existence—leads them to view all stated facts as instruments for furtherance of one ulterior purpose or another. There is good reason to suspect that this Government is actually a conspiracy within a conspiracy; and I for one am reluctant to believe that Stalin himself receives anything like an objective picture of outside world. Here there is ample scope for the type of subtle intrigue at which Russians are past masters. Inability of foreign governments to place their case squarely before Russian policy makers—extent to which they are delivered up in their relations with Russia to good graces of obscure and unknown advisers whom they never see and cannot influence—this to my mind is most disquieting feature of diplomacy in Moscow, and one which Western statesmen would do well to keep in mind if they would understand nature of difficulties encountered here.

Part 3: Projection of Soviet Outlook in Practical Policy on Official Level

We have now seen nature and background of Soviet program. What may we expect by way of its practical implementation?

Soviet policy, as Department implies in its query under reference, is conducted on two planes: (1) official plane represented by actions undertaken officially in name of Soviet Government; and (2) subterranean plane of actions undertaken by agencies for which Soviet Government does not admit responsibility.

Policy promulgated on both planes will be calculated to serve basic policies (a) to (d) outlined in part 1. Actions taken on different planes will differ considerably, but will dovetail into each other in purpose, timing and effect.

On official plane we must look for following:

a. Internal policy devoted to increasing in every way strength and prestige of Soviet state: intensive military-industrialization; maximum development of armed forces; great displays to impress outsiders; continued secretiveness about internal matters, designed to conceal weaknesses and to keep opponents in dark.

b. Wherever it is considered timely and promising, efforts will be made to advance official limits of Soviet power. For the moment, these efforts are restricted to certain neighboring points conceived of here as being of immediate strategic necessity, such as Northern Iran, Turkey, possibly Bornholm. However, other points may at any time come into question, if and as concealed Soviet political power is extended to new areas. Thus a "friendly" Persian Government might be asked to grant Russia a port on Persian Gulf. Should Spain fall under Communist control, question of Soviet base at Gibraltar Strait might be activated. But such claims will appear on official level only when unofficial preparation is complete.

c. Russians will participate officially in international organizations where they see opportunity of extending Soviet power or of inhibiting or diluting power of others. Moscow sees in UNO not the mechanism for a permanent and stable world society founded on mutual interest and aims of all nations, but an arena in which aims just mentioned can be favorably pursued. As long as UNO is considered here to serve this purpose, Soviets will remain with it. But if at any time they come to conclusion that it is serving to embarrass or frustrate their aims for power expansion and if they see better prospects for pursuit of these aims along other lines, they will not hesitate to abandon UNO. This would imply, however, that they felt themselves strong enough to split unity of other nations by their withdrawal, to render UNO ineffective as a threat to their aims or security, and to replace it with an international weapon more effective from their viewpoint. Thus Soviet attitude toward UNO will depend largely on loyalty of other nations to it, and on degree of vigor, decisiveness and cohesion with which these nations defend in UNO the peaceful and hopeful concept of international life, which that organization represents to our way of thinking. I reiterate, Moscow has no abstract devotion to UNO ideals. Its attitude to that organization will remain essentially pragmatic and tactical.

d. Toward colonial areas and backward or dependent peoples, Soviet policy, even on official plane, will be directed toward weakening of power and influence and contacts of advanced Western nations, on theory that in so far as this policy is successful, there will be created a vacuum which will favor Communist-Soviet penetration. Soviet pressure for participation in trusteeship arrangements thus represents, in my opinion, a desire to be in a position to complicate and inhibit exertion of Western influence at such points rather than to provide major channel for exerting of Soviet power. Latter motive is not lacking, but for this Soviets prefer to rely on other channels than official trusteeship arrangements. Thus we may expect to find Soviets asking for admission everywhere to trusteeship or similar arrangements and using levers thus acquired to weaken Western influence among such peoples.

e. Russians will strive energetically to develop Soviet representation in, and official ties with, countries in which they sense strong possibilities of opposition to Western centers of power. This applies to such widely separated points as Germany, Argentina, Middle Eastern countries, etc.

f. In international economic matters, Soviet policy will really be dominated by pursuit of antarchy for Soviet Union and Soviet-dominated adjacent areas taken together. That, however, will be underlying policy. As far as official line is concerned, position is not yet clear. Soviet Government has shown strange reticence since termination hostilities on subject foreign trade. If large scale long term credits should be forthcoming, I believe Soviet Government may eventually again do lip service, as it did in 1930's to desirability of building up international economic exchanges in general. Otherwise I think it possible Soviet foreign trade may be restricted largely to Soviet's own security sphere, including occupied areas in Germany, and that a cold official shoulder may be turned to principle of general economic collaboration among nations.

g. With respect to cultural collaboration, lip service will likewise be rendered to desirability of deepening cultural contacts between peoples, but this will not in practice be interpreted in any way which could weaken security position of Soviet peoples. Actual manifestations of Soviet policy in this respect will be restricted to arid channels of closely shepherded official visits and functions, with superabundance of vodka and speeches and dearth of permanent effects.

h. Beyond this, Soviet official relations will take what might be called "correct" course with individual foreign governments, with great stress being laid on prestige of Soviet Union and its representatives and with punctilious attention to protocol, as distinct from good manners.

Part 4: Following May Be Said as to What We May Expect by Way of Implementation of Basic Soviet Policies on Unofficial, or Subterranean Plane, i.e. on Plane for Which Soviet Government Accepts no Responsibility

Agencies utilized for promulgation of policies in this plane are following:

1. Inner central core of Communist Parties in other countries. While many of persons who compose this category may also appear and act in unrelated public capacities, they are in reality working closely together as an underground operating directorate of world communism, a concealed Comintern tightly coordinated and directed by Moscow. It is important to remember that this inner core is actually working on underground lines, despite legality of parties with which it is associated.

2. Rank and file of Communist Parties. Note distinction is drawn between these and persons defined in paragraph 1. This distinction has become much sharper in recent years. Whereas formerly foreign Communist Parties represented a curious (and from Moscow's standpoint often inconvenient) mixture of conspiracy and legitimate activity, now the conspiratorial element has been neatly concentrated in inner circle and ordered underground, while rank and file—no longer even taken into confidence about realities of movement—are thrust forward as bona fide internal partisans of certain political tendencies within their respective countries, genuinely innocent of conspiratorial connection with foreign states. Only in certain countries where communists are numerically strong do they now regularly appear and act as a body. As a rule they are used to penetrate, and to influence or dominate, as case may be, other organizations less likely to be suspected of being tools of Soviet Government, with a view to accomplishing their purposes through [apparent omission] organizations, rather than by direct action as a separate political party.

3. A wide variety of national associations or bodies which can be dominated or influenced by such penetration. These include: labor unions, youth leagues, women's organizations, racial societies, religious societies, social organizations, cultural groups, liberal magazines, publishing houses, etc.

4. International organizations which can be similarly penetrated through influence over various national components. Labor, youth and women's organizations are prominent among them. Particular, almost vital, importance is attached in this connection to international labor movement. In this, Moscow sees possibility of sidetracking western governments in world affairs and building up international lobby capable of compelling governments to

take actions favorable to Soviet interests in various countries and of paralyzing actions disagreeable to USSR.

5. Russian Orthodox Church, with its foreign branches, and through it the Eastern Orthodox Church in general.

6. Pan-Slav movement and other movements (Azerbaijan, Armenian, Turcoman, etc.) based on racial groups within Soviet Union.

7. Governments or governing groups willing to lend themselves to Soviet purposes in one degree or another, such as present Bulgarian and Yugoslav Governments, North Persian regime, Chinese Communists, etc. Not only propaganda machines but actual policies of these regimes can be placed extensively at disposal of USSR.

It may be expected that component parts of this far-flung apparatus will be utilized, in accordance with their individual suitability, as follows:

a. To undermine general political and strategic potential of major western powers. Efforts will be made in such countries to disrupt national self-confidence, to hamstring measures of national defense, to increase social and industrial unrest, to stimulate all forms of disunity. All persons with grievances, whether economic or racial, will be urged to seek redress not in mediation and compromise, but in defiant violent struggle for destruction of other elements of society. Here poor will be set against rich, black against white, young against old, newcomers against established residents, etc.

b. On unofficial plane particularly violent efforts will be made to weaken power and influence of Western Powers on colonial backward, or dependent peoples. On this level, no holds will be barred. Mistakes and weaknesses of western colonial administration will be mercilessly exposed and exploited. Liberal opinion in Western countries will be mobilized to weaken colonial policies. Resentment among dependent peoples will be stimulated. And while latter are being encouraged to seek independence of Western Powers, Soviet dominated puppet political machines will be undergoing preparation to take over domestic power in respective colonial areas when independence is achieved.

c. Where individual governments stand in path of Soviet purposes pressure will be brought for their removal from office. This can happen where governments directly oppose Soviet foreign policy aims (Turkey, Iran), where they seal their territories off against Communist penetration (Switzerland, Portugal), or where they compete too strongly, like Labor Government in England, for moral domination among elements which it is important for Communists to dominate.

(Sometimes, two of these elements are present in a single case. Then Communist opposition becomes particularly shrill and savage.)

d. In foreign countries Communists will, as a rule, work toward destruction of all forms of personal independence, economic, political or moral. Their system can handle only individuals who have been brought into complete dependence on higher power. Thus, persons who are financially independent—such as individual businessmen, estate owners, successful farmers, artisans and all those who exercise local leadership or have local prestige, such as popular local clergymen or political figures, are anathema. It is not by chance that even in USSR local officials are kept constantly on move from one job to another, to prevent their taking root.

e. Everything possible will be done to set major Western Powers against each other. Anti-British talk will be plugged among Americans, anti-American talk among British. Continentals, including Germans, will be taught to abhor both Anglo-Saxon powers. Where suspicions exist, they will be fanned; where not, ignited. No effort will be spared to discredit and combat all efforts which threaten to lead to any sort of unity or cohesion among other [apparent omission] from which Russia might be excluded. Thus, all forms of international organization not amenable to Communist penetration and control, whether it be the Catholic [apparent omission] international economic concerns, or the international fraternity of royalty and aristocracy, must expect to find themselves under fire from many, and often [apparent omission].

f. In general, all Soviet efforts on unofficial international plane will be negative and destructive in character, designed to tear down sources of strength beyond reach of Soviet control. This is only in line with basic Soviet instinct that there can be no compromise with rival power and that constructive work can start only when Communist power is dominant. But behind all this will be applied insistent, unceasing pressure for penetration and command of key positions in administration and especially in police apparatus of foreign countries. The Soviet regime is a police regime par excellence, reared in the dim half world of Tsarist police intrigue, accustomed to think primarily in terms of police power. This should never be lost sight of in gauging Soviet motives.

Part 5: *Practical Deductions From Standpoint of US Policy*

In summary, we have here a political force committed fanatically to the belief that with US there can be no permanent *modus vivendi,* that it is desirable and necessary that the internal harmony of our society be disrupted, our traditional way of life be destroyed, the international authority of our state be broken, if Soviet power is to be secure. This political force has complete power of disposition over energies of one of world's greatest peoples and resources of world's richest national territory, and is borne along by deep and powerful currents of Russian nationalism. In addition, it has an elaborate and far flung apparatus for exertion of its influence in other countries, an apparatus of amazing flexibility and versatility, managed by people whose experience and skill in underground methods are presumably without parallel in history. Finally, it is seemingly inaccessible to considerations of reality in its basic reactions. For it, the vast fund of objective fact about human society is not, as with us, the measure against which outlook is constantly being tested and re-formed, but a grab bag from which individual items are selected arbitrarily and tendenciously to bolster an outlook already preconceived. This is admittedly not a pleasant picture. Problem of how to cope with this force is undoubtedly greatest task our diplomacy has ever faced and probably greatest it will ever have to face. It should be point of departure from which our political general staff work at present juncture should proceed. It should be approached with same thoroughness and care as solution of major strategic problem in war, and if necessary, with no smaller outlay in planning effort. I cannot attempt to suggest all answers here. But I would like to record my conviction that problem is within our power to solve—and that without recourse to any general military conflict. And in support of this conviction there are certain observations of a more encouraging nature I should like to make:

1. Soviet power, unlike that of Hitlerite Germany, is neither schematic nor adventuristic. It does not work by fixed plans. It does not take unnecessary risks. Impervious to logic of reason, and it is highly sensitive to logic of force. For this reason it can easily withdraw—and usually does—when strong resistance is encountered at any point. Thus, if the adversary has sufficient force and makes clear his readiness to use it, he rarely has to do so. If situations are properly handled there need be no prestige-engaging showdowns.

2. Gauged against Western World as a whole, Soviets are still by far the weaker force. Thus, their success will really depend on degree of

cohesion, firmness and vigor which Western World can muster. And this is factor which it is within our power to influence.

3. Success of Soviet system, as form of internal power, is not yet finally proven. It has yet to be demonstrated that it can survive supreme test of successive transfer of power from one individual or group to another. Lenin's death was first such transfer, and its effects wracked Soviet state for 15 years. After Stalin's death or retirement will be second. But even this will not be final test. Soviet internal system will now be subjected, by virtue of recent territorial expansions, to series of additional strains which once proved severe tax on Tsardom. We here are convinced that never since termination of civil war have mass of Russian people been emotionally farther removed from doctrines of Communist Party than they are today. In Russia, party has now become a great and—for the moment—highly successful apparatus of dictatorial administration, but it has ceased to be a source of emotional inspiration. Thus, internal soundness and permanence of movement need not yet be regarded as assured.

4. All Soviet propaganda beyond Soviet security sphere is basically negative and destructive. It should therefore be relatively easy to combat it by any intelligent and really constructive program.

For these reasons I think we may approach calmly and with good heart problem of how to deal with Russia. As to how this approach should be made, I only wish to advance, by way of conclusion, following comments:

1. Our first step must be to apprehend, and recognize for what it is, the nature of the movement with which we are dealing. We must study it with same courage, detachment, objectivity, and same determination not to be emotionally provoked or unseated by it, with which doctor studies unruly and unreasonable individual.

2. We must see that our public is educated to realities of Russian situation. I cannot over-emphasize importance of this. Press cannot do this alone. It must be done mainly by Government, which is necessarily more experienced and better informed on practical problems involved. In this we need not be deterred by [ugliness] of picture. I am convinced that there would be far less hysterical anti-Sovietism in our country today if realities of this situation were better understood by our people. There is nothing as dangerous or as terrifying as the unknown. It may also be argued that to reveal more information on our difficulties with Russia would reflect unfavorably on Russian-American relations. I feel that if there is any real risk here involved, it is one which

we should have courage to face, and sooner the better. But I cannot see what we would be risking. Our stake in this country, even coming on heels of tremendous demonstrations of our friendship for Russian people, is remarkably small. We have here no investments to guard, no actual trade to lose, virtually no citizens to protect, few cultural contacts to preserve. Our only stake lies in what we hope rather than what we have; and I am convinced we have better chance of realizing those hopes if our public is enlightened and if our dealings with Russians are placed entirely on realistic and matter-of-fact basis.

3. Much depends on health and vigor of our own society. World communism is like malignant parasite which feeds only on diseased tissue. This is point at which domestic and foreign policies meet. Every courageous and incisive measure to solve internal problems of our own society, to improve self-confidence, discipline, morale and community spirit of our own people, is a diplomatic victory over Moscow worth a thousand diplomatic notes and joint communiqués. If we cannot abandon fatalism and indifference in face of deficiencies of our own society, Moscow will profit—Moscow cannot help profiting by them in its foreign policies.

4. We must formulate and put forward for other nations a much more positive and constructive picture of sort of world we would like to see than we have put forward in past. It is not enough to urge people to develop political processes similar to our own. Many foreign peoples, in Europe at least, are tired and frightened by experiences of past, and are less interested in abstract freedom than in security. They are seeking guidance rather than responsibilities. We should be better able than Russians to give them this. And unless we do, Russians certainly will.

5. Finally we must have courage and self-confidence to cling to our own methods and conceptions of human society. After all, the greatest danger that can befall us in coping with this problem of Soviet communism, is that we shall allow ourselves to become like those with whom we are coping.

                                                            KENNAN

◇◇◇

4   **TOP SECRET**

American Relations with the Soviet Union: A Report to the President by the Special Counsel to the President.

September 24, 1946

[Source: Harry S. Truman Papers, Harry S. Truman Library, Independence, Missouri]

This lengthy report, only the conclusion of which is printed here, was prepared on President Truman's orders by his Special Counsel, Clark M. Clifford, after consultation with the Secretaries of State, War, Navy, the Joint Chiefs of Staff, the Attorney General, the Director of Central Intelligence, and other administration officials. Never formally circulated outside the White House, it represents nonetheless a significant early attempt to formulate a comprehensive national policy for dealing with the Soviet Union, building on the analysis of Russian behavior contained in Kennan's "long telegram" (Document 3).

The Clifford report is interesting for its tacit assumption that the United States possessed the capacity to oppose Soviet expansion wherever it occurred and for its confidence in the efficacy of atomic and biological weapons should war break out. Clifford's report also reflects the view, widely shared in Washington during the early days of the Cold War, that the centralized, highly disciplined nature of the Soviet government gave it a considerable advantage over its more loosely organized counterparts in the West.

A slightly different version of this memorandum was published as an appendix to Arthur Krock, *Memoirs: Sixty Years on the Firing Line* (New York: Funk & Wagnalls, 1968).

The primary objective of United States policy toward the Soviet Union is to convince Soviet leaders that it is in their interest to participate in a system of world cooperation, that there are no fundamental causes for war between our two nations, and that the security and prosperity of the Soviet Union, and that of the rest of the world as well, is being jeopardized by aggressive militaristic imperialism such as that in which the Soviet Union is now engaged.

However, these same leaders with whom we hope to achieve an understanding on the principles of international peace appear to believe that a war with the United States and the other leading capitalistic nations is inevitable. They are increasing their military power and the sphere of Soviet influence in preparation for the "inevitable" conflict, and they are trying to weaken and subvert their potential opponents by every means at their disposal. So long as these men adhere to these beliefs, it is highly dangerous to conclude that hope of international peace lies only in "accord," "mutual under-standing," or "solidarity" with the Soviet Union.

Adoption of such a policy would impel the United States to make sacri-fices for the sake of Soviet-U.S. relations, which would only have the effect of raising Soviet hopes and increasing Soviet demands, and to ignore alter-native lines of policy, which might be much more compatible with our own national and international interests.

The Soviet Government will never be easy to "get along with." The American people must accustom themselves to this thought, not as a cause for despair, but as a fact to be faced objectively and courageously. If we find it impossible to enlist Soviet cooperation in the solution of world prob-lems, we should be prepared to join with the British and other Western countries in an attempt to build up a world of our own which will pursue its own objectives and will recognize the Soviet orbit as a distinct entity with which conflict is not predestined but with which we cannot pursue common aims.

As long as the Soviet Government maintains its present foreign policy, based upon the theory of an ultimate struggle between Communism and Capitalism, the United States must assume that the U.S.S.R. might fight at any time for the twofold purpose of expanding the territory under communist control and weakening its potential capitalist opponents. The Soviet Union was able to flow into the political vacuum of the Balkans, Eastern Europe, the Near East, Manchuria and Korea because no other nation was both willing and able to prevent it. Soviet leaders were encouraged by easy suc-cess and they are now preparing to take over new areas in the same way. The Soviet Union, as Stalin euphemistically phrased it, is preparing "for any eventuality."

Unless the United States is willing to sacrifice its future security for the sake of "accord" with the U.S.S.R. now, this government must, as a first step toward world stabilization, seek to prevent additional Soviet aggression. The greater the area controlled by the Soviet Union, the greater the military requirements of this country will be. Our present military plans are based on the assumption that, for the next few years at least, Western Europe, the Middle East, China and Japan will remain outside the Soviet sphere. If the Soviet Union acquires control of one or more of these areas, the military forces required to hold in check those of the U.S.S.R. and prevent still fur-ther acquisitions will be substantially enlarged. That will also be true if any of the naval and air bases in the Atlantic and Pacific, upon which our present plans rest, are given up. This government should be prepared, while scrupulously avoiding any act which would be an excuse for the Soviets to begin a war, to resist vigorously and successfully any efforts of the U.S.S.R. to expand into areas vital to American security.

The language of military power is the only language which disciples of power politics understand. The United States must use that language in order that Soviet leaders will realize that our government is determined to uphold the interests of its citizens and the rights of small nations. Compromise and concessions are considered, by the Soviets, to be evidences of weakness and they are encouraged by our "retreats" to make new and greater demands.

The main deterrent to Soviet attack on the United States, or to attack on areas of the world which are vital to our security, will be the military power of this country. It must be made apparent to the Soviet Government that our strength will be sufficient to repel any attack and sufficient to defeat the U.S.S.R. decisively if a war should start. The prospect of defeat is the only sure means of deterring the Soviet Union.

The Soviet Union's vulnerability is limited due to the vast area over which its key industries and natural resources are widely dispersed, but it is vulnerable to atomic weapons, biological warfare, and long-range air power. Therefore, in order to maintain our strength at a level which will be effective in restraining the Soviet Union, the United States must be prepared to wage atomic and biological warfare. A highly mechanized army, which can be moved either by sea or by air, capable of seizing and holding strategic areas, must be supported by powerful naval and air forces. A war with the U.S.S.R. would be "total" in a more horrible sense than any previous war and there must be constant research for both offensive and defensive weapons.

Whether it would actually be in this country's interest to employ atomic and biological weapons against the Soviet Union in the event of hostilities is a question which would require careful consideration in the light of the circumstances prevailing at the time. The decision would probably be influenced by a number of factors, such as the Soviet Union's capacity to employ similar weapons, which can not now be estimated. But the important point is that the United States must be prepared to wage atomic and biological warfare if necessary. The mere fact of preparedness may be the only powerful deterrent to Soviet aggressive action and in this sense the only sure guaranty of peace.

The United States, with a military potential composed primarily of highly effective technical weapons, should entertain no proposal for disarmament or limitation of armament as long as the possibility of Soviet aggression exists. Any discussion on the limitation of armaments should be pursued slowly and carefully with the knowledge constantly in mind that proposals on outlawing atomic warfare and long-range offensive weapons would greatly limit United States strength, while only moderately affecting the Soviet Union. The Soviet Union relies primarily on a large infantry and artillery force and the result of such arms limitation would be to deprive the United States of its most effective weapons without impairing the Soviet Union's ability to wage a quick war of aggression in Western Europe, the Middle East or the Far East.

The Soviet Government's rigid controls on travellers, and its internal security measures, enable it to develop military weapons and build up military forces without our knowledge. The United States should not agree to arms limitations until adequate intelligence of events in the U.S.S.R. is available and, as long as this situation prevails, no effort should be spared to make our forces adequate and strong. Unification of the services and the adoption of universal military training would be strong aids in carrying out a forthright United States policy.[4] In addition to increasing the efficiency of our armed forces, this program would have a salutary pyschological effect upon Soviet ambitions.

Comparable to our caution in agreeing to arms limitation, the United States should avoid premature disclosure of scientific and technological information relating to war materiel until we are assured of either a change in Soviet policies or workable international controls. Any disclosure would decrease the advantage the United States now has in technological fields and diminish our strength in relation to that of the U.S.S.R.

In addition to maintaining our own strength, the United States should support and assist all democratic countries which are in any way menaced or endangered by the U.S.S.R. Providing military support in case of attack is a last resort; a more effective barrier to communism is strong economic support. Trade agreements, loans and technical missions strengthen our ties with friendly nations and are effective demonstrations that capitalism is at least the equal of communism. The United States can do much to ensure that economic opportunities, personal freedom and social equality are made possible in countries outside the Soviet sphere by generous financial assistance. Our policy on reparations should be directed toward strengthening the areas

4. The National Security Act of 1947 created a National Military Establishment, headed by a Secretary of Defense, with Secretaries of the Army, Navy, and Air Force subordinate to him. Despite repeated Administration requests, Congress never approved a program of universal military training. [Ed. note]

we are endeavoring to keep outside the Soviet sphere. Our efforts to break down trade barriers, open up rivers and international waterways, and bring about economic unification of countries, now divided by occupation armies, are also directed toward the re-establishment of vigorous and healthy non-communist economies.

The Soviet Union recognizes the effectiveness of American economic assistance to small nations and denounces it bitterly by constant propaganda. The United States should realize that Soviet propaganda is dangerous (especially when American "imperialism" is emphasized) and should avoid any actions which give an appearance of truth to the Soviet charges. A determined effort should be made to expose the fallacies of such propaganda.

There are some trouble-spots which will require diligent and considered effort on the part of the United States if Soviet penetration and eventual domination is to be prevented. In the Far East, for example, this country should continue to strive for a unified and economically stable China, a reconstructed and democratic Japan, and a unified and independent Korea. We must ensure Philippine prosperity and we should assist in the peaceful solution, along noncommunistic lines, of the political problems of Southeast Asia and India.

With respect to the United Nations, we are faced with the fact that the U.S.S.R. uses the United Nations as a means of achieving its own ends. We should support the United Nations and all other organizations contributing to international understanding, but if the Soviet Union should threaten to resign at any time because it fails to have its own way, the United States should not oppose Soviet departure. It would be better to continue the United Nations as an association of democratic states than to sacrifice our principles to Soviet threats.

Since our difficulties with the Soviet Union are due primarily to the doctrines and actions of a small ruling clique and not the Soviet people, the United States should strive energetically to bring about a better understanding of the United States among influential Soviets and to counteract the anti-American propaganda which the Kremlin feeds to the Soviet people. To the greatest extent tolerated by the Soviet Government, we should distribute books, magazines, newspapers and movies among the Soviets, beam radio broadcasts to the U.S.S.R., and press for an exchange of tourists, students and educators. We should aim, through intellectual and cultural contacts, to convince Soviet leaders that the United States has no aggressive intentions and that the nature of our society is such that peaceful coexistence of capitalistic and communistic states is possible.

A long-range program of this sort may succeed where individual high-level conversations and negotiations between American and Soviet diplomats may fail in bringing about any basic change in the Soviet outlook. The general pattern of the Soviet system is too firmly established to be altered suddenly by any individual—even Stalin. Conferences and negotiations may continue to attain individual objectives but it appears highly improbable that we can persuade the Soviets, by conferences alone, to change the character of their philosophy and society. If they can be influenced in ways beneficial to our interests, it will be primarily by what we do rather than by what we say, and it is likely to be a slow and laborious process.

Our best chances of influencing Soviet leaders consist in making it unmistakably clear that action contrary to our conception of a decent world order will redound to the disadvantage of the Soviet regime whereas friendly and cooperative action will pay dividends. If this position can be maintained firmly enough and long enough, the logic of it must permeate eventually into the Soviet system.

Cooperation by the Soviets can result in increased trade. The United States Government must always bear in mind, however, that questions as to the extent and nature of American trade should be determined by the overall interests of this country. It should also bear in mind that, while Soviet policy can conceivably be influenced by the hope of obtaining greater economic assistance from this country, it is unlikely that the Soviet Government will entertain sentiments of gratitude for aid once it has been granted and it is unlikely to be induced by goodwill gifts to modify its general policies. For the time being, economic aid granted to the Soviet Government or other governments within its sphere, and the fruits of private trade with persons inside these countries, will go to strengthen the entire world program of the Kremlin. This is also true of the proposals to send American engineers, scientists and technicians to share the benefits of their education and experience with Soviet counterparts. So long as Soviet industry is devoted to building up the Soviet military potential, such proposals have a direct bearing on American security.

Within the United States, communist penetration should be exposed and eliminated whenever the national security is endangered. The armed forces, government agencies and heavy industries are the principal targets for communistic infiltration at present.

Because the Soviet Union is a highly-centralized state, whose leaders exercise rigid discipline and control of all governmental functions, its government acts with speed, consistency, and boldness. Democratic governments are usually loosely organized, with a high degree of autonomy in government departments and agencies. Government policies at times are confused, misunderstood, or disregarded by subordinate officials. The United States can not afford to be uncertain of its policies toward the Soviet Union. There must be such effective coordination within the government that our military and civil policies concerning the U.S.S.R., her satellites, and our Allies are consistent and forceful. Any uncertainty or discrepancy will be seized immediately by the Soviets and exploited at our cost.

Our policies must also be global in scope. By time-honored custom, we have regarded "European Policy," "Near Eastern Policy," "Indian Policy" and "Chinese Policy" as separate problems to be handled by experts in each field. But the areas involved, far removed from each other by our conventional standards, all border on the Soviet Union and our actions with respect to each must be considered in the light of overall Soviet objectives.

Only a well-informed public will support the stern policies which Soviet activities make imperative and which the United States Government must adopt. The American people should be fully informed about the difficulties in getting along with the Soviet Union, and the record of Soviet evasion, misrepresentation, aggression and militarism should be made public.

In conclusion, as long as the Soviet Government adheres to its present policy, the United States should maintain military forces powerful enough to restrain the Soviet Union and to confine Soviet influence to its present area. All nations not now within the Soviet sphere should be given generous economic assistance and political support in their opposition to Soviet penetration. Economic aid may also be given to the Soviet Government and private trade with the U.S.S.R. permitted provided the results are beneficial to our interests and do not simply strengthen the Soviet program. We should continue to work for cultural and intellectual understanding between the United States and the Soviet Union but that does not mean that, under the guise of an exchange program, communist subversion and infiltration in the United States will be tolerated. In order to carry out an effective policy toward the Soviet Union, the United States Government should coordinate its own activities, inform and instruct the American people about the Soviet Union, and enlist their support based upon knowledge and confidence. These actions by the United States are necessary before we shall ever be able to achieve understanding and accord with the Soviet Government on any terms other than its own.

Even though Soviet leaders profess to believe that the conflict between Capitalism and Communism is irreconcilable and must eventually be resolved by the triumph of the latter, it is our hope that they will change their minds and work out with us a fair and equitable settlement when they realize that we are too strong to be beaten and too determined to be frightened.

<><><><><><><><><><><><><><><><><><><><><><><><><><><><><><><><>

5   **T O P   S E C R E T**

United States Assistance to Other Countries from the Standpoint of National Security

JCS 1769/1   *loc. assumes total war*   April 29, 1947

[Source: *Foreign Relations of the United States: 1947,* I, 738–50]

This long report by the Joint Strategic Survey Committee to the Joint Chiefs of Staff, only the "discussion" portion of which is printed here, offers a striking contrast to the Clifford memorandum (Document 4). Here the emphasis is on the limits of American abilities to project power in the world, and on the consequent need to differentiate between areas of peripheral and vital importance to U.S. security. The fact that this report was written just after the President had announced a public policy of aiding "free peoples" everywhere suggests that the Truman Doctrine was more a rhetorical flourish designed to persuade a parsimonious Congress to approve aid to Greece and Turkey than the blueprint for globalism it appeared to be on the surface.

The ranking of interests set forth in JCS 1769/1 to a large extent established priorities for the programs of economic and military assistance implemented in the name of "containment" during the next three years.

1. At the outset, it should be firmly fixed in mind that the mere giving of assistance to other countries will not necessarily enhance the national security of the United States. The results obtained by such assistance will determine whether our national security is strengthened thereby. What, then, are the desired results? These are firm friends located in areas which will be of strategic importance to the United States in the event of war with our ideological enemies, and with economies strong enough to support the military establishments necessary for the maintenance of their own independence and national security.

2. The problem envisages aid for two reasons; namely, urgency of need and importance to the national security of the United States. The past months have proved that United States assistance to some countries whose inhabitants urgently needed aid did not increase the military security of the United States, but that, on the contrary, it was used by governments ideologically opposed to the United States and representing a minority of the people, to strengthen their control of suppressed majorities. For this reason,

it is believed that the question of which countries to exclude from receipt of United States aid is as important as the question of which countries should receive assistance. Keeping in mind that the United States cannot give substantial aid to all countries of the world, it is evident that, if we spread our available resources for aid over too large an area, no country is likely to receive assistance sufficient to be of major importance in the resurgence of its economy and military potential. The primary rule governing assistance by the United States should be that the USSR and every country now under her control should be specifically excluded from assistance. No country under Soviet control should receive assistance from the United States until every vestige of Soviet control has been removed therefrom.

3. The first step in determining the countries which should receive assistance because of their importance to our national security is to establish the areas of primary strategic importance to the United States in the event of ideological warfare.

4. The area of United States defense commitments includes, roughly, the lands and waters from Alaska to the Philippines and Australia in the Pacific and from Greenland to Brazil and Patagonia in the Atlantic. This area contains 40 percent of the land surface of the earth but only 25 percent of the population. The Old World (Europe, Asia and Africa) contains only 60 percent of the land surface of the earth but 75 percent of the population. The potential military strength of the Old World in terms of manpower and in terms of war-making capacity is enormously greater than that of our area of defense commitments, in which the United States is the only arsenal nation. It is obvious, therefore, that in case of an ideological war we must have the support of some of the countries of the Old World unless our military strength is to be overshadowed by that of our enemies.

5. In the case of an ideological war the most vulnerable side of our defense area will be in the Atlantic. Also, unless we can retain allies on the eastern side of the Atlantic strong enough, in the event of an ideological war, to hold the Soviets away from the eastern shores of the Atlantic, the shortest and most direct avenue of attack against our enemies will almost certainly be denied to us. Further, almost all potentially strong nations who can reasonably be expected to ally themselves with the United States in such a war are situated in western Europe. Moreover, two world wars in the past thirty years have demonstrated the interdependence of France, Great Britain and the United States in case of war with central or eastern European powers. In war these nations not only need one another but are in mortal peril if they do not combine their forces. In the past war it was demonstrated that France could not stand without Great Britain and that when France fell the

British Isles were in mortal peril. If Britain had fallen, the Western Hemisphere would have been completely exposed, and the United States would have had to defend itself in the Atlantic before it could have thought of resisting the Japanese conquest of China, the East Indies, the Philippines and the Far Pacific. That the defense of the United States and Canada in North America and of Great Britain and France in western Europe is inseparable from the combined defense of them all is not a question of what men think now, but is something that has been demonstrated by what we have had to do, though tardily, and therefore at greater risk and cost, in actual warfare in the past. In the light of this past experience the burden of proof is upon anyone who opposes the thesis of the interdependence of these four countries. The opponent would have to show that an assault by our ideological opponents on any one of these nations would not be of vital consequence to the other three nations. No one can show this, nor how Britain could live in security if France were not independent and her friend, nor how Canada and the United States could live safely if France and/or Great Britain were under Soviet domination either by reason of military conquest or for the reason that communists had taken over control of their governments. While the conquest or communization of other countries would adversely affect the security of the United States, the conquest or communization of no other country or area would be so detrimental as that of France and/or Great Britain. The maintenance of these two countries in a state of independence, friendly to the United States and with economies able to support the armed forces necessary for the continued maintenance of their independence, is still of first importance to the national security of the United States as well as to the security of the entire Western Hemisphere. This means that the entire area of western Europe is in first place as an area of strategic importance to the United States in the event of ideological warfare.

6. Potentially, the strongest military power in this area is Germany. Without German aid the remaining countries of western Europe could scarcely be expected to withstand the armies of our ideological opponents until the United States could mobilize and place in the field sufficient armed forces to achieve their defeat. With a revived Germany fighting on the side of the Western Allies this would be a possibility. Further, the complete resurgence of German industry, particularly coal mining, is essential for the economic recovery of France—whose security is inseparable from the combined security of the United States, Canada, and Great Britain. The economic revival of Germany is therefore of primary importance from the viewpoint of United States security.

7. France is, however, still the leader of those countries of Europe west

of Germany and all indications are that France will vigorously oppose any substantial revival of German heavy industry. The fear of a revived Germany is still strong in France and this fear is compounded by the activities of French communists who, in accordance with Soviet desires, seek to make post-war Germany weak industrially and militarily. Yet the German people are the natural enemies of the USSR and of communism. If treated without undue harshness by the Western Allies they would in all probability align themselves with the Western Allies in the event of ideological warfare unless the countries of Europe to the west of Germany had previously fallen under communist domination. In this latter case Germany would be between two hostile factions and her alignment in such a war would be problematical.

8. From the viewpoint of the security of the United States it appears that our efforts should be directed toward demonstrating both to the leaders of France and to the leaders of Germany that the emergence of a principal world power to the east of them, ideologically opposed to all of their traditional way of life, whose ultimate aim is world conquest, and which they can successfully oppose only if both are strong and united against the new eastern menace, makes them interdependent just as France, England, Canada, and the United States are interdependent. Further, France, as one of the victors of the past war, must be made to see that diplomatic ideological warfare is now going on and that if the diplomatic war can be won the shooting war will be delayed and perhaps even avoided. Most important of all, France and the United States and Great Britain must acknowledge that the decisive diplomatic contest between totalitarian Russia and the democracies of the West is taking place in Germany today. The western democracies can win this contest only if there is drastic change in their economic policies for Germany. Further, Germany can aid in European recovery and become an ally of the West against their ideological opponents only if her economy is restored. In fact, such a course should appeal to France and Great Britain as well as to the United States in view of the high cost that devolves upon these countries for the mere feeding of the German population so long as German industry and foreign trade are paralyzed. This cost to Great Britain and the United States has been estimated by Mr. Herbert Hoover to be $950,000,000 before July of 1948.

9. Other countries in the Western European area which are of more than ordinary importance to our national security for military or political reasons are Italy, Spain, Belgium, the Netherlands, and Denmark. To assign priority of assistance to these countries on the basis of importance to our national se-

curity is most difficult, but on the basis of urgency of need they appear to line up as follows: Italy, Belgium, the Netherlands, Spain, and Denmark. The reasons for the importance of these countries to our national security, aside from geographic positions, deserve brief mention. Italy and Spain are of primary importance in connection with control of the Mediterranean sea lanes, shortest route to the oil and processing facilities of the Middle East. Further, Italy, like Greece, is a border nation in the current diplomatic ideological war between the western democracies and the Soviets. Denmark has sovereignty over Greenland which, by reason of geographic position, is a major outpost for defense of North America. Belgium controls, in the Belgian Congo, the area containing the largest and richest known deposits of uranium ore in the world.

10. The area of secondary strategic importance to the United States in case of ideological warfare is the Middle East, not only because of the existence of great oil reserves and processing facilities in this area but also because it offers possibilities for direct contact with our ideological enemies. However, a program of aid to Greece and Turkey in this area has already been approved by the Senate of the United States.[5] Other countries in this area—Iran, Iraq, and Saudi Arabia—are of importance, but their need for aid is not urgent and they could not repel Soviet attack until United States military assistance could reach them. In fact, since they could offer practically no military assistance to the United States in case of ideological warfare, direct assistance to these countries can be considered as of minor importance from the viewpoint of United States security. However, in order to retain their good will they should be granted favorable terms for the purchase from the United States of supplies needed for the modernization and improvement of their industries, living conditions and armed forces. Further, technical assistance, both military and civilian, should be granted if they request it.

11. Central and South America and northwest Africa comprise the remainder of the United States Atlantic area of defense commitments. If Western Europe, particularly France and the Low Countries, falls under Soviet domination for any reason, the United States would immediately have to take the action with armed forces necessary to exclude the Soviets from northwest Africa. However, if Western Europe can be kept out of the sphere of Soviet domination and friendly to the United States, no immediate threat to the security of the United States can be expected to develop in western

5. S. 938, passed by the Senate on April 22, 1947. [Ed. note]

Africa. If any event, there are no countries in this area to which direct current assistance should be given.

12. The defense of South America is of vital importance to the national security of the United States. But, since South American contains no principal military power which can help greatly to insure that defense, the United States must regard the defense of South America as a heavy commitment and should seek to alleviate it by actions which will gradually increase the level of military self-sufficiency of South America as a whole.

13. However, the commitment of the United States for the defense of South America can be challenged by only one of the great powers of the Northern Hemisphere, and the fulfillment of our commitment depends upon whether, in our relations with the great powers, we and our friends outweigh our foes. In spite of technological developments it is still true that only a great power can successfully challenge or resist another great power and that, total resources being equal, the strength of a number of small nations will not combine to balance that of one of the great powers. For this reason the bulk of United States assistance should be given to nations who are potentially powerful and also potential allies of the United States.

14. Thus, current *direct* assistance to the individual countries of South America is not of critical importance to our national security at this particular time. However, policies designed to lessen the potential burden of our commitment for the defense of South America are of great importance. There can no longer be doubt that the communist party is gaining strength in that area. In consequence, anything less than complete *rapprochement* between the United States and every one of her neighbors to the south is entirely unacceptable from the viewpoint of United States security. To stand by and watch a fifth column grow stronger and stronger to the south of us is to invite disaster. The United States is, by reason of its strength and political enlightenment, the natural leader of this hemisphere. But, there is always jealousy of the leader and in this case the injurious effects of that jealousy are compounded by the activities of our ideological opponents in that area. Further, the opposition has plainly undertaken to overthrow by one means or another the ideology which we champion. How better to combat us than by taking over the leadership of the southern half of the Western Hemisphere? They are attempting it now and it must be realized that in this hemisphere we cannot combat them by dollar credits alone. Individual and national want is not sufficient in this hemisphere to make this an effective method here. The most important specific act required is the completion and implementa-

tion of a treaty embodying the agreements concerning the defense of the Western Hemisphere which were reached at Chapultepec.[6]

15. Of almost equal importance is the passage of a bill embodying the provisions of H.R. 6326 (79th Congress)[7] which would permit the standardization of the armaments of the American republics by the transfer of United States equipment, and the maintenance of United States military missions in those countries. Apparently the support for such a bill, other than by the War and Navy Departments, has been withdrawn. The public press has suggested that the reason for the withdrawal of support is that implementation of the provisions of the bill might weaken the economies and the political stability of the governments of South America. Whether or not this be so is of little consequence from the viewpoint of national security, since our present policy is reacting unfavorably upon the security of the United States and of the Western Hemisphere. An important fact is that most of the Latin American Governments are dependent upon the military for stability. In consequence, contact with Latin American military men would in reality mean contact with very strong domestic political leaders. It is suggested that it is now advisable to attempt to bring about the economic and the domestic conditions which we desire to see in South America through these men and through passage of a bill similar to H.R. 6326 instead of attempting to attain these ends through direct diplomatic pressure. We need offer these countries no current financial assistance in the interests of our own security. However, in the interest of this same security we should take our hemispheric neighbors into full partnership in the affairs of our hemisphere; should conclude one formal blanket mutual defense treaty with all of them; and should definitely, positively, and tactfully lead them toward true democracy while publicizing the misery and the slavery to the state which would result should they come under the control of our ideological opponents whether by the communization of their governments or by conquest.

16. In the Pacific area of United States defense commitments, from the standpoint of urgent want, Korea, China, and Japan deserve consideration for current United States assistance. From the security viewpoint the primary reasons for current assistance to Korea would be that, as a result of the 38°

---

6. The Act of Chapultepec, signed on March 6, 1945, by the United States and the states of Latin America, pledged joint action to resist aggression during the remainder of the war, and anticipated the negotiation of a treaty institutionalizing such arrangements once the war was over. [Ed. note]

7. H.R. 6326, the Inter-American Military Cooperation Act, was submitted to the Congress on May 6, 1946. It was approved by the House Foreign Affairs Committee, but no further action was taken during that session of Congress. [Ed. note]

(v.2)

Korea, really
big here

parallel agreement,[8] this is the one country within which we alone have for almost two years carried on ideological warfare in direct contact with our opponents, so that to lose this battle would be gravely detrimental to United States prestige, and therefore security, throughout the world. To abandon this struggle would tend to confirm the suspicion that the United States is not really determined to accept the responsibilities and obligations of world leadership, with consequent detriment to our efforts to bolster those countries of western Europe which are of primary and vital importance to our national security. However, this suspicion could quite possibly be dissipated and our prestige in these same western European countries enhanced if a survey of our resources indicated we could not afford to resist our ideological opponents on all fronts and we publicly announced abandonment of further aid to Korea in order to concentrate our aid in areas of greater strategic importance to us.

in case of general war

17. If the present diplomatic ideological warfare should become armed warfare, Korea could offer little or no assistance in the maintenance of our national security. Therefore, from this viewpoint, current assistance should be given Korea only if the means exist after sufficient assistance has been given the countries of primary importance to insure their continued independence and friendship for the United States and the resurgence of their economies.

18. China's greatest military asset is manpower. However, China does not have the industry to equip this manpower for warfare nor does she produce sufficient food to maintain this manpower in fighting condition. Therefore, in the case of warfare with our ideological opponents, China could be a valuable ally only if we diverted to her great quantities of food and equipment manufactured in this country. It is extremely doubtful that the end result would be any great assistance to our war effort. On the other hand, there is in existence in China an army which embraces the ideology of our opponents and which, given assistance by our opponents concurrent with the withdrawal by the United States of assistance to opposing forces in China, could possibly conquer all of China with very grave long-range jeopardy to our national security interests. If, however, we abandoned aid to

8. Agreement reached between Soviet and American military commanders in the last days of World War II providing that Soviet forces would accept the surrender of Japanese troops in Korea north of the 38th parallel, and that American forces would accept the surrender of those south of the parallel. The subsequent inability of the United States and the Soviet Union to agree on a common government for all of Korea resulted in the *de facto* partition of that country, with United States forces occupying the south and Soviet forces occupying the north. [Ed. note]

China in order to concentrate our forces for a crushing offensive from the West against our primary ideological opponents and the success of this offensive resulted in the isolation of communism among the undeveloped countries of the Far East, it might be possible to keep it isolated there by the imposition of an economic quarantine. The assumption that the next war will be ideological and the thesis that current aid shall be given only in the interest of our national security places China very low on the list of countries which should be given such assistance.

19. Japan is the most important arena of ideological struggle within our Pacific area of defense commitments. Like Germany, Japan is a defeated nation and the idea of assistance to her is probably offensive to the majority of our people. However, Japan left to herself grew strong enough to challenge American power in the Pacific. Japan is still a potentially powerful nation and one which we cannot forever keep militarily impotent. Japan is the one nation which could contain large armed forces of our ideological opponents in the Far East while the United States and her allies in the West launched a major offensive in that area. For this very simple reason, on the assumption that the next war will be ideological, of all the countries in the Pacific area Japan deserves primary consideration for current United States assistance designed to restore her economy and her military potential.

20. The question of assistance for the Philippine Republic is unique since the islands have long been closely associated with the United States and since the republic was formed, and remains, under United States guidance. There is need in the Philippines for financial assistance, but the importance of the republic to our national security in case of ideological warfare is not great. Financial assistance should be continued, however, in order to assist in the stabilization of the republic's budget and economy and for the maintenance of United States prestige throughout the Far East. We cannot afford to renounce our primary moral obligation in this area.

21. In view of this general consideration of the areas of primary strategic importance to the United States in the event of ideological warfare, it appears that current assistance should be given if possible to the following countries arranged in order of their *importance to our national security:*

1. Great Britain	7. Italy	13. Japan
2. France	8. Canada	14. China
3. Germany	9. Turkey	15. Korea
4. Belgium	10. Greece	16. The Philippines
5. Netherlands	11. Latin America	
6. Austria	12. Spain	

22. The Joint Chiefs of Staff are currently supporting certain specific objectives, the attainment of which they believe will enhance the national security. These objectives are:

    a. A system of military base rights as approved by the Joint Chiefs of Staff on 4 June 1946 in J.C.S.570/62.[9]

    b. The accomplishment of a treaty formalizing the agreements concerning the security of the Western Hemisphere which were reached at Chapultepec.

    c. The continued availability of the oil of the Middle East.

    d. The elimination from national armaments of atomic and other weapons of mass destruction preceded by the conclusion of agreements which provide effective safeguards against their production and use.

    e. The realization of a United Nations organization capable of playing an effective role in the maintenance of international security, thereby making it possible to scale down the military establishments presently required for maintenance of the security of the individual nations of the world.

    f. The prevention of communist control over those areas from which offensive air, ground and naval action could be most effectively and economically launched against our enemies in the event of ideological warfare.

23. It is axiomatic that any program of aid to other countries of the world should aim at making it easier to attain these security objectives and that no assistance adversely affecting our ability to attain these objectives should be undertaken. The relationship of a program of United States assistance to these security objectives will therefore be treated briefly.

24. The United States desires base rights, considered essential to her security, from Portugal, Ecuador, France and Spain. Of these, base rights from Portugal and Spain are the more essential. There are other base rights listed in Joint Chiefs of Staff papers as required if reasonably obtainable but not absolutely essential to the base system. The majority of these are in the Pacific and have been obtained by the United States by reason of the mandate granted under the United Nations. Those desired in the Atlantic belong to Great Britain, France, Portugal, Cuba, Liberia and Newfoundland. This study envisages United States assistance to Great Britain, France and the Latin American countries. The program should therefore enhance our possibilities of receiving the base rights desired from these countries.

9. For this list of base rights, see SWNCC 38/35, June 5, 1946, *Foreign Relations of the United States: 1946*, I, 1174–77. [Ed. note]

25. A program of aid to other countries should not adversely affect our objective of accomplishing a treaty formalizing the agreements concerning the security of the Western Hemisphere which were reached at Chapultepec. On the contrary, since assistance to the Latin American countries of the Western Hemisphere is envisaged, this objective of the Joint Chiefs of Staff should be made easier of attainment by such assistance.

26. Whether a program of assistance will make it easier for the United States to insure the continued availability of the oil of the Middle East or whether such a program will cause Russia to take equally forehanded action to deny us this oil in event of ideological warfare is problematical. It is true, however, that the availability of this oil in case of war *cannot* be adversely affected by the program of United States assistance and that assistance given to countries in the Middle Eastern area may prevent these countries from falling within the Russian orbit, thereby making the task of protecting this area less difficult if war occurs.

27. The objective of eliminating from national armaments atomic and other weapons of mass destruction will certainly not be adversely affected by United States assistance to other countries. However, this is only one part of the United States objective in this respect and the other part, the conclusion of agreements which provide effective safeguards against the production and use of atomic and other weapons of mass destruction, may be so adversely affected that its realization will be impossible. The elimination of atomic and other weapons of mass destruction would be to Russia's advantage at present so that, instead of resisting this, she will continue her present maneuvers to accomplish it without safeguards if possible. The United States cannot accept elimination without safeguards and therefore, since the Soviets will correctly interpret a program of United States assistance as aimed at containing them, they may become increasingly adamant on the question of safeguards with resultant failure of the United States to attain this objective.

28. The realization of a United Nations capable of playing an effective role in the maintenance of international security, thereby making it possible to scale down the military establishments presently required for maintenance of the security of the individual nations of the world, will be made more difficult by a program of United States assistance to countries strategically important to the United States in the event of ideological warfare. This follows from the fact that the realization of a United Nations capable of playing an important and useful role in the maintenance of world security is entirely dependent upon the achievement of a general over-all understanding and peace settlement by the great nations of the world. A program of United

States assistance to countries outside the Soviet orbit will certainly prevent achievement of the general over-all understanding and peace settlement required for the accomplishment of this objective. However, this result would not necessarily adversely affect our national security since the United Nations as presently constituted can in no way enhance that security. On the contrary, faith in the ability of the United Nations as presently constituted to protect, now or hereafter, the security of the United States would mean only that the faithful have lost sight of the vital security interest of the United States and could quite possibly lead to results fatal to that security. Yet, it is partially an earnest desire to make the United Nations a capable and useful instrument for the maintenance of world security which has led the United States to try to attain a settlement with our ex-enemies before we have stabilized our relations with our allies in the past war, and before we have a clear idea of the role we wish our ex-enemies to play in the post-war world. The drawing up of a comprehensive program of assistance to other countries may clarify United States policy in this regard with possibly very beneficial effect on the national security of the United States.

29. Finally, there can be little doubt that a program of United States assistance will aid in the realization of the objective of preventing communist control over those areas from which offensive air, ground, and naval action could be most effectively and economically launched against our enemies in the event of ideological warfare.

30. It appears, on balance, that a program of United States assistance would be desirable if the major objectives of the Joint Chiefs of Staff are considered as a whole, and that, since the attainment of these objectives would increase our national security, the program is, from the military point of view, highly desirable.

31. An initial step in this study was to list the countries of the world to which assistance should be given in order of urgency of need. For this purpose documents of the Department of State prepared in connection with a preliminary similar study for the State–War–Navy Coordinating Committee have been consulted (J.C.S. 1769—SWNCC 360). These documents support the following listing of countries in order of the *urgency of their need:*

1. Greece	8. Hungary	14. Portugal
2. Turkey	9. Great Britain	15. Czechoslovakia
3. Italy	10. Belgium	16. Poland
4. Iran	11. Luxembourg	17. Latin American
5. Korea	12. Netherlands—	Republics
6. France	N.E.I.	18. Canada
7. Austria	13. The Philippines	

China does not appear on this list although the documents referred to indicate that China will need an undetermined amount of post-UNRRA aid in the near future. The Department of State wishes further time to determine China's real needs before determining a priority for aid to that country. On the basis of actual current needs, however, it is believed that China should be placed after Austria and be followed by Turkey.

32. Notwithstanding the listing given above, no aid of any sort to Hungary or to Czechoslovakia and Poland is advocated. The reason for this is that the United States cannot give aid to all countries requiring aid on the basis of their need in sufficient amounts to have any real effect on the ability of all of these countries to retain, or regain, freedom from predominant Soviet influence. From the military point of view, it is firmly believed that assistance should be concentrated on those countries of primary strategic importance to the United States in case of ideological warfare, excepting in those rare instances which present an opportunity for the United States to gain worldwide approbation by an act strikingly humanitarian; for example, the recent provision of food for the famine areas of Roumania. Therefore, from the viewpoint of the national security of the United States, assistance should be extended to the following countries listed in order arrived at by considering *their importance to United States security and the urgency of their need in combination:*

1. Great Britain	7. Austria	13. Korea
2. France	8. Japan	14. China
3. Germany	9. Belgium	15. The Philippines
4. Italy	10. Netherlands	16. Canada
5. Greece	11. Latin America	
6. Turkey	12. Spain	

(K. ahead of China & Canada)

33. It is emphasized that assistance in each instance should be sufficient to positively assist the nation aided to achieve, or retain, a sound economy, to maintain the armed forces necessary for its continued independence, and to be of real assistance to the United States in case of ideological warfare. This requirement, since the ability of the United States to give assistance is not unlimited, may mean that not all nations listed above will receive assistance. However, it is felt that the requirement is necessary if the national security of the United States is to receive maximum benefit from a United States program of assistance to other nations.

6

The Sources of Soviet Conduct

July 1947

[Source: *Foreign Affairs,* XXV (July, 1947), 572–76, 580–82. Copyright 1947 by the Council on Foreign Relations, Inc., and excerpted by permission.]

Shortly after Kennan became head of the State Department's Policy Planning Staff, an article entitled "The Sources of Soviet Conduct," attributed only to a "Mr. X," appeared in the journal *Foreign Affairs.* The authoritative tone of the piece attracted considerable attention, and word soon leaked out that Kennan had written it not long before assuming his duties on the Planning Staff. This information gave the article the aura of an official pronouncement; the word "containment," which it introduced, quickly became a capsule characterization of postwar American policy toward the Soviet Union.

Kennan had not intended the article to serve this function; it was, rather, a means of placing before the public the analysis of Soviet policy he had initially expressed in his February 1946 "long telegram" (Document 3). Such recommendations for action as Kennan included in the *Foreign Affairs* article did not represent fully his ideas on the course American foreign policy should take, a fact which will become apparent upon comparison of the passages excerpted below with several of Kennan's internal memoranda from the period (see Documents 7 and 8).

The "X" article, like the Truman speech of March 1947, seemed to be a call for resistance to Soviet expansionism on a global basis by any and all means. To this extent, it contributed to confusion as to the meaning of "containment," because the Truman administration did not in fact implement such a policy. The article is also significant as an early expression of Kennan's views on Soviet vulnerabilities—views he would elaborate in NSC 20/1 (Document 22).

. . . [W]e are going to continue for a long time to find the Russians difficult to deal with. [This] does not mean that they should be considered as embarked upon a do-or-die program to overthrow our society by a given date. The theory of the inevitability of the eventual fall of capitalism has the fortunate connotation that there is no hurry about it. The forces of progress can take their time in preparing the final *coup de grâce.* Meanwhile, what is vital is that the "Socialist fatherland"—that oasis of power which has been already won for Socialism in the person of the Soviet Union—should be cherished and defended by all good Communists at home and abroad, its fortunes promoted, its enemies badgered and confounded. The promotion of premature, "adventuristic" revolutionary projects abroad which might embarrass Soviet power in any way would be an inexcusable, even a counter-revolutionary act. The cause of Socialism is the support and promotion of Soviet power, as defined in Moscow.

This brings us to the second of the concepts important to contemporary Soviet outlook. That is the infallibility of the Kremlin. The Soviet concept of power, which permits no focal points of organization outside the Party itself, requires that the Party leadership remain in theory the sole repository of truth. For if truth were to be found elsewhere, there would be justification for its expression in organized activity. But it is precisely that which the Kremlin cannot and will not permit.

The leadership of the Communist Party is therefore always right, and has been always right ever since in 1929 Stalin formalized his personal power by announcing that decisions of the Politburo were being taken unanimously.

On the principle of infallibility there rests the iron discipline of the Communist Party. In fact, the two concepts are mutually self-supporting. Perfect discipline requires recognition of infallibility. Infallibility requires the observance of discipline. And the two together go far to determine the behaviorism of the entire Soviet apparatus of power. But their effect cannot be understood unless a third factor be taken into account: namely, the fact that the leadership is at liberty to put forward for tactical purposes any particular thesis which it finds useful to the cause at any particular moment and to require the faithful and unquestioning acceptance of that thesis by the members of the movement as a whole. This means that truth is not a constant but is actually created, for all intents and purposes, by the Soviet leaders themselves. It may vary from week to week, from month to month. It is nothing absolute and immutable—nothing which flows from objective reality. It is only the most recent manifestation of the wisdom of those in whom the ultimate wisdom is supposed to reside, because they represent the logic of history. The accumulative effect of these factors is to give to the whole subordinate apparatus of Soviet power an unshakable stubbornness and steadfastness in its orientation. This orientation can be changed at will by the Kremlin but by no other power. Once a given party line has been laid down on a given issue of current policy, the whole Soviet governmental machine, including the mechanism of diplomacy, moves inexorably along the prescribed path, like a persistent toy automobile wound up and headed in a given direction, stopping only when it meets with some unanswerable force. The individuals who are the components of this machine are unamenable to argument or reason which comes to them from outside sources. Their whole training has taught them to mistrust and discount the glib persuasiveness of the outside world. Like the white dog before the phonograph, they hear only the "master's voice." And if they are to be called off from the purposes last dictated to them, it is the master who must call them off. Thus the foreign representative cannot hope that his words will make any impression on them. The most that he can hope is that they will be transmitted to those at the top, who are capable of changing the party line. But even those are not likely to be swayed by any normal logic in the words of the bourgeois representative. Since there can be no appeal to common purposes, there can be no appeal to common mental approaches. For this reason, facts speak louder than words to the ears of the Kremlin; and words carry the greatest weight when they have the ring of reflecting, or being backed up by, facts of unchallengeable validity.

But we have seen that the Kremlin is under no ideological compulsion to accomplish its purposes in a hurry. Like the Church, it is dealing in ideological concepts which are of long-term validity, and it can afford to be patient. It has no right to risk the existing achievements of the revolution for the sake of vain baubles of the future. The very teachings of Lenin himself require great caution and flexibility in the pursuit of Communist purposes. Again, these precepts are fortified by the lessons of Russian history: of centuries of obscure battles between nomadic forces over the stretches of a vast unfortified plain. Here caution, circumspection, flexibility and deception are the valuable qualities; and their value finds natural appreciation in the Russian or the oriental mind. Thus the Kremlin has no compunction about retreating in the face of superior force. And being under the compulsion of no timetable, it does not get panicky under the necessity for such retreat. Its political action is a fluid stream which moves constantly, wherever it is permitted to move, toward a given goal. Its main concern is to make sure that it has filled every nook and cranny available to it in the basin of world power. But if it finds unassailable barriers in its path, it accepts these philosophically and accommodates itself to them. The main thing is that there should always be pressure, unceasing constant pressure, toward the desired goal. There is no trace of any feeling in Soviet psychology that that goal must be reached at any given time.

These considerations make Soviet diplomacy at once easier and more difficult to deal with than the diplomacy of individual aggressive leaders like Napoleon and Hitler. On the one hand it is more sensitive to contrary force, more ready to yield on individual sectors of the diplomatic front when that force is felt to be too strong, and thus more rational in the logic and rhetoric of power. On the other hand it cannot be easily defeated or discouraged by a single victory on the part of its opponents. And the patient persistence by which it is animated means that it can be effectively countered not by sporadic acts which represent the momentary whims of democratic opinion but only by intelligent long-range policies on the part of Russia's adversaries—policies no less steady in their purpose, and no less variegated and resourceful in their application, than those of the Soviet Union itself.

In these circumstances it is clear that the main element of any United States policy toward the Soviet Union must be that of a long-term, patient but firm and vigilant containment of Russian expansive tendencies. It is important to note, however, that such a policy has nothing to do with with outward histrionics: with threats or blustering or superfluous gestures of outward "toughness." While the Kremlin is basically flexible in its reaction to political realities, it is by no means unamenable to considerations of prestige. Like almost any other government, it can be placed by tactless and threatening gestures in a position where it cannot afford to yield even though this might be dictated by its sense of realism. The Russian leaders are keen judges of human psychology, and as such they are highly conscious that loss of temper and of self-control is never a source of strength in political affairs. They are quick to exploit such evidences of weakness. For these reasons, it is a *sine qua non* of successful dealing with Russia that the foreign government in question should remain at all times cool and collected and that its demands on Russian policy should be put forward in such a manner as to leave the way open for a compliance not too detrimental to Russian prestige.

III

In the light of the above, it will be clearly seen that the Soviet pressure against the free institutions of the western world is something that can be contained by the adroit and vigilant application of counter-force at a series of constantly shifting geographical and political points, corresponding to the shifts and manœuvres of Soviet policy, but which cannot be charmed or talked out of existence. . . .

. . . [T]he future of Soviet power may not be by any means as secure as Russian capacity for self-delusion would make it appear to the men in the Kremlin. That they can keep power themselves, they have demonstrated. That they can quietly and easily turn it over to others remains to be proved. Meanwhile, the hardships of their rule and the vicissitudes of international life have taken a heavy toll of the strength and hopes of the great people on whom their power rests. It is curious to note that the ideological power of Soviet authority is strongest today in areas beyond the frontiers of Russia, beyond the reach of its police power. This phenomenon brings to mind a comparison used by Thomas Mann in his great novel "Buddenbrooks." Observing that human institutions often show the greatest outward brilliance at a moment when inner decay is in reality farthest advanced, he compared the Buddenbrook family, in the days of its greatest glamour, to one of those stars whose light shines most brightly on this world when in reality it has long since ceased to exist. And who can say with assurance that the strong light still cast by the Kremlin on the dissatisfied peoples of the western world is not the powerful afterglow of a constellation which is in actuality on the wane? This cannot be proved. And it cannot be disproved. But the possibility remains (and in the opinion of this writer it is a strong one) that Soviet power, like the capitalist world of its conception, bears within it the seeds of its own decay, and that the sprouting of these seeds is well advanced.

IV

It is clear that the United States cannot expect in the foreseeable future to enjoy political intimacy with the Soviet régime. It must continue to regard the Soviet Union as a rival, not a partner, in the political arena. It must continue to expect that Soviet policies will reflect no abstract love of peace and stability, no real faith in the possibility of a permanent happy coexistence of the Socialist and capitalist worlds, but rather a cautious, persistent pressure toward the disruption and weakening of all rival influence and rival power.

Balanced against this are the facts that Russia, as opposed to the western world in general, is still by far the weaker party, that Soviet policy is highly flexible, and that Soviet society may well contain deficiencies which will eventually weaken its own total potential. This would of itself warrant the United States entering with reasonable confidence upon a policy of firm containment, designed to confront the Russians with unalterable counter-force at every point where they show signs of encroaching upon the interests of a peaceful and stable world.

But in actuality the possibilities for American policy are by no means limited to holding the line and hoping for the best. It is entirely possible for the United States to influence by its actions the internal developments, both within Russia and throughout the international Communist movement, by which Russian policy is largely determined. This is not only a question of the modest measure of informational activity which this government can conduct in the Soviet Union and elsewhere, although that, too, is important. It is rather a question of the degree to which the United States can create among the peoples of the world generally the impression of a country which knows what it wants, which is coping successfully with the poblems of its internal life and with the responsibilities of a World Power, and which has a spiritual vitality capable of holding its own among the major ideological currents of the time. To the extent that such an impression can be created and maintained, the aims of Russian Communism must appear sterile and quixotic, the hopes and enthusiasm of Moscow's supporters must wane, and added strain must be imposed on the Kremlin's foreign policies. For the palsied decrepitude of the capitalist world is the keystone of Communist philosophy. Even the failure of the United States to experience the early economic depression which the ravens of the Red Square have been predicting with such complacent confidence since hostilities ceased would have deep and important repercussions throughout the Communist world.

By the same token, exhibitions of indecision, disunity and internal disintegration within this country have an exhilarating effect on the whole Communist movement. At each evidence of these tendencies, a thrill of hope and excitement goes through the Communist world; a new jauntiness can be noted in the Moscow tread; new groups of foreign supporters climb on to what they can only view as the band wagon of international politics; and Russian pressure increases all along the line in international affairs.

It would be an exaggeration to say that American behavior unassisted and alone could exercise a power of life and death over the Communist movement and bring about the early fall of Soviet power in Russia. But the United States has it in its power to increase enormously the strains under which Soviet policy must operate, to force upon the Kremlin a far greater degree of moderation and circumspection than it has had to observe in recent years, and in this way to promote tendencies which must eventually find their outlet in either the break-up or the gradual mellowing of Soviet power. For no mystical, Messianic movement—and particularly not that of the Kremlin—can face frustration indefinitely without eventually adjusting itself in one way or another to the logic of that state of affairs.

Thus the decision will really fall in large measure in this country itself. The issue of Soviet-American relations is in essence a test of the over-all worth of the United States as a nation among nations. To avoid destruction the United States need only measure up to its own best traditions and prove itself worthy of preservation as a great nation.

Surely, there was never a fairer test of national quality than this. In the light of these circumstances, the thoughtful observer of Russian-American relations will find no cause for complaint in the Kremlin's challenge to American society. He will rather experience a certain gratitude to a Providence which, by providing the American people with this implacable challenge, has made their entire security as a nation dependent on their pulling themselves together and accepting the responsibilities of moral and political leadership that history plainly intended them to bear.

<><><><><><><><><><><><><><><><><><><><><><><><><><><><><><><><><><>

7   **S E C R E T**

Resumé of World Situation

PPS 13   November 6, 1947

[Source: *Foreign Relations of the United States: 1947,* I, 772–77]

Drafted by Kennan for Secretary of State George C. Marshall, this document provides a clearer explanation than Kennan's *Foreign Affairs* article of how he proposed to implement containment (see Document 6). Several points stand out: (1) Kennan's conviction that because the Soviet Union had no intention of starting a war military force would not be the primary instrument of containment; (2) his expectation that Soviet expansion, both in Europe and the Far East, would generate its own forces of resistance; (3) his concern over the limits of American power, and the resulting need to specify which parts of the world were vital to U.S. security and which were not. The document also anticipated by three months the communist coup in Czechoslovakia, an event Kennan regarded as a defensive Soviet reaction to the success of the European Recovery Program (see Documents 9 and 10).

Summary

1. The danger of war is vastly exaggerated in many quarters. The Soviet Government neither wants nor expects war with us in the foreseeable future. The warmongering campaign in the UN is designed to weaken our world leadership and to prevent the UN from being effectively used as a means of pressure against communistic expansion.

2. The political advance of the communists in Western Europe has been at least temporarily halted. This is the result of several factors, among which the prospect of U.S. aid is an important one.

3. The halt in the communist advance is forcing Moscow to consolidate its hold on Eastern Europe. It will probably have to clamp down completely on Czechoslovakia. For if the political trend in Europe turns against communism, a relatively free Czechoslovakia could become a threatening salient in Moscow's political position in Eastern Europe.

This also means that the Kremlin may very likely order the communist parties in France and Italy to resort to virtual civil war in those countries as soon as our right to have troops in Italy expires. If this happens, an intensified push against Greece may be expected at the same time.

4. In these operations, the Russians will try to keep their hand well concealed and leave us no grounds for formal protest against themselves.

5. Our best answer to this is to strengthen in every way local forces of resistance, and persuade others to bear a greater part of the burden of opposing communism. The present "bi-polarity" will, in the long run, be beyond our resources. It will also over-strain the UN. It is entirely possible that the Russians may soon withdraw from that body if we continue to use it as an instrument for mobilizing world opinion and pressure against them.

6. All in all, our policy must be directed toward restoring a balance of power in Europe and Asia. This means that in the C.F.M. meeting we must insist on keeping Western Germany free of communistic control. We must then see that it is better integrated into Western Europe and that a part of our responsibility for conditions there is shifted to the western European allies and the German people themselves.

I

The world situation is still dominated by the effort undertaken by the Russians in the post-hostilities period to extend their virtual domination over all, or as much as possible, of the Eurasian land mass.

In making this effort the Russians were taking advantage of the power vacuums left by the collapse of Germany and Japan and by the natural wave of radicalism following on the heels of any great military-political upheaval.

It was an integral part of that project to neutralize our own ability to oppose it by weakening in every way our national potential and by undermining confidence everywhere in our motives and our fitness for leadership.

II

That effort has now been brought substantially to a standstill by four factors:

1. Our insistence on a satisfactory peace settlement as a prerequisite to our military evacuation of ex-enemy territories. This has meant that we have offset to some extent the power vacuum on which the Russians had counted in their plans.

2. The recent use, in some instances—or proposed use in some others—

of our economic-aid to strengthen forces of resistance to communist pressure.

3. The Soviet failure to dominate the United Nations and the partial effectiveness of the United Nations in mobilizing world opinion against communist expansion.

4. The natural recession of the wave of post-war radicalism.

In consequence of these factors the Russians have been momentarily blocked in their political advance in the west. If U.S. aid to Europe becomes a reality, they will probably not be able to resume it. But the battle is far from won, and any relaxation of our efforts could still result in a political debacle for the non-communist forces.

III

Of the four factors cited above which have brought communist expansion to a halt, three are the result of our efforts. We have borne almost single-handed the burden of the international effort to stop the Kremlin's political advance. But this has stretched our resources dangerously far in several respects.

The continued occupation of Japan and of portions of Germany and Austria becomes increasingly more difficult for us, and disadvantageous in other respects, as the war recedes.

The program of aid to Europe which we are now proposing to undertake will probably be the last major effort of this nature which our people could, or should, make.

Our use of the United Nations as an instrument for opposing Soviet expansion, prior to the conclusion of peace, has strained that institution severely. It has an increasing tendency to alarm smaller nations and to paralyze, rather than stimulate, their will to play an active part in the organization. Furthermore, if we continue vigorously along this line—and particularly if we try to make effective use of the "little Assembly," [10] there is a real likelihood that the Russians will leave the Organization.

In these circumstances it is clearly unwise for us to continue the attempt to carry alone, or largely singlehanded, the opposition to Soviet expansion. It is urgently necessary for us to restore something of the balance of power

10. The "little Assembly" to which Kennan referred was a proposed Interim Committee of the General Assembly of the United Nations which the United States hoped to establish to circumvent the Soviet-American deadlock in the Security Council. If established as proposed, the new committee would have operated without the veto privilege which encumbered Security Council deliberations and actions. [Ed. note]

in Europe and Asia by strengthening local forces of independence and by getting them to assume part of our burden. The Harvard speech [11] approach was highly effective from this standpoint. But we have done almost nothing to exploit psychologically the initial advantage we have gained. If our effort in Europe is to be successful we must improve radically our machinery and practice in matters of informational policy in Europe and elsewhere.

IV

The halt in the communist advance in Western Europe has necessitated a consolidation of communist power throughout Eastern Europe. It will be necessary for them, in particular, to clamp down completely on Czechoslovakia. As long as communist political power was advancing in Europe, it was advantageous to the Russians to allow to the Czechs the outer appearances of freedom. In this way, Czechoslovakia was able to serve as a bait for nations farther west. Now that there is a danger of the political movement proceeding in the other direction, the Russians can no longer afford this luxury. Czechoslovakia could too easily become a means of entry of really democratic forces into Eastern Europe in general.

The sweeping away of democratic institutions and the consolidation of communist power in Czechoslovakia will add a formidable new element to the underground anti-communist political forces in the Soviet satellite area. For this reason, the Russians proceed to this step reluctantly. It is a purely defensive move.

Once having dug in politically on the Luebeck-Trieste line, the Russians can probably maintain their position there for some time by sheer police methods. But the problem will become an increasingly difficult one for them. It is unlikely that approximately one hundred million Russians will succeed in holding down permanently, in addition to their own minorities, some ninety millions of Europeans with a higher cultural level and with long experience in resistance to foreign rule.

One of the most dangerous moments to world stability will come when some day Russian rule begins to crumble in the eastern European area. The Kremlin may then feel itself seriously threatened internally and may resort to desperate measures. I do not see that situation developing in the immediate future.

11. Secretary of State George C. Marshall's speech at Harvard University, June 5, 1947, announcing the European Recovery Program. [Ed. note]

V

If native forces in western Europe are to take over part of our burden of opposing communism, it is essential that Germany be fitted into this picture.

It is now more unlikely than ever that the Russians would be willing to take their chances on a genuinely democratic, united Germany. Such a Germany, if it were to withstand communist penetration and domination, would, like present day Czechoslovakia, exercise a highly disruptive influence on communist power in eastern Europe. Rather than risk that, the Russians would probably prefer a continuance of the present status, under which they are at least sure of being able to neutralize the political potential of eastern Germany.

They may well attempt various ruses at the coming Council of Foreign Ministers meeting to try to get us out of western Germany under arrangements which would leave that country defenseless against communist penetration. For us to yield to such tactics would plainly undermine the ability of western Europe as a whole to withstand communist pressure and would of course be inconsistent with the aims of our program of aid to Europe.

If pressed along these lines we will therefore have no choice but to disagree again at London and to proceed to make the best of a divided Germany. It will then be essential that we bring the western part of Germany into some acceptable relationship to the other western European countries. Geographically, it is much more their problem than ours; and it is improper and unnatural that we should continue to bear the lion's share of the responsibility for handling it.

This means that we shall have to make a determined effort to bring the French, Belgians, Dutch, Danes, et cetera to an enlightened understanding of the necessities of the German situation; to the acknowledgement of their primary responsibility for integrating western Germany into western Europe, and to a detailed agreement with us as to how this shall be done. In this effort we must expect to give, as well as to receive, concessions.

VI

The Middle East is undoubtedly in for a rocky time. In Palestine, we have a situation which is badly fouled up by the past mistakes of many people, including ourselves. These probably cannot be settled without great unpleasantness, including violence. The further development of this situation is inevitably going to present favorable opportunities for the Russians to fish in muddy waters. These they will exploit to the limit. But if we and the British remain united in the resolve to hold this area free of Soviet control, and agreed as to the methods for doing so, we ought to be able to weather the storm.

VII

The Far Eastern area is in a state of almost total instability. The problem of correcting that instability and bringing some order out of the chaos and uncertainty is an enormous one, which we have scarcely touched. In part, it probably exceeds our capacity. But we will have to make a careful and realistic study of what we can conceivably do, and then proceed to implement that program.

Our most immediate problem is Japan, where our responsibility is directly engaged. It is unlikely that we will reach any early agreement with our Allies on any Japanese peace settlement. We must therefore reckon with the possibility of a continuation of our direct responsibility for Japan for some time into the future.

The basic ideas with which we entered on the occupation of Japan apparently did not take into account the possibility of a hostile Russia and the techniques of communist political penetration. Our occupation policies have consequently been effective in disarming Japan and destroying the old pattern of militarism; but they have not produced, nor are they designed to produce, the political and economic stability which Japanese society will require if it is to withstand communist pressures after we have gone.

Our task now is to correct that deficiency. Until we do that, we cannot safely release Japan from the occupational regime.

All this calls for a thorough re-examination of our occupation policies.

In China there is not much we can do, in present circumstances but to sweat it out and to try to prevent the military situation from changing too drastically to the advantage of the communist forces. We must bear in mind that a frustration of communist aims in the west will probably lead to increased Soviet pressure in the Far East. But there are definite limitations on both the military and economic capabilities of the Russians in that area. We should not ignore these limitations or over-rate the Soviet threat.

As to Korea, there is no longer any real hope of a genuinely peaceful and free democratic development in that country. Its political life in the coming period is bound to be dominated by political immaturity, intolerance and violence. Where such conditions prevail, the communists are in their element.

Therefore, we cannot count on native Korean forces to help us hold the line against Soviet expansion. Since the territory is not of decisive strategic importance to us, our main task is to extricate ourselves without too great a loss of prestige. In doing so, however, we should remember that it makes no sense to yield in Korea and then to try to insist on the elimination of Soviet influence behind Korea, in northern Manchuria.

VIII

As to the over-all international situation, the extreme anxiety felt in many quarters about the danger of war rests on an incorrect appraisal of Soviet intentions. The Kremlin does not wish to have another major war and does not expect to have one. Their warmongering campaign in the United Nations is a smoke-screen, designed to scare off our friends and to discredit us.

If aid to Europe gets favorable reaction in the coming Special Session of Congress,[12] Moscow will probably order the French and Italian communists, as a last resort, to proceed to civil war, in the hopes that this will bring chaos in Europe and dissuade us from proceeding with the aid program. Such tactics will probably not be implemented until after mid-December, when our right to have forces in Italy will have expired. That is also the time when we may expect the culmination of communist-satellite pressure in Greece.

The Russians do not expect these actions to lead to war with us. They will try to keep their own hand carefully disguised and to leave us in the frustrated position of having no one to oppose but local communists, or possibly the satellites.

They are aware that civil war in France and Italy may lead to serious reverses for the communist parties of those countries. This does not bother them very much. If United States aid is successful, these parties will not be much immediate use to them, anyway. And the hard cores of the parties are prepared to go underground again, if need be.

In playing this sort of a game they are admittedly operating very close to the line: closer than they themselves probably realize. They normally work with a disciplined movement; and they are accustomed to feeling that they can always withdraw if they see that they have reached the limits of the other fellow's patience. The greatest danger in this case is that they may

12. Special session of the 80th Congress, called to consider interim aid to Europe under the European Recovery Program, which met from November 17, 1947, to December 19, 1947. [Ed. note]

overestimate the discipline of their satellites in the Balkans, and that the latter may get out of hand, once violence begins, and go so far as to engage our interests directly.

Our best answer to all of this will be to stiffen local forces of resistance, wherever we can, and to see first whether they cannot do the work. There is a good chance that they can, particularly in France and Italy. Only if they show signs of failing, do we have to consider more direct action.

But even then, we should be free to call the play and to determine whether that action is to be directed against Russia or only against Russian stooge forces. The latter would be strongly preferable, in principle—and would *not* necessarily lead to war with Russia.

All in all, there is no reason to expect that we will be forced suddenly and violently into a major military clash with Soviet forces.

<><><><><><><><><><><><><><><><><><><><><><><><><><><><><><><><><><><><><>

8   **T O P   S E C R E T**

Review of Current Trends: U.S. Foreign Policy

PPS 23   February 24, 1948

[Source: *Foreign Relations of the United States: 1948,* I (part 2), 526–28]

Like PPS 13 (Document 7) PPS 23 was a review by Kennan of the overall world situation. Excerpts from it dealing with the implementation of containment in specific areas are printed elsewhere in this collection (see Documents 11, 19, and 25). In the portion printed here, Kennan endeavored to set the policy of containment in perspective by distinguishing between "universalist" and "particularist" traditions in American foreign policy. Kennan's analysis foreshadowed the distinction between the "realist" and "legalistic-moralistic" approaches to diplomacy which he later stressed in his published writings. It also reflected the dilemma faced by American policy makers as they sought to integrate a foreign policy based on balance-of-power considerations with principles of collective security underlying the United Nations Charter.

VII. International Organization

A broad conflict runs through U.S. policy today between what may be called the universalistic and the particularized approaches to the solution of international problems.

The *universalistic* approach looks to the solution of international problems by providing a universalistic pattern of rules and procedures which would be applicable to all countries, or at least all countries prepared to join, in an identical way. This approach has the tendency to rule out *political* solutions (that is, solutions related to the peculiarities in the positions and attitudes of the individual peoples). It favors legalistic and mechanical solutions, applicable to all countries alike. It has already been embodied in the United Nations, in the proposed ITO Charter, in UNESCO, in the PICAO, and in similar efforts at universal world collaboration in given spheres of foreign policy.

This universalistic approach has a strong appeal to U.S. public opinion; for it appears to obviate the necessity of dealing with the national peculiarities and diverging political philosophies of foreign peoples; which many of our people find confusing and irritating. In this sense, it contains a strong vein of escapism. To the extent that it could be made to apply, it would relieve us of the necessity of dealing with the world as it is. It assumes that if all countries could be induced to subscribe to certain standard rules of behavior, the ugly realities—the power aspirations, the national prejudices, the irrational hatreds and jealousies—would be forced to recede behind the protecting curtain of accepted legal restraint, and that the problems of our foreign policy could thus be reduced to the familiar terms of parliamentary procedure and majority decision. The outward form established for international dealings would then cover and conceal the inner content. And instead of being compelled to make the sordid and involved political choices inherent in traditional diplomacy, we could make decisions on the lofty but simple plane of moral principle and under the protecting cover of majority decision.

The *particularized* approach is one which is skeptical of any scheme for compressing international affairs into legalistic concepts. It holds that the content is more important than the form, and will force its way through any formal structure which is placed upon it. It considers that the thirst for power is still dominant among so many peoples that it cannot be assuaged or controlled by anything but counter-force. It does not reject entirely the idea of alliance as a suitable form of counter-force; but it considers that if alliance is to be effective it must be based upon real community of interest and outlook, which is to be found only among limited groups of governments, and not upon the abstract formalism of universal international law or international organization. It places no credence in the readiness of most peoples to wage war or to make national sacrifices in the interests of an abstraction called "peace". On the contrary, it sees in universal undertakings a series of obligations which might, in view of the shortsightedness and timidity of other governments, prevent this country from taking vigorous and incisive measures for its own defense and for the defense of concepts of international relations which might be of vital importance to world stability as a whole. It sees effective and determined U.S. policy being caught, at decisive moments, in the meshes of a sterile and cumbersome international parliamentarianism, if the universalistic concepts are applied.

Finally, the particularized approach to foreign policy problems distrusts the theory of national sovereignty as it expresses itself today in international organization. The modern techniques of aggressive expansion lend themselves too well to the pouring of new wine into old vessels—to the infusion of a foreign political will into the personality of an ostensibly independent nation. In these circumstances, the parliamentary principle in world affairs can easily become distorted and abused as it has been in the case of White Russia, the Ukraine and the Russian satellites.[13] This is not to mention the problem of the distinction between large and small states, and the voice that they should have, respectively, in world affairs.

This Government is now conducting a dual policy, which combines elements of both of these approaches. This finds its reflection in the Department of State, where the functional (or universalistic) concept vies with the geographic (or particularized) in the framing and conduct of policy, as well as in the principles of Departmental organization.

This duality is something to which we are now deeply committed. I do not mean to recommend that we should make any sudden changes. We cannot today abruptly renounce aspirations which have become for many people here and abroad a symbol of our belief in the possibility of a peaceful world.

But it is my own belief that in our pursuance of a workable world order we have started from the wrong end. Instead of beginning at the center, which is our own immediate neighborhood—the area of our own political and economic tradition—and working outward, we have started on the periphery of the entire circle, i.e., on the universalistic principle of the UN, and have attempted to work inward. This has meant a great dispersal of our effort, and has brought perilously close to discredit those very concepts of a universal world order to which we were so attached. If we wish to preserve those concepts for the future we must hasten to remove some of the strain we have placed upon them and to build a solid structure, proceeding from a central foundation, which can be thrust up to meet them before they collapse of their own weight.

13. White Russia (Byelorussia) and the Ukraine, constituent republics of the Union of Soviet Socialist Republics, were given individual representation in the United Nations General Assembly in an agreement made at Yalta. [Ed. note]

This is the significance of the ERP, the idea of European union, and the cultivation of a closer association with the U.K. and Canada. For a truly stable world order can proceed, within our lifetime, only from the older, mellower and more advanced nations of the world—nations for which the concept of order, as opposed to power, has value and meaning. If these nations do not have the strength to seize and hold real leadership in world affairs today, through that combination of political greatness and wise restraint which goes only with a ripe and settled civilization, then, as Plato once remarked: ". . . cities will never have rest from their evils,—no, nor the human race, as I believe."

≥ 3 ≤

IMPLEMENTATION: EUROPE, 1947–49

As APPLIED in Europe between 1947 and 1949, the policy of "containment" linked the problem of recovery from World War II with that of maintaining political equilibrium in the face of expanding Soviet influence. Kennan had suggested in the "X" article that in the end a self-confident Europe would provide the best possible bulwark against Soviet aggressive tendencies; by 1947 he and other influential policy makers had become convinced that without American help in rebuilding Europe's war-shattered economies such self-confidence would never develop. In PPS 1, 4, and 23 (Documents 9, 10, and 11), Kennan and the Policy Planning Staff worked out in detail the rationale behind this approach.

The events of early 1948, however—the Soviet coup in Czechoslovakia in February, the brief but sharp "war scare" in March, and the imposition of the Berlin blockade in June—made it clear that economic assistance alone would not restore the equilibrium the United States sought. Accordingly, three additional approaches to the problem of European instability were set in motion in the spring and summer of 1948. One was the institutionalization of covert-action capabilities for the Central Intelligence Agency, a measure endorsed by the National Security Council at Kennan's request (Document 12). The second approach, about which Kennan had considerable reservations, involved the formation of an independent West German state (Documents 14, 15). The third and most ambitious approach, about which Kennan also had doubts, envisaged furnishing military assistance to the nations of Western Europe through the framework of a multilateral security organization (Documents 13, 16, 17, and 18).

The reservations entertained by Kennan and the Policy Planning Staff regarding these last two initiatives stemmed from the fear that they would impair prospects for a political settlement with the Russians in Europe. But in these cases Kennan's advice was not heeded; the year 1949 saw the formation of both NATO and the Federal Republic of Germany.

9   **S E C R E T**

Policy with Respect to American Aid to Western Europe

PPS 1   May 23, 1947

[Source: *Foreign Relations of the United States: 1947,* III, 224–30]

JCS 1769/1 (Document 5) had rated the countries of Western Europe first among potential recipients of American aid. In their initial deliberations, the State Department's Policy Planning Staff considered how the United States might provide such assistance. PPS 1 established three principles which were to guide future policy: (1) that psychological malaise stemming from the dislocations of war and reconstruction, not the danger of Soviet military attack or international communism, constituted the chief threat to the European balance of power; (2) that the United States could most effectively solve this problem by furnishing economic, not military, assistance; and (3) that such aid could most efficiently be provided through a program run largely by the Europeans themselves.

PPS 1 contained many of the ideas and even some of the language used by Secretary of State George C. Marshall at Harvard University on June 5, 1947, when he first publicly proposed the European Recovery Program, or "Marshall Plan," as it came to be known. The document also represented a less than subtle critique of the sweeping language President Truman had used in March 1947 to justify aid to Greece and Turkey—language that had failed to differentiate between vital and peripheral interests, a distinction basic to the underlying assumptions of both JCS 1769/1 and PPS 1.

I. General

1. The Policy Planning Staff has selected the question of American aid to western Europe as the first subject of its attention. This does not mean that the Staff is unmindful of the importance or urgency of problems in other areas or of its mission to coordinate long-term policy on a global basis. It means simply that western Europe appears to be the area for which long-term planning might most advantageously begin.

2. The Policy Planning Staff does not see communist activities as the root of the difficulties of western Europe. It believes that the present crisis results in large part from the disruptive effect of the war on the economic, political, and social structure of Europe and from a profound exhaustion of physical plant and of spiritual vigor. This situation has been aggravated and rendered far more difficult of remedy by the division of the continent into east and west. The Planning Staff recognizes that the communists are exploiting the European crisis and that further communist successes would create serious danger to American security. It considers, however, that American effort in

aid to Europe should be directed not to the combatting of communism as such but to the restoration of the economic health and vigor of European society. It should aim, in other words, to combat not communism, but the economic maladjustment which makes European society vulnerable to exploitation by any and all totalitarian movements and which Russian communism is now exploiting. The Planning Staff believes that American plans should be drawn to this purpose and that this should be frankly stated to the American public.

3. The Policy Planning Staff sees in this general question of American aid to western Europe two problems: a long-term one and a short-term one. The long-term problem is that of how the economic health of the area is to be restored and of the degree and form of American aid for such restoration. The short-term problem is to determine what effective and dramatic action should be taken in the immediate future to halt the economic disintegration of western Europe and to create confidence that the overall problem can be solved and that the United States can and will play its proper part in the solution.

.   .   .   .

II. The Short-Term Problem

5. With respect to the short-term problem, the Planning Staff feels that we should select some particular bottleneck or bottlenecks in the economic pattern of western Europe and institute immediate action which would bring to bear the full weight of this Government on the breaking of those bottlenecks. The purpose of this action would be on the one hand psychological—to put us on the offensive instead of the defensive, to convince the European peoples that we mean business, to serve as a catalyst for their hope and confidence, and to dramatize for our people the nature of Europe's problems and the importance of American assistance. On the other hand, this action would be designed to make a real contribution to the solution of Europe's economic difficulties.

The Planning Staff attaches great importance to this project and considers it almost essential to the success of the general scheme. It fears that unless something of this sort is done at once the result may be a further deterioration of morale in Europe which will seriously jeopardize the long-term program. For this reason it recommends that most careful and intensive consideration be given at once to this project.

.   .   .   .

III. The Long-Term Problem

6. The Policy Planning Staff recognizes that the long-term problem is one of enormous complexity and difficulty. . . . In the belief, however, that this Government cannot afford to delay the adoption of some overall approach to the solution of the problem, the following tentative views are set forth:

   a. It is necessary to distinguish clearly between a program for the economic revitalization of Europe on the one hand, and a program of American support of such revitalization on the other. It would be neither fitting nor efficacious for this Government to undertake to draw up unilaterally and to promulgate formally on its own initiative a program designed to place western Europe on its feet economically. This is the business of the Europeans. The formal initiative must come from Europe; the program must be evolved in Europe; and the Europeans must bear the basic responsibility for it. The role of this country should consist of friendly aid in the drafting of a European program and of the later support of such a program, by financial and other means, at European request.

   b. The program which this country is asked to support must be a joint one, agreed to by several European nations. While it may be linked to individual national programs, such as the Monnet plan in France,[1] it must, for psychological and political as well as economic reasons, be an internationally agreed program. The request for our support must come as a joint request from a group of friendly nations, not as a series of isolated and individual appeals.

   c. This European program must envisage bringing western Europe to a point where it will be able to maintain a tolerable standard of living on a financially self-supporting basis. It must give promise of doing the whole job. The program must contain reasonable assurance that if we support it, this will be the last such program we shall be asked to support in the foreseeable future.

   d. The overall European program must embrace, or be linked to, some sort of plan for dealing with the economic plight of Britain. The plan must be formally a British one, worked out on British initiative and British responsibility, and the role of the United States, again, must be to give friendly support.

   e. This does not mean that the United States need stand aside or remain aloof from the elaboration of the overall European program.

---

1. A plan for revitalizing the postwar French economy, proposed by the economist Jean Monnet. [Ed. note]

As a member of the United Nations and particularly of the Economic Commission for Europe,[2] and as a power occupying certain European territories, it is entitled and obliged to participate in working out the program. Our position as an occupying power also makes it incumbent upon us to cooperate whole-heartedly in the execution of any program that may be evolved. For this reason, and because we must know as soon as possible to what extent such a program is technically feasible, we must undertake an independent and realistic study of the entire problem of European rehabilitation. But we must insist, for the sake of clarity, for the sake of soundness of concept, and for the sake of the self-respect of European peoples, that the initiative be taken in Europe and that the main burden be borne by the governments of that area. With the best of will, the American people cannot really help those who are not willing to help themselves. And if the requested initiative and readiness to bear public responsibility are not forthcoming from the European governments, then that will mean that *rigor mortis* has already set in on the body politic of Europe as we have known it and that it may be already too late for us to change decisively the course of events.

f. While this program must necessarily center in the European area, it will admittedly have widespread ramifications in other areas. It will also have important connotations for the UN, and we should bear constantly in mind the need for maximum utilization of UN machinery.

g. American support for such a program need not be confined to financial assistance. It may involve considerable practical American cooperation in the solution of specific problems.

h. With respect to any program which this Government may eventually be asked to support, it will be necessary for it to insist on safeguards to assure

first, that everything possible be done to whittle down the cost of such support in dollars;

secondly, that the European Governments use the full force of their authority to see that our aid is employed in a purposeful and effective way; and

thirdly, that maximum reimbursement be made to this country in

2. The Economic Commission for Europe, made up of the United States and seventeen European countries, was created by the United Nations Economic and Social Council on March 28, 1947, for the purpose of aiding the economic reconstruction of Europe. [Ed. note]

any forms found to be economically feasible and in United States interest.

i. The problem of where and in what form the initiative for the formulation of a European program should be taken is admittedly a tremendously difficult and delicate one. It cannot be definitely predetermined by us. Presumably an effort would first be made to advance the project in the Economic Commission for Europe, and probably as a proposal for general European (not just western European) cooperation; but then it would be essential that this be done in such a form that the Russian satellite countries would either exclude themselves by unwillingness to accept the proposed conditions or agree to abandon the exclusive orientation of their economies. If the Russians prove able to block any such scheme in the Economic Commission for Europe, it may be necessary for the key countries of western Europe to find means of conferring together without the presence of the Russians and Russian satellites. In general, however, the question of where and how this initiative should be taken is primarily one for the European nations, and we should be careful not to seek unduly to influence their decision.

·   ·   ·   ·   ·   ·   ·

IV. Clarifying Implications of "Truman Doctrine"

8. Steps should be taken to clarify what the press has unfortunately come to identify as the "Truman Doctrine", and to remove in particular two damaging impressions which are current in large sections of American public opinion. These are:

a. That the United States approach to world problems is a defensive reaction to communist pressure and that the effort to restore sound economic conditions in other countries is only a by-product of this reaction and not something we would be interested in doing if there were no communist menace;

b. That the Truman Doctrine is a blank check to give economic and military aid to any area in the world where the communists show signs of being successful. It must be made clear that the extension of American aid is essentially a question of political economy in the literal sense of that term and that such aid will be considered only in cases where the prospective results bear a satisfactory relationship to the expenditure of American resources and effort. It must be made clear that in the case of Greece and Turkey we are dealing with a critical area where the failure to take action would have had particularly serious consequences, where a successful action would promise particularly far-reaching results, and where the overall cost was relatively small; and that in other areas we should have to apply similar criteria.

<><><><><><><><><><><><><><><><><><><><><><><><><><><><><><><><><>

10   **TOP SECRET**

Certain Aspects of the European Recovery Problem from the United States Standpoint (Preliminary Report)

PPS 4   July 23, 1947

[Source: Records of the Policy Planning Staff held in the Department of State's Foreign Affairs Documentation and Reference Center, Washington, D.C.]

Following Secretary of State Marshall's speech at Harvard University on June 5, 1947, the Policy Planning Staff turned its attention to a detailed consideration of how the European Recovery Program might work. The result was PPS 4, a document more than forty pages long, excerpts from which are printed below.

PPS 4 provides as complete an expression as exists from this period of why Washington officials considered European stability a vital national interest. It also emphasizes the limitations of American resources, and insists that the European Recovery Program should not be viewed as a precedent for American policy in other parts of the world.

This Government will soon be called upon to discuss with European governments the problem of European recovery and to determine the part which the United States should take in its solution.

The purpose of this report is to examine the elements of the problem in their relation to the interests of the United States and to suggest some of the considerations by which this Government might usefully be guided in determining its attitude in the questions at issue.

I. The Source of United States Interest

The factors which have impeded the general recovery of European economy since V-E day need no elaborate description. They have been widely analyzed and discussed in the United States. For purposes of this report, it is sufficient to note that they include, in addition to certain long-term trends of

European development, the following factors, most of which have arisen directly from the recent war:

a. The physical and psychic exhaustion of people everywhere;

b. the feelings of disillusionment, insecurity and apathy occasioned by the developments of the post-hostilities period and particularly by the tendency toward division of the continent between east and west;

c. the destruction and depreciation of physical plant and equipment;

d. the depletion of financial reserves, particularly in foreign exchange and external assets;

e. social and economic dislocation, including the breakdown of the pre-war institutional patterns and the destruction of the machinery of economic intercourse;

f. the prolonged delay in adjusting German economy to production for peaceful purposes.

In consequence of these factors, and of other lesser ones, we face a situation today in which important industrial and population centers of the continent are unable to recover by dint of their own efforts the living standards which their peoples enjoyed prior to the war. In many instances, they are not even in a position to prevent, unaided, a further deterioration of the conditions under which their peoples are obliged to live.

Further deterioration might be disastrous to Europe. It might well bring such hardship, such bewilderment, such desperate struggle for control over inadequate resources as to lead to widespread repudiation of the principles on which modern European civilization has been founded and for which, in the minds of many, two world wars have been fought. The principles of law, of justice, and of restraint in the exercise of political power, already widely impugned and attacked, might then be finally swept away—and with them the vital recognition that the integrity of society as a whole must rest on respect for the dignity of the individual citizen. The implications of such a loss would far surpass the common apprehensions over the possibility of "communist control." There is involved in the continuation of the present conditions in Europe nothing less than the possibility of a renunciation by Europeans of the values of individual responsibility and political restraint which has become traditional to their continent. This would undo the work of centuries and would cause such damage as could only be overcome by the effort of further centuries.

United States interests in the broadest sense could not fail to be profoundly affected by such a trend of events.

In the first place, the United States people have a very real economic interest in Europe. This stems from Europe's role in the past as a market and as a major source of supply for a variety of products and services.

But beyond this, the traditional concept of U.S. security has been predicated on the sort of Europe now in jeopardy. The broad pattern of our recent foreign policy, including the confidence we have placed in the United Nations, has assumed the continuation in Europe of a considerable number of free states subservient to no great power, and recognizing their heritage of civil liberties and personal responsibility and determined to maintain this heritage. If this premise were to be invalidated, there would have to be a basic revision of the whole concept of our international position—a revision which might logically demand of us material sacrifices and restraints far exceeding the maximum implications of a program of aid to European reconstruction. But in addition, the United States, in common with most of the rest of the world, would suffer a cultural and spiritual loss incalculable in its long-term effects.

It is on the recognition of these realities that U.S. interest in European recovery is founded. And it is from this recognition that any assessment of the proper role of the United States in a European recovery program must proceed.

.   .   .   .

IV. General Considerations Governing United States Aid

The principal considerations which should determine the nature of United States aid to a European recovery program are the following:

a. Our aid should cover only that area of the total needs of the program which clearly cannot be met by other resources available to the participating nations. Claims on U.S. supplies should be carefully screened to see that there is no other source from which the desired supplies could advantageously be obtained.

b. Our aid should be concentrated, as far as possible, in a few key items which will have the maximum immediate effect in promoting European recovery. This will contribute to simplicity and clarity of concept. It will also have the advantage of restricing the number of fields in which this Government becomes associated with the needs and problems of European governments. By restricting U.S. aid to a few key items, it will be possible to leave to the Europeans the responsiblity for handling the needs of their economies in a multitude of lesser items; and at the same time U.S. assistance in meeting the major needs will free resources through which the minor ones can more easily be met. Particular attention should be given, in selecting the items for U.S. aid, to the critical bottlenecks which impede general European production and distribution.

c. The emphasis of the whole program of U.S. aid should be to help Europe to help herself. Every effort should be made to avoid forms of assistance which would increase, rather than decrease, the abnormal economic dependence of these areas on the United States. Whenever there is a choice between supplying Europe with goods for consumption and supplying her with the means to produce those goods herself, the latter course should be chosen unless cost is prohibitive.

d. Our aid should be directed wherever possible to those branches of economic activity—as for example, coal—the effects of which are apt to relate not just to a single country but to be radiated generally across international borders and to affect European economy as a whole. These branches of activity will tend to be identical with those which the European nations themselves will have chosen to approach through international, rather than purely national, programs. If U.S. aid is directed generally to such branches of activity, the problem of allocations as between individual European countries will be simplified; our aims in extending assistance will be clearer to everyone; we will have in effect a collective endorsement by the European nations of the need for the particular type of aid in question; and it will be harder for troublemakers everywhere to misrepresent the motives, and to disrupt the effect, of such assistance as we may grant.

e. Our aid must be closely related to our resources and to the needs of a healthy domestic economy. In this respect, careful consideration must be given to the eventual results of the studies which the President has ordered to be conducted on the relation of foreign aid to our domestic economy.[3] If the results of these studies indicate, as they may, that certain restrictions of domestic consumption and the reimposition of certain economic controls are necessary to the carrying out of a program of aid to Europe, then the inconveniences involved will have to be weighed against the probable consequences of our failure to extend such aid at this time.

3. On June 22, 1947, President Truman announced the formation of three committees, headed respectively by Secretary of the Interior Julius Krug, Edwin G. Nourse, chairman of the Council of Economic Advisers, and Secretary of Commerce W. Averell Harriman, to study U.S. capabilities for implementing the proposed European Recovery Program and the impact that program would have on the American economy. [Ed. note]

IX. *Further Implications of United States Aid to Europe*

Measures as far-reaching as those discussed in this report should be care-fully examined for their implications and incidental effects in areas of U.S. interest other than those to which they are immediately directed. In this re-spect the following considerations deserve attention:

A. UNITED STATES DOMESTIC ECONOMY

A European aid program will have implications for United States econ-omy with respect to both cost and benefits.

The costs need no elucidation. They may include not only the financial sacrifice which must be made by the taxpayers of this country but also the restraints in the form of controls on exports, and possibly on consumption, which may have to be established.

As against these costs there should be weighed not only the negative fac-tor of the alternatives but also the positive factor of the possible benefits to U.S. economy. Only if European recovery can be achieved will there be possible the development of a world trade situation in which Europe and the U.S. can enjoy normal economic relations on a mutually beneficial basis. Past experience has taught us that the U.S. cannot achieve full prosperity in a world of depression.

To many, the probable costs of a program along the lines envisaged in this report may seem severe. But they would be short-term costs, calculated in years. The possible benefits would be mainly long-term benefits, calcu-lated at least in decades; and no one can doubt that if they are forthcoming at all, they will outweigh the costs many times.

B. THE UNITED NATIONS

The interest of the United States in developing the United Nations and its specialized and related agencies as rapidly as possible to the point where they may effectively discharge their responsibilities for promoting and har-monizing international cooperative action in the economic field has been re-peatedly made clear. . . .

In the case of European recovery, the urgency of effective international action is such that delay might be fatal. The European nations which have taken the initiative in organizing discussion of common economic problems on an international basis in response to Secretary Marshall's suggestion[4] found it advisable to inaugurate these discussions through a temporary organization rather than through UN bodies. This decision was one which deserves respect in view of the background of circumstances against which it was taken; and events subsequent to the inauguration of the preliminary discussions have tended to confirm the necessity for this approach at this time. This should not, however, constitute a reason for doubt or discouragement as to the long-run usefulness of the UN bodies in this field. On the contrary, if there can be evolved at this time a constructive international approach to the economic problems which are weighing so heavily on the peoples of Europe, this in itself could not fail to bring about conditions within which the UN could operate most effectively. In the meantime, UN organs and related agencies can play many useful roles in relation to specific aspects of European recovery. . . .

. . . .

This Government should also continue to press for the speedy building up of the appropriate UN bodies in order that they may take over their full share of the burden as rapidly as possible.

C. UNITED STATES FOREIGN POLICY IN GENERAL

Further U.S. aid to Europe would not in itself constitute any basic change in U.S. foreign policy. The international environment in which our foreign policy must operate has always been, and must always be, a changing one. By the same token, our policy can never be static. There must be an unceasing process of adaptation to new conditions. The considerations set forth in this report refer merely to an attempt at such adjustment in one specific instance. There are, and will continue to be, areas outside of Europe which will have need of U.S. cooperation in their development. These needs will have to be faced, like those of Europe, on their merits. But Europe's needs are, in their aggregate, clear in outline, readily susceptible of short-term solution, and of urgent importance to the interests of this country and of world recovery in general. And for that reason, they lend themselves to immediate and special treatment.

There is no reason to believe that the approaches here applied to European problems will find any wide application elsewhere. With one or two exceptions, notably Korea and Japan, where specific U.S. obligations may call for

4. Marshall's Harvard speech, June 5, 1947. [Ed. note]

further assistance along patterns similar to those outlined here with respect to Europe, the needs of peoples of other areas differ, for the most part, in certain fundamental respects from those of peoples in Europe.

The problem in Europe is basically one of releasing the capacity for self-help already present in certain highly advanced countries. This is a short-term problem.

In the case of many non-European areas, what is needed is not the release of existing energies but the creation of new ones. This is a long-term problem and one which calls for much more in the way of assistance directly from the American people, in the form of technical and managerial guidance and private investment, than of financial assistance by our Government. It is here that there will be particular need of new organizational machinery, . . . through which the technical skills of the people of this country can be channelled.

It may be argued that a program for Europe might prejudice the availability of supplies for distribution elsewhere, in excess of existing programs. This is a valid point; and the amounts which this country can safely make available to Europe should be carefully related to what is known of demands existing or those which may be raised elsewhere over the same period and which might seem to be of equal urgency and importance, but there is no likelihood that demands of this particular nature will be large.

In general, the extent of the calls on this country is so great in relation to our responses that we could not contemplate assistance to others on any universal basis, even if this were desirable. A beginning would have to be made somewhere, and the best place for a beginning is obviously in Europe.

By the same token, a program of U.S. aid to Europe should not be viewed as an attempt at a total solution of the world dollar problem. It is not that. Even if Europe be effectively aided, a problem would still remain in the need of other countries for products and services from this country beyond what they are able to give to us and what we are willing to take from them in return. The so-called dollar problem is a reflection of a profound temporary disparity in productive capacity between this country and the world around it. That disparity cannot be removed by anything this country alone can do. But if Europe's exchange situation could be substantially relieved by the combined effort of the Europeans and ourselves, this would have a cumulative effect, and the rest of the world would benefit indirectly from this improvement and its problems would be reduced to dimensions which would make it much easier for everyone to deal with.

The undertaking of a program of aid for Europe would not mean termination or suspension of efforts to find ways of relieving the problem of the dollar exchange shortage elsewhere. It would merely mean that this Government had agreed to join others in tackling the core of this problem in an organized and intensive manner.

If the considerations outlined in this report have implications for U.S. policy in areas other than Europe, these implications do not lie, for the most part, in parallels between action in Europe and action elsewhere, but rather in the importance of Europe itself to the regeneration of confidence everywhere in the possibility of progress and peaceful development in international life. The older cultural centers of Europe are the meteorological centers in which much of the climate of international life is produced and from which it proceeds. Until hope has been restored in Europe, there can be no real revival of confidence and security in the affairs of the world at large.

X. Conclusion

. . . [I]t is none too soon to begin the charting of a course of U.S. policy with relation to European recovery which would do justice both to the immediate national interests of this country and to the abiding concern which the people of the United States feel for the continued vitality and prosperity of the European community.

---

11   **TOP SECRET**

Review of Current Trends: U.S. Foreign Policy

PPS 23   February 24, 1948

[Source: *Foreign Relations of the United States: 1948,* I (part 2), 510–12, 515–21]

By early 1948, it had become evident that the prospect of U.S. economic aid had contributed significantly to a restoration of self-confidence in Europe. Kennan now addressed himself, in the excerpts from PPS 23 printed below (other excerpts are printed as Documents 8, 19, and 25), to the question of what American political objectives in Western Europe and the Mediterranean should be. The ultimate goal, he argued, should be a reconstitution of political authority in Europe independent of domination by either the United States or the Soviet Union. To this end, he strongly endorsed the concept of European union, and stressed the need to associate Britain with that enterprise, even at the expense of some loosening of ties with Canada and the United States. That part of Germany not under Soviet control would also have to be integrated into this system, Kennan argued; the alternatives of a divided but perpetually intransigent Germany on the one hand, and a unified but potentially aggressive Germany on the other, risked to an unacceptable degree such stability as had been attained in postwar Europe. Kennan also concerned himself with the dangers of instability in the Mediterranean, where in both Greece and Italy there existed large and active communist parties eager to seize power. His recommendation for dealing with this problem involved the use of United States military forces as a political instrument with which to encourage conflicts of interest between the Soviet Union and the indigenous communists in that part of the world. These excerpts conclude with Kennan's recommendations on the delicate Palestine question, another issue involving the need to balance strategic considerations against those of international (and, in this case, domestic) politics.

I. United States, Britain, and Europe

On the assumption that Western Europe will be rescued from communist control, the relationships between Great Britain and the continental countries, on the one hand, and between Great Britain and the United States and Canada on the other, will become for us a long-term policy problem of major significance. The scope of this problem is so immense and its complexities so numerous that there can be no simple and easy answer. The solutions will have to be evolved step by step over a long period of time. But it is not too early today for us to begin to think out the broad outlines of the pattern which would best suit our national interests.

In my opinion, the following facts are basic to a consideration of this problem.

1. Some form of political, military, and economic union in Western Europe will be necessary if the free nations of Europe are to hold their own against the people of the east united under Moscow rule.

2. It is questionable whether this union could be strong enough to serve its designed purpose unless it had the participation and support of Great Britain.

3. Britain's long term economic problem, on the other hand, can scarcely be solved just by closer association with the other Western European countries, since these countries do not have, by and large, the food and raw material surpluses she needs; this problem could be far better met by closer association with Canada and the United States.

4. The only way in which a European union, embracing Britain but excluding eastern Europe, could become economically healthy would

be to develop the closest sort of trading relationships either with this hemisphere or with Africa.

It will be seen from the above that we stand before something of a dilemma. If we were to take Britain into our own U.S.-Canadian orbit, according to some formula of "Union now", this would probably solve Britain's long term economic problem and create a natural political entity of great strength. But this would tend to cut Britain off from the close political association she is seeking with continental nations and might therefore have the ultimate effect of rendering the continental nations more vulnerable to Russian pressure. If, on the other hand, the British are encouraged to seek salvation only in closer association with their continental neighbors, then there is no visible solution of the long term economic problem of either Britain or Germany, and we would be faced, at the termination of ERP, with another crises of demand on this country for European aid.

To me, there seem only two lines of emergence from this dilemma. They are not mutually exclusive and might, in fact, supplement each other very well.

In the first place, Britain could be encouraged to proceed vigorously with her plans for participation in a European union, and we could try to bring that entire union, rather than just Britain alone, into a closer economic association with this country and Canada. We must remember, however, that if this is to be really effective, the economic association must be so intimate as to bring about a substantial degree of currency and customs union, plus relative freedom of migration of individuals as between Europe and this continent. Only in this way can the free movement of private capital and labor be achieved which will be necessary if we are to find a real cure for the abnormal dependence of these areas on governmental aid from this country. But we should also note carefully the possible implications of such a program from the standpoint of the ITO Charter. As I see it, the draft charter, as well as the whole theory behind our trade agreements program, would make it difficult for us to extend to the countries of western Europe special facilities which we did not extend in like measure to all other ITO members and trade agreement partners.

A second possible solution would lie in arrangements whereby a union of Western European nations would undertake jointly the economic development and exploitation of the colonial and dependent areas of the African Continent. The realization of such a program admittedly presents demands which are probably well above the vision and strengths and leadership capacity of present governments in Western Europe. It would take considerable prodding from outside and much patience. But the idea itself has much to recommend it. The African Continent, is relatively little exposed to communist pressures; and most of it is not today a subject of great power rivalries. It lies easily accessible to the maritime nations of Western Europe, and politically they control or influence most of it. Its resources are still relatively undeveloped. It could absorb great numbers of people and a great deal of Europe's surplus technical and administrative energy. Finally, it would lend to the idea of Western European union that tangible objective for which everyone has been rather unsuccessfully groping in recent months.

However this may be, one thing is clear: if we wish to carry through with the main purpose of the ERP we must cordially and loyally support the British effort toward a Western European union. And this support should consist not only of occasional public expressions of approval. The matter should be carefully and sympathetically discussed with the British themselves and with the other governments of Western Europe. Much could be accomplished in such discussions, both from the standpoint of the clarification of our own policy and in the way of the exertion of a healthy and helpful influence on the Europeans themselves. In particular, we will have accomplished an immense amount if we can help to persuade the Western Europeans of the necessity of treating the Germans as citizens of Europe.

With this in mind, I think it might be well to ask each of our missions in Western Europe to make a special study of the problem of Western European union, both in general and with particular reference to the particular country concerned, and to take occasion, in the course of preparation of this study, to consult the views of the wisest and most experienced people they know in their respective capitals. These studies should be accompanied by their own recommendations as to how the basic problem could best be approached. A digest of such studies in this Department should yield a pretty sound cross-section of informed and balanced opinion on the problem in question.

.   .   .   .

III. Germany

The coming changes with respect to the responsibility for military government in Germany provide a suitable occasion for us to evolve new long-term concepts of our objectives with respect to that country. We cannot rely on the concepts of the existing policy directives. Not only were these designed to meet another situation, but it is questionable, in many instances, whether they were sound in themselves.

The planning to be done in this connection will necessarily have to be many-sided and voluminous. But it is possible to see today the main outlines of the problem we will face and, I think, of the solutions we must seek.

In the long run there can be only three possibilities for the future of western and central Europe. One is German domination. Another is Russian domination. The third is a federated Europe, into which the parts of Germany are absorbed but in which the influence of the other countries is sufficient to hold Germany in her place.

If there is no real European federation and if Germany is restored as a strong and independent country, we must expect another attempt at German domination. If there is no real European federation and if Germany is *not* restored as a strong and independent country, we invite Russian domination, for an unorganized Western Europe cannot indefinitely oppose an organized Eastern Europe. The only reasonably hopeful possibility for avoiding one of these two evils is some form of federation in western and central Europe.

Our dilemma today lies in the fact that whereas a European federation would be by all odds the best solution from the standpoint of U.S. interests, the Germans are poorly prepared for it. To achieve such a federation would be much easier if Germany were partitioned, or drastically decentralized, and if the component parts could be brought separately into the European union. To bring a unified Germany, or even a unified western Germany, into such a union would be much more difficult; for it would still over-weigh the other components, in many respects.

Now a partition of the Reich might have been possible if it had been carried out resolutely and promptly in the immediate aftermath of defeat. But that moment is now past, and we have today another situation to deal with. As things stand today, the Germans are psychologically not only unprepared for any breakup of the Reich but in a frame of mind which is distinctly unfavorable thereto.

In any planning we now do for the future of Germany we will have to take account of the unpleasant fact that our occupation up to this time has been unfortunate from the standpoint of the psychology of the German people. They are emerging from this phase of the post-hostilities period in a state of mind which can only be described as sullen, bitter, unregenerate, and pathologically attached to the old chimera of German unity. Our moral and political influence over them has not made headway since the surrender. They have been impressed neither by our precepts nor by our example. They are not going to look to us for leadership. Their political life is probably going to proceed along the lines of a polarization into extreme right and extreme left, both of which elements will be, from our standpoint, unfriendly, ugly to deal with, and contemptuous of the things we value.

We cannot rely on any such Germany to fit constructively into a pattern of European union of its own volition. Yet without the Germans, no real European federation is thinkable. And without federation, the other countries of Europe can have no protection against a new attempt at foreign domination.

If we did not have the Russians and the German communists prepared to take advantage politically of any movement on our part toward partition we could proceed to partition Germany regardless of the will of the inhabitants, and to force the respective segments to take their place in a federated Europe. But in the circumstances prevailing today, we cannot do this without throwing the German people politically into the arms of the communists. And if that happens, the fruits of our victory in Europe will have been substantially destroyed.

Our possibilities are therefore reduced, by the process of exclusion, to a policy which, without pressing the question of partition in Germany, would attempt to bring Germany, or western Germany, into a European federation, but do it in such a way as not to permit her to dominate that federation or jeopardize the security interests of the other western European countries. And this would have to be accomplished in the face of the fact that we cannot rely on the German people to exercise any self-restraint of their own volition, to feel any adequate sense of responsibility vis-à-vis the other western nations, or to concern themselves for the preservation of western values in their own country and elsewhere in Europe.

I have no confidence in any of the old-fashioned concepts of collective security as a means of meeting this problem. European history has shown only too clearly the weakness of multilateral defensive alliances between complete sovereign nations as a means of opposing desperate and determined bids for domination of the European scene. Some mutual defense arrangements will no doubt be necessary as a concession to the prejudices of the other Western European peoples, whose thinking is still old fashioned and unrealistic on this subject. But we can place no reliance on them as a deterrent to renewed troublemaking on the part of the Germans.

This being the case, it is evident that the relationship of Germany to the other countries of western Europe must be so arranged as to provide mechanical and automatic safeguards against any unscrupulous exploitation of Germany's preeminence in population and in military-industrial potential.

The first task of our planning will be to find such safeguards.

In this connection, primary consideration must be given to the problem of the Ruhr. Some form of international ownership or control of the Ruhr industries would indeed be one of the best means of automatic protection against the future misuse of Germany's industrial resources for aggressive purposes. There may be other devices which would also be worth exploring.

A second line of our planning will have to be in the direction of the maximum interweaving of German economy with that of the remainder of Europe. This may mean that we will have to reverse our present policies, in certain respects. One of the most grievous mistakes, in my opinion, of our post-hostilities policy was the renewed extreme segregation of the Germans and their compression into an even smaller territory than before, in virtual isolation from the remaining peoples of Europe. This sort of segregation and compression invariably arouses precisely the worst reaction in the German character. What the Germans need is not to be thrust violently in upon themselves, which only heightens their congenital irrealism and self-pity and defiant nationalism, but to be led out of their collective egocentrism and encouraged to see things in larger terms, to have interests elsewhere in Europe and elsewhere in the world, and to learn to think of themselves as world citizens and not just as Germans.

Next, we must recognize the bankruptcy of our moral influence on the Germans, and we must make plans for the earliest possible termination of those actions and policies on our part which have been psychologically unfortunate. First of all, we must reduce as far as possible our establishment in Germany; for the residence of large numbers of representatives of a victor nation in a devastated conquered area is never a helpful factor, particularly when their living habits and standards are as conspicuously different as are those of Americans in Germany. Secondly, we must terminate as rapidly as possible those forms of activity (denazification, re-education, and above all the Nuremberg Trials) which tend to set [us] up as mentors and judges over internal German problems. Thirdly, we must have the courage to dispense with military government as soon as possible and to force the Germans to accept responsibility once more for their own affairs. They will never begin to do this as long as we will accept that responsibility for them.

The military *occupation* of western Germany may have to go on for a long time. We may even have to be prepared to see it become a quasi-permanent feature of the European scene. But military *government* is a different thing. Until it is removed, we cannot really make progress in the direction of a more stable Europe.

Finally, we must do everything possible from now on to coordinate our policy toward Germany with the views of Germany's immediate western neighbors. This applies particularly to the Benelux countries, who could probably easily be induced to render valuable collaboration in the implementation of our own views. It is these neighboring countries who in the long run must live with any solutions we may evolve; and it is absolutely essential to any successful ordering of western Europe that they make their full contribution and bear their full measure of responsibility. It would be better for us in many instances to temper our own policies in order to win their support than to try to act unilaterally in defiance of their feelings.

With these tasks and problems before us it is important that we should do nothing in this intervening period which would prejudice our later policies. The appropriate offices of the Department of State should be instructed to bear this in mind in their own work. We should also see to it that it is borne in mind by our military authorities in the prosecution of their policies in Germany. These considerations should be observed in any discussions we hold with representatives of other governments. This applies particularly to the forthcoming discussions with the French and the British.

IV. Mediterranean

As the situation has developed in the past year, the Soviet chances for disrupting the unity of western Europe and forcing a political entry into that area have been *deteriorating* in *northern Europe,* where the greater political maturity of the peoples is gradually asserting itself, but *holding their own,* if not actually increasing, *in the south* along the shores of the Mediterranean. Here the Russians have as assets not only the violent chauvinsim of their Balkan satellites but also the desperate weakness and weariness of the Greek and Italian peoples. Conditions in Greece and Italy today are peculiarly favorable to the use of fear as a weapon for political action, and hence to the tactics which are basic and familiar to the communist movement.

It cannot be too often reiterated that this Government does not possess the weapons which would be needed to enable it to meet head-on the threat to national independence presented by the communist elements in foreign countries. This poses an extremely difficult problem as to the measures which our Government can take to prevent the communists from achieving success in the countries where resistance is lowest.

The Planning Staff has given more attention to this than to any single problem which has come under its examination. Its conclusions may be summed up as follows:

1. The use of U.S. regular armed force to oppose the efforts of indige-

nous communist elements within foreign countries must generally be considered as a risky and profitless undertaking, apt to do more harm than good.

2. If, however, it can be shown that the continuation of communist activities has a tendency to attract U.S. armed power to the vicinity of the affected areas, and if these areas are ones from which the Kremlin would definitely wish U.S. power excluded, there is a possibility that this may bring into play the defensive security interests of the Soviet Union and cause the Russians to exert a restraining influence on local communist forces.

The Staff has therefore felt that the wisest policy for us to follow would be to make it evident to the Russians by our actions that the further the communists go in Greece and Italy the more surely will this Government be forced to extend the deployment of its peacetime military establishment in the Mediterranean area.

There is no doubt in our minds but that if the Russians knew that the establishment of a communist government in Greece would mean the establishment of U.S. air bases in Libya and Crete, or that a communist uprising in northern Italy would lead to the renewed occupation by this country of the Foggia field, a conflict would be produced in the Kremlin councils between the interests of the Third Internationale, on the one hand, and those of the sheer military security of the Soviet Union, on the other. In conflicts of this sort, the interests of narrow Soviet nationalism usually win. If they were to win in this instance, a restraining hand would certainly be placed on the Greek and Italian communists.

This has already been, to some extent, the case. I think there is little doubt that the activity of our naval forces in the Mediterranean (including the stationing of further Marines with those forces), plus the talk of the possibility of our sending U.S. forces to Greece, has had something to do with the failure of the satellites, up to this time, to recognize the Markos Government, and possibly also with the Kremlin's reprimand to Dimitrov.[5] Similarly, I think the statement we made at the time of the final departure of our troops from Italy was probably the decisive factor in bringing about the abandonment of the plans which evidently existed for a communist uprising in Italy prior to the spring elections.

5. Markos Vafiades was President and Minister of War in the "First Provisional Democratic Government of Free Greece," the Soviet puppet government established there late in 1947. Georgi Dimitrov was Prime Minister of Bulgaria and Secretary-General of the Bulgarian Communist Party. [Ed. note]

For this reason, I think that our policy with respect to Greece and Italy, and the Mediterranean area in general, should be based upon the objective of demonstration to the Russians that:

a. the reduction of the communist threat will lead to our military withdrawal from the area; but that

b. further communist pressure will only have the effect of involving us more deeply in a military sense.

V. Palestine and the Middle East

The Staff views on Palestine have been made known in a separate paper.[6] I do not intend to recapitulate them here. But there are two background considerations of determining importance, both for the Palestine question and for our whole position in the Middle East, which I should like to emphasize at this time.

1. THE BRITISH STRATEGIC POSITION IN THE MIDDLE EAST

We have decided in this Government that the security of the Middle East is vital to our own security. We have also decided that it would not be desirable or advantageous for us to attempt to duplicate or to take over the strategic facilities now held by the British in that area. We have recognized that these facilities would be at our effective disposal anyway, in the event of war, and that to attempt to get them transferred, in the formal sense, from the British to ourselves would only raise a host of new and unnecessary problems, and would probably be generally unsuccessful.

This means that we must do what we can to support the maintenance of the British of their strategic position in that area. This does *not mean* that we must support them in every individual instance. It does *not mean* that we must back them up in cases where they have got themselves into a false position or where we would thereby be undertaking extravagant political commitments. It *does mean* that any policy on our part which tends to strain British relations with the Arab world and to whittle down the British position in the Arab countries is only a policy directed against ourselves and against the immediate strategic interests of our country.

6. The reference here is to PPS 19 of January 20, 1948, entitled "Position of the United States with Respect to Palestine" (not printed); and to PPS 21 of February 11, 1948, entitled "The Problem of Palestine" (not printed). [Ed. note]

2. THE DIRECTION OF OUR OWN POLICY

The pressures to which this Government is now subjected are ones which impel us toward a position where we would shoulder major responsibility for the maintenance, and even the expansion, of a Jewish state in Palestine. To the extent that we move in this direction, we will be operating directly counter to our major security interests in that area. For this reason, our policy in the Palestine issue should be dominated by the determination to avoid being impelled along this path.

We are now heavily and unfortunately involved in this Palestine question. We will apparently have to make certain further concessions to our past commitments and to domestic pressures.

These concessions will be dangerous ones; but they will not necessarily be catastrophic if we are thoroughly conscious of what we are doing, and if we lay our general course toward the avoidance of the possibility of the responsibility I have referred to. If we do not lay our course in that direction but drift along the lines of least resistance in the existing vortex of cross currents, our entire policy in the Middle Eastern area will unquestionably be carried in the direction of confusion, ineffectiveness, and grievous involvement in a situation to which there cannot be—from our standpoint—any happy ending.

I think it should be stated that if this Government is carried to a point in the Palestine controversy where it is required to send U.S. forces to Palestine in any manner whatsoever, or to agree either to the international recruitment of volunteers or the sending of small nation forces which would include those of Soviet satellites, then in my opinion, the whole structure of strategic and political planning which we have been building up for the Mediterranean and Middle Eastern areas would have to be re-examined and probably modified or replaced by something else. For this would then mean that we had consented to be guided, in a highly important question affecting those areas, not by national interest but by other considerations. If we tried, in the face of this fact, to continue with policy in adjacent areas motivated solely by national interest, we would be faced with a duality of purpose which would surely lead in the end to a dissipation and confusion of effort. We cannot operate with one objective in one area, and with a conflicting one next door.

If, therefore, we decide that we are obliged by past commitments or UN decision or any other consideration to take a leading part in the enforcement in Palestine of any arrangement opposed by the great majority of the inhabitants of the Middle Eastern area, we must be prepared to face the implications of this act by revising our general policy in that part of the world. And since the Middle East is vital to the present security concepts on which this Government is basing itself in its worldwide military and political planning, this would further mean a review of our entire military and political policy.

.   .   .   .

12   **T O P S E C R E T**

National Security Council Directive on Office of Special Projects

NSC 10/2   June 18, 1948

[Source: Records of the National Security Council held at the Secretariat, Executive Office Building, Washington, D.C.]

An additional dimension of U.S. containment policy involved the development of covert-action capabilities. In NSC 4/A of December 14, 1947 (not printed), the National Security Council authorized the newly organized Central Intelligence Agency to conduct clandestine psychological operations—primarily activities involving the use of unattributed, forged, and/or subsidized publications.[7] But in May 1948, in the wake of the Czech coup and the growing Berlin crisis, Kennan recommended broadening this authority to include covert political action as well. The National Security Council approved Kennan's suggestion, and in NSC 10/2 established the Office of Special Projects (soon to be renamed the Office of Policy Coordination) within the CIA. The document also defined the term "covert operations" to include a wide variety of activities ranging from propaganda and economic pressure to sabotage, subversion, and unconventional warfare.

NSC 10/2 emphasized the need to conduct covert operations in a manner consistent with the political and military objectives of the United States, and therefore specified close consultation between the Chief of the Office of Special Projects, the Director of Central Intelligence, the Departments of State and Defense, and the National Security Council. In furtherance of this injunction to cooperation, the directive made the Secretary of State, and not the Director of the CIA, responsible for nominating the Chief of the Office of Special Projects. "It did not work out at all the way I had conceived it," Kennan admitted in 1975. "We had thought that this would be a facility which could be used when and if an occasion arose when it might be needed. There might be years when we wouldn't have to do anything like this. But if the occasion arose we wanted somebody in the Government who would have the funds, the experience, the expertise to do these things and to do them in a proper way."[8]

7. Anne Karalekas, "History of the Central Intelligence Agency," in U.S. Congress, Senate (94th Cong., 2nd sess.), Select Committee to Study Government Operations with respect to Intelligence Activities, *Final Report: Supplementary Detailed Staff Reports on Foreign and Military Intelligence: Book IV* (Washington: 1976), p. 26n.
8. Quoted *ibid.*, p. 31.

1. The National Security Council, taking cognizance of the vicious covert activities of the USSR, its satellite countries and Communist groups to discredit and defeat the aims and activities of the United States and other Western powers, has determined that, in the interests of world peace and US national security, the overt foreign activities of the US Government must be supplemented by covert operations.

2. The Central Intelligence Agency is charged by the National Security Council with conducting espionage and counter-espionage operations abroad. It therefore seems desirable, for operational reasons, not to create a new agency for covert operations, but in time of peace to place the responsibility for them within the structure of the Central Intelligence Agency and correlate them with espionage and counter-espionage operations under the over-all control of the Director of Central Intelligence.

3. Therefore, under the authority of Section 102(d)(5) of the National Security Act of 1947,[9] the National Security Council hereby directs that in time of peace:

    a. A new office of Special Projects shall be created within the Central Intelligence Agency to plan and conduct covert operations; and in coordination with the Joint Chiefs of Staff to plan and prepare for the conduct of such operations in wartime.

    b. A highly qualified person, nominated by the Secretary of State, acceptable to the Director of Central Intelligence and approved by the National Security Council, shall be appointed as Chief of the Office of Special Projects.

    c. The Chief of the Office of Special Projects shall report directly to the Director of Central Intelligence. For purposes of security and of flexibility of operations, and to the maximum degree consistent with efficiency, the Office of Special Projects shall operate independently of other components of Central Intelligence Agency.

    d. The Director of Central Intelligence shall be responsible for:

        (1) Ensuring, through designated representatives of the Secretary of State and of the Secretary of Defense, that covert operations are planned and conducted in a manner consistent with US foreign and military policies and with overt activities. In disagreements arising between the Director of Central Intelligence

9. Public Law 253 of July 26, 1947. Section 102 (d)(5) provides that the Central Intelligence Agency, under the direction of the National Security Council, shall "perform such other functions and duties related to intelligence affecting the national security as the National Security Council may from time to time direct." [Ed. note]

and the representative of the Secretary of State or the Secretary of Defense over such plans, the matter shall be referred to the National Security Council for decision.

(2) Ensuring that plans for wartime covert operations are also drawn up with the assistance of a representative of the Joint Chiefs of Staff and are accepted by the latter as being consistent with and complementary to approved plans for wartime military operations.

(3) Informing, through appropriate channels, agencies of the US Government, both at home and abroad (including diplomatic and military representatives in each area), of such operations as will affect them.

e. Covert operations pertaining to economic warfare will be conducted by the Office of Special Projects under the guidance of the departments and agencies responsible for the planning of economic warfare.

f. Supplemental funds for the conduct of the proposed operations for fiscal year 1949 shall be immediately requested. Thereafter operational funds for these purposes shall be included in normal Central Intelligence Agency Budget requests.

4. In time of war, or when the President directs, all plans for covert operations shall be coordinated with the Joint Chiefs of Staff. In active theaters of war where American forces are engaged, covert operations will be conducted under the direct command of the American Theater Commander and orders therefor will be transmitted through the Joint Chiefs of Staff unless otherwise directed by the President.

5. As used in this directive, "covert operations" are understood to be all activities (except as noted herein) which are conducted or sponsored by this government against hostile foreign states or groups or in support of friendly foreign states or groups but which are so planned and conducted that any US Government responsibility for them is not evident to unauthorized persons and that if uncovered the US Government can plausibly disclaim any responsibility for them. Specifically, such operations shall include any covert activities related to: propaganda; economic warfare; preventive direct action, including sabotage, anti-sabotage, demolition, and evacuation measures; subversion against hostile states, including assistance to underground resistance movements, guerrillas and refugee liberations groups, and support of indigenous anti-communist elements in threatened countries of the free world. Such operations shall not include armed conflict by recognized military

forces, espionage, counter-espionage, and cover and deception for military operations.

6. This Directive supersedes the directive contained in NSC 4-A, which is hereby cancelled.

◇◇◇

13   **T O P   S E C R E T**

The Position of the United States with Respect to Providing Military Assistance to Nations of the Non-Soviet World

NSC 14/1   July 1, 1948

[Source: *Foreign Relations of the United States: 1948,* I (part 2), 585–88]

In addition to stimulating the authorization of covert-action capabilities, the Czech coup and the Berlin blockade raised the question of whether self-confident, economically viable societies could develop in Europe in the face of the apparently overwhelming Soviet military presence. The original concept of containment had relied primarily on economic assistance to accomplish its objectives, but by the summer of 1948 it appeared as though military aid would also be necessary. At that time the United States was already providing military assistance on a country-by-country basis to the Philippines, China, Greece, Turkey, and certain Latin American countries. In NSC 14 series papers, the National Security Council attempted to evolve a more general approach to this problem in a manner consistent with the priorities established a year earlier in JCS 1769/1 (Document 5). In doing so, the Council anticipated many of the issues that would arise in implementing the Military Assistance Act of 1949.

Reprinted here are excerpts from a revised version of NSC 14 adopted by the National Security Council on July 1, 1948, with conclusions approved by President Truman on July 10, 1948.

The Problem

1. To assess and appraise the position of the United States with respect to providing military assistance in the form of supplies, equipment and technical advice to nations of the non-Soviet world.

Analysis

2. The success of certain free nations in resisting aggression by the forces of Soviet directed world communism is of critical importance to the security of the United States. Some of these nations require not only economic assistance but also strengthened military capabilities if they are to continue and make more effective their political resistance to communist subversion from

within and Soviet pressure from without and if they are to develop ultimately an increased military capability to withstand external armed attack. Although they possess considerable military potential in manpower and resources, these nations are industrially incapable of producing intricate modern armaments and equipment in the necessary quantities. Consequently if they are to develop stronger military capabilities it is essential that their own efforts be effectively coordinated and be supplemented by assistance in the form of military supplies, equipment and technical advice from the United States.

3. Such military assistance from the United States would not only strengthen the moral and material resistance of the free nations, but would also support their political and military orientation toward the United States, augment our own military potential by improvement of our armaments industries, and through progress in standardization of equipment and training increase the effectiveness of military collaboration between the United States and its allies in the event of war.

. . . .

Conclusions

8. Certain free nations the security of which is of critical importance to the United States require strengthened military capabilities, if they are to present effective political resistance to communist aggression now, and military resistance later if necessary.

9. Therefore, the United States should assist in strengthening the military capabilities of these nations to resist communist expansion provided they make determined efforts to resist communist expansion and such assistance contributes effectively to that end. . . .

. . . .

11. Any US military-assistance program should be predicated to the maximum practicable extent upon the self-help and mutual assistance of recipient states.

12. The military assistance program should be governed by the following considerations:

    a. The program should not jeopardize the fulfillment of the minimum materiel requirements of the United States armed forces, as determined by the Joint Chiefs of Staff.

    b. The program should not be inconsistent with strategic concepts approved by the Joint Chiefs of Staff.

   c. Certain factors, such as the need for strengthening the morale and internal security of recipient nations and protecting various US interests abroad, may in exceptional cases become over-riding political considerations modifying the strict application of paragraphs a and b above.

   d. Continuing support for the program should be planned to include supply of needed replacements, spare parts and ammunition so long as our security interests dictate.

   e. The program should be properly integrated with the ECA [10] program, and should not be permitted to jeopardize the economic stability of the United States or other participating nations. The program should be subject to review and recommendation by the National Security Resources Board in order to insure a sound balancing of requirements under the military aid program with US domestic requirements.

   f. The program should adequately safeguard US classified material.

13. In measures of military assistance additional to those already provided for in specific legislation or in existing governmental undertakings, first priority should be given to Western Europe.

14. Countries participating in military assistance programs should be encouraged so far as consistent with the progressive stabilization of their economies:

   a. To cooperate in integrating their armaments industries with a view ultimately to maintaining and re-supplying their own equipment when economic conditions permit.

   b. To standardize their weapons and materiel to the maximum practical extent and, so far as practicable in the future, to US accepted types.

   c. To provide strategic raw materials to the United States in return for military assistance.

   d. To compensate the supplying nation for the military assistance which they receive whenever and to what extent feasible.

15. The military assistance program, in conjunction with the materiel needs of the US armed forces, will require the partial rehabilitation of the US armaments industry.

---

10. Economic Cooperation Administration, the agency of the American government that supervised Marshall Plan aid to Europe. It was succeeded at the end of 1951 by tne Mutual Security Administration. [Ed. note]

◇◇

14   **S E C R E T**

Department of State Policy Statement: Germany

August 26, 1948

[Source: *Foreign Relations of the United States: 1948,* II, 1315–19]

Discussions anticipating American military association with Western Europe naturally raised questions regarding the future of Germany. Frustrated by the Russians' refusal to accept Western suggestions for a political settlement in that divided country, representatives of the United States, the United Kingdom, and France met in London from February 23 to March 6 and from April 20 to June 1, 1948, to decide upon a course of action to be followed in their respective zones of occupation. Their decision—to authorize the convening of constituent assemblies looking toward formation of a West German federal republic—was announced on June 7.[11]

The rationale behind this decision to accept the *de facto* partition of Germany is set forth in the following policy statement prepared for internal use within the Department of State early in the summer of 1948, but dated August 26 of that year.

．   ．   ．   ．   ．   ．   ．

The US has endeavored since 1946 to inaugurate procedures leading to negotiation of a general peace settlement for Germany. Proposals which had, in all essentials, been agreed upon by the three western powers were rejected in both the 1947 Moscow and London meetings of the CFM by the USSR. The main issue between the USSR and the western powers, particularly the US, was the role to be assigned the other Allied governments in the preparation of a German peace treaty. The US held that all of the Allied countries, large and small, were entitled to participate at appropriate stages in the preparation of the treaty, a view in which the other western powers concurred. The USSR wished to confine the drafting and final formulation of the treaty to the four CFM powers concerned, while closely restricting the rights of consultation and participation to a limited number of the other Allied governments. Prolonged attempts to arrive at an agreed procedure, both at Moscow and London, met with failure.

Another major difficulty was the definitive settlement of German frontiers. The US has always held and still maintains that decisions on frontiers must await the peace settlement. It has proposed the creation of international boundary commissions to examine all boundary claims and problems and make recommendations to the CFM. The USSR has repeatedly insisted that

11. See *Foreign Relations of the United States: 1948,* II, 313–17.

the present administrative boundary between Germany and Poland, as fixed at Potsdam, must be considered as final and is not open to review. The US, while recognizing Poland's right to territorial compensation from Germany, stands upon the Potsdam provision that "the final delimitation of the western frontier of Poland should await the peace settlement." It is concerned that the frontiers of Germany should not become "impenetrable barriers" to trade, nor dangerously exacerbate irredentist sentiment. In particular the US believes that a revision of the present Oder-Neisse line to Germany's advantage is essential in view of the present economic-demographic situation of Germany. We have agreed to support the claim of the USSR to northern East Prussia in the peace settlement. In the west the US believes that, with the exception of the Saar, only minor border rectifications to eliminate existing anomalies with respect to trade or communications should be considered; it is opposed to territorial cessions as compensation for war damage or loss. The US has approved the detachment of the Saar district from Germany and its economic integration with France.

There is little likelihood of a definitive German settlement in the immediate future. The London Agreements, if and when implemented, might be considered in the nature of a provisional settlement governing western Germany. The US maintains that responsibility for failure to reach a final German settlement must rest at the door of the USSR, which has consistently obstructed agreement by insisting upon conditions unacceptable to the three western powers. These powers are proceeding with measures which they consider indispensable for the areas of Germany under their control. The US holds that all such measures are of a tentative and provisional character pending the time when a general settlement can be agreed upon by all the powers which at present exercise sovereign rights over Germany.

After three years of occupation the chief premise upon which US policy with respect to Germany was originally based has broken down. This was the assumption that German problems, both immediate and long-term, were susceptible to solution on the basis of four power agreement. It has become clear that such agreement is unlikely in the early or foresee[a]ble future in view of the obstructive and intransigent attitude of the USSR with regard to German and European problems. The US has been confronted with two alternatives. It could accept stalemate without action and thus permit Germany to sink deeper into political and economic chaos, with the attendant threat to the general welfare and security, or it could concert a provisional settlement of German problems together with those governments which were willing to reach agreement in the common interest. The US has chosen this second alternative.

US policy must be judged in the light of present realities. No ideal solution embracing the whole of Germany is at present possible. German policy is of necessity influenced by over-riding policy with respect to western Europe. Such policy dictates that Germany must not be drawn into the Soviet orbit or reconstructed as a political instrument of Soviet policy. It requires that Germany be brought into close association with the democratic states of western Europe and that it be enabled to contribute to and participate in European economic recovery. These objectives clearly cannot be achieved through quadripartite action. Hence it has become necessary to embark on an extensive program of reconstruction in association with the UK, France and the Benelux countries which have a special and immediate concern with western Germany. The London agreements mark the first broad, constructive step toward a resolution of the German problem since Potsdam. They are of necessity provisional and in no way preclude ultimate Allied agreement on a final settlement. But it is believed that the London program, when effectuated, will mean substantial progress toward such a settlement.

Despite all efforts since the end of the war Germany remains a major unresolved problem of US foreign policy. Such objectives as demilitarization, denazification and punishment of war criminals have been in the main achieved. But in matters of basic reconstruction there have been only beginnings, or tentative and provisional measures. Germany still lacks political or economic unity, or any vestige of a national government. The German economy operates at a dangerously low level and the bizonal area survives only through subsidies furnished mainly by the US. Democratization of political and cultural life has proceeded at a painfully slow pace. The determination of frontiers and of long-range controls upon German economic and political life still awaits a peace treaty. The re-integration of the German economy into that of Europe will only be achieved with the working out of the European Recovery Program. The end of the occupation is not in sight, and Germany will continue as a major concern and responsibility of the US for a period as yet unforeseen.

·   ·   ·   ·   ·   ·   ·

Failure to achieve a definitive solution of the German problem which is central to a general European settlement has given rise to a critical situation. Germany has become an area of strategic importance in the East-West conflict over the shaping of Europe's future. The significance of current developments rests primarily in the fact that the US, with its associates, has seized the initiative in Germany. This has resulted in vigorous Soviet counter-measures. The rights and prerogatives of the western powers in

Berlin are being challenged and every effort is being made to make their position there untenable. The evolution of the London program for western Germany can be expected to meet with Soviet protest and opposition at every stage. The success of the program will depend upon other uncertain factors—the rapidity of economic recovery, the cooperativeness of the Germans and the support of the French who have not been won over to whole-hearted approval of the agreements and may seek to modify them in further negotiation. There is a definite risk that implementation of the program will widen and confirm the cleavage between the western powers and the USSR and effect a virtual partition of Germany for the time being. The decision of the US to embark upon a program entailing these risks and uncertainties has been reached with full realization of the difficulties involved but with the conviction that even greater risks and dangers would result from failure to act promptly and effectively in dealing with urgent German problems.

Future developments in Germany cannot be predicted with any degree of assurance. There will doubtless be continued tension in US-USSR relations which would reach a critical stage if the USSR should resort to coercive measures to expel the western powers from Berlin. The US is now completely committed to a far-reaching program of political and economic reconstruction for western Germany, with the door always open to Soviet collaboration in such a program if extended to all Germany. The next few years will be of critical importance in the working out of the London agreements and the ERP in Germany, with Soviet antagonism a constant factor, even if a major crisis is avoided. Unless there develops a totally unanticipated change in the Soviet attitude toward the west, and unless Soviet designs in Germany are drastically modified, there seems to be little prospect of a general German settlement in the near future. Germany will probably remain divided. The Soviet zone and the west will then continue to develop, economically and constitutionally, in divergent directions, although the forces of economic interdependence and German national sentiment will operate in some measure to counteract disunion. Germany will remain an important, perhaps the most important area of conflict in the struggle between east and west for the shaping of the new Europe.

15   **S E C R E T**

Policy Questions Concerning a Possible German Settlement

PPS 37   August 12, 1948

[Source: *Foreign Relations of the United States: 1948*, II, 1288–96]

Discussions on the future of Germany for the first time brought the Policy Planning Staff into disagreement with the rest of the Department of State on a substantive issue. In PPS 23 of February 24, 1948 (see Document 11) Kennan had advocated the integration of Germany into a European federation. But by August, he had come to view prospects for such a development as dim. Kennan's alternative, proposed in PPS 37, was to seek a German settlement on the basis of a withdrawal of all occupation forces and the emergence of a unified Germany as a strong, independent state.

Reaction to Kennan's proposal within the State Department was not favorable. John D. Hickerson, Director of the Office of European Affairs, wrote Kennan that "it would be highly dangerous to agree to unite Germany along the lines you propose until Western Europe is stronger, both economically and militarily." Jacques J. Reinstein, Special Assistant Secretary of State for Economic Affairs, argued that "unless an agreement regarding Germany is thought likely to alter fundamentally the objectives of Soviet foreign policy, it would be wiser to develop Western Germany politically and economically as part of a Western European system under the supervision and protection of the Western Allies . . . than at this time to cast Germany loose in the hope that things will work out for the best." [12] The Policy Planning Staff did work out a much more elaborate version of Kennan's plan, [13] but the alternative of seeking an independent, unified Germany was ultimately rejected in favor of creating a separate West German state, closely tied to the West.

The debate over PPS 37 reflected what was to become a fundamental dilemma for American policy makers: should the objective of containment be the re-creation of Europe as an independent center of power, free from both Russian and American control, or the division of Europe into Soviet and American spheres of influence?

.   .   .   .   .   .

If the present talks [14] were to lead to a four-power meeting, it appears to us that we would not be able to plan adequately for such a meeting until we had made a broad political decision on the following question:

Is it in our national interest to press *at this time* for a sweeping settlement

12. *Foreign Relations of the United States: 1948*, II, 1287–88, 1320–38. See also Kennan, *Memoirs: 1925–1950* (Boston: Little, Brown, 1967), pp. 418–29, 442–48.

13. PPS 37/1, "Position to be Taken by the United States at a CFM Meeting," November 15, 1948, printed in *Foreign Relations of the United States: 1948*, II, 1320–38.

14. Discussions among the four powers occupying Germany, held in Moscow in August 1948. [Ed. note]

of the German problem which would involve the withdrawal of Allied forces from at least the major portion of Germany, the termination of military government and the establishment of a German Government with real power and independence? Or should we, and could we, be content to carry on for the time being, as we have been doing, with a divided Germany, holding the line with our own forces and our own prestige while we endeavor to strengthen western Europe?

Before discussing the merits of this question, I would like to make certain comments about it.

First, it is basically a question of timing. Some day our forces must leave central Europe. Some day Soviet forces must leave. Some day Germany must again become a sovereign and independent entity. The question is "when"? Is this the best time for these things to happen? Or can we hope that there will be a future time which will be more favorable?

Secondly, it seems to us, on the basis of our preliminary study, that there is no acceptable middle ground between these two solutions. We doubt the possibility of unifying Germany under four-power control. We feel that Germany can be unified only by the departure of the major Allies from the German scene and not by further efforts on their part to collaborate in the military government of Germany; that there will be no unification as long as the zonal boundaries remain; and that the zonal boundaries will remain, in one form or another, as long as Russian forces remain. Therefore, if Allied forces remain at all in the heart of Germany, there will be zones and there will be a divided Germany. In these circumstances, we shall have no choice but to proceed with the vigorous implementation of the London Conference program, the Russians will set up a rival Government in their zone; and the fight will be on for fair.

· · · · · · ·

I would also like, before going into the argumentation pro and con, to spell out in a little greater detail what we have in mind by the first of these alternatives. It differs in certain important respects from the position with which we have approached previous CFM conferences. The main points of difference are these:

a. We are no longer thinking in terms of the establishment of German unity by quadripartite agreement, to be administered under quadripartite control, as a prerequisite for the later establishment of a provisional German Government and for a gradual reduction of the powers of military government. We have in mind, for reasons indicated above, the early abandonment of military government, establishment of a German government with real powers, and withdrawal of the occupying forces entirely from the major portion of Germany. Allied forces, under this concept, might still be kept on the periphery of Germany, as for example in the Rhineland and in Silesia, but only on a garrison status, without civil affairs responsibility. Their function would be to serve as a sanction for the observance by a German Government of the necessary demilitarization controls. Some form of quadripartite controls of this nature would of course be provided for.

b. We think it would be well if we could get away from the idea that there must be a peace treaty. We see no theoretical justification for any "treaty of peace" between the Allies and the Germans, and feel that it complicates unnecessarily the real issues of the German settlement. The four Allies are the custodians of German sovereignty, as a result of the conquest and subjugation of Germany. They can turn over, whenever they want and to whom they want, the total of, or any part of, that sovereignty. There is no need for any compact with the Germans. . . .

.　　.　　.　　.　　.　　.　　.

Now for the relative advantages and disadvantages of a broad settlement such as that outlined above.

The advantages are the following:

1. *It would avoid congealment of Europe along the present lines.*

We can no longer retain the present line of division in Europe and yet hope to keep things flexible for an eventual retraction of Soviet power and for the gradual emergence from Soviet control, and entrance into a free European community, of the present satellite countries. The recent London Conference and Western Union[15] developments have demonstrated that if Europe continues divided, both we and the Russians will have to take measures which will tend to fix and perpetuate, rather than to overcome, that division. We have been able to avoid this congealment thus far only because the reconstruction of Europe had not progressed far enough to give this effect to the measures taken on both sides. Today, we have come to a point where our measures are bound to have more lasting effect. If we carry on

15. A fifty-year alliance established by Great Britain, France, Belgium, the Netherlands, and Luxemburg at Brussels on March 17, 1948, providing for joint action in case of armed attack and for economic cooperation. [Ed. note]

along present lines, Germany must divide into eastern and western governments and western Europe must move toward a tight military alliance with this country which can only complicate the eventual integration of the satellites into a European community. From such a trend of developments, it would be hard—harder than it is now—to find "the road back" to a united and free Europe.

2. It would solve the Berlin situation without detriment to ourselves or to the Berlin population.

We could then withdraw from Berlin without loss of prestige, and the people of the western sectors would not be subjected to Soviet rule, because the Russians would also be leaving the city.

3. It would permit us to take advantage of a peculiarly favorable political situation in Germany.

All reports indicate that the Berlin conflict has radically improved political sentiment throughout Germany, from the western standpoint. This is particularly true among the people of Berlin itself, whose feelings would have special importance if a German Government were to be set up in that city. It is the initial period which will probably be decisive in future German political development. Communist chances for success depend largely on their ability to seize power at the start. The present would therefore be a favorable moment to effect the transition from military government to German political responsibility. There may not be another such moment.

4. It would bring about a certain withdrawal of Soviet forces toward the east.

Getting the Soviet forces out of the major portion of the present Soviet zone should go some distance toward assuaging the fears of the members of the Brussels Union, providing U.S. forces remain somewhere in or near Germany. It might actually be possible to arrange for the stationing of U.S. and Soviet garrison forces at points where they could be supplied by sea, thus obviating the necessity for supply lines through Poland. But even though this were not possible, the Russians would still, under the arrangement contemplated, not be able to deploy their forces in strength or hold large scale maneuvers outside their own frontiers except on the territory of their ally, Poland, which would be less satisfactory to them and less menacing to the western European countries than the present situation.

5. *It would greatly reduce the size and cost of our military establishment in Germany,* [16] *and the scope of its responsibilities.*

To these advantages, of a positive nature, should be added the following disadvantages of the alternative course: namely, of carrying on with a divided Europe. If we carry on as we have been doing:

1. *The Berlin situation would still be with us, in one form or another.*

We may get an agreement at this time which would bring about a removal of the restrictions on our access to Berlin in the prospect of four-power negotiations; but if the negotiations are not successful and if we revert to the London program, it must be regarded as almost certain that the Russians will continue to do everything in their power to make it difficult for us in Berlin. In other words, there is no satisfactory solution of the Berlin situation under the divided set-up.

2. *It would mean the establishment of a rival German government in the Soviet zone, with corresponding complications for the political progress of our western zones.*

3. *We would face a growing problem in our relations with the western zone Germans.*

Available information indicates that there is developing among the Germans a strong current of political restiveness and a determination to regain responsibility for the conduct of their own affairs. . . .

4. *The ERP action for Germany must lead to unsatisfactory results.*

Without the loosening up of the situation in Europe and without a considerable development of east-west trade, there is no prospect of German viability. ERP will certainly not eliminate the dependence upon ourselves of the western zones of a divided Germany. If we are not to be faced with an ugly problem upon the termination of the ERP program we must find some way to broaden the background of German recovery and to relieve ourselves of the excessive responsibility we now bear for German economy. . . . In carrying on with an effort to bring recovery to the western portions alone of a divided Germany, we are really working for the unattainable. It has been politically worthwhile to do this, up to the present; but we must remember that at sometime we have got to get ourselves out of this box.

16. Including its present military government appendages. [Note in source text]

5. *Continuance of the present situation raises questions with regard to future appropriations.*

At the present time, the most vital elements of our German policy are absolutely dependent on the willingness of Congress to make recurring appropriations for the occupation and military government of Germany. This involves an element of uncertainty which is bound to increase with time. Somewhere there must be a time-limit to Congress's willingness to support this operation. A sudden shift of congressional sentiment could now place us in an extremely embarrassing position, which would be detrimental to our whole situation in Europe. Any step which would reduce this financial burden would therefore have a positive value.

So much for the disadvantages of carrying on with present arrangements and for the advantages of seeking a broad settlement over Germany.

How about the other side of the picture? What are the disadvantages of trying to get a general German settlement at this time and the advantages of carrying on with a policy based on the development of western Germany and western Europe?

First: the disadvantages of a general German settlement at this time, along the lines discussed above:

1. *To turn political responsibility over to a German Government at this time would be to assume a new and great risk.*

The Germans, from all accounts, are confused, embittered, self-pitying and unregenerate. Western concepts of democracy have only a slender foundation among them. There is a very good prospect that they will move toward a strongly nationalistic and authoritarian form of government. We cannot be sure that a new German regime would not enter into political deals with Moscow at the expense of the west, or that it will not be captured by the German communists.

2. *To set up a German Government at this time would complicate the ERP program.*

It would be much simpler, for the short term, if the ERP relationship could be restricted to the western zones, as already established. The addition of the Soviet Zone to the present ERP area would only create a need for increased appropriations and complicate the whole political-administrative framework of the recovery program.

3. To set up a German Government at this time would complicate the Western Union discussions.

As long as western Germany is occupied by western forces, the role of Germany in the concept of "western union" can be conveniently ignored. If a united Germany were again to become a political entity, the relationship of that entity to the other western European countries would have to be clarified. For this the French are poorly prepared. They would scarcely welcome German participation. Yet a repudiation of the Germans by the west might automatically impel them into the Soviet camp.

4. This sort of a settlement would mean the reestablishment of Germany as the only great state in central Europe.

In other words, in the absence of some real union of the European nations, this would reestablish, in essence, the status quo of 1920, and invite the same ensuing disasters. The mere proposal of it would be bound to alarm and dismay the French. It would create the framework from which Germany could some day renew the attempt to dominate the continent. In this sense, it would raise the question as to what we had gained, in the long term, by our recent war effort.

5. Since half-way measures will be difficult here, it means turning over to the Germans more power than most of us have really contemplated at this time.

A gradual transfer of power would be difficult even if we were doing this all ourselves and did not have Russians to bother about. Given the impossibility of real four-power collaboration in these matters, it becomes almost impossible. We will thus find ourselves compelled to turn over to the Germans powers on a scale for which neither we nor the western Europeans are psychologically prepared.

To these considerations should be added the positive advantages of carrying on as we are. They are the following:

1. We have the London program ready for implementation.

A lot of careful effort and considerable anguish has gone into the preparation and adoption of this program. It would be easier not to have to abandon it. The same applies to all the other inter-zonal arrangements we have made with the British and French.

2. *We would be able to carry on normally with the ERP and Western Union programs.*

3. *The western Europeans, particularly the French, would continue to have the reassurance of knowing that our forces were stationed in the heart of Europe.*

4. *There could be no question of the extension of Russian police power into the heart of Germany.*

It is quite apparent from the above that we are faced here with a painfully difficult decision, with respect to which the pertinent considerations are so closely balanced as to present a real dilemma. To this dilemma there can be no wholly satisfactory solution. What I am about to say I therefore say with great reservation and with the realization that there is a great deal to be said against it.

It is my own view that, balancing all the considerations set forth above, it would be better for us to seek and accept at this time, if we can get it, the broad general settlement of the German question described above. Of course, if we cannot get it, we should proceed vigorously with the London program.

The reasons by which I arrive at this view are reflected, for the most part, in the above discussion. But I wish to mention specifically those considerations which seem to me to be the prevailing ones.

The solution I favor is unquestionably, for the immediate future, the harder of the two. So often, the course of action and change is harder than the course of inaction. But I doubt that there is any easy way out of our involvement in Germany, now or at any time. And I doubt that there will be a future time when this disengagement will be any easier for us than it is today. This is a case where we must try hard not to think statically, in terms of the situation we now have before us, but dynamically, in terms of the trends of development in Germany and elsewhere which will determine the background of our action in future. It is my feeling that if the division of Europe cannot be overcome peacefully at this juncture, when the lines of cleavage have not yet hardened completely across the continent, when the Soviet Union (as I believe) is not yet ready for another war, when the anticommunist sentiment in Germany is momentarily stronger than usual, and when the Soviet satellite area is troubled with serious dissension, uncertainty and disaffection, then it is not likely that prospects for a peaceful resolution of Europe's problems will be better after a further period of waiting. Even if we can wait (which is possible), even if the other Europeans can wait (which is more doubtful), I do not think that the Germans can. I believe that something is happening, and cannot help but happen, in the political evolution of the Germans which we will either have to recognize and give scope to or make it our business to suppress. And I would not like to see us do the latter.

The strongest arguments against the course which I favor are those which relate to the danger of the reestablishment of a unified Germany and the risk which surrounds the behavior of such a Germany in the future as a powerful member of the European community. These are serious arguments, the force of which cannot be denied. I myself have never felt that the reestablishment of Germany in this way was the desirable answer to the German problem.

But beggars can't be choosers. The fact of the matter is that there is no solution of this German problem except in terms of a federated Europe into which the several parts of Germany could be absorbed. Without such a Europe, the partition of Germany would be a futile attempt at retrogression. Such a Europe can be created only by the Europeans, not by us. But they have not yet created it; and it looks as though it would be a long time before they did.

Plainly, no such constructive solution of the German problem will, or could, be found in the face of the tragic east–west differences which now divide Europe. This is the real reason why Germany must be given back to the Germans. The inability of the recent Allies to agree on the treatment or the future of Germany obliges them, by a sort of iron logic, to restore the power of decision to the Germans themselves. For the development of life in Europe cannot await the composure of east–west differences. Something must be done; and something will be done, whether we like it or not.

Frustrated as we are in our efforts to agree with Moscow about the future of Germany,—faced with the weariness and timidity and lack of leadership among the western European allies which prevents them from making real progress towards a federation of at least the western European peoples,—saddled ourselves with responsibility for the early restoration of hope and progress among the western Germans,—I do not see that we have any choice but to strive for a general relinquishment of Allied responsibilities in Germany and for the assumption of the risk of granting to the Germans the ability to manage their own affairs. If we cannot get agreement to this, we shall at least have made the gesture, which is important.

In considering such a course, we can of course envisage continued allied controls designed to enforce complete demilitarization. These should serve

in some measure to obviate, or at least to postpone, the danger of a resurgence of German aggression. Beyond that, there is a good chance that the
two great military defeats of the last World Wars will have left their mark on
the Germans, and that the peak of the German will and ability to subjugate
Europe may prove to have passed with the Hitler era. In any case, such automatic controls as we devise could be reinforced by a really vigorous and
serious effort on our part to understand the background of German political
thought and to influence it in directions compatible with our interests. It is
my impression that this is something we have not yet seriously attempted to
do.

The above is my personal view in the light of such information as the
Staff now has before it. I would certainly not recommend that any decision
be taken on so momentous a question before a considerably broader foundation of advice has been obtained. If the present Moscow talks lead to an
agreement envisaging four-power negotiations, then measures should be
taken at once to bring to bear on this subject the best opinion of our appropriate representatives in Europe. And the matter should certainly be
thoroughly explored with Republican leaders; for whoever wins the elec-
tion is going to have to live with the results of whatever decision we take today.

<>~<>~<>~<>~<>~<>~<>~<>~<>~<>~<>~<>~<>~<>~<>~<>~<>~<>~<>~<>~<>~<>~

16   **T O P   S E C R E T**

Washington Exploratory Conversations on Security

September 9, 1948

[Source: *Foreign Relations of the United States: 1948*, III, 237–45]

Representatives of Belgium, Luxembourg, France, the Netherlands, the United
Kingdom, Canada, and the United States conducted a series of discussions from July
6, 1948, to September 9, 1948, concerning common defense issues. Known as the
Washington Security Talks, the meetings led quickly to mature plans for a North
Atlantic mutual defense association. By September 9, 1948, the date of the fifteenth
meeting, the representatives had developed a comprehensive rationale for a proposed
association, and in a memorandum subsequently referred to as "the Washington
paper," they forwarded the rationale to their respective governments for study and
comment. The document explicitly recognized the tie between the security of Eu-
ope and that of North America, denigrated the possibility of "peaceful coexistence"
with Soviet communism, and surveyed the practical problems of defining a North
Atlantic security area. In an annex to the memorandum, not printed here, the rep-

resentatives appended specific suggestions for provisions of a treaty, suggestions that paralleled very closely the eventual articles of the North Atlantic Treaty of April 4, 1949.

.   .   .   .

Developments in the international situation since the end of hostilities make clear the urgent need for further measures which will contribute effectively to peace and security.

The establishment of the O.E.E.C. and the signature of the Brussels Treaty [17] are important achievements which indicate the intent of the peace-loving countries of Europe to work together in their common interest, and additional steps designed to bring about a substantial and permanent degree of cooperation and unity among these countries would materially improve the present position. But the situation demands further measures: those nations having a primary interest in the security of the North Atlantic area should collaborate in the development of a regional or collective defence arrangement for that area. Such action should be taken within the framework of the Charter of the United Nations.

I. The Situation in Europe as it Affects Security

1. The war, by weakening the Western European countries and by creating a vacuum in Germany has increased the strength of the Soviet Union relative to the strength of Western Europe. This has resulted in a situation in which the security of this area is immediately threatened and that of North America is seriously affected.

2. Soviet ideology is self-admittedly expansionist. Moreover, according to this ideology and doctrine the peaceful coexistence of the Soviet and non-Soviet worlds is impossible on any permanent basis. The Kremlin leaders aim at the maximum extension of their power and influence. International communism serves them as a powerful instrument for the achievement of this aim.

3. The westward expansion of Soviet power since the defeat of Hitler has rendered the Soviet Union strategically capable at the present time of dominating the continent of Europe by force. Soviet forces are so grouped and

17. Treaty of Economic, Social, and Cultural Collaboration and Collective Self-Defense (Brussels Treaty), signed March 17, 1948, and put into effect August 25, 1948, establishing the Western Union of France, Great Britain, Belgium, the Netherlands, and Luxembourg. The OEEC was the original European organization formed in 1948 to administer Marshall Plan aid. [Ed. note]

organized that they could take the initiative in military action at short notice. The military strength of the Soviet satellite countries of Eastern Europe has been so organized as to make a material contribution to Soviet striking power. These factors support the Kremlin program of intimidation designed to attain the domination of Europe. The Communist International under the new title of the Cominform[18] is again active in the field of indirect aggression.

4. While there is no evidence to suggest that the Soviet Government is planning armed aggression as an act of policy, there is always the danger that, in the tense situation existing at the present time, some incident might occur which would lead to war. War might also come about by a miscalculation of western intentions on the part of the Soviet Government. Alternatively, a sudden decision by the Kremlin leaders to precipitate war might result from fear: (1) that their own personal power was being undermined, or (2) that Soviet strength in relation to that of the western nations was declining, or (3) that these nations had aggressive intentions toward the Soviet Union.

5. Soviet plans have suffered a political setback as a result of the implementation of the European recovery program, the growing determination of the western powers to draw together for their well-being and mutual protection, and recent developments in Europe such as the trend of events in Greece and Tito's breach with the Cominform. There remains, however, a justified sense of insecurity among the peoples of Western Europe. The continued presence of U.S. forces in Western Europe is important since an attack upon them would bring the United States immediately and directly into war. Nevertheless, something more is needed to counteract the fear of the peoples of Western Europe that their countries might be overrun by the Soviet Army before effective help could arrive.

6. The U.S.S.R. under Kremlin dictatorship, utilizing the technique of indirect aggression and the threat of direct aggression, is an implacable enemy of western civilization and the present situation in Europe must be regarded as extremely insecure. The problem is to consider how the countries of Western Europe and those of the North American continent can most effectively join together for mutual aid against this common danger and achieve security. The immediate purpose is, in the first place, to prevent a Soviet attack; in this respect weak measures might only be provocative; firm measures may well prove a deterrent. In the second place, it is to restore

18. Communist Information Bureau. [Ed. note]

confidence among the peoples of Western Europe. United States and Canadian association in some North Atlantic security arrangement would be a major contribution to this.

II. Territorial Scope of a North Atlantic Security Arrangement and Its Relationship to the Security of Other Nations

1. A North Atlantic security system composed exclusively of the United States, Canada and the present parties to the Brussels Treaty would not be fully effective. On the other hand, even the combined military resources of these nations would be inadequate to warrant their assuming hard and fast commitments for the security of a large number of geographically scattered countries. A line must be drawn somewhere. The problem is to devise an arrangement which would best meet the security needs of the nations here represented without over-extending their military capabilities.

2. To be fully satisfactory, a North Atlantic security system would have to provide not only for the security of the countries mentioned above but also for that of the North Atlantic territories of Denmark (especially Greenland), Norway, Iceland, Portugal (especially the Azores) and Ireland, which, should they fall into enemy hands, would jeopardize the security of both the European and the North American members and seriously impede the flow of the reciprocal assistance between them.

3. Furthermore, other free European nations must be taken into account in view of: (1) the effect on the security of the nations participating in these talks should the political or territorial integrity of these other nations be menaced; (2) the necessity for maintaining and strengthening their Western orientation; and (3) the importance of avoiding any Soviet miscalculation to the effect that these nations could be absorbed into the Soviet orbit with impunity.

4. The circumstances and capabilities of the North Atlantic and Western European countries vary widely. Taking these variations into account rather than attempting to fit each nation into a uniform rigid pattern may provide the solution. It is suggested that the concept should include different categories of nations: (1) those whose membership in a North Atlantic Pact would involve maximum commitments for reciprocal assistance (with due regard for the resources of each party), and participation in the development of coordinated military potential; (2) those whose membership in the Pact would only involve limited commitments as, for example, to provide facilities for the common defense in return for commitments by the full members

to defend their territories; and (3) other nations, not members of the Pact, a threat to whose political or territorial integrity would require action by the full members. The division of nations between these categories need not be rigidly fixed but should permit flexibility.

5. Full membership in a North Atlantic security sytem would involve undertakings for mutual assistance in the event of armed attack upon any party, provision for consultation if the security of any party was otherwise threatened directly or indirectly, and provision for the establishment of agencies to implement the treaty. The original full members would be Canada, the U.S., the parties to the Brussels Treaty and such other members of the North Atlantic community as are ready to undertake the requisite obligations and are acceptable.

6. While it might well be desirable to have Norway, Denmark, Portugal, Iceland, and Ireland as full members, these countries may not now be prepared to accept fully the requisite responsibilities. They should be consulted before conclusion of the Pact and, if they are not then willing to assume such responsibilities, they should be invited to accede to the Pact with limited commitments, the exact nature of which would be determined in negotiation with them. The nature of such commitments might vary as between countries but would be generally such that: (a) the full members would agree to regard an attack on any of these countries as an attack against themselves; (b) these countries would agree to defend their own territories to the limit of their capabilities and to make available such facilities as are within their power, whenever required, in order to provide for the protection of the North Atlantic area.

7. Provision should be made by which the parties may by agreement invite any other state in or bordering upon Western Europe, the maintenance of whose territorial or political integrity is of direct concern to the security of the parties, to accede to the treaty on conditions to be agreed between them and the state so invited. These new participating countries might enter the pact either as full members, or with limited commitments as indicated above, or under such special arrangements as might be necessary owing to their geographical position or to their international obligations (Sweden, Italy).

8. The case of Italy presents a particular problem. It is not a North Atlantic country and it is subject to the military limitations imposed by the Peace Treaty. On the other hand its territory is of strategic importance to the nations here represented and its Western orientation must be maintained and strengthened. The United States representatives felt that a satisfactory solu-

tion of the problem of Italy must be found, either within the formula referred to in the preceding paragraph or otherwise.

9. The original full parties to the North Atlantic Pact would issue a joint statement at the time of its conclusion to the effect that any threat of aggression, direct or indirect, against any other OEEC country (including Western Germany, Austria, and Trieste) would be regarded by them as a development calling for consultation with the object of taking any measures which may be necessary.

10. It was recognized that the ultimate relationship of Spain and Western Germany (if Germany remains divided) to a North Atlantic security arrangement must eventually be determined but that it would be premature to attempt to do so at this time.

III. Nature of a Possible North Atlantic Security Arrangement

Any North Atlantic security arrangement should be clearly and specifically defined, since the respective governments and peoples must know exactly what the arrangement is and what advantages and obligations are involved. The obligations and commitments of each party should of course be undertaken by constitutional process. With the exceptions noted in the preceding section, the security arrangements should be generally reciprocal in nature. The preference expressed in the U.S. Senate on June 11, 1948[19] that U.S. association with any such arrangements be effected by treaty has been noted, as well as the Canadian position in regard to such an association stated by the Prime Minister of Canada in the House of Commons on March 17, 1948.[20]

2. The presence of U.S. troops in Germany not only entails U.S. participation in the security problems of Europe but also would in most contingencies, as long as they remain, involve the U.S. in any hostilities were they to break out there. The problem is, however, to recommend a long-term arrangement binding the parties to meet aggression jointly from whatever quarter and at whatever time. If the arrangement is to fill this requirement and those outlined above and to contribute to the restoration of confidence

19. Senate Resolution 239, the Vandenberg Resolution. [Ed. note]

20. The Canadian prime minister, William Lyon MacKenzie King, speaking on the occasion of the signing of the Brussels Treaty, had indicated Canada's readiness to participate in a mutual defense arrangement in these words: "The people of all free countries may be assured the Canada will play her full part in every movement to give substance to the conception of an effective system of collective security by the development of regional pacts under the charter of the United Nations." Quoted in Robert A. Spencer, *Canada in World Affairs: From UN to NATO, 1946–1949* (Toronto: Oxford University Press, 1959), p. 253. [Ed. note]

among the peoples of Western Europe, it would not be possible to base it on the presence of U.S. troops in Germany.

3. No alternative to a treaty appears to meet the esential requirements.

4. Consideration has been given to the question of whether or not conclusion of such a treaty might be considered provocative by the Soviet Government. Any arrangement linking the defense of Western Europe with that of the U.S. and Canada would reduce the chances of successful Soviet expansionist moves and would therefore encounter Soviet opposition as bitter as that which the European recovery program has encountered. Half measures might prove both ineffectual and provocative, whereas unmistakably clear determination to resist should serve to deter, and minimize the risk of, armed aggression. Soviet criticism could be offset by fitting the arrangement squarely into the framework of the United Nations and by providing not merely for defense but also for the advancement of the common interests of the parties and the strengthening of the economic, social and cultural ties which bind them.

5. Furthermore the existence of a treaty containing unmistakably clear provisions binding the parties to come to each other's defense in case of attack would hearten the peoples and leaders of the countries concerned. It would assist them to surmount the difficulties still besetting them, particularly in Western Europe where confidence is essential to full economic recovery.

6. Inasmuch as the conclusion of such a treaty might increase the existing tension with the Soviet Government, the Western European countries are the more anxious that the assistance given to an attacked country should be immediate, and military as well as economic and political. It also seems necessary that, within the limits of sound military practice, the military and other measures to be taken immediately by each participating country should be planned and decided beforehand by the agencies established for effective implementation of the treaty. It was appreciated that some of these military matters were being studied in London at the present time and that the military meetings there might be considered as indicative of the sort of consultation which might take place under the treaty, in the military and other fields.

7. Consideration was also given to the effect of the conclusion of such a treaty upon the security of other free European nations which may not become parties. It must be made clear that its conclusion in no way implies any lack of interest on the part of the parties in the security of such countries. This difficulty could to some extent be met by providing in the treaty for consultation in the event the security of any of the parties is threatened by armed attack upon a non-signatory or by any other fact or situation.

8. The foregong considerations have led to agreement upon the following basic criteria for such an arrangement:

    (1) It should be within the framework of the United Nations Charter, demonstrate the determination of the parties fully to meet their obligations under the Charter and encourage the progressive development of regional or collective defense arrangements.

    (2) It should contribute, through increasing the individual and collective capacities of the parties for self-defense, to the maintenance of peace and the greater national security of the parties.

    (3) It should make unmistakably clear the determination of the respective peoples jointly to resist aggression from any quarter.

    (4) It should define the area within which aggression against any party would bring the provisions for mutual assistance into operation.

    (5) It should be based on and promote continuous and effective self-help and mutual aid in all fields.

    (6) It should be more than an arrangement for defense alone; it should serve both to preserve the common civilization and to promote its development by increasing the collaboration between the signatories and advancing the conditions of stability and well-being upon which peace depends.

    (7) It should provide adequate machinery for implementing its terms, in particular for organized coordination and strengthening of the defense capacities of the parties, beginning immediately it comes into force.

9. In addition, the representatives of the European countries emphasized that it was particularly desirable that the arrangement should provide for the speediest practicable measures of material assistance in case of an armed attack, including individual military assistance by each of the members accepting full commitments as soon as such an attack is launched against any of them.

10. The U.S. representatives emphasized that U.S. association with any security arrangement must be within the framework of the Resolution adopted by the U.S. Senate on June 11, 1948 (S. Res. 239, 80th Congress, 2nd session). Of the four conditions specified by that Resolution three are covered by the basic criteria cited above: (1) that the arrangements must be within the framework of the Charter, (2) that U.S. association with it must be by constitutional procress, and (3) that the arrangement must be based upon continuous and effective self-help and mutual aid. It was made clear that the third condition meant that U.S. assistance must supplement rather than take the place of the maximum efforts of the other nations on behalf of

themselves and each other, and that assistance must be reciprocal. The fourth condition was that the arrangement should affect (i.e. increase) the national security of the U.S. In this connection the U.S. representatives made clear their belief that a North Atlantic security arrangement, if it is to increase adequately the security of North America and provide the Western European countries with adequate assurance that North American ground and air forces and supplies could effectively be brought to their assistance in time of war, should include the North Atlantic territories of Denmark (Greenland), Iceland, Ireland, Norway and Portugal (the Azores).

11. The United States representatives also considered that some of the articles of the Rio Treaty, which had been approved by the U.S. Senate,[21] provided a useful basis for the formulation of an arrangement which would meet the requirements. At the same time they fully recognized the relevance of provisions of the Brussels Treaty. They considered certain articles of the Rio Treaty, notably those concerning voting procedure,[22] unsuited to an arrangement for the North Atlantic area.

12. The United States representatives emphasized that the United States could not constitutionally enter into any treaty which would provide that the United States would be at war without a vote of Congress. All representatives stressed that their respective constitutional processes must be observed and agreed that, as in any similar treaty, the question of fact as to whether or not an armed attack had occurred would be a matter for individual determination.

13. The Canadian representatives emphasized the importance which they attached to provisions, in any treaty which might be concluded, for the encouragement of cooperation in fields other than security. Such cooperation would contribute directly to general security. In other words, they felt that the purpose of a treaty should not be merely negative and that it should create the dynamic counter-attraction of a free, prosperous and progressive society as opposed to the society of the Communist world. The treaty should provide a basis for the organization of an overwhelming preponderance of moral, economic and military force and a sufficient degree of unity to assure that this preponderance of force may be so used as to guarantee that the free nations will not be defeated one by one.

14. The conclusion of an arrangement of this general character appears

21. The Senate advised ratification of the Inter-American Treaty of Reciprocal Assistance on December 8, 1947. [Ed. note]

22. The Rio Treaty permitted decisions on sanctions and other matters to be taken by a two-thirds vote of signatories who had ratified the treaty, and made such decisions binding on all signatories. The principal of unanimity was adopted in NATO. [Ed. note]

practicable. There is attached an outline of provisions which it might include.[23]

◇◇

17   **T O P   S E C R E T**

Considerations Affecting the Conclusion of a North Atlantic Security Pact

PPS 43   November 23, 1948

[Source: *Foreign Relations of the United States: 1948*, III, 284–88]

In PPS 43, the Policy Planning Staff addressed the question of a North Atlantic Security Pact, a possibility brought clearly into view by the Washington discussions of late summer (see Document 16). PPS 43 reflected a somewhat grudging acceptance of the concept, not because the staff perceived a significant Soviet military threat to Western Europe, but because they believed that only such a pact could dispel European ''subjective'' fears of such an attack. The staff emphasized that economic aid was still more important for Europe than military support, and that an alliance would not modify the nature or danger of Soviet policies. Further, the Policy Planning Staff argued that the pact should be limited to states bordering on the North Atlantic, lest the effectiveness of the pact be vitiated by lack of focus and conflicts among member states.

Both PPS 43 and PPS 37 (Document 15) reflect Kennan's growing divergence from the course of United States foreign policy, particularly his questioning of measures that might retard an eventual political settlement with the Russians.

The Policy Planning Staff wishes to invite attention to certain considerations which it feels should be borne in mind in connection with the forthcoming negotiations for a North Atlantic Security Pact, and to advance certain recommendations which flow therefrom:

1. MISCONCEPTIONS AS TO THE SIGNIFICANCE OF THE PACT

There is danger that we will deceive ourselves, and permit misconceptions to exist among our own public and in Europe, concerning the significance of the conclusion of such a pact at this time.

It is particularly difficult to assess the role of such a pact in our foreign policy for the reason that there *is* valid long-term justification for a formalization, by international agreement, of the natural defense relationship among the countries of the North Atlantic community. Such a formalization could

23. Printed in *Foreign Relations of the United States: 1948*, III, 245–48. [Ed. note]

contribute to the general sense of security in the area;
facilitate the development of defensive power throughout the area; and
act as a deterrent to outside aggressive forces.

It is therefore desirable, quite aside from the situation of the moment in Europe, that we proceed deliberately, and with careful study to the elaboration and negotiation of such an agreement.

On the other hand, it is important to understand that the conclusion of such a pact is not the main answer to the present Soviet effort to dominate the European continent, and will not appreciably modify the nature or danger of Soviet policies.

A military danger, arising from possible incidents or from the prestige engagement of the Russians and the western powers in the Berlin situation, does exist, and is probably increasing rather than otherwise. But basic Russian intent still runs to the conquest of western Europe by political means. In this program, military force plays a major role only as a means of intimidation.

The danger of political conquest is still greater than the military danger. If a war comes in the foreseeable future, it will probably be one which Moscow did not desire but did not know how to avoid. The political war, on the other hand, is now in progress; and, if there should not be a shooting war, it is this political war which will be decisive.

A North Atlantic Security Pact will affect the political war only insofar as it operates to stiffen the self-confidence of the western Europeans in the face of Soviet pressures. Such a stiffening is needed and desirable. But it goes hand in hand with the danger of a general preoccupation with military affairs, to the detriment of economic recovery and of the necessity for seeking a peaceful solution to Europe's difficulties.

This preoccupation is already widespread, both in Europe and in this country. It is regrettable; because it addresses itself to what is not the main danger. We have to deal with it as a reality; and to a certain extent we have to indulge it, for to neglect it would be to encourage panic and uncertainty in western Europe and to play into the hands of the communists. But in doing so, we should have clearly in mind that the need for military alliances and rearmament on the part of the western Europeans is primarily a *subjective* one, arising in their own minds as a result of their failure to understand correctly their own position. Their best and most hopeful course of action, if they are to save themselves from communist pressures, remains the struggle for economic recovery and for internal political stability.

Compared to this, intensive rearmament constitutes an uneconomic and regrettable diversion of effort. A certain amount of rearmament can be subjectively beneficial to western Europe. But if this rearmament proceeds at any appreciable cost to European recovery, it can do more harm than good. The same will be true if concentration on the rearmament effort gradually encourages the assumption that war is inevitable and that therefore no further efforts are necessary toward the political weakening and defeat of the communist power in central and eastern Europe.

2. THE TERRITORIAL SCOPE OF THE PACT

The Policy Planning Staff is of the opinion that the scope of a pact of this sort should be restricted to the North Atlantic area itself, and that attempts to go further afield and to include countries beyond that area might have undesirable consequences.

The possibility of a mistake in this respect is particularly acute because we ourselves showed uncertainty on this point in the preliminary discussions of the past summer, and the final record of the results of those discussions left open the possibility of the Pact's being extended beyond the North Atlantic area.[24]

This point was included largely at the insistence of the United States group. While it might do no great harm to have this possibility left open in the final text of the Pact, the Policy Planning Staff did not then, and does not now, agree with the thinking that lay behind this insistence.

The Staff considers that a North Atlantic security pact might properly embrace any country whose homeland or insular territories are washed by the waters of the North Atlantic, or which form part of a close union of states which meets this description. Under this concept, for example, Luxembourg would properly come into such a pact through its membership in the Benelux group. But to go beyond this, and to take in individual continental countries which do not meet this description would, in the opinion of the Staff, be unsound, for the following reasons.

In the first place, the admission of any single country beyond the North Atlantic area would be taken by others as constituting a precedent, and would almost certainly lead to a series of demands from states still further afield that they be similarly treated. Failure on our part to satisfy these further demands would then be interpreted as lack of interest in the respective countries, and as evidence that we had "written them off" to the Russians.

24. A footnote in the original at this point quoted in full Section II, paragraph 7, of the "Washington paper," Document 16. [Ed. note]

Beyond the Atlantic area, which is a clean-cut concept, and which embraces a real community of defense interest firmly rooted in geography and tradition, there is no logical stopping point in the development of a system of anti-Russian alliances until that system has circled the globe and has embraced all the non-communist countries of Europe, Asia and Africa.

To get carried into any such wide system of alliances would lead only to one of two results; either all these alliances become meaningless declarations, after the pattern of the Kellogg Pact,[25] and join the long array of dead-letter pronouncements through which governments have professed their devotion to peace in the past; or this country becomes still further over-extended, politically and militarily. In the first case, we would have made light of our own word and damaged the future usefulness of Article 51 of the United Nations Charter. In addition, we would have weakened the integrity and significance of our own defense relationship with our neighbors of the north Atlantic community. In the second case, we would be flying in the face of the solemn warning recently given by the Joint Chiefs of Staff concerning the increasing discrepancy between our commitments and our military resources.[26]

A particularly unfortunate effect of going beyond the North Atlantic area would be that we would thereby raise for every country in Europe the question: to belong or not to belong. An issue would thus be raised which would be in many cases unneccessary and potentially embarrassing, and in some cases outright dangerous. If individual countries rejected membership or were refused membership, the Russians could make political capital out of this, either way. If, on the other hand, most of the ERP countries were permitted to join, and did so, this would amount to a final militarization of the present dividing-line through Europe. Such a development would be particularly unfortunate, for it would create a situation in which no alteration, or obliteration, of that line could take place without having an accentuated military significance. This would reduce materially the chances for Austrian and German settlements, and would make it impossible for any of the satellite countries even to contemplate anything in the nature of a gradual withdrawal from Russian domination, since any move in that direction would take on the aspect of a provocative military move.

25. The Kellogg-Briand Pact between France and the United States, and, eventually, virtually all the other nations of the world was signed at Paris on August 27, 1928. It condemned recourse to war as an instrument of national policy. [Ed. note]

26. The reference is to a memorandum of the Joint Chiefs of Staff of November 2, 1948, which became a part of NSC 35, dated November 17, 1948, entitled "Existing International Commitments Involving the Possible Use of Armed Forces," printed in *Foreign Relations of the United States: 1948,* I (part 2), 656–62. [Ed. note]

Unquestionably, there is already a strong tendency in this direction; and it may not be possible for us to prevent a progressive congealment of the present line of division. But our present policy is still directed (and in the opinion of the Staff, rightfully so) toward the eventual peaceful withdrawal of both the United States and the U.S.S.R. from the heart of Europe, and accordingly toward the encouragement of the growth of a third force which can absorb and take over the territory between the two.

Unless we are prepared consciously to depart from this policy, to renounce hope of a peaceful solution of Europe's difficulties, and to plan our foreign policy deliberately on the assumption of a coming military conflict, we should not do things which tend to fix, and make unchangeable by peaceful means, the present line of east-west division.

The Staff feels that, rather than extending membership in the pact to non-North Atlantic powers, a much sounder way of enhancing the sense of security of other European countries would be through the implementation of the suggestion, contained in Paragraph 9 of Part II of the record of the recent informal discussions,[27] that the members of the pact jointly made known their interest in the security of the given country.

This view of the Staff is without prejudice to the question of the desirability of the United States associating itself with any further regional agreements, as for example a Mediterranean pact, which question lies outside the scope of this paper.

Recommendations

In the light of the above, the Policy Planning Staff recommends:

    a. That it be accepted as the view of this Government:

        (1) That there is a long-term need for a permanent formalization of the defense relationship among the countries of the North Atlantic area;

        (2) That the conclusion of a North Atlantic Security Pact just at this time will have a specific short-term value in so far as it may serve to increase the sense of security on the part of the members of the Brussels Pact and of other European countries; but

27. This paragraph of the "Washington paper" read as follows: "The original full parties to the North Atlantic Pact would issue a joint statement at the time of its conclusion to the effect that any threat of aggression, direct or indirect, against any other OEEC country (including Western Germany, Austria, and Trieste) would be regarded by them as a development calling for consultation with the object of taking any measures which may be necessary." (See Document 16.) [Ed. note]

(3) That, nevertheless, the conclusion of the Pact is not the main answer to the Russian effort to achieve domination over western Europe, which still appears to be primarily political in nature. The conclusion and implementation of such a pact should therefore not be considered as a replacement for the other steps which are being taken and should be taken to meet the Russian challenge, nor should they be given priority over the latter.

b. That steps be taken to see that this view of the significance of a possible North Atlantic Security Pact be made available for background to all higher officials of the Department, to Missions in the field, and to the informational organs of this Department and other Government Departments, with a view to keeping it before the public and to combatting opposite concepts.

c. That it be the policy of this Government not to encourage adherence to a North Atlantic Security Pact of any country not properly a part of the North Atlantic community.

<><><><><><><><><><><><><><><><><><><><><><><><><><><><><><><><><><><>

18

The North Atlantic Pact: Collective Defense and the Preservation of Peace, Security and Freedom in the North Atlantic Community

March 20, 1949

[Source: *Foreign Relations of the United States: 1949*, IV, 240–41]

Despite the misgivings of Kennan and the Policy Planning Staff, the organization of a North Atlantic defense community went forward more along the lines sketched in the "Washington paper" than those advocated in PPS 43 (see Documents 16 and 17). In March 1949, just weeks before the signing of the North Atlantic Treaty, the Department of State issued a statement making clear its view of the relation among the several economic and military elements of containment as implemented in Western Europe. Excerpts from the statement appear below.

·   ·   ·   ·   ·   ·   ·

The Atlantic Pact and the European Recovery Program

The North Atlantic Pact is a necessary complement to the broad economic coordination now proceeding under the European Recovery Program, but there is no formal connection between the Pact and the ERP since the latter includes countries which will not participate in the Pact.

In the view of the United States, the Pact and the ERP are both essential to the attainment of a peaceful, prosperous, and stable world. The economic recovery of Europe, the goal of the ERP, will be aided by the sense of increased security which the Pact will promote among these countries. On the other hand, a successful ERP is the essential foundation upon which the Pact, and the increased security to be expected from it, must rest.

The Atlantic Pact and Military Assistance

A military assistance program is now being considered by the executive branch of the Government. This program, another measure for securing peace for the United States and other peace-loving nations, envisages aid to the members of the Pact as well as other friendly states of the free world. As President Truman stated to the Congress in March 1947: "I believe that it must be the policy of the United States to support free peoples who are resisting attempted subjugation by armed minorities or by outside pressures. . . . Totalitarian regimes imposed upon free peoples, by direct or indirect aggression, undermine the foundations of international peace and hence the security of the United States." [28] Since May 1947, military assistance has been provided to several countries under this policy.

While the North Atlantic Pact does not expressly commit the United States to furnish military assistance to the other Parties of the Pact, the decision to do so by the United States would be one way in which this nation could logically contribute to the mutual aid concept expressed in article 3 of the Pact. [29] It is not intended, however, that one nation should carry on its shoulders the entire burden of maintenance of the security of the North Atlantic area. The United States is one of the contributors to this effort. The United States is fully aware that it does not have available unlimited supplies and that it is essential that its own armed forces be adequately equipped. Allocation of such military equipment as is available for transfer to other countries must be made in such a manner as will serve the over-all security interests of the United States.

In accordance with the principle of self-help and mutual aid, the other members of the Pact have already taken action to further the security of the

28. President Truman's address to the Congress in support of aid to Greece and Turkey, March 12, 1947. [Ed. note]

29. Article 3 of the North Atlantic Pact provided that "In order more effectively to achieve the objectives of this Treaty, the Parties, separately and jointly, by means of continuous and effective self-help and mutual aid, will maintain and develop their individual and collective capacity to resist armed attack." [Ed. note]

North Atlantic area. Their efforts toward reestablishing sound economies are a vital provision of self-help in the security arrangements. The military budgets already carried by many of these countries, despite the tremendous load of economic recovery expenditures which they are undertaking, are an added expression of their intention of helping themselves and of not relying solely or even principally on United States assistance to maintain their own security and that of the North Atlantic area.

The Pact and European Integration

Economic and Political Cooperation. The North Atlantic Pact is made possible by the strides the Western nations of Europe have taken toward economic recovery and toward economic, political, and military cooperation. The core of the economic recovery effort is the European Recovery Program and the Organization for European Economic Cooperation (OEEC), composed of the sixteen countries receiving American aid through the United States Economic Cooperation Administration (ECA). The sixteen countries in the OEEC and represented on its Council are the United Kingdom, Austria, Belgium, Denmark, France, Greece, Iceland, Ireland, Italy, Luxembourg, the Netherlands, Norway, Portugal, Sweden, Switzerland, and Turkey. Western Germany also participates fully in the OEEC. The Charter of the OEEC pledges the continuing effort of these countries to increase production, modernize industry, stabilize their finances, and balance their accounts with the outside world in order to make their full contribution to world economic security. Lines of action to increase cooperation through 1952 have been prepared. Support and aid to this integration has also come from the United Nations Economic Commission for Europe, of which the United States is a member.

·   ·   ·   ·   ·   ·   ·

❧ 4 ❧

IMPLEMENTATION: THE SOVIET UNION AND THE COMMUNIST WORLD, 1948–49

here, they are "approaches," not policy

ALTHOUGH AMERICAN OFFICIALS regarded restoration of the balance of power in Europe as their first priority, such a position by no means precluded efforts to reach accommodations with the Soviet Union where opportunities existed to do so. The documents printed in this section illustrate three different approaches to the problem of dealing with the U.S.S.R. once the European balance had been reconstituted. PPS 23 (Document 19) represents Kennan's case for direct negotiations with the Russians on the resolution of outstanding issues. NSC 7 (Document 20) rejects negotiations, favoring instead a "worldwide counteroffensive" against both the Soviet Union and international communism. A third approach is reflected in PPS 35, NSC 20/1, and NSC 58 (Documents 21, 22, and 24), all of which draw on the implications of Yugoslavia's split with the Soviet Union in the summer of 1948 to propose strategies that might promote friction between Moscow and its putative ideological sympathizers throughout the world.

B.S.

Also printed in this section is NSC 20/4 (Document 23), a paper reflecting aspects of all three approaches. Approved by President Truman in November 1948, NSC 20/4 became the definitive expression of United States policy toward the Soviet Union until it was superseded by NSC 68 in the spring of 1950.

<><><><><><><><><><><><><><><><><><><><><><><><><><><><><><>

19   **TOP SECRET**

Review of Current Trends: U.S. Foreign Policy

PPS 23   February 24, 1948

[Source: *Foreign Relations of the United States: 1948,* I (part 2), 521–23, 528]

Kennan never intended for the United States and its allies merely to limit the geographical expansion of Soviet influence and restore the balance of power in Europe.

Gaddis writes a brief for Kennan

At some point, he believed, it would be necessary to resume substantive negotiations with the Russians with a view to resolving outstanding differences. Behind this assumption was Kennan's conviction that neither the United States nor the Soviet Union could indefinitely maintain the advanced positions they had occupied since the end of World War II; sooner or later, he thought, a reciprocal withdrawal of forces would have to take place. As indicated in these excerpts from PPS 23, Kennan regarded negotiations as feasible even with Stalin—if conducted realistically by professional diplomats on topics where there might be mutual interest in reaching agreements. In the relative importance he attached to negotiations Kennan parted company with other top Washington policy makers, most of whom harbored greater skepticism than he about what diplomatic contacts with Moscow could accomplish, and tended to emphasize instead the need to build up alliances against Soviet power.

(Acheson thought no negotiation possible)

VI. U.S.S.R

If the Russians have further success in the coming months in their efforts at penetration and seizure of political control of the key countries outside the iron curtain (Germany, France, Italy, and Greece), they will continue, in my opinion, to be impossible to deal with at the council table. For they will see no reason to settle with us at this time over Germany when they hope that their bargaining position will soon be improved.

If, on the other hand, their situation outside the iron curtain does not improve—if the ERP aid arrives in time and in a form to do some good and if there is a general revival of confidence in western Europe, than a new situation will arise and the Russians will be prepared, for the first time since the surrender, to do business seriously with us about Germany and about Europe in general. They are conscious of this and are making allowance for this possibility in their plans. I think, in fact, that they regard it as the more probable of the two contingencies.

When that day comes, i.e. when the Russians will be prepared to talk realistically with us, we will be faced with a great test of American statesmanship, and it will not be easy to find the right solution. For what the Russians will want us to do will be to conclude with them a sphere-of-influence agreement similar to the one they concluded with the Germans in 1939. It will be our job to explain to them that we cannot do this and why. But we must also be able to demonstrate to them that it will still be worth their while:

    a. to reduce communist pressures elsewhere in Europe and the Middle East to a point where we can afford to withdraw all our armed forces from the continent and the Mediterranean; and

b. to acquiesce thereafter in a prolonged period of stability in Europe.

I doubt that this task will be successfully accomplished if we try to tackle it head-on in the CFM or at any other public meeting. Our public dealings with the Russians can hardly lead to any clear and satisfactory results unless they are preceded by preparatory discussions of the most secret and delicate nature with Stalin. I think that those discussions can be successfully conducted only by someone who:

    a. has absolutely no personal axe to grind in the discussions, even along the lines of getting public credit for their success, and is prepared to observe strictest silence about the whole proceeding; and

    b. is thoroughly acquainted not only with the background of our policies but with Soviet philosophy and strategy and with the dialectics used by Soviet statesmen in such discussions.

(It would be highly desirable that this person be able to conduct conversations in the Russians' language. In my opinion, this is important with Stalin.)

These discussions should not be directed toward arriving at any sort of secret protocol or any other written understanding. They should be designed to clarify the background of any written understanding that we may hope to reach at the CFM table or elsewhere. For we know now that the words of international agreements mean different things to the Russians than they do to us; and it is desirable that in this instance we should thresh out some common understanding of what would really be meant by any further written agreements we might arrive at.

The Russians will probably not be prepared to "talk turkey" with us until after the elections. But it would be much easier to talk to them at that time if the discussions did not have to be inaugurated too abruptly and if the ground had been prepared beforehand.

      ·   ·   ·   ·   ·   ·   ·

. . . But we must bear in mind that this understanding would necessarily have to be limited and coldly realistic, could not be reduced to paper, and could not be expected to outlast the general international situation which had given rise to it.

I may add that I think such an understanding would have to be restricted pretty much to the European and western Mediterranean areas. I doubt that it could be extended to apply to the Middle East and Far East. The situation in these latter areas is too unsettled, the prospects for the future too confusing, the possibilities of one sort or another too vast and unforeseeable, to admit of such discussions. The only exception to this might be with respect to

Japan. It might conceivably be possible for us to achieve some arrangement whereby the economic exchanges between Japan and Manchuria might be revived in a guarded and modified form, by some sort of barter arrangement. This is an objective well worth holding in mind, from our standpoint. But we should meanwhile have to frame our policies in Japan with a view to creating better bargaining power for such discussions than we now possess.

·   ·   ·   ·   ·   ·   ·

We are still faced with an extremely serious threat to our whole security, in the form of the men in the Kremlin. These men are an able, shrewd and utterly ruthless group, absolutely devoid of respect for us or our institutions. They wish for nothing more than the destruction of our national strength. They operate through a political organization of unparalleled flexibility, discipline, cynicism and toughness. They command the resources of one of the world's greatest industrial and agricultural nations. Natural force, independent of our policies, may go far to absorb and eventually defeat the efforts of this group. But we cannot depend upon this. Our own diplomacy has a decisive part to play in this connection. The problems involved are new to us, and we are only beginning to adjust ourselves to them. We have made some progress; but we are not yet nearly far enough advanced. Our operations in foreign affairs must attain a far higher degree of purposefulness, of economy of effort, and of disciplined coordination if we are to be sure of accomplishing our purposes.

·   ·   ·   ·   ·   ·   ·

<><><><><><><><><><><><><><><><><><><><><><><><><><><><><><><>

20   **T O P   S E C R E T**

The Position of the United States with Respect to Soviet-Directed World Communism

NSC 7   March 30, 1948

[Source: *Foreign Relations of the United States: 1948,* I (part 2), 546–50]

In addition to the problems of dealing with the Soviet Union itself, Washington officials had to consider the relationship of that country to the international communist movement. NSC 7, prepared by the staff of the National Security Council in consultation with representatives from the Army, Navy, Air Force, State Department, National Security Resources Board, and the Central Intelligence Agency, represented one of the first comprehensive efforts within the government to do this. The document is significant first in its assumption of congruent interests among the Soviet

Union and members of the international communist movement, a position events in Yugoslavia soon called into question; second, in its failure to include Chinese Communist activities within the scope of ''Soviet-directed world communism''; and third, in its insistence that the internal communist threat in the United States approached the external threat in importance.

The Problem

1. To assess and appraise the position of the United States with respect to Soviet-directed world communism, taking into account the security interests of the United States.

Analysis

2. The ultimate objective of Soviet-directed world communism is the domination of the world. To this end, Soviet-directed world communism employs against its victims in opportunistic coordination the complementary instruments of Soviet aggressive pressure from without and militant revolutionary subversion from within. Both instruments are supported by the formidable material power of the USSR and their use is facilitated by the chaotic aftermath of the war.

3. The defeat of the Axis left the world with only two great centers of national power, the United States and the USSR. The Soviet Union is the source of power from which international communism chiefly derives its capability to threaten the existence of free nations. The United States is the only source of power capable of mobilizing successful opposition to the communist goal of world conquest. Between the United States and the USSR there are in Europe and Asia areas of great potential power which if added to the existing strength of the Soviet world would enable the latter to become so superior in manpower, resources and territory that the prospect for the survival of the United States as a free nation would be slight. In these circumstances the USSR has engaged the United States in a struggle for power, or ''cold war,'' in which our national security is at stake and from which we cannot withdraw short of eventual national suicide.

4. Already Soviet-directed world communism has achieved alarming success in its drive toward world conquest. It has established satellite police states in Poland, Yugoslavia, Albania, Hungary, Bulgaria, Rumania, and Czechoslovakia; it poses an immediate threat to Italy, Greece, Finland, Korea, the Scandanavian countries, and others. The USSR has prevented the conclusion of peace treaties with Germany, Austria, and Japan; and has

made impossible the international control of atomic energy and the effective functioning of the United Nations. Today Stalin has come close to achieving what Hitler attempted in vain. The Soviet world extends from the Elbe River and the Adriatic Sea on the west to Manchuria on the east, and embraces one-fifth of the land surface of the world.

5. In addition, Soviet-directed world communism has faced the non-Soviet world with something new in history. This is the worldwide Fifth Column directed at frustrating foreign policy, dividing and confusing the people of a country, planting the seeds of disruption in time of war, and subverting the freedom of democratic states. Under a multitude of disguises, it is capable of fomenting disorders, including armed conflicts, within its victim's territory without involving the direct responsibility of any communist state. The democracies have been deterred in effectively meeting this threat, in part because communism has been allowed to operate as a legitimate political activity under the protection of civil liberties.

6. In its relations with other nations the USSR is guided by the communist dogma that the peaceful co-existence of communist and capitalist states is in the long run impossible. On the basis of this postulate of ultimate inevitable conflict, the USSR is attempting to gain world domination by subversion, and by legal and illegal political and economic measures, but might ultimately resort to war if necessary to gain its ends. Such a war might be waged openly by the USSR with her satellites, or might be waged by one or a combination of the satellites with the avowed neutrality or disapproval of the USSR, though with her covert support. However, the Soviet Union so far has sought to avoid overt conflict, since time is required to build up its strength and concurrently to weaken and divide its opponents. In such a postponement, time is on the side of the Soviet Union so long as it can continue to increase its relative power by the present process of indirect aggression and internal subversion.

7. In view of the nature of Soviet-directed world communism, the successes which it has already achieved, and the threat of further advances in the immediate future, a defensive policy cannot be considered an effectual means of checking the momentum of communist expansion and inducing the Kremlin to relinquish its aggressive designs. A defensive policy by attempting to be strong everywhere runs the risk of being weak everywhere. It leaves the initiative to the Kremlin, enabling it to strike at the time and place most suitable to its purpose and to effect tactical withdrawals and diversions. It permits the Kremlin to hold what it has already gained and leaves its power potential intact.

8. As an alternative to a defensive policy the United States has open to it

the organization of a world-wide counter-offensive against Soviet-directed world communism. Such a policy would involve first of all strengthening the military potential of the United States, and secondly, mobilizing and strengthening the potential of the non-Soviet world. A counter-offensive policy would gain the initiative and permit concentration of strength on vital objectives. It would strengthen the will to resist of anti-communist forces throughout the world and furnish convincing evidence of US determination to thwart the communist design of world conquest. It should enlist the support of the American people and of the peoples of the non-Soviet world. It would be consistent with the national objectives of the United States. This policy, in fact, would be the most effective way of deterring the USSR from further aggression. Such aggression might ultimately require the United States, in order to sustain itself, to mobilize all of its resources against the continued threat of war, resulting in the creation of a vast armed camp within its borders. In the latter eventuality, rigid economies, regimentation and a fear psychosis might easily promote the very conditions in the United States that we are determined to eliminate elsewhere in the world. The measures adopted under a counter-offensive policy need not be inconsistent with the purposes and principles of the United Nations. We would continue to support the United Nations within the limits of its capabilities, and seek to strengthen it.

Conclusions

9. The defeat of the forces of Soviet-directed world communism is vital to the security of the United States.

10. This objective cannot be achieved by a defensive policy.

11. The United States should therefore take the lead in organizing a world-wide counter-offensive aimed at mobilizing and strengthening our own and anti-communist forces in the non-Soviet world, and at undermining the strength of the communist forces in the Soviet world.

12. As immediate steps in the counter-offensive, the United States should take the following measures:

A. DOMESTIC

(1) Strengthen promptly the military establishment of the United States by:

    (a) Initiation of some form of compulsory military service.

    (b) Reconstitution of the armaments industry.

(2) Maintain overwhelming US superiority in atomic weapons. (In the

event of international agreement on the control of atomic weapons this conclusion should be reconsidered.)

(3) Urgently develop and execute a firm and coordinated program (to include legislation if necessary) designed to suppress the communist menace in the United States in order to safeguard the United States against the disruptive and dangerous subversive activities of communism.

(4) To the extent necessary to implement (1) above, initiate civilian and industrial mobilization.

(5) Vigorously prosecute a domestic information program, designed to insure public understanding and non-partisan support of our foreign policy.

B. FOREIGN

(1) In our counter-offensive efforts, give first priority to Western Europe. This should not preclude appropriate efforts in the case of other countries of Europe and the Middle East, which are immediately threatened by world communism and where loss of freedom would most seriously threaten our national security.

(2) Urgently adopt and implement the European Recovery Program.

(3) Strongly endorse the Western Union and actively encourage its development and expansion as an anti-communist association of states.

(4) Work out an appropriate formula which will provide for:
   (a) Military action by the United States in the event of unprovoked armed attack against the nations in the Western Union or against other selected non-Communist nations.
   (b) Initiation of political and military conversations with such nations with a view to coordination of anti-Communist efforts.

(5) Assist in building up the military potential of selected non-communist nations by the provision of machine tools to rehabilitate their arms industries, technical information to facilitate standardization of arms, and by furnishing to the extent practicable military equipment and technical advice.

(6) When we have developed a program for suppressing the communist menace in the United States (12A.(3) above), cooperate closely with governments which have already taken such action and encourage other governments to take like action.

(7) Encourage and assist private United States citizens and organizations in fostering non-communist trade union movements in those countries where that would contribute to our national security. Measures of assistance should include consideration of individual income tax deductions for that purpose.

(8) Intensify the present anti-communist foreign information program.

(9) Develop a vigorous and effective ideological campaign.

(10) Develop, and at the appropriate time carry out, a coordinated program to support underground resistance movements in countries behind the iron curtain, including the USSR.

(11) Establish a substantial emergency fund to be used in combatting Soviet-directed world communism.

(12) Make unmistakably clear to the Kremlin at an opportune time, and in an appropriate manner, United States determination to resist Soviet and Soviet-directed communist aggression so as to avoid the possibility of an "accidental" war through Soviet miscalculation of how far the Western Powers might be pushed.

13. Effectuation of the above policies requires bi-partisan support.

<><><><><><><><><><><><><><><><><><><><><><><><><><><><><><><><><>

21   **S E C R E T**

The Attitude of This Government Toward Events in Yugoslavia

PPS 35   June 30, 1948

[Source: *Foreign Relations of the United States: 1948,* IV, 1079–81]

PPS 35, written within days after news broke of the Tito-Stalin split, constituted the first explicit recognition within the U.S. government of the possibility that a communist state might exist independent of Moscow's control. From this realization that the international communist movement was no longer a monolith, the Policy Planning Staff developed a strategy for taking advantage of such fissures, actual and potential, to achieve the goals of containment (see also Documents 22 and 24).

Secretary of State Marshall approved PPS 35 on July 1, 1948, and as NSC 18 it was submitted to the National Security Council, where action on the document was neither requested nor taken.

Discussion

1. The defiance of the Kremlin by the leaders of the Yugoslav Communist Party creates an entirely new problem of foreign policy for this Government. For the first time in history we may now have within the international community a communist state resting on the basis of Soviet organizational principles and for the most part on Soviet ideology, and yet independent of Moscow.

If the Soviet satellite area disintegrates further, either now or in the more distant future, this situation may arise in other instances as well. For this reason, the attitude we take now may constitute an important precedent.

Furthermore, our attitude at this time may have an important influence on *whether* the rift between Tito and Moscow spreads to Russia's relations with other members of the satellite area or serves to weld those other members still more tightly to the Kremlin.

It necessary, therefore, that this Department and its representatives abroad be extremely circumspect in the handling of all matters which might be taken to reflect this Government's attitude toward the Tito-Stalin imbroglio.

2. It is essential to bear in mind certain outstanding facts which are already apparent in this situation:

(a) Yugoslavia remains a communist state, dedicated to an ideology of hostility and contempt toward the "bourgeois capitalist world", and committed at home to government by the methods of communist totalitarian dictatorship. Its leaders have continued to demonstrate right up to this moment a sincere concern for the unity of the communist world in the face of "capitalist imperialism". It would therefore be a frivolous and undignified error on our part to assume that because Tito had fallen out with Stalin he could now be considered our "friend".

(b) The disunity within the communist world which has been demonstrated by these events must be profoundly humiliating and disagreeable to *all* the parties concerned. Efforts will certainly be made, from one side or both, to patch up the rift for the sake of appearances. It is too early to hazard any guesses as to the success of these efforts. But it can be stated with assurance that even though they might be outwardly and momentarily successful, the damage done to the movement by this episode can probably never be entirely repaired. A new factor of fundamental and profound significance has been introduced into the world communist movement by the demonstration that the Kremlin can be successfully defied by one of its own minions. By this act, the aura of mystical omnipotence and infallibility which has surrounded the Kremlin power has been broken. The possibility of defection from Moscow, which has heretofore been unthinkable for foreign communist leaders, will from now on be present in one form or another in the mind of every one of them.

(c) The Russians will seek intently for any mistakes in the handling of this situation by the western countries which can be exploited as a means of bringing pressure to bear on Tito to come back into the fold and as a means of discouraging other satellite figures from following Tito's example.

If the western world now fawns on Tito this will be exploited by Moscow to arouse feelings of disgust and revulsion throughout the international communist movement and among Tito's own followers. This would help to undermine his position with his own followers and to bring Yugoslavia back into the fold. Such a course would also arouse strong, and justifiable, criticism in this country.

If, on the other hand, the western world is too cold toward Tito, ridicules him in his present international loneliness, and repulses any advances that may be made by him toward closer association with the west, this will be used by the Moscow communists as proof that foreign communists have no alternative but to stay with Moscow: that desertion only places them at the mercy of the wolves of capitalism.

Conclusions

1. The Department and all its representatives should observe extreme circumspection in discussing the Yugoslav differences with the Cominform. Bearing in mind that Yugoslavia is still a communist state and is still led by men who have consistently adopted an arrogant and hostile attitude toward this country and the western world in general, we should not detract from the dignity of our own position by exhibiting an excessive friendliness toward the Yugoslav leaders or indulging in exaggerated hopes that they will soon become an integral part of the western world. On the other hand, we should be careful not to create the impression that Tito has been held up to ridicule by the west just *because* he has been eliminated from the communist family.

2. The line which should be adhered to by representatives of the Department in private conversation, with respect to the attitude of this Government, should be substantially as follows:

This Government would welcome a genuine re-emergence of Yugoslavia as a political personality in its own right. Its attitude toward a Yugoslav Government which had cut loose from Moscow would depend primarily on the behavior of that government with regard to this country, to the other European countries, and to the international community in general. We recognize that Yugoslavia's internal regime continues to be one which is deeply distasteful to our people and that as long as such a regime exists, Yugoslav-

American relations can never take on quite the cordiality and intimacy which we would wish. On the other hand, we also recognize that if Yugoslavia is not to be subservient to an outside power its internal regime is basically its own business. The character of that regime would not, in these circumstances, stand in the way of a normal development of economic relations between Yugoslavia and this country or—as far as we are concerned—between Yugoslavia and the countries of western Europe provided Yugoslavia is willing to adopt a loyal and cooperative attitude in its international relationships. However, the question of Yugoslavia's economic relationship with the countries of western Europe who are participating in the European Recovery Program is primarily a matter for those countries themselves rather than for us. If the Yugoslavs should demonstrate a wish to establish better relations with the west, this Government would not stand in the way of such a development.

3. The line which should be adhered to by representatives of this Department in discussing the *interpretation* of events in Yugoslavia should be substantially as follows:

Tito's defiance of the Cominform does not mean that Yugoslavia has "come over" to the west. Yugoslavia remains a communist state and its negative attitude toward the western democracies is as yet unchanged. Efforts will certainly be made to patch up the differences between Belgrade and Moscow. It is too early to predict what the success of these efforts will be. In any case, however, the international communist movement will never be able to make good entirely the damage done by this development. For the first time in the history of the movement, a servant of the international communist movement controlling territory, armed forces and a political organization, has defied, with at least temporary success, the authority of the Kremlin. This example will be noted by other communists everywhere. Eventually, the non-Russian communists will come to appreciate that they have no future as the servants of Kremlin policies.

Recommendation

The Policy Planning Staff recommends that the above conclusions be made the basis of a guidance directive to the Office of the Assistant Secretary for Public Affairs, and of instructions to all diplomatic missions and to important consular offices, to the end that representatives of this Government will exhibit a uniform reaction to the recent developments in Yugoslavia.

◇◇

22   **T O P   S E C R E T**

U.S. Objectives with Respect to Russia

NSC 20/1   August 18, 1948

[Source: Records of the National Security Council on deposit in the Modern Military Records Branch, National Archives, Washington, D.C.]

NSC 20/1 originated in response to a request from Secretary of Defense James V. Forrestal for a "comprehensive statement of national policy" with regard to the Soviet Union, on the grounds that until such a statement was prepared, "no logical decisions can be reached as to the proportion of our resources which should be devoted to military purposes. . . ." [1] Drafted by the Policy Planning Staff, this document represented the most complete exposition up to that time of the objectives the policy of containment was supposed to accomplish.

The document established two basic goals for U.S. policy toward the Soviet Union: (1) reduction of the power and influence of the U.S.S.R. to the point that they would no longer threaten international stability; and (2) accomplishment of a fundamental change in the theory and practice of international relations as applied by the Soviet government. Unlike NSC 7 (Document 20), NSC 20/1 stressed the distinction between the Soviet Union and the international communist movement, and, in line with the reasoning in PPS 35 (Document 21), held out the possibility of driving a wedge between the two of them as a means of implementing U.S. policy objectives.

NSC 20/1 emphasized the desirability of achieving containment's desired results by means short of war, although it recognized the possibility that war might come, whether by inadvertence or design. The final portion of the document dealt with the question of what U.S. policy should be in that eventuality. It is noteworthy for its stress on the neutralization, rather than the elimination, of Soviet power, and for its implied rejection of the World War II doctrine of unconditional surrender.

I. Introduction

It is plain that Russia, both as a force in its own right and as a center for the world communist movement, has become for the time being the outstanding problem of U.S. foreign policy, and that there is deep dissatisfaction and concern in this country over the aims and methods of the Soviet leaders. The policies of this Government are therefore determined in considerable measure by our desire to modify Soviet policies and to alter the international situation to which they have already led.

1. Forrestal to Sidney W. Souers, July 10, 1948, quoted in NSC 20, "Appraisal of the Degree and Character of Military Preparedness Required by the World Situation," July 12, 1948, *Foreign Relations of the United States: 1948,* I (part 2) 589–592.

However, there has yet been no clear formulation of basic U.S. objectives with respect to Russia. And it is particularly important, in view of the preoccupation of this Government with Russian affairs, that such objectives be formulated and accepted for working purposes by all branches of our Government dealing with the problems of Russia and communism. Otherwise, there is a possibility of serious dissipation of the national effort on a problem of outstanding international importance.

II. Background Considerations

There are two concepts of the relationship of national objectives to the factors of war and peace.

The first holds that national objectives be constant and should not be affected by changes in the country's situation as between war and peace; that they should be pursued constantly by means short of war or by war-like means, as the case may be. This concept was best expressed by Clausewitz, who wrote that, "War is a continuation of policy, intermingled with other means."

The opposite concept is that which sees national objectives in peace and national objectives in war as essentially unrelated. According to this concept, the existence of a state of war creates its own specific political objectives, which generally supersede the normal peacetime objectives. This is the concept which has generally prevailed in this country. Basically, it was the concept which prevailed in the last war, where the winning of the war itself, as a military operation, was made the supreme objective of U.S. policy, other considerations being subordinated to it.

In the case of American objectives with respect to Russia, it is clear that neither of these concepts can prevail entirely.

In the first place, this Government has been forced, for purposes of the political war now in progress, to consider more definite and militant objectives toward Russia even now, in time of peace, than it ever was called upon to formulate with respect either to Germany or Japan in advance of the actual hostilities with those countries.

Secondly, the experience of the past war has taught us the desirability of gearing our war effort to a clear and realistic concept of the long-term political objectives which we wish to achieve. This would be particularly important in the event of a war with the Soviet Union. We could hardly expect to conclude such a war with the same military and political finality as was the case in the recent war against Germany and Japan. Unless, therefore, it were clear to everyone that our objectives did not lie in military victory for its own sake, it might be hard for the U.S. public to recognize what would in reality be a favorable issue of the conflict. The public might expect much more in the way of military finality than would be necessary, or even desirable, from the standpoint of the actual achievement of our objectives. If people were to get the idea that our objectives were unconditional surrender, total occupation and military government, on the patterns of Germany and Japan, they would naturally feel that anything short of these achievements was no real victory at all, and might fail to appreciate a really genuine and constructive settlement.

Finally, we must recognize that Soviet objectives themselves are almost constant. They are very little affected by changes from war to peace. For example, Soviet territorial aims with respect to eastern Europe, as they became apparent during the war, bore a strong similarity to the program which the Soviet Government was endeavoring to realize by measures short of war in 1939 and 1940, and in fact to certain of the strategic-political concepts which underlay Czarist policy before World War I. To meet a policy of such constancy, so stubbornly pursued through both war and peace, it is necessary that we oppose it with purposes no less constant and enduring. Broadly speaking, this lies in the nature of the relationship between the Soviet Union and the outside world, which is one of permanent antagonism and conflict, taking place sometimes within a framework of formal peace and at other times within the legal framework of war.

On the other hand, it is clear that a democracy cannot effect, as the totalitarian state sometimes does, a complete identification of its peacetime and wartime objectives. Its aversion to war as a method of foreign policy is so strong that it will inevitably be inclined to modify its objectives in peacetime, in the hope that they may be achieved without resort to arms. When this hope and this restraint are removed by the outbreak of war, as a result of the provocation of others, the irritation of democratic opinion generally demands either the formulation of further objectives, often of a punitive nature, which it would not have supported in time of peace, or the immediate realization of aims which it might otherwise have been prepared to pursue patiently, by gradual pressures, over the course of decades. It would therefore be unrealistic to suppose that the U.S. Government could hope to proceed in time of war on the basis of exactly the same set of objectives, or at least with the same time-table for realization of objectives, which it would have in time of peace.

At the same time, it must be recognized that the smaller the gap between peacetime and wartime purposes, the greater the likelihood that a successful military effort will be politically successful as well. If objectives are really sound from the standpoint of national interest, they are worth consciously formulating and pursuing in war as in peace. Objectives which come into being as a consequence of wartime emotionalism are not apt to reflect a balanced concept of long-term national interest. For this reason, every effort should be made in government planning now, in advance of any outbreak of hostilities, to define our present peacetime objectives and our hypothetical wartime objectives with relation to Russia, and to reduce as far as possible the gap between them.

III. Basic Objectives

Our basic objectives with respect to Russia are really only two:
a. To reduce the power and influence of Moscow to limits in which they will no longer constitute a threat to the peace and stability of international society; and
b. To bring about a basic change in the theory and practice of international relations observed by the government in power in Russia.

If these two objectives could be achieved, the problem which this country faces in its relations with Russia would be reduced to what might be considered normal dimensions.

Before discussing the manner in which these objectives could be pursued in peace and in war, respectively, let us first examine them in somewhat greater detail.

1. THE GEOGRAPHIC REDUCTION OF RUSSIAN POWER AND INFLUENCE

There are two spheres in which the power and the influence of Moscow have been projected beyond the borders of the Soviet Union in ways detrimental to the peace and stability of international society.

The first of these spheres is what may be defined as the satellite area: namely, the area in which decisive political influence is exercised by the Kremlin. It should be noted that in this area, which is, as a whole, geographically contiguous to the Soviet Union, the presence, or proximity, of Soviet armed power has been a decisive factor in the establishment and maintenance of Soviet hegemony.

The second of these spheres embraces the relation between, on the one hand, the power center which controls the Soviet Union and, on the other, groups or parties in countries abroad, beyond the limits of the satellite area, which look to Russia for their political inspiration and give to it, consciously or otherwise, their basic loyalty.

In both of these spheres the projection of Russian power beyond its legitimate limits must be broken up if the achievement of the first of the objectives listed above is to be effectively served. The countries in the satellite area must be given the opportunity to free themselves fundamentally from Russia domination and from undue Russian ideological inspiration. And the myth which causes millions of people in countries far from the Soviet borders to look to Moscow as the outstanding source of hope for human betterment must be thoroughly exploded and its workings destroyed.

It should be noted that in both cases the objective can conceivably be achieved for the most part without raising issues in which the prestige of the Soviet state, as such, need necessarily be decisively engaged.

In the *second* of the two spheres, a *complete retraction* of undue Russian power should be possible without necessarily engaging the more vital interests of the Russian state; for in this sphere Moscow's power is exerted through carefully concealed channels, the existence of which Moscow itself denies. Therefore, a withering away of the structure of power which was formerly known as the Third International, and which has survived the disuse of that name, need involve no formal humiliation of the government in Moscow and no formal concessions on the part of the Soviet State.

The same is *largely true* of the *first* of these two spheres, but not entirely. In the satellite area, to be sure, Moscow likewise denies the formal fact of Soviet domination and attempts to conceal its mechanics. As has now been demonstrated in the Tito incidents, a breakdown of Moscow control is not necessarily regarded as an event affecting the respective *states* as such. In this instance, it is treated as a party affair by both sides; and particular care is taken everywhere to emphasize that no question of *state* prestige is involved. The same could presumably happen everywhere else throughout the satellite area without involving the formal dignity of the Soviet State.

We are confronted, however, with a more difficult problem in the actual extensions of the borders of the Soviet Union which have taken place since 1939. These extensions cannot in all cases be said to have been seriously detrimental to international peace and stability; and in certain instances it can probably be considered, from the standpoint of our objectives, that they can be entirely accepted for the sake of the maintenance of peace. In other cases, notably that of the Baltic countries, the question is more difficult. We cannot really profess indifference to the further fate of the Baltic peoples.

This has been reflected in our recognition policy to date with respect to those countries. And we could hardly consider that international peace and stability will really have ceased to be threatened as long as Europe is faced with the fact that it has been possible for Moscow to crush these three small countries which have been guilty of no real provocation and which have given evidence of their ability to handle their own affairs in a progressive manner, without detriment to the interests of their neighbors. It should therefore logically be considered a part of U.S. objectives to see these countries restored to something at least approaching a decent state of freedom and independence.

It is clear, however, that their complete independence would involve an actual cession of territory by the Soviet Government. It would therefore raise an issue directly involving the dignity and the vital interests of the Soviet State as such. It is idle to imagine that this could be brought about by means short of war. If, therefore, we are to consider that the basic objective outlined above is one which would be valid for peace as well as for war, then we must logically state that under conditions of peace our objective would be merely to induce Moscow to permit the return to the respective Baltic countries of all of their nationals who have been forcibly removed therefrom and the establishment in those countries of autonomous regimes generally consistent with the cultural needs and national aspirations of the peoples in question. In the event of war, we might, if necessary, wish to go further. But the answer to this question would depend on the nature of the Russian regime which would be dominant in that area in the wake of another war; and we need not attempt to decide it in advance.

In saying, consequently, that we should reduce the power and influence of the Kremlin to limits in which they will no longer constitute a threat to the peace and stability of international society, we are entitled to consider that this is an objective which can be logically pursued not only in the event of a war but also in time of peace and by peaceful means, and that in the latter case it need not necessarily raise issues of prestige for the Soviet Government which would automatically make war inevitable.

2. THE CHANGE IN THEORY AND PRACTICE OF INTERNATIONAL RELATIONS AS OBSERVED IN MOSCOW

Our difficulty with the present Soviet Government lies basically in the fact that its leaders are animated by concepts of the theory and practice of international relations which are not only radically opposed to our own but are clearly inconsistent with any peaceful and mutually profitable development of relations between that government and other members of the international community, individually and collectively.

Prominent among these concepts are the following:

(a) That the peaceful coexistence and mutual collaboration of sovereign and independent governments, regarding and respecting each other as equals, is an illusion and an impossibility;

(b) That conflict is the basis of international life wherever, as is the case between the Soviet Union and capitalist countries, one country does not recognize the supremacy of the other;

(c) That regimes which do not acknowledge Moscow's authority and ideological supremacy are wicked and harmful to human progress and that there is a duty on the part of right-thinking people everywhere to work for the overthrow or weakening of such regimes, by any and all methods which prove tactically desirable;

(d) That there can be, in the long run, no advancement of the interests of both the communist and non-communist world by mutual collaboration, these interests being basically conflicting and contradictory; and

(e) That spontaneous association between individuals in the communist-dominated world and individuals outside that world is evil and cannot contribute to human progress.

Plainly, it is not enough that these concepts should cease to dominate Soviet, or Russian, theory and practice in international relations. It is also necessary that they should be replaced by something approximating their converses.

These would be:

(a) That it *is* possible for sovereign and equal countries to exist peaceably side by side and to collaborate with each other without any thought or attempt at domination of one by the other;

(b) That conflict is *not* necessarily the basis of international life and that it may be accepted that peoples *can* have common purposes without being in entire ideological agreement and without being subordinated to a single authority;

(c) That people in other countries *do* have a legitimate right to pursue national aims at variance with Communist ideology, and that it is the *duty* of right-thinking people to practice tolerance for the ideas of others, to observe scrupulous non-interference in the internal affairs of others on the basis of reciprocity, and to use only decent and honorable methods in international dealings;

(d) That international collaboration *can,* and *should,* advance the interests of both parties even though the ideological inspiration of the two parties is not identical; and

(e) That the association of individuals across international borders *is* desirable and should be encouraged as a process contributing to general human progress.

Now the question at once arises as to whether the acceptance of such concepts in Moscow is an objective which we can seriously pursue and hope to achieve without resort to war and to the overthrow of the Soviet Government. We must face the fact that the Soviet Government, as we know it today, is, and will continue to be a constant threat to the peace of this nation and of the world.

It is quite clear that the present leaders of the Soviet Union can themselves never be brought to view concepts such as those indicated above as intrinsically sound and desirable. It is equally clear that for such concepts to become dominant throughout the Russian communist movement would mean, in present circumstances, an intellectual revolution within that movement which would amount to a metamorphosis of its political personality and a denial of its basic claim to existence as a separate and vital force among the ideological currents of the world at large. Concepts such as these could become dominant in the Russian communist movement only if, through a long process of change and erosion, that movement had outlived in name the impulses which had originally given it birth and vitality and had acquired a completely different significance in the world than that which it possesses today.

It might be concluded, then (and the Moscow theologians would be quick to put this interpretation on it), that to say that we were seeking the adoption of these concepts in Moscow would be equivalent to saying that it was our objective to overthrow Soviet power. Proceeding from that point, it could be argued that this is in turn an objective unrealizable by means short of war, and that we are therefore admitting that our objective with respect to the Soviet Union is eventual war and the violent overthrow of Soviet power.

It would be a dangerous error to accept this line of thought.

In the first place, there is no time limit for the achievement of our objectives under conditions of peace. We are faced here with no rigid periodicity of war and peace which would enable us to conclude that we must achieve our peacetime objectives by a given date "or else". The objectives of national policy in times of peace should never be regarded in static terms. In so far as they are basic objectives, and worthy ones, they are not apt to be ones capable of complete and finite achievement, like specific military objectives in war. The peacetime objectives of national policy should be thought of rather as lines of direction than as physical goals.

In the second place, we are entirely within our own rights, and need feel no sense of guilt, in working for the destruction of concepts inconsistent with world peace and stability and for their replacement by ones of tolerance and international collaboration. It is not our business to calculate the internal developments to which the adoption of such concepts might lead in another country, nor need we feel that we have any responsibility for those developments. If the Soviet leaders find the growing prevalence of a more enlightened concept of international relations to be inconsistent with the maintenance of their internal power in Russia, that is their responsibility, not ours. That is a matter for their own consciences, and for the conscience of the peoples of the Soviet Union. We are not only within our moral rights but within our moral duty in working for the adoption everywhere of decent and hopeful concepts of international life. In doing so, we are entitled to let the chips fall where they may in terms of internal development.

We do not know for certain that the successful pursuit by us of the objectives in question would lead to the disintegration of Soviet power; for we do not know the time factor here involved. It is entirely possible that under the stress of time and circumstance certain of the original concepts of the communist movement might be gradually modified in Russia as were certain of the original concepts of the American revolution in our own country.

We are entitled, therefore, to consider, and to state publicly, that it is our objective to bring to the Russian people and government, by every means at our disposal, a more enlightened concept of international relations, and that in so doing we are not taking any position, as a government, with respect to internal conditions in Russia.

In the case of war, there could clearly be no question of this nature. Once a state of war had arisen between this country and the Soviet Union, this Government would be at liberty to pursue the achievement of its basic objectives by whatever means it might choose and by whatever terms it might wish to impose upon a Russian authority or Russian authorities in the event of a successful issue of military operations. Whether these terms would embrace the overthrow of Soviet power would be only a question of expediency, which will be discussed below.

This second of the two basic objectives is therefore also one likewise susceptible of pursuit in time of peace as in time of war. This objective, like the first, may accordingly be accepted as an underlying one, from which the formulation of our policy, in peace as in war, may proceed.

IV. The Pursuit of Our Basic Objectives in Time of Peace

In discussing the interpretation which would be given to these basic objectives in time of peace or in time of war respectively, we are confronted with a problem of terminology. If we continue to speak of the particular orientation lines of our policy in peace or in war as "objectives", we may find ourselves falling into a semantic confusion. Solely for the purposes of clarity, therefore, we will make an arbitrary distinction. We will speak of objectives only in the sense of the basic objectives outlined above, which are common both to war and peace. When we refer to our guiding purposes as applied specifically in our wartime or peactime policy, respectively, we will speak of "aims" rather than of "objectives".

What then would be the aims of U.S. national policy with respect to Russia in time of peace?

These should flow logically from the two main objectives discussed above.

1. THE RETRACTION OF RUSSIAN POWER AND INFLUENCE

Let us first consider the retraction of undue Russian power and influence. We have seen that this divided into the problem of the satellite area and the problem of communist activities and Soviet propaganda activities in countries farther afield.

With respect to the satellite area, the aim of U.S. policy in time of peace is to place the greatest possible strain on the structure of relationships by which Soviet domination of this area is maintained and gradually, with the aid of the natural and legitimate forces of Europe, to maneuver the Russians out of their position of primacy and to enable the respective governments to regain their independence of action. There are many ways in which this aim can be, and is being, pursued. The most striking step in this direction was the original proposal for the ERP, as stated in Secretary Marshall's Harvard speech on June 5, 1947. By forcing the Russians either to permit the satellite countries to enter into a relationship of economic collaboration with the west of Europe which would inevitably have strengthened east-west bonds and weakened the exclusive orientation of these countries toward Russia or to force them to remain outside this structure of collaboration at heavy economic sacrifice to themselves, we placed a severe strain on the relations between Moscow and the satellite countries and undoubtedly made more awkward and difficult maintenance by Moscow of its exclusive authority in the satellite capitals. Everything, in fact, which operates to tear off the veil with which Moscow likes to screen its power, and which forces the Russians to reveal the crude and ugly outlines of their hold over the governments of the satellite countries, serves to discredit the satellite governments with their own peoples and to heighten the discontent of those peoples and their desire for free association with other nations.

The disaffection of Tito, to which the strain caused by the ERP problem undoubtedly contributed in some measure, has clearly demonstrated that it *is* possible for stresses in the Soviet-satellite relations to lead to a real weakening and disruption of the Russian domination.

It should therefore be our aim to continue to do all in our power to increase these stresses and at the same time to make it possible for the satellite governments gradually to extricate themselves from Russian control and to find, if they so wish, acceptable forms of collaboration with the governments of the west. This can be done by skillful use of our economic power, by direct or indirect informational activity, by placing the greatest possible strain on the maintenance of the iron curtain, and by building up the hope and vigor of western Europe to a point where it comes to exercise the maximum attraction to the peoples of the east, and by other means too numerous to mention.

We cannot say, of course, that the Russians will sit by and permit the satellites to extricate themselves from Russian control in this way. We cannot be sure that at some point in this process the Russians will not choose to resort to violence of some sort: i.e., to forms of military re-occupation or possibly even to a major war, to prevent such a process from being carried to completion.

It is not our desire that they should do this; and we, for our part, should do everything possible to keep the situation flexible and to make possible a liberation of the satellite countries in ways which do not create any unanswerable challenge to Soviet prestige. But even with the greatest of circumspection we cannot be sure that they will not choose to resort to arms. We cannot hope to influence their policy automatically or to produce any guaranteed results.

The fact that we embark on a policy which *can* lead to these results does not mean that we are setting our course toward war; and we should be extremely careful to make this plain on all occasions and to refute accusations of this character. The fact of the matter is that, granted the relationship of antagonism which is still basic to the entire relationships between the Soviet Government and non-communist countries at this time, war is an ever-present possibility and *no* course which this Government might adopt would appreciably diminish this danger. The converse of the policy set forth above, namely to accept Soviet domination of the satellite countries and to do nothing to oppose it, would not diminish in any way the danger of war. On the contrary, it can be argued with considerable logic that the long-term danger of war will inevitably be greater if Europe remains split along the present lines than it will be if Russian power is peacefully withdrawn in good time and a normal balance restored to the European community.

It may be stated, accordingly, that our first aim with respect to Russia in time of peace is to encourage and promote by means short of war the gradual retraction of undue Russian power and influence from the present satellite area and the emergence of the respective eastern European countries as independent factors on the international scene.

However, as we have seen above, our examination of this problem is not complete unless we have taken into consideration the question of areas now behind the Soviet border. Do we wish, or do we not, to make it our objective to achieve by means short of war any modification of the borders of the Soviet Union? We have already seen in Chapter III the answer to this question.

We should encourage by every means at our disposal the development in the Soviet Union of institutions of federalism which would permit a revival of the national life of the Baltic peoples.

It may be asked: Why do we restrict this aim to the Baltic peoples? Why do we not include the other national minority groups of the Soviet Union? The answer is that the Baltic peoples happen to be the only peoples whose traditional territory and population are now entirely included in the Soviet Union and who have shown themselves capable of coping successfully with the responsibilities of statehood. Moreover, we still formally deny the legitimacy of their violent inclusion in the Soviet Union, and they therefore have a special status in our eyes.

Next we have the problem of the disruption of the myth by which the people in Moscow maintain their undue influence and actual disciplinary authority over millions of people in countries beyond the satellite area. First a word about the nature of this problem.

Before the revolution of 1918, Russian nationalism was solely Russian. Except for a few eccentric European intellectuals of the 19th Century, who even then professed to a mystical faith in Russia's power to solve the ills of civilization,[2] Russian nationalism had no appeal to people outside Russia. On the contrary, the relatively mild despotism of the 19th Century Russian

2. Karl Marx was not one of these people. He was not, as he himself put it, "one of those who believed that the old Europe could be revived by Russian blood." [Note in source text]

rulers was perhaps better known and more universally deplored in the western countries than has since been the case with the far greater cruelties of the Soviet regime.

After the revolution, the Bolshevik leaders succeeded, through clever and systematic propaganda, in establishing throughout large sections of the world public certain concepts highly favorable to their own purposes, including the following: that the October Revolution was a popular revolution; that the Soviet regime was the first real worker's government; that Soviet power was in some way connected with ideals of liberalism, freedom and economic security; and that it offered a promising alternative to the national regimes under which other peoples lived. A connection was thus established in the minds of many people between Russian communism and the general uneasiness arising in the outside world from the effects of urbanization and industrialization, or from colonial unrest.

In this way Moscow's doctrine became to some extent a domestic problem for every nation in the world. In Soviet power, western statesmen are now facing something more than just another problem of foreign affairs. They are facing also an internal enemy in their own countries—an enemy committed to the undermining and eventual destruction of their respective national societies.

To destroy this myth of international communism is a dual task. It takes two parties to create an inter-action such as that which exists between the Kremlin, on the one hand, and the discontented intellectuals in other countries (for it is the intellectuals rather than the "workers" who make up the hard core of communism outside the USSR), on the other. It is not enough to tackle this problem by aiming to silence the propagator. It is even more important to arm the listener against this sort of attack. There is some reason why Moscow propaganda is listened to so avidly, and why this myth takes hold so readily, among many people far from the boundaries of Russia. If it were not Moscow these people listened to, it would be something else, equally extreme and equally erroneous, though possibly less dangerous. Thus the task of destroying the myth on which international communism rests is not just an undertaking relating to the leaders of the Soviet Union. It is also something relating to the non-Soviet world, and above all to the particular society of which each of us forms a part. To the extent to which we can dispel the confusion and misunderstandings on which these doctrines thrive—to the extent that we can remove the sources of bitterness which drive people to irrational and utopian ideas of this sort—we will succeed in breaking down the ideological influence of Moscow in foreign countries.

On the other hand, we must recognize that *only a portion* of international communism outside Russia is the result of environmental influence and subject to correction accordingly. Another portion represents something in the nature of a natural mutation of species. It derives from a congenital fifth-columnism with which a certain small percentage of people in every community appear to be affected, and which distinguishes itself by a negative attitude toward the native society and a readiness to follow any outside force which opposes it. This element will always be present in any society for unscrupulous outsiders to work on; and the only protection against its dangerous misuse will be the absence of the will on the part of great-power regimes to exploit this unhappy margin of human nature.

Fortunately, the Kremlin has thus far done more than we ourselves could ever have done to dispel the very myth by which it operates. The Yugoslav incident is perhaps the most striking case in point; but the history of the Communist International is replete with other instances of the difficulty non-Russian individuals and groups have encountered in trying to be the followers of Moscow doctrines. The Kremlin leaders are so inconsiderate, so relentless, so over-bearing and so cynical in the discipline they impose on their followers that few can stand their authority for very long.

The Leninist-Stalinist system is founded, basically, on the power which a desperate, conspiratorial minority can always wield, at least temporarily, over a passive and unorganized majority of human beings. For this reason, the Kremlin leaders have had little concern, in the past, about the tendency of their movement to leave in its train a steady backwash of disillusioned former followers. Their aim was not to have communism become a mass movement but rather to work through a small group of faultlessly disciplined and entirely expendable followers. They were always content to let those peoples go who could not stomach their particular brand of discipline.

For a long time, this worked reasonably well. New recruits were easy to obtain; and the Party lived by a steady process of natural selection-out, which left within its ranks only the most fanatically devoted, the most unimaginative, and the most obtusely unscrupulous natures.

The Yugoslav case has now raised a great question mark as to how well this system will work in the future. Heretofore, heresy could safely be handled by police repression within the limits of Soviet power or by a tested process of excommunication and character-assassination outside those limits. Tito has demonstrated that in the case of the satellite leaders, neither of these methods is necessarily effective. Excommunication of communist leaders who are beyond the effective range of Soviet power and who themselves have territory, police power, military power, and disciplined followers, can split the whole communist movement, as nothing else was ever able to do, and cause the most grievous damage to the myth of Stalin's omniscience and omnipotence.

Conditions are therefore favorable to a concentrated effort on our part designed to take advantage of Soviet mistakes and of the rifts that have appeared, and to promote the steady deterioration of the structure of moral influence by which the authority of the Kremlin has been carried to peoples far beyond the reach of Soviet police power.

We may say, therefore, that our second aim with respect to Russia in time of peace is, by informational activity and by every other means at our disposal, to explode the myth by which people remote from Russian military influence are held in a position of subservience to Moscow and to cause the world at large to see and understand the Soviet Union for what it is and to adopt a logical and realistic attitude toward it.

2. THE ALTERATION OF RUSSIAN CONCEPTS OF INTERNATIONAL AFFAIRS

We come now to the interpretation, in terms of peacetime policy, of our second major objective: namely, to bring about an alteration of the concepts of international relations prevalent in Moscow governing circles.

As has been seen above, there is no reasonable prospect that we will ever be able to alter the basic political psychology of the men now in power in the Soviet Union. The malevolent character of their outlook on the outside world, their repudiation of the possibility of permanent peaceful collaboration, their belief in the inevitability of the eventual destruction of the one world by the other: these things must remain, if only for the simple reason that the Soviet leaders are convinced that their own system will not stand comparison with the civilization of the west and that it will never be secure until the example of a prosperous and powerful western civilization has been physically obliterated and its memory discredited. This is not to mention the fact that these men are committed to the theory of inevitable conflict between the two worlds by the strongest of all commitments: namely, the fact that they have inflicted the punishment of death or of great suffering and hardship on millions of people in the name of this theory.

On the other hand, the Soviet leaders are prepared to recognize *situations,* if not arguments. If, therefore, situations can be created in which it is clearly not to the advantage of their power to emphasize the elements of conflict in their relations with the outside world, then their actions, and even the tenor of their propaganda to their own people, *can* be modified. This was made

evident in the recent war when the circumstances of their military association with the western powers had the effect just described. In this instance,
the modification of their policies was of relatively short duration; for with
the end of hostilities they thought they saw an opportunity for gaining important objectives of their own regardless of the feelings and views of the
western powers. This meant that the situation which had caused them to
modify their policies no longer appeared to them to exist.

If, however, analogous situations could again be created in the future and
the Soviet leaders compelled to recognize their reality, and if these situations
could be maintained for a longer time, i.e., for a period long enough to en-
compass a respectable portion of the organic process of growth and change
in Soviet political life, then they might have a permanent modifying effect
on the outlook and habits of Soviet power. Even the relatively brief and per-
functory lip service done during the recent war to the possibility of collaboration among the major allies left a deep mark on the consciousness of the
Russian public, and one which has undoubtedly caused serious difficulties to
the regime, since the end of the war, in its attempt to revert to the old
policies of hostility and subversion toward the western world. Yet all this
occurred in a period in which there was absolutely no turnover of any importance in the Soviet leadership and no normal evolution of internal political
life in the Soviet Union. Had it been necessary for the Soviet Government to
observe these policies of circumspection and moderation toward the west for
so long a period that the present leaders would have had to yield to other
ones and that there would have been some normal evolution of Soviet political life in the face of these necessities, then it is possible that some real
modification in Soviet outlook and behavior might eventually have been
achieved.

It flows from this discussion that whereas we will not be able to alter the
basic political psychology of the present Soviet leaders, there is a possibility
that if we can create situations which, if long enough maintained, may cause
them to soft-pedal their dangerous and improper attitude toward the west and
to observe a relative degree of moderation and caution in their dealings with
western countries. In this case, we could really say that we had begun to
make progress toward a gradual alteration of the dangerous concepts which
now underlie Soviet behavior.

Again, as in the case of the retraction of Soviet power, and, in fact, as in
the case of any sound program of resistance to Soviet attempts at the destruction of western civilization, we must recognize that the Soviet leaders
may see the writing on the wall and may prefer to resort to violence rather

than to permit these things to occur. It must be reiterated: that is the risk which we run not just in this, but in any sound policy toward the Soviet Union. It is inherent in the present nature of the Soviet Government; and nothing we may do can alter or remove it. This is not a problem new to the foreign relations of the United States. In the *Federalist Papers,* Alexander Hamilton stated:

"Let us recollect that peace or war will not always be left to our option; that however moderate or unambitious we may be, we cannot count upon the moderation, or hope to extinguish the ambition, of others."

In setting out, therefore, to alter the concepts by which the Soviet Government now operates in world affairs, we must again concede that the question of whether this aim can be achieved by peaceful means cannot be answered entirely by ourselves. But this does not excuse us from making the attempt.

We must say, therefore, that our third aim with respect to Russia in time of peace is to create situations which will compel the Soviet Government to recognize the practical undesirability of acting on the basis of its present concepts and the necessity of behaving, at least outwardly, as though it were the converse of those concepts that were true.

This is of course primarily a question of keeping the Soviet Union politically, militarily, psychologically weak in comparison with the international forces outside of its control and of maintaining a high degree of insistence among the non-communist countries on the observance by Russia of the ordinary international decencies.

3. SPECIFIC AIMS

The aims listed above are all general in nature. To attempt to make them specific would lead us into an endless maze of attempts at verbal classification and would probably be more confusing than clarifying. For this reason, no attempt will be made here to spell out the possible forms of specific application of these aims. Many of these forms will easily suggest themselves to any who give thought to the interpretation of these general aims in terms of practical policy and action. It will be seen for example, that a major factor in the achievement of all of these aims without exception, would be the degree to which we might succeed in penetrating or disrupting the iron curtain.

However, the question of specific interpretation may be considerably clarified by a brief indication of the negative side of the picture: in other words, by pointing out what our aims are *not.*

First of all, it is not our primary aim in time of peace to set the stage for a war regarded as inevitable. We do not regard war as inevitable. We do not repudiate the possibility that our overall objectives with respect to Russia may be successfully pursued without resort to war. We have to recognize the possibility of war, as something flowing logically and at all times from the present attitude of the Soviet leaders; and we have to prepare realistically for that eventuality.

But it would be wrong to consider that our policy rested on an assumption of an inevitability of war and was confined to preparations for an armed conflict. That is not the case. Our task at present, in the absence of a state of war automatically brought about by the actions of others, is to find means of pursuing our objectives successfully without resort to war ourselves. It includes preparations for a possible war, but we regard these as only subsidiary and precautionary rather than as the primary element of policy. We are still hoping and striving to achieve our objectives within the framework of peace. Should we at any time come to the conclusion (which is not excluded) that this is really impossible and that the relations between communist and non-communist worlds cannot proceed without eventual armed conflict, then the whole basis of this paper would be changed and our peacetime aims, as set forth herein, would have to be basically altered.

Secondly, it is not our peacetime aim to overthrow the Soviet Government. Admittedly, we are aiming at the creation of circumstances and situations which would be difficult for the present Soviet leaders to stomach, and which they would not like. It is possible that they might not be able, in the face of these circumstances and situations, to retain their power in Russia. But it must be reiterated: that is their business, not ours. This paper implies no judgment as to whether it is possible for the Soviet Government to behave with relative decency and moderation in external affairs and yet to retain its internal power in Russia. Should the situations to which our peacetime aims are directed actually come into being and should they prove intolerable to the maintenance of internal Soviet power and cause the Soviet Government to leave the scene, we would view this development without regret; but we would not assume responsibility for having sought it or brought it about.

V. The Pursuit of our Basic Objectives in Time of War

This chapter treats of our aims with respect to Russia in the event that a state of war should arise between the United States and the USSR. It proposes to set forth what we would seek as a favorable issue of our military operations.

1. THE IMPOSSIBILITIES

Before entering into a discussion of what we *should* aim to achieve in a war with Russia, let us first be clear in our own minds about those things which we *could not hope* to achieve.

In the first place we must assume that it will not be profitable or practically feasible for us to occupy and take under our military administration the entire territory of the Soviet Union. This course is inhibited by the size of that territory, by the number of its inhabitants, by the differences of language and custom which separate its inhabitants from ourselves, and by the improbability that we would find any adequate apparatus of local authority through which we could work.

Secondly, and in consequence of this first admission, we must recognize that it is not likely that the Soviet leaders would surrender unconditionally to us. It is possible that Soviet power might disintegrate during the stress of an unsuccessful war, as did that of the tsar's regime during World War I. But even this is not likely. And if it did not so disintegrate, we could not be sure that we could eliminate it by any means short of an extravagant military effort designed to bring all of Russia under our control. We have before us in our experience with the Nazis an example of the stubbornness and tenacity with which a thoroughly ruthless and dictatorial regime can maintain its internal power even over a territory constantly shrinking as a consequence of military operations. The Soviet leaders would be capable of concluding a compromise peace, if pressed, and even one highly unfavorable to their own interests. But it is not likely that they would do anything, such as to surrender unconditionally, which would place themselves under the complete power of a hostile authority. Rather than do that, they would probably retire to the most remote village of Siberia and eventually perish, as Hitler did, under the guns of the enemy.

There is a strong possibility that if we were to take the utmost care, within limits of military feasibility, not to antagonize the Soviet people by military policies which would inflict inordinate hardship and cruelties upon them, there would be an extensive disintegration of Soviet power during the course of a war which progressed favorably from our standpoint. We would certainly be entirely justified in promoting such a disintegration with every means at our disposal. This does not mean, however, that we could be sure of achieving the complete overthrow of the Soviet regime, in the sense of the removal of its power over *all* the present territory of the Soviet Union.

Regardless of whether or not Soviet power endures on any of the present Soviet territory we cannot be sure of finding among the Russian people any other group of political leaders who would be entirely "democratic" as we understand that term.

While Russia has had her moments of liberalism, the concepts of democracy are not familiar to the great mass of the Russian people, and particularly not to those who are temperamentally inclined to the profession of government. At the present time, there are a number of interesting and powerful Russian political groupings, among the Russian exiles, all of which do lip service to principles of liberalism, to one degree or another, and any of which would probably be preferable to the Soviet Government, from our standpoint, as the rulers of Russia. But just how liberal these groupings would be, if they once had power, or what would be their ability to maintain their authority among the Russian people without resort to methods of police terror and repression, no one knows. The actions of people in power are often controlled far more by the circumstances in which they are obliged to exercise that power than by the ideas and principles which animated them when they were in the opposition. In turning over the powers of government to any Russian group, it would never be possible for us to be certain that those powers would be exercised in a manner which our own people would approve. We would therefore always be taking a chance, in making such a choice, and incurring a responsibility which we could not be sure of meeting creditably.

Finally, we cannot hope really to impose our concepts of democracy within a short space of time upon any group of Russian leaders. In the long run, the political psychology of any regime which is even reasonably responsive to the will of the people must be that of the people themselves. But it has been vividly demonstrated through our experience in Germany and Japan that the psychology and outlook of a great people cannot be altered in a short space of time at the mere dictate or precept of a foreign power, even in the wake of total defeat and submission. Such alteration can flow only from the organic political experience of the people in question. The best that can be done by one country to bring about this sort of alteration in another is to change the environmental influences to which the people in question are subjected, leaving it to them to react to those influences in their own way.

All of the above indicates that we could not expect, in the aftermath of successful military operations in Russia, to create there an authority entirely submissive to our will or entirely expressive of our political ideals. We must reckon with the strong probability that we would have to continue to deal, in one degree or another, with Russian authorities of whom we will not entirely approve, who will have purposes different from ours, and whose views and desiderata we will be obliged to take into consideration whether we like them or not. In other words, we could not hope to achieve any total assertion of our will on Russian territory, as we have endeavored to do in Germany and in Japan. We must recognize that whatever settlement we finally achieve must be a *political* settlement, *politically* negotiated.

So much for the impossibilities. Now what would be our possible and desirable aims in the event of a war with Russia? These, like the aims of peace, should flow logically from the basic objectives set forth in Chapter III.

2. THE RETRACTION OF SOCIET POWER

The first of our war aims must naturally be the destruction of Russian military influence and domination in areas contiguous to, but outside of, the borders of any Russian state.

Plainly, a successful prosecution of the war on our part would automatically achieve this effect throughout most, if not all, of the satellite area. A succession of military defeats to the Soviet forces would probably so undermine the authority of the communist regimes in the eastern European countries that most of them would be overthrown. Pockets might remain, in the form of political Tito-ism, i.e., residual communist regimes of a purely national and local character. These we could probably afford to by-pass. Without the might and authority of Russia behind them, they would be sure either to disappear with time or to evolve into normal national regimes with no more and no less of chauvinism and extremism than is customary to strong national governments in that area. We would of course insist on the cancellation of any formal traces of abnormal Russian power in that area, such as treaties of alliance, etc.

Beyond this, however, we have again the problem of *the extent to which we would wish Soviet borders modified as a result of a successful military action in our part. We must face frankly the fact that we cannot answer this question at this time.* The answer depends almost everywhere on the type of regime which would be left, in the wake of military operations, in the particular area in question. Should this regime be one which held out at least reasonably favorable prospects of observing the principles of liberalism in internal affairs and moderation in foreign policy, it might be possible to leave under its authority most, if not all, of the territories gained by the Soviet Union in the recent war. If, as is more probable, little dependence could be placed on the liberalism and moderation of a post-hostilities Russian authority, it might be necessary to alter these borders quite extensively. This must simply be chalked up as one of the questions which will have to be left open until the development of military and political events in Russia reveals to us the full nature of the post-war framework in which we will have to act.

We then have the question of the Soviet myth and of the ideological authority which the Soviet Government now exerts over people beyond the present satellite area. In the first instance, this will of course depend on the question of whether or not the present All-Union Communist Party continues to exert authority over any portion of the present Soviet territory, in the aftermath of another war. We have already seen that we cannot rule out this possibility. Should communist authority disappear, this question is automatically solved. It must be assumed, however, that in any event an unsuccessful issue of the war itself, from the Soviet standpoint, would probably deal a decisive blow to this form of the projection of Soviet power and influence.

However that may be, we must leave nothing to chance; and it should naturally be considered that one of our major war aims with respect to Russia would be *to destroy thoroughly the structure of relationships by which the leaders of the All-Union Communist Party have been able to exert moral and disciplinary authority over individual citizens, or groups of citizens, in countries not under communist control.*

3. THE ALTERATION OF THE RUSSIAN CONCEPTS OF INTERNATIONAL RELATIONS

Our next problem is again that of the concepts by which Russian policy would be governed in the aftermath of a war. How would we assure ourselves that Russian policy would henceforth be conducted along lines as close as possible to those which we have recognized above as desirable? This is the heart of the problem of our war aims with respect to Russia; and it cannot be given too serious attention.

In the first instance this is a problem of the future of Soviet power: that is, of the power of the communist party in the Soviet Union. This is an extremely intricate question. There is no simple answer to it. We have seen that while we would welcome, and even strive for, the complete disintegration and disappearance of Soviet power, we could not be sure of achieving this entirely. We could therefore view this as a maximum, but not a minimum, aim.

Assuming, then, that there might be a portion of Soviet territory on which we would find it expedient to tolerate the continued existence of Soviet power, upon the conclusion of military operations, what should be our relationship to it? Would we consent to deal with it at all? If so, what sort of terms would we be willing to make?

First of all, we may accept it as a foregone conclusion that we would not be prepared to conclude a full-fledged peace settlement and/or resume regular diplomatic relations with any regime in Russia dominated by any of the present Soviet leaders or persons sharing their cast of thought. We have had too bitter an experience, during the past fifteen years, with the effort to act as though normal relations were possible with such a regime; and if we should now be forced to resort to war to protect ourselves from the consequences of their policies and actions, our public would hardly be in a mood to forgive the Soviet leaders for having brought things to this pass, or to resume the attempt at normal collaboration.

On the other hand, if a communist regime were to remain on any portion of Soviet territory, upon the conclusion of military operations, we could not afford to ignore it entirely. It could not fail to be, within the limits of its own possibilities, a potential menace to the peace and stability of Russia itself and of the world. The least we could do would be to see to it that its possibilities for mischief were so limited that it could not do serious damage, and that we ourselves, or forces friendly to us, would retain all the necessary controls.

For this, two things would probably be necessary. The first would be the actual physical limitation of the power of such a residual Soviet regime to make war or to threaten and intimidate other nations or other Russian regimes. Should military operations lead to any drastic curtailment of the territory over which the communists held sway, particularly such a curtailment as would deprive them of key factors in the present military-industrial structure of the Soviet Union, this physical limitation would automatically flow from that. Should the territory under their control not be substantially diminished, the same result could be obtained by extensive destruction of important industrial and economic targets from the air. Possibly, both of these means might be required. However that may be,

we may definitely conclude that we could not consider our military operations successful if they left a communist regime in control of enough of the present military-industrial potential of the Soviet Union to enable them to wage war on comparable terms with any neighboring state or with any rival authority which might be set up on traditional Russian territory.

The second thing required, if Soviet authority is to endure at all in the traditional Russian territories, will probably be some sort of terms defining at least its military relationship to ourselves and to the authorities surrounding it. In other words, it may be necessary for us to make some sort of deal with a regime of this sort. This may sound distasteful to us now, but it is quite possible that we would find our interests better protected by such a deal than by the all-out military effort which would be necessary to stamp out Soviet power entirely.

It is safe to say that such terms would have to be harsh ones and distinctly humiliating to the communist regime in question. They might well be something along the lines of the Brest-Litovsk settlement of 1918[3] which deserves careful study in this connection. The fact that the Germans made this settlement did not mean that they had really accepted the permanency of the Soviet regime. They regarded the settlement as one which rendered the Soviet regime momentarily harmless to them and in a poor position to face the problems of survival. The Russians realized that this was the German purpose. They agreed to the settlement only with the greatest of reluctance, and with every intention of violating it at every opportunity. But the German superiority of force was real; and the German calculations realistic. Had Germany not suffered defeat in the west soon after the conclusion of the Brest-Litovsk agreement, it is not likely that the Soviet Government would have been able to put up any serious opposition to the accomplishment of German purposes with respect to Russia. It is in this sense that it might be necessary for this Government to deal with the Soviet regime in the latter phases of an armed conflict.

It is impossible to forecast what the nature of such terms should be. The smaller the territory left at the disposal of such a regime, the easier the task of imposing terms satisfactory to our interests. Taking the worst case, which would be that of the retention of Soviet power over all, or nearly all, of present Soviet territory, we would have to demand:

   (a) *Direct military terms* (surrender of equipment, evacuation of key areas, etc.) designed to assure military helplessness for a long time in advance;

   (b) *Terms designed to produce a considerable economic dependence on the outside world;*

3. Treaty of Brest-Litovsk, signed March 3, 1918, ended hostilities between Soviet Russia and the Central Powers on the basis of provisions that included the independence of the Ukraine, Georgia, Finland, the transfer to the Central Powers of Poland, the Baltic States, and portions of Byelorussia, and the cession of Kars, Ardahan, and Batum to Turkey. As part of the armistice agreement between Germany and the Western Powers on November 11, 1918, Germany was forced to repudiate this treaty. [Ed. note]

(c) *Terms designed to give necessary freedom, or federal status, to national minorities* (we would at least have to insist on the complete liberation of the Baltic States and on the granting of some type of federal status to the Ukraine which would make it possible for a Ukrainian local authority to have a large measure of autonomy); and

(d) *Terms designed to disrupt the iron curtain* and to assure a liberal flow of outside ideas and a considerable establishment of personal contact between persons within the zone of Soviet power and persons outside it.

So much for our aims with respect to any residual *Soviet* authority. There remains the question of what our aims would be with respect to any *non-communist* authority which might be set up on a portion or all of Russian territory as a consequence of the events of war.

First of all, it should be said that regardless of the ideological basis of any such non-communist authority and regardless of the extent to which it might be prepared to do lip service to the ideals of democracy and liberalism, we would do well to see that in one way or another the basic purposes were assured which flow from the demands listed above. In other words, we should set up automatic safeguards to assure that even a regime which is non-communist and nominally friendly to us:

(a) Does not have strong military power;

(b) Is economically dependent to a considerable extent on the outside world;

(c) Does not exercise too much authority over the major national minorities; and

(d) Imposes nothing resembling the iron curtain over contacts with the outside world.

In the case of such a regime, professing hostility to the communists and friendship toward us, we should doubtless wish to take care to impose these conditions in a manner which would not be offensive or humiliating. But we would have to see to it that in one way or another they *were* imposed, if our interests and the interests of world peace were to be protected.

We are therefore safe in saying that it should be our aim in the event of war with the Soviet Union, to see to it that when the war was over no regime on Russian territory is permitted:

(a) To retain military force on a scale which could be threatening to any neighboring state;

(b) To enjoy a measure of economic autarchy which would permit the erection of the economic basis of such armed power without the assistance of the western world;

(c) To deny autonomy and self-government to the main national minorities; or

(d) To retain anything resembling the present iron curtain.

If these conditions are assured, we can adjust ourselves to any political situation which may ensue from the war. We will then be safe, whether a Soviet government retains the bulk of Russian territory or whether it retains only a small part of such territory or whether it disappears altogether. And we will be safe even though the original democratic enthusiasm of a new regime is short-lived and tends to be replaced gradually by the a-social concepts of international affairs to which the present Soviet generation has been educated.

The above should be adequate as an expression of our war aims *in the event that political processes in Russia take their own course* under the stresses of war and that we are not obliged to assume major responsibility for the political future of the country. But there are further questions to be answered for *the event that Soviet authority should disintegrate* so *rapidly* and so radically as to leave the country in chaos, making it encumbent upon us as the victors to make political choices and to take decisions which would be apt to shape the political future of the country. For this eventuality there are three main questions which must be faced.

4. PARTITION VS. NATIONAL UNITY

First of all, would it be our desire, in such a case, that the present territories of the Soviet Union remain united under a single regime or that they be partitioned? And if they are to remain united, at least to a large extent, then what degree of federalism should be observed in a future Russian government? What about the major minority groups, in particular the Ukraine?

We have already taken note of the problem of the Baltic states. The Baltic states should not be compelled to remain under any communist authority in the aftermath of another war. Should the territory adjacent to the Baltic states be controlled by a Russian authority other than a communist authority, we should be guided by the wishes of the Baltic peoples and by the degree of moderation which that Russian authority is inclined to exhibit with respect to them.

In the case of the Ukraine, we have a different problem. The Ukrainians are the most advanced of the peoples who have been under Russian rule in modern times. They have generally resented Russian domination; and their nationalistic organizations have been active and vocal abroad. It would be easy to jump to the conclusion that they should be freed, at last, from Russian rule and permitted to set themselves up as an independent state.

We would do well to beware of this conclusion. Its very simplicity condemns it in terms of eastern European realities.

It is true that the Ukrainians have been unhappy under Russian rule and that something should be done to protect their position in future. But there are certain basic facts which must not be lost sight of. While the Ukrainians have been an important and specific element in the Russian empire, they have shown no signs of being a "nation" capable of bearing successfully the responsibilities of independence in the face of great Russian opposition. The Ukraine is not a clearly defined ethnical or geographic concept. In general, the Ukrainian population made up of originally in large measure out of refugees from Russian or Polish despotism shades off imperceptibly into the Russian or Polish nationalities. There is no clear dividing line between Russia and the Ukraine, and it would be impossible to establish one. The cities in Ukrainian territory have been predominantly Russian and Jewish. The real basis of "Ukrainianism" is the feeling of "difference" produced by a specific peasant dialect and by minor differences of custom and folklore throughout the country districts. The political agitation on the surface is largely the work of a few romantic intellectuals, who have little concept of the responsibilities of government.

The economy of the Ukraine is inextricably intertwined with that of Russia as a whole. There has never been any economic separation since the territory was conquered from the nomadic Tatars and developed for purposes of a sedentary population. To attempt to carve it out of the Russian economy and to set it up as something separate would be as artificial and as destructive as an attempt to separate the Corn Belt, including the Great Lakes industrial area, from the economy of the United States.

Furthermore, the people who speak the Ukrainian dialect have been split, like those who speak the White Russian dialect, by a division which in eastern Europe has always been the real mark of nationality: namely, religion. If any real border can be drawn in the Ukraine, it should logically be the border between the areas which traditionally give religious allegiance to the Eastern Church and those which give it to the Church of Rome.

Finally, we cannot be indifferent to the feelings of the Great Russians themselves. They were the strongest national element in the Russian Empire, as they now are in the Soviet Union. They will continue to be the strongest national element in that general area, under any status. Any long-term U.S. policy must be based on their acceptance and their cooperation. The Ukrainian territory is as much a part of their national heritage as the Middle West is of ours, and they are conscious of that fact. A solution which attempts to separate the Ukraine entirely from the rest of Russia is bound to incur their resentment and opposition, and can be maintained, in the last analysis, only by force. There is a reasonable chance that the Great Russians could be induced to tolerate the renewed independence of the Baltic states. They tolerated the freedom of those territories from Russian rule for long periods in the past; and they recognize, subconsciously if not otherwise, that the respective peoples are capable of independence. With respect to the Ukrainians, things are different. They are too close to the Russians to be able to set themselves up successfully as something wholly different. For better or for worse, they will have to work out their destiny in some sort of special relationship to the Great Russian people.

It seems clear that this relationship can be at best a federal one, under which the Ukraine would enjoy a considerable measure of political and cultural autonomy but would not be economically or militarily independent. Such a relationship would be entirely just to the requirements of the Great Russians themselves. It would seem, therefore, to be along these lines that U.S. objectives with respect to the Ukraine should be framed.

It should be noted that this question has far more than just a distant future significance. Ukrainian and Great Russian elements among the Russian emigré-opposition groups are already competing vigorously for U.S. support. The manner in which we receive their competing claims may have an important influence on the development and success of the movement for political freedom among the Russians. It is essential, therefore, that we make our decision now and adhere to it consistently. And that decision should be neither a pro-Russian one nor a pro-Ukrainian one, but one which recognizes the historical geographic and economic realities involved and seeks for the Ukrainians a decent and acceptable place in the family of the traditional Russian Empire, of which they form an inextricable part.

It should be added that while, as stated above, we would not deliberately encourage Ukrainian separatism, nevertheless if an independent regime were to come into being on the territory of the Ukraine through no doing of ours, we should not oppose it outright. To do so would be to undertake an undesirable responsibility for internal Russian developments. Such a regime would be bound to be challenged eventually from the Russian side. If it were to maintain itself successfully, that would be proof that the above analysis was wrong and that the Ukraine does have the capacity for, and the moral right to, independent status. Our policy in the first instance should be to maintain an outward neutrality, as long as our own interests—military or otherwise—were not immediately affected. And only if it became clear that an undesirable deadlock was developing, we would encourage a composing of the differences along the lines of a reasonable federalism. The same would apply to any other efforts at the achievement of an independent status on the part of other Russian minorities. It is not likely that any of the other minorities could successfully maintain real independence for any length of time. However, should they attempt it (and it is quite possible that the Caucasian minorities would do this), our attitude should be the same as in the case of the Ukraine. We should be careful not to place ourselves in a position of open opposition to such attempts, which would cause us to lose permanently the sympathy of the minority in question. On the other hand, we should not commit ourselves to their support to a line of action which in the long run could probably be maintained only with our military assistance.

5. THE CHOICE OF A NEW RULING GROUP

In the event of a disintegration of Soviet power, we are certain to be faced with demands for support on the part of the various competing political elements among the present Russian opposition groups. It will be almost impossible for us to avoid doing things which would have the effect of favoring one or another of these groups over its rivals. But a great deal will depend on ourselves, and on our concept of what we are trying to accomplish.

We have already seen that among the existing and potential opposition groups there is none which we will wish to sponsor entirely and for whose actions, if it were to obtain power in Russia, we would wish to take responsibility.

On the other hand, we must expect that vigorous efforts will be made by various groups to induce us to take measures in Russian internal affairs which will constitute a genuine commitment on our part and make it possible for political groups in Russia to continue to demand our support. *In the light of these facts, it is plain that we must make a determined effort to avoid taking responsibility for deciding who would rule Russia in the wake of a disintegration of the Soviet regime.* Our best course would be to permit all the exiled elements to return to Russia as rapidly as possible and to see to it, in so far as this depends on us, that they are all given roughly equal opportunity to establish their bids for power. Our basic position must be that in the final analysis the Russian people will have to make their own choices, and that we do not intend to influence those choices. We should therefore avoid having protégés, and should try to see to it that all of the competing groups receive facilities for putting their case to the Russian people through the media of public information. It is probable that there will be violence between these groups. Even in this instance, we should not interfere unless our military interests are affected or unless there should be an attempt on the part of one group to establish its authority by large-scale and savage repression along totalitarian lines, affecting not just the opposing political leaders but the mass of the population itself.

6. THE PROBLEM OF "DE-COMMUNIZATION"

In any territory which is freed of Soviet rule, we will be faced with the problem of the human remnants of the Soviet apparatus of power.

It is probable that in the event of an orderly withdrawal of Soviet forces from present Soviet territory, the local communist party apparatus would go underground, as it did in the areas taken by the Germans during the recent war. It would then probably reemerge in part in the form of partisan bands and guerrilla forces. To this extent, the problem of dealing with it would be a relatively simple one; for we would need only to give the necessary arms and military support to whatever non-communist Russian authority might control the area and permit that authority to deal with the communist bands through the traditionally thorough procedures of Russian civil war.

A more difficult problem would be presented by minor communist party members or officials who might be uncovered and apprehended, or who might throw themselves on the mercy of our forces or of whatever Russian authority existed in the territory.

Here, again, we should refrain from taking upon ourselves the responsibility of disposing of these people or of giving direct orders to the local authorities as to how to do so. We would have a right to insist that they be disarmed and that they not come into leading positions in government unless they had given clear evidence of a genuine change of heart. But basically this must remain a problem for whatever Russian authority may take the place of the communist regime. We may be sure that such an authority will be more capable than we ourselves would be to judge the danger which ex-communists would present to the security of the new regime, and to dispose of them in such ways as to prevent their being harmful in the future. Our main concern should be to see that no communist regime, as such, is re-established in areas which we have once liberated and which we have decided should remain liberated from communist control. Beyond that, we should be careful not to become entangled in the problem of "de-communization."

The basic reason for this is that the political processes of Russia are strange and inscrutable. They contain nothing that is simple, and nothing that can be taken for granted. Rarely, if ever, are the colors straight black or white. The present communist apparatus of power probably embraces a large proportion of those persons who are fitted by training and inclination to take part in the processes of government. Any new regime will probably have to utilize the services of many of these people in order to be able to govern at all. Furthermore, we are incapable of assessing in each individual case the motives which have brought individuals in Russia into association with the communist movement. We are also incapable of assessing the degree to which such association will appear discreditable or criminal to other Russians, in retrospect. It would be dangerous for us to proceed on the basis of any fixed assumptions in such matters. We must always remember that to be the subject of persecution at the hands of a foreign government inevitably makes local martyrs out of persons who might otherwise only have been the objects of ridicule.

We would be wiser, therefore, in the case of territories freed from communist control, to restrict ourselves to seeing to it that individual ex-communists do not have the opportunity to reorganize as armed groups with pretenses to political power and that the local non-communist authority is given plenty of arms and help in any measures which they may desire to take with respect to them.

We may say, therefore, that we would not make it our aim to carry out with our own forces, on territory liberated from the communist authorities, any large-scale program of de-communization, and that in general we would leave this problem to whatever local authority might supplant Soviet rule.

<><><><><><><><><><><><><><><><><><><><><><><><><><><><><><><><><><><><><>

23   **T O P   S E C R E T**

U.S. Objectives with Respect to the USSR to Counter Soviet Threats to U.S. Security

NSC 20/4   November 23, 1948

[Source: *Foreign Relations of the United States: 1948,* I (part 2), 663–69]

NSC 20/4 was the final product of the review of American policy toward the Soviet Union initiated by Secretary of Defense Forrestal in the summer of 1948. Although it reiterates in modified form the conclusions reached in NSC 20/1 (Document 22), it does so without elaborating much of the reasoning which went into that predecessor document. President Truman approved NSC 20/4, as printed below, on November 24, 1948, and it remained the definitive statement of United States policy toward the Soviet Union until April 1950, when NSC 68 appeared.

The Problem

1. To assess and appraise existing and foreseeable threats to our national security currently posed by the USSR; and to formulate our objectives and aims as a guide in determining measures required to counter such threats.

Analysis of the Nature of the Threats

2. The will and ability of the leaders of the USSR to pursue policies which threaten the security of the United States constitute the greatest single danger to the U.S. within the foreseeable future.

3. Communist ideology and Soviet behavior clearly demonstrate that the ultimate objective of the leaders of the USSR is the domination of the world. Soviet leaders hold that the Soviet communist party is the militant vanguard of the world proletariat in its rise to political power, and that the USSR, base of the world communist movement, will not be safe until the non-communist nations have been so reduced in strength and numbers that communist influence is dominant throughout the world. The immediate goal of top priority since the recent war has been the political conquest of western Europe. The resistance of the United States is recognized by the USSR as a major obstacle to the attainment of these goals.

4. The Soviet leaders appear to be pursuing these aims by:

    a. Endeavoring to insert Soviet-controlled groups into positions of power and influence everywhere, seizing every opportunity presented by weakness and instability in other states and exploiting to the utmost the techniques of infiltration and propaganda, as well as the coercive power of preponderant Soviet military strength.

    b. Waging political, economic, and psychological warfare against all elements resistant to communist purposes, and in particular attempting to prevent or retard the recovery of and cooperation among western European countries.

    c. Building up as rapidly as possible the war potential of the Soviet orbit in anticipation of war, which in communist thinking is inevitable.

Both the immediate purposes and the ultimate objectives of the Soviet leaders are inimical to the security of the United States and will continue to be so indefinitely.

5. The present Soviet ability to threaten U.S security by measures short of war rests on:

a. The complete and effective centralization of power throughout the USSR and the international communist movement.

b. The persuasive appeal of a pseudo-scientific ideology promising panaceas and brought to other peoples by the intensive efforts of a modern totalitarian propaganda machine.

c. The highly effective techniques of subversion, infiltration and capture of political power, worked out through a half a century of study and experiment.

d. The power to use the military might of Russia, and of other countries already captured, for purposes of intimidation or, where necessary, military action.

e. The relatively high degree of political and social instability prevailing at this time in other countries, particularly in the European countries affected by the recent war and in the colonial or backward areas on which these European areas are dependent for markets and raw materials.

f. The ability to exploit the margin of tolerance accorded the communists and their dupes in democratic countries by virtue of the reluctance of such countries to restrict democratic freedoms merely in order to inhibit the activities of a single faction and by the failure of those countries to expose the fallacies and evils of communism.

6. It is impossible to calculate with any degree of precision the dimensions of the threat to U.S. security presented by these Soviet measures short of war. The success of these measures depends on a wide variety of currently unpredictable factors, including the degree of resistance encountered elsewhere, the effectiveness of U.S. policy, the development of relationships within the Soviet structure of power, etc. Had the United States not taken vigorous measures during the past two years to stiffen the resistance of western European and Mediterranean countries to communist pressures, most of western Europe would today have been politically captured by the communist movement. Today, barring some radical alteration of the underlying situation which would give new possibilities to the communists, the communists appear to have little chance of effecting at this juncture the political conquest of any countries west of the Luebeck-Trieste line. The unsuccessful outcome of this political offensive has in turn created serious problems for them behind the iron curtain, and their policies are today probably motivated in large measure by defensive considerations. However, it cannot be assumed that Soviet capabilities for subversion and political aggression will decrease in the next decade, and they may become even more dangerous than at present.

7. In present circumstances the capabilities of the USSR to threaten U.S. security by the use of armed forces[4] are dangerous and immediate:

    a. The USSR, while not capable of sustained and decisive direct military attack against U.S. territory or the Western Hemisphere, is capable of serious submarine warfare and of a limited number of one-way bomber sorties.

    b. Present intelligence estimates attribute to Soviet armed forces the capability of over-running in about six months all of Continental Europe and the Near East as far as Cairo, while simultaneously occupying important continental points in the Far East. Meanwhile, Great Britain could be subjected to severe air and missile bombardment.

    c. Russian seizure of these areas would ultimately enhance the Soviet war potential, if sufficient time were allowed and Soviet leaders were able to consolidate Russian control and to integrate Europe into the Soviet system. This would permit an eventual concentration of hostile power which would pose an unacceptable threat to the security of the United States.

8. However, rapid military expansion over Eurasia would tax Soviet logistic facilities and impose a serious strain on Russian economy. If at the same time the USSR were engaged in war with the United States, Soviet capabilities might well, in face of the strategic offensives of the United States, prove unequal to the task of holding the territories seized by the Soviet forces. If the United States were to exploit the potentialities of psychological warfare and subversive activity within the Soviet orbit, the USSR would be faced with increased disaffection, discontent, and underground opposition within the area under Soviet control.

9. Present estimates indicate that the current Soviet capabilities mentioned in 7a above will progressively increase and that by no later than 1955 the USSR will probably be capable of serious air attacks against the United States with atomic, biological and chemical weapons, of more extensive submarine operations (including the launching of short-range guided missiles), and of airborne operations to seize advance bases. However, the USSR could not, even then, successfully undertake an invasion of the United States as long as effective U.S. military forces remained in being.

---

4. Soviet military capabilities as set forth in this paper, while constituting potential threats to U.S. security which must be recognized, do not represent an evaluated estimate of Soviet intentions to utilize these capabilities, do not take into account the effect of counter action, and are based upon the assumption of no important change in the territory under Soviet control or in the type of that control.[Note in source text]

Soviet capabilities for overrunning western Europe and the Near East and for occupying parts of the Far East will probably still exist by 1958.

10. The Soviet capabilities and the increases thereto set forth in this paper would result in a relative increase in Soviet capabilities vis-à-vis the United States and the Western democracies unless offset by factors such as the following:

    a. The success of ERP.

    b. The development of Western Union and its support by the United States.

    c. The increased effectiveness of the military establishments of the United States, Great Britain, and other friendly nations.

    d. The development of internal dissension within the USSR and disagreements among the USSR and orbit nations.

11. The USSR has already engaged the United States in a struggle for power. While it cannot be predicted with certainty whether, or when, the present political warfare will involve armed conflict, nevertheless there exists a continuing danger of war at any time.

    a. While the possibility of planned Soviet armed actions which would involve this country cannot be ruled out, a careful weighing of the various factors points to the probability that the Soviet Government is not now planning any deliberate armed action calculated to involve the United States and is still seeking to achieve its aims primarily by political means, accompanied by military intimidation.

    b. War might grow out of incidents between forces in direct contact.

    c. War might arise through miscalculation, through failure of either side to estimate accurately how far the other can be pushed. There is the possibility that the USSR will be tempted to take armed action under a miscalculation of the determination and willingness of the United States to resort to force in order to prevent the development of a threat intolerable to U.S. security.

12. In addition to the risk of war, a danger equally to be guarded against is the possibility that Soviet political warfare might seriously weaken the relative position of the United States, enhance Soviet strength and either lead to our ultimate defeat short of war, or force us into war under dangerously unfavorable conditions. Such a result would be facilitated by vacillation, appeasement or isolationist concepts in our foreign policy, leading to loss of our allies and influence; by internal disunity or subversion; by economic in-

stability in the form of depression or inflation; or by either excessive or inadequate armament and foreign aid expenditures.

13. To counter threats to our national security and to create conditions conducive to a positive and in the long term mutually beneficial relationship between the Russian people and our own, it is essential that this government formulate general objectives which are capable of sustained pursuit both in time of peace and in the event of war. From the general objectives flow certain specific aims which we seek to accomplish by methods short of war, as well as certain other aims which we seek to accomplish in the event of war.

Conclusions

THREATS TO THE SECURITY OF THE UNITED STATES

14. The gravest threat to the security of the United States within the foreseeable future stems from the hostile designs and formidable power of the USSR, and from the nature of the Soviet system.

15. The political, economic, and psychological warfare which the USSR is now waging has dangerous potentialities for weakening the relative world position of the United States and disrupting its traditional institutions by means short of war, unless sufficient resistance is encountered in the policies of this and other non-communist countries.

16. The risk of war with the USSR is sufficient to warrant, in common prudence, timely and adequate preparation by the United States.

   a. Even though present estimates indicate that the Soviet leaders probably do not intend deliberate armed action involving the United States at this time, the possibility of such deliberate resort to war cannot be ruled out.

   b. Now and for the foreseeable future there is a continuing danger that war will arise either through Soviet miscalculation of the determination of the United States to use all the means at its command to safeguard its security, through Soviet misinterpretation of our intentions, or through U.S. miscalculation of Soviet reactions to measures which we might take.

17. Soviet domination of the potential power of Eurasia, whether achieved by armed aggression or by political and subversive means, would be strategically and politically unacceptable to the United States.

18. The capability of the United States either in peace or in the event of war to cope with threats to its security or to gain its objectives would be severely weakened by internal developments, important among which are:

a. Serious espionage, subversion and sabotage, particularly by concerted and well-directed communist activity.
b. Prolonged or exaggerated economic instability.
c. Internal political and social disunity.
d. Inadequate or excessive armament or foreign aid expenditures.
e. An excessive or wasteful usage of our resources in time of peace.
f. Lessening of U.S. prestige and influence through vacillation or appeasement or lack of skill and imagination in the conduct of its foreign policy or by shirking world responsibilities.
g. Development of a false sense of security through a deceptive change in Soviet tactics.

U.S. OBJECTIVES AND AIMS VIS-À-VIS THE USSR

19. To counter the threats to our national security and well-being posed by the USSR, our general objectives with respect to Russia, in time of peace as well as in time of war, should be:
    a. To reduce the power and influence of the USSR to limits which no longer constitute a threat to the peace, national independence and stability of the world family of nations.
    b. To bring about a basic change in the conduct of international relations by the government in power in Russia, to conform with the purposes and principles set forth in the UN charter.
In pursuing these objectives due care must be taken to avoid permanently impairing our economy and the fundamental values and institutions inherent in our way of life.

20. We should endeavor to achieve our general objectives by methods short of war through the pursuit of the following aims:
    a. To encourage and promote the gradual retraction of undue Russian power and influence from the present perimeter areas around traditional Russian boundaries and the emergence of the satellite countries as entities independent of the USSR.
    b. To encourage the development among the Russian peoples of attitudes which may help to modify current Soviet behavior and permit a revival of the national life of groups evidencing the ability and determination to achieve and maintain national independence.
    c. To eradicate the myth by which people remote from Soviet military influence are held in a position of subservience to Moscow and to cause the world at large to see and understand the true nature of the USSR and the Soviet-directed world communist party, and to adopt a logical and realistic attitude toward them.

    d. To create situations which will compel the Soviet Government to recognize the practical undesirability of acting on the basis of its present concepts and the necessity of behaving in accordance with precepts of international conduct, as set forth in the purposes and principles of the UN charter.

21. Attainment of these aims requires that the United States:

    a. Develop a level of military readiness which can be maintained as long as necessary as a deterrent to Soviet aggression, as indispensable support to our political attitude toward the USSR, as a source of encouragement to nations resisting Soviet political aggression, and as an adequate basis for immediate military commitments and for rapid mobilization should war prove unavoidable.

    b. Assure the internal security of the United States against dangers of sabotage, subversion, and espionage.

    c. Maximize our economic potential, including the strengthening of our peace-time economy and the establishment of essential reserves readily available in the event of war.

    d. Strengthen the orientation toward the United States of the non-Soviet nations; and help such of those nations as are able and willing to make an important contribution to U.S. security, to increase their economic and political stability and their military capability.

    e. Place the maximum strain on the Soviet structure of power and particularly on the relationships between Moscow and the satellite countries.

    f. Keep the U.S. public fully informed and cognizant of the threats to our national security so that it will be prepared to support the measures which we must accordingly adopt.

22. In the event of war with the USSR we should endeavor by successful military and other operations to create conditions which would permit satisfactory accomplishment of U.S. objectives without a predetermined requirement for unconditional surrender. War aims supplemental to our peace-time aims should include:

    a. Eliminating Soviet Russian domination in areas outside the borders of any Russian state allowed to exist after the war.

    b. Destroying the structure of relationships by which the leaders of the All-Union Communist Party have been able to exert moral and disciplinary authority over individual citizens, or groups of citizens, in countries not under communist control.

c. Assuring that any regime or regimes which may exist on traditional Russian territory in the aftermath of war:
   (1) Do not have sufficient military power to wage aggressive war.
   (2) Impose nothing resembling the present iron curtain over contacts with the outside world.

d. In addition, if any bolshevik regime is left in any part of the Soviet Union, insuring that it does not control enough of the military-industrial potential of the Soviet Union to enable it to wage war on comparable terms with any other regime or regimes which may exist on traditional Russian territory.

e. Seeking to create postwar conditions which will:
   (1) Prevent the development of power relationships dangerous to the security of the United States and international peace.
   (2) Be conducive to the successful development of an effective world organization based upon the purposes and principles of the United Nations.
   (3) Permit the earliest practicable discontinuance within the United States of wartime controls.

23. In pursuing the above war aims, we should avoid making irrevocable or premature decisions or commitments respecting border rearrangements, administration of government within enemy territory, independence for national minorities, or post-war responsibility for the readjustment of the inevitable political, economic, and social dislocations resulting from the war.

◇◇

24 **T O P S E C R E T**

United States Policy Toward the Soviet Satellite States in Eastern Europe

NSC 58   September 14, 1949

[Source: Records of the National Security Council on deposit in the Modern Military Records Branch, National Archives, Washington, D.C.]

NSC 58, which originated in the Department of State, applied the strategy of encouraging fissures within the international communist movement as outlined in NSC 20/1 (Document 22) to the specific area of Eastern Europe. Contrary to charges subsequently made against the Truman Administration, the document shows no inconsistency between the concepts of ''containment'' and ''liberation,'' if that latter phrase means what the authors of NSC 58 called ''a heretical drifting-away process on the

part of the satellite states.'' NSC 58 also reinforced the argument, advanced originally in PPS 1 (Document 9), that the object to be contained was Soviet expansionism, not international communism. Although the United States might prefer non-
communist governments in Eastern Europe, it could work with communist
governments independent of Moscow's control in the interest of further restricting
Soviet power. Finally, NSC 58 made explicit an idea implicit in NSC 20/1 and
in Kennan's ''X'' article: that the Kremlin leaders' invariable tendency to alienate
those with whom they sought to deal rendered Soviet expansion vulnerable to
overextension and eventual fragmentation.

On December 13, 1949, President Truman approved a modified version of this
document, NSC 58/2, the conclusions of which were still classified at the time this
volume was prepared.

The Problem

To find means of improving and intensifying our efforts to reduce and
eventually to cause the elimination of dominant Soviet influence in the satellite states of Albania, Bulgaria, Czechoslovakia, Hungary, Poland and Rumania.

Analysis

1. Since VE Day we have (a) checked the westward advance of Soviet
power, at least for the time being, at a line running from Lübeck to Trieste
and (b) made substantial strides in developing Western Europe as a counter-
force to Communism. These are defensive accomplishments. The time is
now ripe for us to place greater emphasis on the offensive to consider
whether we cannot do more to cause the elimination or at least a reduction
of predominant Soviet influence in the satellite states of Eastern Europe.

2. These states are in themselves of secondary importance on the European scene. Eventually they must play an important role in a free and integrated Europe; but in the current two-world struggle they have meaning
primarily because they are in varying degrees politico-military adjuncts of
Soviet power and extend that power into the heart of Europe. They are a part
of the Soviet monolith.

3. It is assumed that there is general agreement that, so long as the
U.S.S.R. represents the only major threat to our security and to world stability, our objective with respect to the U.S.S.R.'s European satellites must be
the elimination of Soviet control from those countries and the reduction of
Soviet influence to something like normal dimension.

GENERAL COMMENT REGARDING SATELLITES

4. The criterion which we employ in defining a "satellite" state is amenability to Kremlin direction. Thus Albania, Bulgaria, Czechoslovakia, Hungary, Poland and Rumania are by this definition satellite states. Yugoslavia is not because, although it is a Communist state, it is not at present subservient to the Kremlin and an integral part of the Soviet system. Nor is Finland; because, notwithstanding the existence of a large Soviet naval base on its territory, Finland has demonstrated on the whole a greater degree of resistance to than compliance with Soviet pressure and has, in particular, been able to resist internal police domination by the MVD.

5. Certain generalizations can be made about the satellite states. For the most part, they were overrun by the Soviet Army during or after the war. Their present governments were established by Kremlin dictate or under Moscow guidance. And they are all minority governments dominated by Communists. In particular, internal police power, which is the key factor in a Communist power system, is under Moscow control.

6. Moreover, the satellite states have under Soviet compulsion reoriented their economies from the west to the east. The Kremlin forced this readjustment with the purpose of exploiting the satellites for the aggrandizement of Soviet economic-military might and preventing their contact with the West. Moreover, the satellite economies are being steadily Sovietized. The Soviet pattern of state monopoly of trade and industry and of collectivized agriculture is being rapidly forced on these countries.

7. The cultural life of the satellite peoples, too, is being steadily Sovietized. A common pattern in education, religion, science and the fine arts is being pressed on the mind and spirit of Eastern Europe.

8. These developments do not have popular support in the satellite countries. The majority of the population in these states look upon their governments and the Soviet Union as an oppressive rather than an emancipating force.

THE ANATOMY OF SOVIET POWER IN THE SATELLITE STATES

9. What is the anatomy of Soviet power in these countries? The four basic factors making for Soviet influence and control are:

    a. Certain traditional ties, such as Pan-Slavism and the Orthodox Church, and in some segments of the satellite population a common fear of the resurgence of German aggression;

    b. The presence or encircling propinquity of recognized elements of the Soviet armed forces and security troops;

    c. Kremlin penetration and domination of the government, the party, and all other mass organizations (including economic enterprises) through both Soviet and satellite nationals;

    d. A common body of communist ideology adhered to by the ruling groups.

10. Where they exist, the traditional ties of race and culture are systematically utilized by the Kremlin as a binding force. Similarly, fear of the resurgence of German aggression is vigorously exploited by the Russians to hold these satellites in the Soviet sphere. The shabby old fabric of Pan-Slavism has been patched and tailored to serve as a rather ineffectual ethnographic and cultural comforter over Eastern Europe. The corrupt Othodox Church, which had provided a loose religious affinity between Russia and some of the Balkan countries, has been recorrupted and forced away from the œcumenical concept and in the direction of recognizing the primacy of the Moscow Patriarchate, which in turn is thoroughly subservient, in fact if not in spirit, to the Communist Party and the MVD.

11. The presence of Soviet armed forces and security troops in certain satellites and their near-encirclement of all of them exert an intimidating influence throughout the orbit. Where Soviet forces are garrisoned within satellite states, they serve to reinforce the authority of puppet officials.

12. Stalinist penetration of the governments and mass organizations of satellite states is a tangible mechanical instrument of Soviet power. It is the Kremlin's reinsurance against ideological corrupt[i]bility on the part of satellite officials, the guarantee that its political, economic and cultural policies will be implemented. The termiting of all satellite organizations, but particularly the leader positions in police organizations, by Stalinist agents means that no satellite citizen in a position of responsibility is immune from the Kremlin's displeasure. This produces a degree of sensitive subservience which could never be achieved through ideological hypnotism alone.

13. There are three discernible strata in the accreted ideology of Marx, Lenin and Stalin. There is first the traditional conglomerate of Marxist-Leninist philosophy based on dialectical materialism. Quackery that it is, it is nevertheless an outlook on the world adhered to in common not only by the U.S.S.R. and its satellites but also by such non-conformists as Tito and the Trotskyites. Whatever differences may divide them, whatever opportunist accommodations they may be forced to make to the mammon of private capitalism, they are united in common detestation of the infidel bourgeoisie.

14. The second stratum is the Leninist-Stalinist blueprint for the capture

and retention of power. It is the working formula for totalitarianism, the modern science of revolution, coup d'etat and tyranny. From the Russian revolution to the Czech coup, this formula has been proved effective. It is not, however, of itself a force binding the satellites to the U.S.S.R.

15. The third stratum is specifically designed as a magnetic law to hold the satellites in the Kremlin's orbit. It is the Stalinist dogma that (a) the non-Soviet world is unalterably hostile to not only the U.S.S.R. but all of the "New Democracies" simply because their goal is Communism, (b) the U.S.S.R. is the socialist fatherland, leading a movement predestined to triumph over the non-Soviet world, (c) the satellite states can survive and realize their destiny only through identification of their interests with those of the U.S.S.R., faithfully following the infallible and invincible leadership of the Kremlin, and (d) the citizens of the satellites therefore owe primary allegiance to the U.S.S.R. It is this dogma which provides the rationalization for the imposition of Soviet imperialism in all of its aspects, political, economic and cultural, and for satellite acceptance of a colonial status. It should also be noted that the inclination of the West—a quite understandable one—to act on the basis of (a) above tends to reinforce this myth and causes the satellite leaders to believe that they have no future outside of the Stalinist camp.

16. Three of the basic factors identified in preceding paragraphs: (a) military intimidation, (b) penetration and (c) the Stalinist dogma are the root cause and the conditioning force of other mechanisms of Kremlin power and influence in the satellites. Such derivative factors as the Council of Mutual Economic Assistance[5] (and the reverse of this medal: the prohibition of satellite participation in ERP), standardization of military equipment, defensive alliances and common propaganda lines would not necessarily have developed had it not been for these three basic factors. While the derivative factors are of secondary importance in an analysis of the real anatomy of Soviet power, they are of great practical significance in considering what we can do toward reducing Soviet influence and control in the satellite states. It is in that context, later in this paper, that these mechanisms, particularly the economic, will be examined.

17. Returning to the basic factors, where are the weak points in this anatomy of Soviet influence and control? The weakness of the traditional ties between the U.S.S.R. and its satellites lies in their comparatively shallow hold

5. The Council of Mutual Economic Assistance was formed in January 1949 by representatives of the Soviet Union, Bulgaria, Hungary, Poland, Rumania, and Czechoslovakia for the purpose of exchanging experience and technical assistance in the economic field. [Ed. note]

and in the traditional conflicts of the area, which have historically always outweighed the cohesive influences at work. Pan-Slavism may have some meaning in Bulgaria but it is an absurdity in Albania. And certainly the long-standing national antagonisms of the Poles, Rumanians and Hungarians toward the Russians—not to mention mutual antipathies among the satellites themselves—are strong counter-currents to the new Stalinist internationalism.

18. The Kremlin's weakness with respect to its armed forces stationed in countries of the Soviet orbit lies in the fact that they are there on a legally impermanent basis—unless new treaty provisions are made or the satellite states in which they are stationed are absorbed into the U.S.S.R. The removal of Soviet troops will, under present circumstances, leave the other instruments of Soviet influence and control without legal resort to the ultimate recourse of massive force.

19. Few weaknesses exist in the crucial factor of Stalinist penetration. With Kremlin agents permeating party and state structures and with mutual suspicion and denunciation having become, as they are in the U.S.S.R., ingrained in all human relationships, this channel of influence and control appears well-nigh invulnerable. Its only weakness would appear to lie in its self-stultification and demoralization—the recurring necessity to purge personnel—and in the nationalist resistance which constant Soviet interference partially generates and inflames. Such, after all, has been the experience in certain of the minority "nations" of the U.S.S.R.—the Ukraine and the Baltic states. Moscow penetration and interference in these sub-states provoked resistance, most of which could be suppressed by individual or small-scale secret-police measures. But some revolts were of such magnitude as to require employment of the Red Army and State Security troops. Furthermore, the elements of the Red Army and State Security troops employed were not native to the "nation" in which they were used. This experience raises again the question of the efficacy of Stalinist agent penetration in the event the Soviet Army is withdrawn behind the borders of the U.S.S.R.

20. The weakness of the ideological hold which the Kremlin exerts over the satellite leaders lies in the Stalinist dogma of subservience to the U.S.S.R., particularly the dictum that satellite interests cannot and must not conflict with those of the U.S.S.R. That myth, happily, is the weakest segment of the accreted ideology of Marx, Lenin and Stalin. It engenders essentially the same popular reactions that colonialism has produced throughout history, for it is in fact a form of colonialism. The myth quickly loses its attraction for all those with real roots in the local scene once it becomes appar-

ent that satellite interests, particularly in the economic field, must be subordinated to the imperious needs of the Soviet sovereign. This development must also have its effect on even those satellite leaders who view Moscow as the center of a new internationalism. The Stalinist dogma undoubtedly had validity in the minds of satellite leaders when they were revolutionaries seeking power. At that time, there was little conflict between their interests and those of the Kremlin; they were wholly dependent upon Moscow and could hope to realize their revolutionary aims—and personal ambitions—only through subserving the interests of the U.S.S.R. But now that they have the appearance and considerable of the substance of power, subtle new forces come into play. Power, even the taste of it, is as likely to corrupt Communist as bourgeois leaders. Considerations of national as well as personal interest materialize and come into conflict with the colonial policy pursued by the Soviet interests. When this happens, satellite officials may still remain, by force of other factors, Kremlin captives; but at least they are not entirely willing ones.

THE LESSON OF TITO

21. In examining the problem before us, it is instructive to analyze the reasons for Tito's present independence of Moscow control. How does it happen that Yugoslavia is not solidly aligned with the U.S.S.R. and its satellites?

22. The answer obviously does not lie in the realm of ideology. Yugoslavia's state philosophy, like that of the U.S.S.R. and its satellites, is Marxism-Leninism. Furthermore, Tito rose to power and now retains it by a sedulous application of the Leninist-Stalinist blueprint for totalitarianism. It is only in the third ideological stratum—that of subservience to the interests of the U.S.S.R.—that Tito openly deviates ideologically from the satellites. How has he been able to do it?

23. The key to Tito's successful rejection of Kremlin control lies in the fact that (a) the Yugoslav Communist Party was largely his personal creation, (b) the Soviet Army did not occupy Yugoslavia and establish there an ultimate repository of Kremlin force, and (c) he had been able from the outset to prevent effective Stalinist penetration of his party and governmental apparati.

24. This having been the case, Tito and his associates were able to develop a party, secret police and army who had confidence in themselves, particularist pride in their own achievements—and whose first loyalty was to themselves. They have therefore been thus far, in the conflict and showdown

with the U.S.S.R., immune to Stalinist disciplinary action against their persons. It is ironical that the Kremlin-Cominform attack has served to strengthen the domestic position of Tito and his cohorts and to solidify popular support around them.

25. Why did a rift occur between Tito and the Soviet bloc? The answer lies both in the nature of the Yugoslavs and in the nature of Soviet imperialism. The Kremlin made a gross miscalculation regarding the Yugoslav Communists. It underestimated the tough recalcitrant Yugoslav character and the organizational ability of the Titoists to resist Soviet pressure. With a heavy hand the Kremlin strove to force its colonial policy on Yugoslavia. As it did so it engaged its prestige against the Titoists. As arrogant Soviet pressure mounted, Yugoslav resistance increased until the open break occurred.

26. Notwithstanding the bitterness of their present quarrel, the Marxist-Leninist bond between the Kremlin and the Titoists remains. Let us not delude ourselves into thinking that Tito might like us better for being the butt of a Communist family feud. The best that we can hope from Tito is crafty self-interest in playing both sides, similar to that practiced by Franco in his relations with the Axis and the Allies during the last war. Uncongenial as such a relationship may be, it is far less inimical to us and other nations of good will than a Yugoslavia cemented into the Soviet monolith.

27. The Communist Reformation in Yugoslavia occurred quickly and sharply defined because of the especial conditions described in the preceding paragraphs. Conditions do not now exist in the satellite states which would permit them promptly to follow the pattern of Yugoslavia. The leaders of the satellite states did not come to power primarily through their own efforts. Most of them were transplanted from Moscow by the Red Army and Soviet secret police. The satellite leaders do not therefore have the particularist esprit de corps of the Titoists. Rather their parties and governments are thoroughly penetrated by Stalinists with the result that any conspiracy against Kremlin control is quickly detected, isolated and crushed. Furthermore, their armies contain informers and agents. And finally, Soviet armed forces are stationed on satellite territories or around their borders.

COURSES OPEN TO US

28. In seeking to bring about the elimination of Soviet power from the satellite states, two principal courses of action are conceivable. One is war; the other is measures short of war.

29. Resort to war as a course of action is raised in this paper solely for the purpose of making clear that it should be rejected as a practical alterna-

tive. This course is rejected, if for no other reason, because it is organically not feasible for this Government to initiate a policy of creating a war. It therefore follows that this paper is necessarily addressed to measures short of war. However, if war in Eastern Europe is forced upon us, that is a different matter and one which would create a wholly new situation beyond the compass of this paper. It scarcely need be added that we should always be prepared for such a contingency.

30. There remains then the category of measures short of war. Before discussing them, we should at the outset have clearly in mind another set of alternatives between which we must make a conscious choice. In attempting to cause an elimination of Soviet power in these countries, we obviously cannot expect a vacuum to result. The type of government which might succeed to power is intimately related to the removal of Kremlin influence and control. Therefore, should it be our aim to replace, as a first step, Kremlin authority with (a) governments immediately friendly to us or (b) any governments free of Moscow domination, even though they be Communist regimes?

31. Our ultimate aim must, of course, be the appearance in Eastern Europe of non-totalitarian administrations willing to accommodate themselves to, and participate in, the free world community. Strong tactical considerations, however, argue against setting up this goal as an immediate objective. None of the Eastern European countries, except Czechoslovakia, has ever known any but authoritarian government. Democracy in the western sense is alien to their culture and tradition. Moreover, the non-totalitarian leadership, such as it is, in the satellite states has been thoroughly fragmented and crushed. It has little chance of coming to power save through armed intervention from the west. Were we to set as our immediate goal the replacement of totalitarianism by democracy, an overwhelming portion of the task would fall on us, and we would find ourselves directly engaging the Kremlin's prestige and provoking strong Soviet reaction, possibly in the form of war or at least in vigorous indirect aggression. At best, we would find ourselves deeply enmeshed in the eastern European situation and saddled with an indefinitely continuing burden of political, economic and military responsibility for the survival of the uncertain regimes which we had placed in power.

32. If, however, we are willing that, as a first step, schismatic Communist regimes supplant the present Stalinist governments, we stand a much better chance of success. Admittedly, it would be a difficult task to attempt to bring about a severance of satellite ties with the Kremlin. But it would not

be nearly so difficult as challenging at the outset, not only the whole complex of Communist ideology and method, but also the long heritage of authoritarianism.

33. The more feasible immediate course, then, is to foster a heretical drifting-away process on the part of the satellite states. However weak they may now appear, grounds do exist for heretical schisms. We can contribute to the widening of these rifts without assuming responsibility. And when the final breaks occur, we would not be directly involved in engaging Soviet prestige; the quarrel would be between the Kremlin and the Communist Reformation.

34. Such a development could conceivably grow to the point where there would be two opposing blocs in the Communist world—a Stalinist group and a non-conformist faction, either loosely allied or federated under Tito's leadership. A situation of this description might eventually provide us with an opportunity to operate on the basis of a balance of forces in the Communist world and to foster the tendencies toward accommodation with the West implicit in such a state of affairs.

35. With the foregoing in mind, let us now consider the most evidently beneficial course which we can follow. The obvious first step, perhaps even an essential prerequisite, is the creation of circumstances bringing about the withdrawal of Soviet troops from satellite countries. The conclusion of an Austrian peace settlement would remove the most evident present justification for Soviet troops in Hungary and Rumania. Similarly, an agreement by the four powers with respect to Germany, if and when it is achieved, should include provisions assuring preferably an elimination but at least a reduction of Soviet garrisons in Germany and Poland. These developments should go a long way toward loosening the Kremlin's hold not only on the states affected but also on adjoining satellites. There is no guarantee, of course, that such a move might not be followed by Soviet-satellite treaty arrangements or the Soviet Union's incorporating some or all of the satellites in the U.S.S.R., thus providing a new legal basis for the retention of Soviet forces in those countries. In such an eventuality, a new situation would have been created necessitating a full reexamination of this paper.

36. A second course open before us is to attack the weaknesses in the Stalinist penetration of satellite governments and mass organizations. In the light of what has been said, this will be no easy task. The weaknesses discussed in paragraph 19 do represent, however, a vulnerable sector on this front, especially if Soviet armed forces are withdrawn behind the borders of the U.S.S.R. The basic problem would seem to be to bring about the isola-

tion, not only in satellite society, but particularly in the Communist Parties, of the Stalinist elements, and as they are identified and isolated, to create conditions which will reduce and eventually eliminate their power. [Security deletion in source text] The propensity of the revolution to devour its own, the suspicions of the Kremlin regarding its agents and the institutions of denunciation, purge and liquidation are grave defects in the Soviet system which have never been adequately exploited.

37. This course is intimately related to and partly dependent upon the third course of action open to us—an attack on the ideological front, specifically directed at the Stalinist dogma of satellite dependence upon and subservience to the U.S.S.R. This key doctrine should be unremittingly attacked all across the board in its political, economic and cultural applications. On the positive side, the reverse of the Stalinist dogma—nationalism—should be encouraged. The offensive should be maintained not only on the overt but also the covert plane.

38. The subsidiary mechanisms of Soviet control touched upon in paragraph 16 are of varying vulnerability. It is difficult to see, for example, how we can bring pressure to bear against such mechanisms as Soviet military missions in satellite states. The political and cultural fields, however, offer possibilities for the exertions of our influences. For instance, through formal diplomatic channels and within the U.N., we have some opportunity to bring pressures to bear on the political ties between the satellite governments and the U.S.S.R. And in our general ideological offensive mentioned in the preceding paragraph, we should not neglect pressing the attack, necessarily indirectly in most cases, against specific instrumentalities such as the various ''popular'' organizations in the satellite states.

39. But it is probably in the economic realm that we can most concretely make our influence felt. All of the Soviet economic mechanisms of control, particularly the CMEA, are affected by the policies which we follow with regard to such matters as East-West trade, purchase of gold and export controls. The potential effectiveness of our economic tactics is widespread. If we can succeed in jolting the CMEA structure, the repercussions are bound to be felt in the political, military and cultural spheres. We do not have at hand and are therefore not operating on the basis of a thorough study of all of the elements of the problem. Not until we have completed an exhaustive study of all of the economic—and political—factors involved can we mobilize this economic potential and utilize it for maximum effect. This is a tactical problem which should immediately be worked out in detail.

FACTORS AFFECTING OUR CHOICE

40. The broad courses of action open to us are qualified by a series of other factors. They are considerations of (a) timing and tempo, (b) our long-term goals, (c) our world position, (d) our relations with the U.S.S.R., and (e) the relative vulnerability of the various satellites.

41. Although the time is now ripe for us to move to the offensive, this does not mean that we should attempt to move at a maximum pace. The tempo at which we move is necessarily qualified by the basic pragmatic approach which we have to foreign relations. The truism, sometimes ignored in the public mind, is here recognized that our pace must be accommodated to what the situation in the satellites warrants.

42. A course of encouraging schisms within the Communist world cannot be pursued without reserve because such a course is a tactical expediency which, however necessary, must never be permitted to obscure our basic long-term objectives—a non-totalitarian system in Eastern Europe. The problem is to facilitate the development of heretical Communismm without at the same time seriously impairing our chances for ultimately replacing this intermediate totalitarianism with tolerant regimes congenial to the Western World. Nor must we slacken, rather we should increase, the support and refuge which we may be able to offer to leaders and groups in these countries who are western-minded.

43. Considerations of our international position, particularly with respect to the U.N., impose further limitations on our policy with respect to the satellites. We cannot, for example, come out in unqualified support of Tito or Titoism any more than we can take such a stand in favor of Franco and Fascism. Furthermore, we cannot pursue a wholly unilateral course because we have committed ourselves to the collective idea, because our western allies have far-reaching legitimate interests in Eastern Europe and because the full effectiveness of our operations depends upon their cooperation.

44. Our relations with the U.S.S.R. are another consideration which must be taken into account. The satellite question is a function of our main problem—relations with the U.S.S.R. No examination of a proposed course of action toward the satellites is complete without thorough consideration of the probable effects it might have on the U.S.S.R. Proposed operations directed at the satellites must consequently be measured against the kind and degree of retaliation which they are likely to provoke from the Kremlin. They must not exceed in provocative effect what is calculated suitable in the given situation.

45. Finally, considerations of the relative vulnerability of the various satellites must enter into our calculations. No one course of action can be applied alike to all satellites. Obviously our policy both with regard to methods and tempo must differ among the several orbit countries. These are tactical problems which must be flexibly worked out by the operating elements within this Government.

Conclusions

46. Our over-all aim with respect to the satellite states should be the gradual reduction and eventual elimination of preponderant Soviet power from Eastern Europe without resort to war.

47. We should, as the only practical immediate expedient, seek to achieve this objective through fostering Communist heresy among the satellite states, encouraging the emergence of non-Stalinist regimes as temporary administrations, even though they be Communist in nature.

48. It must, however, be our fixed aim that eventually these regimes must be replaced by non-totalitarian governments desirous of participating with good faith in the free world community.

49. More specifically, bearing in mind all of the qualifications set forth in the analysis of this paper, we should:

   a. Seek to bring about retraction of Soviet military forces behind the borders of the U.S.S.R.;
   b. Endeavor to cause an increasing isolation of the confirmed Stalinists from the nationalist elements of the party and from popular support in the satellite states toward the end that their power be reduced;
   c. Attack the Stalinist dogma of satellite subservience to the U.S.S.R. and encourage nationalism;
   d. Bring fully to bear on the Soviet-satellite relationship the economic forces which we control or influence.

50. The operating elements within this Government should forthwith begin tactical planning and implementation of such plans in conformity with the strategic concept set forth in this paper. In connection with economic planning, it will be necessary first to undertake the study mentioned in paragraph 39.

≋ 5 ≋

IMPLEMENTATION: THE FAR EAST, 1947–49

AMERICAN POLICY in the Far East between 1947 and 1949 proceeded from three assumptions: (1) that although it was in the interest of the United States to prevent the domination of Asia by a single hostile power, that task was secondary in importance to the objective of maintaining stability in Europe; (2) that because of its limited resources, the United States should avoid military involvement on the Asian mainland, concentrating instead on holding island strongpoints; (3) that the expanding influence of the Soviet Union constituted the chief threat to the balance of power in the Far East, and that the United States could best counter it by aligning its policies with the forces of nationalism there.

PPS 23 (Document 25) contains Kennan's overall assessment of the Far Eastern situation as of February 1948; in it he remarks on the importance of distinguishing between peripheral and vital interests, and warns against accepting responsibilites in Asia beyond the limits of American capabilities. PPS 28/2 (Document 26) outlines a strategic concept for the United States in the western Pacific based on liquidating commitments on the mainland.

The NSC 49 series (Documents 27 and 28) addresses the role Japan would play in this postwar security system; NSC 22, NSC 22/1, NSC 34, and PPS 39/1 (Documents 29, 30, 31, and 32) reflect contending points of view within the government regarding the future of China. Both groups of documents illustate the tendency of the Joint Chiefs of Staff to concentrate on relatively short-term military considerations and that of the State Department to be concerned with longer-term political and economic problems.

The chapter concludes with two documents from the NSC 48 series, NSC 48/1 and NSC 48/2 (Documents 33 and 34), which represented an effort to integrate previous decisions into a comprehensive statement of American policy in Asia.

<><><><><><><><><><><><><><><><><><><><><><><><><><><><><><><><><><><>

25   **T O P   S E C R E T**

Review of Current Trends: U.S. Foreign Policy

PPS 23   February 24, 1948

[Source: *Foreign Relations of the United States: 1948,* I (part 2), 523–26]

This excerpt from PPS 23 provides a clear exposition of Kennan's general views on the application of containment in Asia. (For other excerpts from PPS 23, see Documents 8, 11, and 19). As he had in his earlier "Review of the World Situation" (Document 7), Kennan stressed the limited ability of the United States to affect events in the Far East, and the danger of overextension unless distinctions between vital and peripheral interests were kept firmly in mind. Calling for the abandonment of pretensions to moral or ideological leadership in that part of the world, Kennan advocated an American policy based on economic and military assistance in selected areas—notably the island bastions of Japan and the Philippines, which he viewed as the cornerstones of a future security system in the Pacific.

VII. Far East

My main impression with regard to the position of this Government with regard to the Far East is that we are greatly over-extended in our whole thinking about what we can accomplish, and should try to accomplish, in that area. This applies, unfortunately, to the public in our country as well as to the Government.

It is urgently necessary that we recognize our own limitations as a moral and ideological force among the Asiatic peoples.

Our political philosophy and our patterns for living have very little applicability to masses of people in Asia. They may be all right for us, with our highly developed political traditions running back into the centuries and with our peculiarly favorable geographic position; but they are simply not practical or helpful, today, for most of the people in Asia.

This being the case, we must be very careful when we speak of exercising "leadership" in Asia. We are deceiving ourselves and others when we pretend to have the answers to the problems which agitate many of these Asiatic peoples.

Furthermore, we have about 50% of the world's wealth but only 6.3% of its population. This disparity is particularly great as between ourselves and the peoples of Asia. In this situation, we cannot fail to be the object of envy and resentment. Our real task in the coming period is to devise a pattern of relationships which will permit us to maintain this position of disparity without positive detriment to our national security. To do so, we will have to dispense with all sentimentality and day-dreaming; and our attention will have to be concentrated everywhere on our immediate national objectives. We need not deceive ourselves that we can afford today the luxury of altruism and world-benefaction.

For these reasons, we must observe great restraint in our attitude toward the Far Eastern areas. The peoples of Asia and of the Pacific area are going to go ahead, whatever we do, with the development of their political forms and mutual interrelationships in their own way. This process cannot be a liberal or peaceful one. The greatest of the Asiatic peoples—the Chinese and the Indians—have not yet even made a beginning at the solution of the basic demographic problem involved in the relationship between their food supply and their birth rate. Until they find some solution to this problem, further hunger, distress and violence are inevitable. All of the Asiatic peoples are faced with the necessity for evolving new forms of life to conform to the impact of modern technology. This process of adaptation will also be long and violent. It is not only possible, but probable, that in the course of this process many peoples will fall, for varying periods, under the influence of Moscow, whose ideology has a greater lure for such peoples, and probably greater reality, than anything we could oppose to it. All this, too, is probably unavoidable; and we could not hope to combat it without the diversion of a far greater portion of our national effort than our people would ever willingly concede to such a purpose.

In the face of this situation we would be better off to dispense now with a number of the concepts which have underlined our thinking with regard to the Far East. We should dispense with the aspiration to "be liked" or to be regarded as the repository of a high-minded international altruism. We should stop putting ourselves in the position of being our brothers' keeper and refrain from offering moral and ideological advice. We should cease to talk about vague and—for the Far East—unreal objectives such as human rights, the raising of the living standards, and democratization. The day is not far off when we are going to have to deal in straight power concepts. The less we are then hampered by idealistic slogans, the better.

We should recognize that our influence in the Far Eastern area in the coming period is going to be primarily military and economic. We should make a careful study to see what parts of the Pacific and Far Eastern world are absolutely vital to our security, and we should concentrate our policy on seeing to it that those areas remain in hands which we can control or rely on. It is my own guess, on the basis of such study as we have given the problem so far, that Japan and the Philippines will be found to be the corner-stones of such a Pacific security system and that if we can contrive to retain effective control over these areas there can be no serious threat to our security from the East within our time.

Only when we have assured this first objective, can we allow ourselves the luxury of going farther afield in our thinking and our planning.

If these basic concepts are accepted, then our objectives for the immediate coming period should be:

a. to liquidate as rapidly as possible our unsound commitments in China and to recover, vis-à-vis that country, a position of detachment and freedom of action;

b. to devise policies with respect to Japan which assure the security of those islands from communist penetration and domination as well as from Soviet military attack, and which will permit the economic potential of that country to become again an important force in the Far East, responsive to the interests of peace and stability in the Pacific area; and

c. to shape our relationship to the Philippines in such a way as to permit to the Philippine Government a continued independence in all internal affairs but to preserve the archipelago as a bulwark of U.S. security in that area.

Of these three objectives, the one relating to Japan is the one where there is the greatest need for immediate attention on the part of our Government and the greatest possibility for immediate action. It should therefore be made the focal point of our policy for the Far East in the coming period.

<><><><><><><><><><><><><><><><><><><><><><><><><><><><><><><><><><>

26   **T O P   S E C R E T**

Conversation between General of the Army MacArthur and Mr. George F. Kennan

PPS 28/2   March 5, 1948

[Source: *Foreign Relations of the United States: 1948,* VI, 700–702]

Early in 1948 Kennan traveled to Japan for consultations with General Douglas MacArthur, Supreme Commander of Alllied Powers Japan (SCAP). During these conversations MacArthur outlined his strategic concept for the Far East, a plan which, like Kennan's, involved holding island air and naval bases to enable the

United States to prevent anti-American offensive operations from the Asian mainland. MacArthur's formulation would appear as official policy almost two years later in Secretary of State Dean Acheson's "defensive perimeter" speech to the National Press Club, January 12, 1950.

Excerpts from Kennan's record of his conversation with MacArthur on March 5, 1948, as included in PPS 28/2 of May 26, 1948, are printed below.

. . . .

Turning to the question of security, the General outlined his views on the position of the Pacific area in the pattern of our national defense. He said that the strategic boundaries of the United States were no longer along the western shores of North and South America; they lay along the eastern shores of the Asiatic continent. Accordingly, our fundamental strategic task was to make sure that no serious amphibious force could ever be assembled and dispatched from an Asiatic port. In the past the center of our defense problem had lain farther south, in the neighborhood of the Philippines. It had now shifted to the north, since it was now only toward the north that a threat of the development of amphibious power could mature.

The General then described the area of the Pacific in which, in his opinion, it was necessary for us to have striking force. This was a U-shaped area embracing the Aleutians, Midway, the former Japanese mandated islands, Clark Field in the Philippines, and above all Okinawa. Okinawa was the most advanced and vital point in this structure. From Okinawa he could easily control every one of the ports of northern Asia from which an amphibious operation could conceivably be launched. This was what was really essential. Naval facilities were important; but the air striking power was vital for the purpose in question. With adequate force at Okinawa, we would not require the Japanese home islands for the purpose of preventing the projection of amphibious power from the Asiatic mainland. That did not mean, of course, that it was not important to us to see that the strategic facilities of the Japanese islands remained denied to any other power. All the islands of the Western Pacific were of vital importance to us.

For these reasons, he attached great importance to Okinawa, and felt it absolutely necessary that we retain unilateral and complete control of the Ryukyu chain south of Latitude 29. . . .

. . . .

As for the Japanese islands, he did not believe that it would be feasible for us to retain bases anywhere in Japan after the conclusion of a treaty of peace. For us to do so would be to admit the equally legitimate claim of others to do likewise. He could assure me that the others would be only too anxious to take advantage of this. Not only the Russians but the other Allies would want some sort of base on Japanese territory. The only way to prevent this was for us to keep out.

As for the needs of our Navy, this was the one subject on which he felt some doubts about the adequacy of his own knowledge of the problem. He understood the Navy's desire to have facilities in this area and appreciated the necessity for it. He realized that the Navy did not like the prospect of making Okinawa its advance base, principally because the island was swept by typhoons and did not provide adequate protection, not to mention the absence of the usual port development. He felt, however, that these difficulties could be overcome. It would be possible to build a breakwater which would give better protection to vessels lying there; and it would always be possible for them to stand out to sea if necessary, under typhoon conditions.

<><><><><><><><><><><><><><><><><><><><><><><><><><><><><><><><><>

27, 28

Strategic Evaluation of United States Security Needs in Japan

NSC 49 series   June 15, 1949–September 30, 1949

Upon his return from the Far East in the spring of 1948, Kennan convinced both the Joint Chiefs of Staff and the Department of State that changes in occupation policy would be necessary if Japan were to emerge as a firmly pro-Western power in the intensifying Cold War. Kennan's recommendations, approved with slight modifications by President Truman on May 6, 1949,[1] stressed reducing the number of American occupation forces in the country, modifying those aspects of occupation policy not conducive to Japanese economic recovery, and working toward the eventual conclusion of a nonpunitive peace treaty that would leave U.S. military bases on Okinawa intact.

Agreement on these points left unclear the post-treaty status of Japan, however, and in the NSC 49 series, Washington officials addressed themselves to this question. Two excerpts from the NSC 49 series are printed below: (1) NSC 49 of June 15, 1949, which set forth the views of the Joint Chiefs of Staff; and (2) NSC 49/1 of October 4, 1949, which provided the views of the State Department. Both documents emphasize the importance of ensuring a pro-Western orientation for post-occupation Japan; significantly, though, they differ on the nature of the potential threat to that country, with the Joint Chiefs of Staff according high priority to the danger of external attack, and the State Department concentrating on the risks of internal political, economic, and social disorder.

1. NSC 13/3, "Recommendations with Respect to U.S. Policy toward Japan," *Foreign Relations of the United States: 1949*, VII (part 2), 730–36.

27   **T O P   S E C R E T**

Strategic Evaluation of United States Security Needs in Japan

NSC 49   June 15, 1949

[Source: *Foreign Relations of the United States: 1949,* VII (part 2), 774–77]

1. The Japanese Islands are of high strategic importance to United States security interests in the Far East, primarily because of their geographic location with respect to the trade routes of the North Pacific, the exits and entrances of the Sea of Japan, the East China and Yellow Seas, and, to a lesser degree, the ports of Asia north of the Shanghai-Woosung area, inclusive. Japan, also because of her geographic location, could under USSR control be used as a base for aggressive action directly against United States bases in the Western Pacific, in anticipation of step-by-step advances eastward and to the Southeast Asia region. Conversely, United States control of Japan, either directly or indirectly, will not only deny to the USSR an extremely important strategic base for aggressive or defensive action but also, in the event of war, will make available to us strategic outposts for early denial to the USSR, and eventually for control or neutralization by us, of the Sea of Japan and the Yellow and East China Seas. In addition, it would provide us with staging areas from which to project our military power to the Asiatic mainland and to USSR islands adjacent thereto.

2. Japan's strategic importance is increased by her manpower and her industrial potentials. These several potentials could, under readily foreseeable circumstances, and, despite the logistic demand that would need to be met in making her support useful, have great influence either for or against the interests of the United States in the event of global war.

3. The ability of the Japanese to wage both aggressive and defensive war was proven in the last world conflict. It is almost inconceivable that the Japanese manpower potential would be permitted to continue in peaceful pursuits in the event of another global conflict. Under USSR control, Japan probably would provide both the arsenal personnel and the manpower for aggressive military campaigns in the Pacific and to the southwest. If United States influence predominates, Japan can be expected, with planned initial United States assistance, at least to protect herself and, provided logistic necessities can be made available to her, to contribute importantly to military operations against the Soviets in Asia, thus forcing the USSR to fight on the Asiatic front as well as elsewhere.

4. From the military point of view, the ultimate minimum United States

position in the Far East vis-à-vis the USSR, one to which we are rapidly being forced, requires at least our present degree of control of the Asian offshore island chain. In the event of war, this island chain should constitute in effect a system of strong outposts for our strategic position. It would have only limited offensive value, however, and might well be untenable, if any major portion of the chain, such as Japan, were unavailable at the outset of the struggle.

5. The ability of the United States to derive full strategic advantage from the potentialities of Japan and to deny Japan's ultimate exploitation by the USSR will depend largely on the course we follow from now on with respect to Japan. This course should, accordingly, take into account the essential objectives, from the military viewpoint, of denying Japan to the Soviets and of maintaining her orientation toward the Western Powers.

·   ·   ·   ·   ·   ·   ·

7. In view of the fact that NSC 13/3 reserved a final United States position concerning the post treaty arrangements for Japanese military security "until the peace negotiations are upon us", and since agreement of the Joint Chiefs of Staff with the terms of the position set forth in that paper was with the understanding that it was, generally speaking, an interim position (and one which could not, when drafted, take into account the subsequent debacle in China), it is believed that some general discussion, in addition to the specific comment above, is in order.

8. From the military viewpoint, it is clear, as discussed initially in this memorandum, that the developing chaos on the Asiatic mainland, together with its communistic trend, makes it vital that, with or without a peace treaty, the orientation of Japan towards the West be assured. At the same time, the difficulty of achieving and maintaining such assurance has increased and it can be foreseen that economic and political pressure may well cause the problem to become very great indeed. This makes the question of Japanese internal security more important than ever. In turn, and commensurate with the degree to which Japanese western orientation is maintained, Japan's capacity for self-defense must be developed against the time when it may be determined by the Soviets that overt aggression by them or their satellites is their only means for gaining control over Japan.

9. With these points in mind, the Joint Chiefs of Staff are of the opinion, from the military point of view, that a peace treaty would, at the present time, be premature since the continuing Soviet policy of aggressive communist expansion makes it essential that Japan's democracy and western orientation first be established beyond all question, and since global develop-

ments are still in such a state of flux that measures leading to the risk of loss of control of any area might seriously affect our national security.

10. If peace negotiations are to be undertaken in the near future, they believe that the following safeguards should be included in order that our own national security interests may not be jeopardized and in order that the Far East communistic expansion plans of the Soviets may be held in check at least as far as Japan is concerned:

    a. There should be prior assurance of Japan's economic, psychological, and political stability, and of her democracy and western orientation;

    b. Japan's internal security forces must be adequate not only for maintenance of order but for protection against sabotage of vital installations. This may involve stronger internal security forces than were thought to be essential prior to the current overrunning of China;

    c. Since there can be no guarantee in the present world situation of the sovereignty of a defenseless Japan, there should be plans, as previously recommended by the Joint Chiefs of Staff, for limited Japanese armed forces for self-defense to be effectuated in war emergency, and, in any case, unless the general situation makes it clearly unnecessary, prior to departure of occupation forces from Japan; and

    d. No definite time should be set in the peace treaty for withdrawal of occupation forces. Rather, they should be phased out gradually and occupation should be terminated only after it has been determined and agreed that conditions are sufficiently satisfactory to justify termination.

---

28   **TOP SECRET**

Department of State Comments on NSC 49

NSC 49/1   September 30, 1949

[Source: *Foreign Relations of the United States: 1949,* VII (part 2), 871–73]

.   .   .   .

With respect to paragraph 5 of the JCS paper,[2] the Department of State would add that, from the political, as well as the military point of view, our

2. NSC 49. [Ed. note]

essential objectives with respect to Japan are its denial to the Soviet Union and the maintenance of Japan's orientation toward the Western powers.

The Department of State would emphasize the inter-relation between these two objectives. The denial of Japan to the USSR depends not only on the military capabilities and intentions of the U.S. but also on the attitude—the orientation—of the Japanese people. The effectiveness, cost and duration of the U.S. effort required to insure a denial of Japan to the USSR are directly affected by the attitude of the Japanese.

The Department of State does not doubt that, in the event of an overt Soviet attack on Japan in the foreseeable future—the contingency which must necessarily be foremost in the thinking of the JCS—the military effort of the U.S. would be the decisive factor. The Department of State believes that the JCS would agree, however, that the degree of effort required of the U.S. would be radically conditioned by the orientation of the Japanese.

In the event that the present world situation continues much as at present, the denial of Japan to the USSR constitutes a problem of combatting, not overt attack and invasion, but concealed aggression. The threat to Japan in these circumstances comes from agitation, subversion and *coup d'etat*. The threat is that of a conspiracy inspired by the Kremlin, but conducted by Japanese. It is essentially a conspiracy from within—and whether it succeeds depends primarily on the political, economic and social health of Japan itself. It is these problems which are foremost in the thinking of the Department of State in planning U.S. policy toward Japan for the present—and the foreseeable future.

The orientation of any people toward a foreign country is a subjective politico-psychological condition. It is the product of domestic political, economic and social factors, together with the nature and quality of a nation's relations with foreign countries. This being the case, the U.S. can neither impose nor enforce a pro-western orientation on any foreign people, including the Japanese. We can contribute to such an orientation only through (a) fostering in Japan, so far as we are able, conditions conducive to a pro-western orientation and (b) conducting our relations with Japan in such a way that, in the developing scene within Japan, we continue to be respected and, if possible, regarded with favor.

A word of caution should be advanced at this point regarding Japanese pro-western orientation. Such an orientation is, of course, our optimum objective. There are, however, many gradations between a pro-western orientation and the other extreme—an anti-U.S. and pro-Soviet attitude. The history of Japan and the ominous difficulties which lie before that country cause the Department of State to question whether this optimum objective can be realistically regarded as attainable. It is suggested that we may eventually find it necessary, through force of circumstances, to adopt the objective of a strongly nationalist, anti-Soviet Japan which we would regard without favor but as decidedly preferable to a Japan oriented toward the USSR.

In the meantime, the Department of State concurs with the opinion expressed by the JCS in paragraph 8 of its paper that the U.S. should do everything possible in an attempt to assure a continuance and development of the present generally favorable attitude of Japan toward the West. It is also in accord with the JCS conviction that Japanese internal security is more important than ever and that Japan's capacity for self-defense must at the proper time be developed. It shares the belief of the JCS that the spreading chaos on the mainland of Asia[3] heightens the importance of Japan to us.

The Department of State does not wholly concur with the opinion of the JCS that

a peace treaty would, at the present time, be premature since the continuing Soviet policy of aggressive communist expansion makes it essential that Japan's democracy and western orientation first be established beyond all question, and since global developments are still in such a state of flux that measures leading to the risk of loss of control of any area might seriously affect our national security.

The Department of State dissents from this judgment and the first of the two reasons advanced in support of it because they are, in terms of political realities, mutually exclusive. The only hope for the preservation and advancement of such democracy and western orientation as now exist in Japan lies in the early conclusion of a peace settlement with that country. From the political point of view, the achievements of our objectives with respect to Japan are now less likely to be thwarted by proceeding promptly to a peace treaty than by continuance of the occupation regime, provided that essential U.S. military needs in Japan are assured in the treaty or other concurrent arrangements.

The problem before us, the Department of State would submit, is to contribute through a peace treaty and a new relationship with Japan to the development within that country of indigenous resistance to Communism and of

3. The JCS reasoning in paragraph 7 that the debacle in China could not have been taken into account in the drafting of NSC 13/3, dated May 6, 1949, is difficult to follow. NSC 34, dated October 13, 1948, forecast the general course of the debacle and was, in so far as the Department of State was concerned, taken into account in the drafting of NSC 13/3. [Note in the source text.] NSC 34 is excerpted below as Document 31. [Ed. note]

spontaneous orientation toward the west, while at the same time making sure that our essential military requirements with respect to Japan are provided for and that the Japanese are given sufficient military strength of a police nature to check infiltration and to withstand efforts of Kremlin-inspired groups to seize power by force or intimidation. . . .

<><><><><><><><><><><><><><><><><><><><><><><><><><><><><><><><><>

29, 30

Possible Courses of Action for the U.S. with Respect to the Critical Situation in China

NSC 22 series   July 26, 1948–February 2, 1949

At no point during the period 1948–49 did Washington officials accord China the same priority they gave to Japan or Western Europe, despite the increasingly precarious position of Chiang Kai-shek's Nationalist government in the face of Mao Tsetung's Communist insurgency. This relative lack of concern stemmed from an awareness both of the immensity of China's problem and of the limited resources available to the United States in the Far East at a time when energies were being focused on the task of European recovery.

Not everyone in Washington shared this set of priorities, however; beginning in 1947 supporters of the Nationalist cause lobbied energetically, against the Truman Administration's wishes, for aid to Chiang Kai-shek. Their efforts bore fruit with the passage in April 1948 of the China Aid Act, which appropriated $275 million in economic aid and an additional fund of $125 million to be used at China's discretion for the purchase of military equipment.

With this development in mind, Secretary of the Army Kenneth C. Royall on July 26, 1948, submitted a paper (NSC 22, printed below) to the National Security Council outlining alternative courses of action for the United States in China. Two weeks later, the Joint Chiefs of Staff commented on NSC 22; their observations (NSC 22/1, printed below) constitute the strongest case made within the government at the time for a continuation of economic and military aid to Chiang Kai-shek.

29   **T O P   S E C R E T**

Possible Courses of Action for the U.S. with Respect to the Critical Situation in China

NSC 22   July 26, 1948

[Source: *Foreign Relations of the United States: 1949,* VIII, 118–22]

Problem

1. To assess the critical situation in China in light of current events; and state the critical questions facing the U.S. Government with possible alternative courses of action.

Analysis

2. a. The broad objectives of current U.S. policy toward China are understood to be:

    (1) Recognition of the National Government as the legal government of a sovereign China.

    (2) China should eliminate, by political agreement, conflict of armed forces within her territories as a Chinese responsibility to the United Nations in ameliorating the threat to world stability and peace.

    (3) China should undertake steps to broaden the base of the National Government to make it truly representative of the Chinese people in achieving the goal of a united and democratic China.

    (4) The U.S. Government desires to assist China as she moves toward peace, unity and genuinely democratic government.

    (5) The U.S. Government desires to assist China in the development of an effective Army and Navy, so limited in size as not to become an undue burden on the Chinese economy, and to this end maintains advisory missions. This assistance, however, will not extend to direct participation in the Chinese civil war.

     .   .   .   .

j. In light of the existing situation, the following critical questions face the U.S. Government:

    (1) What will be the effect on the security of the United States should the present Chinese National Government collapse?

    (2) What should be the attitude of the U.S. toward forestalling collapse of the present Chinese National Government?

    (3) What should be the attitude of the U.S. with respect to recognizing and/or aiding regional governments in China, should this transpire?

3. The following courses of action would appear to be open to the U.S.

   a. *U.S. aid might be increased to the maximum extent feasible.* This course of action would undoubtedly commit the resources of the United States to an extent which could be ill afforded at present, particularly in the light of the ERP. It is also questionable, owing to the rapid deterioration of the military and economic situation, as to whether commensurate benefits would ensue.

   b. *U.S. aid might be withdrawn.* Such a course of action would undoubtedly precipitate the fall of the National Government and accelerate the financial and economic deterioration now in process. This step would appear to nullify the will of the Congress which has legislated aid to China to the amount of $100,000,000 for the current year.

   c. *Continuation of U.S. aid on basis of programs now authorized.* This course of action would recognize the interest of Congress in continuing the ECA aid program as well as maintain, before the world, the semblance of adhering to announced U.S. policy toward China. Such a course could not produce the favorable decision required in the short time available to the Chinese National Government; nevertheless, it would be in the nature of "buying time" until the overall world situation is clarified.

   d. *United States recognition and aid might be shifted from the National Government of China to appropriate regional regimes that may arise as a result of the collapse of the present national government.* Under this course decision would have to be made as to whether to affiliate with certain separatist movements or remain aloof until such time as they might of their own accord arise out of the collapse of the present government. The process of encouraging separatist movements would be contrary to the expressed policy of the U.S.

---

30   **T O P   S E C R E T**

Possible Courses of Action for the U.S. with Respect to the Critical Situation in China

NSC 22/1   August 6, 1948

[Source: *Foreign Relations of the United States: 1948,* VIII, 131–35]

In accordance with your informal request, the Joint Chiefs of Staff have studied NSC 22, a paper entitled "Possible Courses of Action for the United States with Respect to the Critical Situation in China", and are in general agreement with the analysis therein of the present critical situation in China and with the statement, following the analysis, of the critical questions now facing the United States Government with respect to China.

.   .   .   .

While it is clear that the present Chinese National Government may collapse and that it would be out of the question for the United States to provide assistance, both material and military, on the massive scale that would be required for complete and early stabilization of China, it is not correctly a foregone conclusion that it is too late for worthwhile continuation of United States aid on the basis of programs now authorized.

The situation is worse than it was, but it is not, in the opinion of the Joint Chiefs of Staff, so bad that any further effort on the part of the United States would be useless. Thus, it is all the more important to continue the present authorized programs, rather than to encourage, if not assure, collapse by withdrawal of aid.

As earlier stated, carefully planned, selective and well-supervised assistance to the Chinese National Government, with safegaurds against misuse of such assistance and with inclusion of military equipment assistance, should make the Chinese assistance programs useful and effective.

The Joint Chiefs of Staff do not predict that this will necessarily turn the tide. They are convinced, however, that it will at least delay and postpone further deterioration and that the importance to our national security of the issues involved justifies, therefore, continuation of authorized assistance programs with special emphasis on the efficient and early implementation of the military aid program.

.   .   .   .

In view of all the preceding discussion, the Joint Chiefs of Staff recommend, with respect to the first three alternative United States courses of action, that the third alternative, continuation of United States aid on the basis of programs now authorized, continue to be accepted as the United States course of action.

With respect to the fourth alternative, shift of recognition and aid to appropriate regional regimes if the present Chinese National Government collapses, the Joint Chiefs of Staff believe that decision should properly be made in the light of the existing situation if and when collapse occurs. They believe, however, that at that time favorable consideration should be given to the above fourth alternative, since they are convinced that no matter how unfavorable ultimate developments in China may be, nor how possible it may be that they cannot be indefinitely forestalled, the buying of time by expenditures within reason will constitute, as in the case of the recommended continuation of authorized aid programs, true economy in terms of our national security.

<>∼<><><><><><><><><><><><><><><><><><><><><><><><><><><><><><>

31   **S E C R E T**

United States Policy Toward China

NSC 34   October 13, 1948

[Source: *Foreign Relations of the United States: 1948,* VIII, 146–55]

The Department of State expressed its view on the further extension of aid to Chiang Kai-shek in NSC 34, submitted to the National Security Council on October 13, 1948. Based on an earlier Policy Planning Staff study (PPS 39), this document advanced a much more pessimistic evaluation than that of the Joint Chiefs of Staff regarding Nationalist prospects for retaining power; it also implied that the Chiefs had considerably underestimated the costs to the United States of supporting that effort. NSC 34 injected a significant new argument into the debate, moreover, with its prediction that even if Mao Tse-tung did gain power, China would not become a reliable Soviet satellite. In taking this position, the Policy Planning Staff extended to the Far East a conclusion it had already drawn from events in Yugoslavia (see PPS 35, Document 21): that the international communist movement was not a monolith, and that the United States should retain the option, where appropriate, of not opposing communist regimes which chose to assert their independence from Moscow's control. In any case, the Staff concluded that because China lacked modern economic power and military technology, a communist regime there would pose no immediate threat to American security.

·   ·   ·   ·   ·   ·   ·

THE KREMLIN AND CHINA

Before analyzing Soviet objectives and strategy with respect to China, it would be useful to attempt an appraisal of that country from the point of view of the Kremlin.

In economic terms the Kremlin is certainly covetous of Manchuria's, and to a lesser degree, North China's, natural resources, both to deny them to Japan and to develop the Soviet Far East. As for the bulk of China proper, the Kremlin is hardly likely to view it other than as a vast poorhouse, responsibility for which is to be avoided.

Nor is there any reason to believe that the unromantic men in the Kremlin cherish any illusions regarding China's power potential; in any war in the foreseeable future China could at best be a weak ally or at worst an inconsequential enemy. Under certain conditions, however, parts of China, specifically Manchuria and Sinkiang, might serve as an avenue of attack on the USSR by a third power. The Kremlin, extremely sensitive about its land borders, must therefore regard Manchuria and Sinkiang as gaps in its buffer defense zone.

But it is the political situation in China which must arouse the aggressive interest of the Kremlin. In the struggle for world domination—a struggle which the Kremlin pursues essentially through political action (even in civil war)—the allegiance of China's millions is worth striving for. That allegiance is worth struggling for if only to deny it to the free world. In positive terms, China is worth having because capture of it would represent an impressive political victory and, more practically, acquisition of a broad human glacis from which to mount a political offensive against the rest of East Asia.

The Kremlin's objective with respect to China, therefore, is to expand its influence there and eventually to control all of the territory comprising China.

In pursuit of this objective the Kremlin's strategy is to (1) disrupt and then liquidate all active opposition to the expansion of communism and (2) bring under as tight control as possible all native communist elements and their collaborators. In seeking to defeat opposition, two of the most powerful indigenous political forces in China are employed: the sentiment of nationalism (anti-imperialism) is used against foreign opposition and the urge towards reform and a new order is used against native opposition—the National Government. And because one of the cardinal lines of attack is anti-imperialism, the USSR has been extremely careful to avoid any appearance of overt intervention; it has relied on indigenous elements, the Chinese Communists and affiliated groups, to carry on the fight.

The process of bringing the Chinese Communists and their collaborators under Kremlin control has already begun. It has been done, in at least one case—that of Li Li-san [4]—by introducing a presumed Stalinist into a posi-

4. Li Li-san, also known as Li Ming and Li Ming-jen, in 1948 was political adviser to General Lin Piao, who commanded Communist troops in Manchuria. American observers considered Li and other such advisers with Soviet ties to be part of a Soviet scheme to infiltrate the

tion of power. It is also being done by a reduction in the size of the territory answerable to the Communists in China proper. This is a bolshevik adaptation of the classic doctrine of divide and rule. There are indications that at least western and northern Manchuria and Sinkiang are intended to be separatist regimes answerable directly to Moscow (thus, at the same time, filling the gaps in the Soviet buffer defense zone). Furthermore the Chinese Communists have been denied overlordship over certain Manchurian Mongols, but permitted so far a communist suzerainty over Jehol Mongols.

It may be asked why such precautions are necessary if, as we are sometimes told, all communist parties—including the Chinese—obediently follow Moscow directives and are abject tools of the Kremlin. The answer is that Stalin and his Politbureau confreres do not have much faith in human nature. Their inclination towards cynicism is confirmed by experience—from the very process through which each of them came to power to the edifying truancy of comrade Tito. It is quite true that a common body of ideology is a strong bond; but to the old conspirators of the Kremlin the questions to ask about any foreign communist party are: who controls the party apparatus; who controls the secret police; who controls (if they exist) the armed forces; and does the foreign leader love power more than he fears the Kremlin?

If the answers to these questions as applied to China are as unsatisfactory to the Kremlin as they turned out to be in the case of Yugoslavia, Moscow faces a considerable task in seeking to bring the Chinese Communists under its complete control, if for no other reason than that Mao Tse-tung has been entrenched in power for nearly ten times the length of time that Tito has.

If on the other hand all elements of the Chinese Communist machine are Kremlin-controlled and Mao is now fearfully loyal, Moscow still cannot be satisfied with the situation. China is too big, too populous. Even Mao and his colleagues cannot be permitted eventually to acquire all of it—the temptation might be too great for them, especially as they would have, in part, risen to power on the heady wine of nationalism. The Kremlin prefers, where possible, not to take chances in such matters.

Finally, it may be said that the primary concern of the Kremlin with regard to China is not how the Chinese Communists can be helped to defeat opposition, to win the civil war—they are doing about as well as could be expected on that score—but how to ensure complete and lasting control over them and their collaborators. No one is more keenly aware than the Kremlin of the skill, subtlety and patience necessary to accomplish this. Still green in

Chinese Communist Party in preparation for a purge of anti-Soviet Chinese Communists. [Ed. note]

the Kremlin's memory is its own inept 1927 venture in open intervention,[5] its impetuous masterminding of an Asiatic revolution from Moscow, only to have the revolution "betrayed" by an intimate collaborator—Chiang Kai-shek.

THE AMERICAN ROLE IN CHINA
.   .   .   .

It is perhaps not surprising that as Chiang's fortunes declined the U.S. Government tended to commit itself more deeply to him, for we had come to equate Chiang with what we sought—a strong unified China. Therefore it was natural that in part as a gesture of faith in the future of the National Government this Government should have insisted in the depths of World War II that China should be accorded the position of one of the five Great Powers of the post-war world. It is also understandable that we should have continued to support Chiang in civil war long after it was evident that he could not win it.

This continuing exclusive commitment to Chiang is understandable, but it is not good diplomacy. It binds this Government to a single course, leaving it no alternative, no latitude for maneuver. This loss of initiative may not be fatal if the tide of events is running in one's favor. In the present situation in China, however, the tide is against us and we need the freedom to tack, or perhaps even to lie at anchor until we are quite sure of our bearings.

Conclusions

THE DISTANT FUTURE

From the analysis in this paper of demographic and economic factors[6] it is concluded that for years to come China will probably be plagued by (1) an implacable population pressure, which is likely to result in (2) a general standard of living around and below the subsistence level, which in turn will tend to cause (3) popular unrest, (4) economic backwardness, (5) cultural lag, and (6) an uncontrolled crude birth rate.

The political alternatives which this vicious cycle will permit for China's future are chaos or authoritarianism. Democracy cannot take root in so harsh an environment.

5. Soviet attempts to back Communist factions in seizing control of China's amorphous revolutionary movement in the middle 1920s culminated in a bloody episode in Shanghai in 1927, in which Chiang Kai-shek and other non-Communist revolutionaries expelled the Communists and their Soviet advisers into the countryside. [Ed. note]

6. This analysis was in opening sections of the paper, not printed here. [Ed. note]

Authoritarianism may be able to break the cycle by drastic means, such as forcible "socialization". At best, such measures could be put into effect only at heavy and long protracted cost to the whole social structure; at worst they could provoke such rebellion as to recreate a state of chaos.

THE IMMEDIATE FUTURE

It follows from the analysis in preceding sections that the Kuomintang and the National Government have so declined in strength that they may be assumed to be on the verge of losing their long struggle with the Chinese Communists.

The question naturally arises: late as it is, might not the Kuomintang and National Government as now constituted yet save themselves and might not American aid reverse the course of the civil war? The answer to the first half of the question is, "No"; it began to be evident ten years ago and is now abundantly clear that the Chiang-Kuomintang-National Government combination lacks the political dynamism to win out. The answer to the second half of the question is "It might, but only if the U.S. would provide as much aid as was necessary for as long as was necessary".

The aid which we have extended . . . has been insufficient to check the communist advance, much less reverse its course. How much more aid would be needed is less likely to be a problem of arithmetic progression than one approaching geometric progression. "All-out aid" amounts to overt intervention. Overt intervention multiplies resistance to the intervener. The ramified forces of new nationalism and traditional Chinese xenophobia would be likely to rally to the Communists, whose ties with the USSR are obscured in Chinese eyes by the Communists' violent anti-imperialism. Open U.S. intervention would, as it militarily strengthened Chiang, tend politically to strengthen the Communists. Thus, the more we openly intervened in the deep-rooted Chinese revolution, the more we would become politically involved, the more the National Government would tend to be regarded in Chinese eyes as a puppet—and thus discreditable, the greater our task would become, and the more the intervention would cost.

Eventually, assuming optimistically that the American people did not balk at the political and financial price, that the Communists were defeated on the field of battle and that the National Government was made supreme over a unified China—what then? Would we have ensured that the National Government would not promptly go to pieces on us again? What guarantee would we have that the revolution—the basic causes of which our action could not cure—would not begin all over again, and once more be exploited by the Kremlin? And when could we expect to get out from under the dreary load of political, military and financial responsibility for the National Government of China?

"All-out aid" to the National Government is therefore a course of action of huge, indefinite and hazardous proportions. The American Government cannot rightly gamble thus with American prestige and resources.

We then face up to the probability that the disappearance of the National Government as we now know it is only a matter of time. . . .

.   .   .   .

It is a nice piece of irony that at precisely the time the Chinese Communist leadership is most likely to wish to conceal its ties from Moscow, the Kremlin is most likely to be exerting utmost pressure to bring the Chinese Communists under complete control. The possibilities which such a situation would present us, provided we have regained freedom of action, need scarcely be spelled out.

This brings us to conclusions which may be drawn regarding our role in China.

U.S. POLICY

The traditional American aims with respect to China—(a) international respect for the territorial and administrative integrity of China, (b) equal opportunity, and (c) encouraging the development of a friendly and unified China—may be accepted as an expression of our long-range aspirations.

Given the realities of the situation in China and the limitations on our own capabilities, it is evident that our traditional aims are not now and will not be for some time to come susceptible of achievement. We therefore need for the foreseeable future a policy which can serve as a pragmatic guide through the Chinese maze.

It would, however, be misleading at this stage to attempt any detailed charting of a course to be followed for the next several years. The current situation is so chaotic and that which would follow the disappearance of the present National Government would be so fluid that any definite prescription for action would be bogus. Until the world situation is much clearer, particularly with respect to the USSR and China, our policy for the immediate future must be defined in the most flexible and elementary terms. For the foreseeable future, therefore, U.S. policy toward China should be:

a. to continue to recognize the National Government as now constituted;

b. with the disappearance of the National Government as we now know it, to make our decision regarding recognition in the light of circumstances at the time;

c. to prevent so far as is possible China's becoming an adjunct of Soviet politico-military power.

PRINCIPLES GOVERNING U.S. TACTICS

In the implementation of the foregoing policy, we should bear in mind the following principles, which should govern our tactics.

We must realize that there are operating in China tremendous, deep-flowing indigenous forces which are beyond our power to control. We must therefore accept the fact that there are considerable limitations on what we can do to affect the course of events in China. If we undertake or are maneuvered into action counter to basic Chinese forces these limitations will multiply and we will tend to defeat ourselves; conversely if we act so as to take advantage of these natural forces our influence will be multiplied.

Likewise, we must understand that the capabilities of the Kremlin to influence and utilize China for its overall purpose are severely qualified by the demographic, economic and political considerations discussed in this paper. It is impossible that the Kremlin could in the space of the next crucial five years mobilize China's resources and manpower to the extent that they would constitute a serious threat to U.S. security. It remains to be proved that the Kremlin could, if it survives as a predatory international force, accomplish this over the long run. If Soviet imperialism does not survive, Chinese communism will be of minor security concern to us for it has potentially grave significance to us only as a possible adjunct of Soviet politico-military power.

It follows from the preceding two paragraphs that China's destiny is largely in its own hands. The salvation or destruction of China lies essentially with the Chinese—not with foreigners.

In long-range planning for other countries of the Far East we must take into account that for some time to come China will be a chaotic and undependable factor on the Far Eastern scene.

Because China is unpredictable, we must not become irrevocably committed to any one course of action or any one faction in China and we must be willing to cut our losses when it becomes evident that any involvement is likely to prove to be a losing proposition.

We must place no reliance on the subjective attitude of any Chinese faction or government toward the U.S. Fear and favor always have and still do control fundamentally the attitude of foreign governments toward us, but only if expertly wielded.

If our strength is to be respected rather than scorned, it must be exercised in a form which is effective; it must not be dissipated by misapplication. There are four general forms in which our strength can be applied: military, economic, political and cultural. We must recognize that our military strength cannot be effectively applied excepting at prohibitive cost. The Kremlin has, by relying primarily on politico-cultural measures and avoiding overt intervention, enjoyed a phenomenal success in riding the ground-swell of the Chinese revolution. In the battle for the mind of China the most effective application of our strength will be through political, cultural and economic forms.

Economic favor becomes tribute if it continues to be given without exactions. While we must have favors in hand, in the shape of economic aid authorizations, for the post-Chiang situation, they must not be pre-committed. The Executive must have the flexibility to give or withhold fully or in part. Only thus will U.S. politico-economic influence be felt.

<><><><><><><><><><><><><><><><><><><><><><><><><><><><><><>

32   **C O N F I D E N T I A L**

United States Policy Toward China

PPS 39/1   November 23, 1948

[Source: *Foreign Relations of the United States: 1948,* VIII, 208–11]

Frustrated by the unsympathetic reaction NSC 34 had received from the Department of Defense, Kennan elaborated on the ideas expressed in that document in PPS 39/1, a memorandum approved by the Policy Planning Staff but not intended as an official expression of the State Department position. In PPS 39/1, Kennan attempted to define criteria for when the United States should and should not intervene in the internal affairs of other countries. Significantly, he proposed as the most important consideration in such decisions not morality, or even the requirements of the balance of power, but simply the prospects that such intervention would produce results commensurate with probable costs.

The following are the views of the Policy Planning Staff on the assertion, now frequently heard both inside and outside the Government, that we have no policy with relation to the present course of events in China, and that it is urgently necessary that we devise one.

1. There is no requirement either in United States diplomatic tradition, or in the general rules which govern intercourse between states, that a government have "a policy" with respect to internal events in another country. On the contrary, it is a traditional principle of this Government, deeply sanc-

tioned in practice and in public opinion, to refrain from interference in the internal affairs of other countries. Non-intervention in internal affairs is therefore our normal practice; and we do not consider that we are automatically obliged to take measures to influence decisively the course of internal events in other countries. There are, to be sure, instances in which such intervention has been found to be in the national interest. But these are the exceptions and not the rule. Whoever proposes or urges such intervention should properly bear the burden of proof

   a. that there is sufficiently powerful national interest to justify our departure in the given instance from a rule of international conduct which has been proven sound by centuries of experience and which we would wish others to observe with respect to ourselves, and

   b. that we have the means to conduct such intervention successfully and can afford the cost in terms of the national effort it involves.

2. In the case at hand, there is no question but that it is regrettable, and prejudicial to United States interest, that the recognized Chinese Government should be losing ground rapidly, in civil conflict, to elements largely inspired and dominated by Moscow. On the other hand, whether this process will lead to a complete domination of China by the Communists without at the same time promoting powerful "Tito" tendencies within the Communist movement, is doubtful. There is also little likelihood that the Communists, however much of China they may come to control, could develop and exploit its resources in a manner seriously dangerous to the security interests of this country. Thus, while the growing power of the Chinese Communists represents an important political development and a serious deterioration, from our standpoint, of the general situation in Asia, it is not likely to be catastrophic to United States interests.

3. Although the detriment to United States national interest involved in present developments in China, as mentioned above, would probably be sufficient to warrant intervention on the part of this country, we do not today have the means to intervene successfully in this situation. The successes of the Chinese Communists are due only in small degree to aid extended by Moscow. Of greater importance is Moscow's moral support and ideological inspiration, but even this is secondary. The main factor in the Communist advances is the inner weakness and decay of the Central Government in China. The relative change in forces which is in progress in that country is in part reflection of deep trends of internal development which themselves have nothing to do either with Russia or with the United States and which can be little altered by anything that either of those two powers may do.

4. It is plain, given the dimensions of the framework in which the civil war in China is proceeding, that in any successful attempt to repulse Communist advances the major effort must be made by the Chinese themselves, and any aid granted them by this country must be marginal to their own effort. However, the weaknesses of the Chinese Government are today so pronounced, and its resultant tendency to lean on outside aid is so overwhelming that it is quite plain that in any serious effort to turn the tide of events in that country and to eliminate the Communists from the control of Chinese territory (including Manchuria) it would be our effort which would have to be the major one and the Chinese effort which would be marginal. We must recognize that in China, as in other countries, but possibly more than anywhere else, there is a compelling tendency to regard United States aid not as a welcome addition to a continuing local effort but as a means of relieving the respective local regime of both responsibility and effort.

5. It must be emphasized that this state of affairs stems not only from national traits of long standing but also and predominantly from a pervasive and organic weakness which no sudden reform measures or personal leadership could overcome. The many and conflicting suggestions advanced for suddenly remedying the deficiencies of the Chinese Government and rendering it able to withstand Communist pressures condemn themselves. Most of them are obviously gross over-simplifications which can stem only from ignorance or naïveté. The evils which limit the military and political effectiveness of the Central Government are ones profoundly rooted in the present stage of development of Chinese society, and many of them will doubtless reappear to limit the effectiveness of any Chinese Communist regime which assumes authority in the central and southern regions of China.

6. In the light of these facts, it is unrealistic and indefensible, in the view of this staff, to assume that we could decisively affect the course of events in China without taking upon ourselves the major responsibility and the major part of the expenditure of energy and funds and goods which that would involve. As far as the Staff is aware, this Government does not have before it any official estimate, from competent quarters, of what it would involve in the way of military effort on our part to assume the major burden of containing and repulsing Communist forces in China. Such estimates as we have seen from outside quarters or from individual opinions of officials in the Government have generally been based on the theory that the Chinese Government was capable of making the major effort necessary for this purpose and only required from this country marginal assistance in shipments of

arms and military advice. In the absence of any official estimates on this point, based on a realistic view of the background situation, it would have been, and would be today, frivolous and irresponsible to venture into any program of economic or military aid designed to enable the Chinese Central Government to defeat the Communist forces and reestablish its authority throughout the country.

7. Actually, and particularly in view of the fact that what would be called for from this country would be not only arms and money but a major output in terms of executive and military personnel, it would seem clear even to the casual inquirer that any attempt to assume the major burden of the government's cause in the Chinese Civil War would be plainly beyond what Congress or the people of this country could realistically be expected to sanction and support at this time.

8. In the light of the above, the Policy Planning Staff strongly doubts that there is a practical possibility of exercising any serious influence on the course of events in China through the extension of further military or economic aid to the Central Government at this time. If this view is correct, then our policy toward China must, in so far as it envisages any intervention in Chinese internal affairs, be based rather on other possible expedients, as for example use of our economic bargaining power to extract specific concessions, aid to local factions or authorities, etc.

9. Since it is also clear that the policy of this country cannot be predicated on the resistance to Communism which the Central Government may put up, it follows that our actions will have to be adjusted to the needs of specific local situations. This will mean that we cannot have "a policy" toward China as a whole, except to favor authorities which take a relatively cooperative view toward United States interests and to disfavor those which do not. Such a policy must be translated into action on a day by day basis in accordance with the changes of the moment. It cannot be explicitly defined on paper in a form which can serve as a guide for months or years ahead. It is outstandingly a matter which calls for operational skill and flexibility.

10. In summary, there is plainly no great difference of opinion as to what we would like to see happen in China. We would wish to see the Communists defeated and replaced, in the territories they now occupy, by other Chinese authorities not inspired or directed by any foreign government, and not animated by any basic hostility to this country.

On the other hand, our means for influencing directly the course of events in China are extremely limited. It is plain, in particular, that there is little we can do to influence these events through the programs of economic aid and military aid to the Central Chinese Government.

This being the case, we must reconcile ourselves to the possibility that there may be further serious deterioration of the situation and that we may be powerless to prevent it.

However, we may hope that eventually static factors of geography, history, tradition, social conditions, etc., will absorb and contain much of the Communist effort. Meanwhile, we should search diligently for opportunities to make our influence usefully felt, if only in local theatres of activity.

<><><><><><><><><><><><><><><><><><><><><><><><><><><><><><><><><><><><><>

33, 34

US Policy Toward Asia

NSC 48 series   December 23–30, 1949

In the NSC 48 series, the National Security Council attempted to weave the disparate threads of United States Far Eastern policy into a general statement of objectives and recommendations for action. NSC 48/1, prepared by the staff of the National Security Council and presented to that body on December 23, 1949, represented the culmination of that process.

NSC 48/1 defined the American interest in Asia in terms of maintaining a balance of power on the continent. It viewed the Soviet Union as the principal threat to that balance, but carefully avoided attributing all revolutionary activity in Asia to Kremlin machinations. Rather, it argued, such movements stemmed primarily from the growing strength of nationalism and could, with proper handling, be used as instruments with which to resist Soviet expansionism. For this reason the document advised against any attempt to deny Formosa to the Chinese Communists, on the grounds that such interference in the Chinese civil war on the Nationalists' behalf could only drive Mao Tse-tung's government into further dependence on the Russians. NSC 48/1 also argued that Japan would more reliably serve as a counterweight to Soviet influence in Asia if allowed to develop its own political and economic ties to the mainland, regardless of ideological differences.

President Truman approved the conclusions of NSC 48/1 in modified form (as NSC 48/2) on December 29, 1949. Secretary of State Dean Acheson in turn drew heavily from these documents in his famous speech to the National Press Club on January 12, 1950, in which he also outlined publicly the "defensive perimeter" concept that had grown out of the Kennan-MacArthur conversations of March 1948 (see Document 26).

NSC 48/2 remained the definitive expression of U.S. Far Eastern policy only briefly, for the sudden outbreak of fighting in Korea in June 1950 brought about virtually overnight a reversal of policy on Formosa, an increase in aid to the French in Indochina, the involvement by November of 1950 of U.S. and Chinese Communist forces in direct military conflict, and, as a result, the abandonment of any significant effort to achieve American objectives in Asia by exploiting Sino-Soviet antagonism.

Yergin say 48/2 reversed policy

33   **T O P   S E C R E T**

The Position of the United States with Respect to Asia

NSC 48/1   December 23, 1949

[Source: U.S. Department of Defense, *United States-Vietnam Relations, 1945–1967* (Washington, 1971), VIII, 226–64]

The Problem

1. To assess and appraise the position of the United States with respect to Asia[7] on the basis of our national security interests.

Analysis

GENERAL CONSIDERATIONS

2. The peoples and countries of Asia have in common a heavy pressure of population on scanty or underdeveloped natural resources and a consequent meager standard of living: disruption experienced in the war: the vigorous nationalistic spirit which characterizes newly independent states or restive colonies: and active discontent with their prevailing social, economic and political institutions. In other words the Asians share poverty, nationalism, and revolution. The United States position with respect to Asia is therefore that of a rich and powerful country dealing with a have-not and sensitively nationalistic area, and of competition together with friendly countries against the USSR for influence on the form and direction of the Asiatic revolutions.

3. Asia is an area of significant potential power—political, economic and military. The development in this region of stable and independent countries friendly to the United States and seeking to direct their potential power into constructive channels would enhance the security of Asia and strengthen the world position of the United States. Conversely, the domination of Asia by a nation or coalition of nations capable of exploiting the region for purposes of self-aggrandizement would threaten the security of Asia and of the United States. Recognition of these principles has been implicit in our traditional policies toward Asia: We have consistently favored a system of independent states and opposed aggrandizement of any powers which threatened eventual domination of the region.

7. For the purposes of this report "Asia" is defined as that part of the continent of Asia south of the USSR and east of Iran together with the major off-shore islands—Japan, Formosa, the Philippines, Indonesia and Ceylon. [Note in source text]

4. Our over-all objective with respect to Asia must be to assist in the development of truly independent, friendly, stable and self-sustaining states in conformity with the purposes and principles of the United Nations Charter. In order to achieve this, we must concurrently oppose the domination of Asia by any single country or coalition. It is conceivable that in the course of time a threat of domination may come from such nations as Japan, China, or India, or from an Asiatic bloc. But now and for the foreseeable future it is the USSR which threatens to dominate Asia through the complementary instruments of communist conspiracy and diplomatic pressure supported by military strength. For the foreseeable future, therefore, our immediate objective must be to contain and where feasible to reduce the power and influence of the USSR in Asia to such a degree that the Soviet Union is not capable of threatening the security of the United States from that area and that the Soviet Union would encounter serious obstacles should it attempt to threaten the peace, national independence or stability of the Asiatic nations.

containment r rollback

POLITICAL CONSIDERATIONS

5. Asia is in the throes of political upheaval. Communist attempts to capture leadership of this revolution, nationalism and the revolt against colonial rule, the emergence of new nations, the decline of western influence, the absence of a stabilizing balance of power, the prevalence of terrorism, economic distress and social unrest, and the repercussions of the struggle between the Soviet world and the free world are currently disruptive forces. The conditions now prevailing in Asia render the realization of United States objectives there difficult and facilitate expansion of the area of both communist control and Soviet influence.

6. The USSR is now an Asiatic power of the first magnitude with expanding influence and interests extending throughout continental Asia and into the Pacific. Since the defeat of Japan, which ended a balance of power that had previously restrained Russian pressures in China and the Pacific, the Soviet Union has been able to consolidate its strategic position until the base of Soviet power in Asia now comprises not only the Soviet Far East, but also China north of the Great Wall, Northern Korea, Sakhalin, and the Kuriles. The islands of Japan and the subcontinent shared by India and Pakistan are the major Asian power centers remaining outside the Soviet orbit. If Japan, the principal component of a Far Eastern war-making complex, were added to the Stalinist bloc, the Soviet Asian base could become a source of strength capable of shifting the balance of world power to the disadvantage of the United States. Should India and Pakistan fall to communism, the

United States and its friends might find themselves denied any foothold on the Asian mainland.

7. While the military advantages of this position to the USSR are great, the general Far Eastern situation also gives the USSR significant political advantages. In estimating the degree of political pressure that the USSR may exert from its present position in Asia, it should be remembered that its proteges deal with Asiatic peoples who are traditionally submissive to power when effectively applied and habituated to authoritarian government and the suppression of the individual. Moreover, the USSR in Asia as elsewhere with relatively little overt interference in other states, at relatively small cost, and at limited risk, is able to give assistance and impetus to native communist movements. The political offensive of the Kremlin or its proteges also tends to gather additional momentum as each new success increases the vulnerability of the next target.

8. Japan has ceased to be a world power, but retains the capability of becoming once more a significant Asiatic power. Whether its potential is developed and the way in which it is used will strongly influence the future patterns of politics in Asia. As a result of the occupation, Japan's political structure has been basically altered and notable steps have been taken toward the development of democratic institutions and practices. Despite these advances, however, traditional social patterns, antithetical to democracy, remain strong. The demonstrated susceptibility of these patterns to totalitarian exploitation is enhanced by economic maladjustment which may grow more serious as a result of population increases and of obstacles to the expansion of trade.

9. Although, in terms of the Japanese context, an extreme right-wing movement might be more effective in exploiting traditional patterns and current dislocations than one of the extreme left, a number of factors combine to make the threat of Communism a serious one. These factors include the close proximity to a weak and disarmed Japan of Communist areas with the attendant opportunities for infiltration, clandestine support of Japanese Communist efforts, and diplomatic pressure backed by a powerful threat; the potential of Communist China as a source of raw materials vital to Japan and a market for its goods; and the existence in Japan of an ably-led, aggressive, if still relatively weak, Communist movement which may be able to utilize Japanese tendencies toward passive acceptance of leadership to further its drive for power while at the same time exploiting economic hardship to undermine the acceptability to the Japanese of other social patterns that are antithetical to Communist doctrines.

10. Even if totalitarian patterns in Japan were to reassert themselves in

the form of extreme right-wing rather than Communist domination, the prospect would remain that Japan would find more compelling the political and economic factors moving it toward accommodation to the Soviet orbit internationally, however anti-Communist its internal policies, than those that move it toward military alliance with the United States. Extreme right-wing domination of Japan, moreover, although less immediately menacing to the United States than Communist control would represent a failure, particularly marked in the eyes of other non-Communist Asiatic countries, of a major United States political effort.

11. A middle of the road regime in Japan retaining the spirit of the reform program, even if not necessarily the letter, would in the long-run prove more reliable as an ally of the United States than would an extreme right-wing totalitarian government. Under such a regime the channels would be open for those elements in Japan that have gained most from the occupation to exercise their influence over government policy and to mold public opinion. Such a regime would undoubtedly wish to maintain normal political and economic relations with the Communist bloc and, in the absence of open hostilities, would probably resist complete identification either with the interests of the United States or the Soviet Union. The existence of such a regime, however, will make possible the most effective exercise of United States political and economic influence in the direction of ensuring Japan's friendship, its ability to withstand external and internal Communist pressure, and its further development in a democratic direction.

12. The basic United States non-military objectives in Japan therefore, remain the promotion of democratic forces and economic stability before and after the peace settlement. To further this objective the United States must seek to reduce to a minimum occupation or post-occupation interference in the processes of Japanese Government while at the same time providing protection for the basic achievements of the occupation and the advice and assistance that will enable the Japanese themselves to perpetuate these achievements; provide further economic assistance to Japan and, in concert with its allies, facilitate the development of mutually beneficial economic relations between Japan and all other countries of the world; make it clear to Japan that the United States will support it against external aggression while at the same time avoiding the appearance that its policies in Japan are dictated solely by considerations of strategic self-interest and guarding against Japan's exploitation of its strategic value to the United States for ends contrary to United States policy interests; and promote the acceptance of Japan as a peaceful, sovereign member of the community of nations.

13. The United States has taken the lead in assisting the efforts of the

Korean people to regain that independence promised them at Cairo.[8] In NSC 8/2,[9] approved by the President on March 23, 1949, it was agreed that "if the significant gains made thus far, in terms both of the welfare and aspirations of the Korean people and of the national interest of the United States are to be consolidated, the United States must continue to give political support and economic, technical, military and other assistance to the Republic of Korea." The principal objective of this policy is to strengthen that Government to the point where it can (1) successfully contain the threat of expanding Communist influence and control arising out of the existence in north Korea of an aggressive Soviet-dominated regime, and (2) serve as a nucleus for the eventual peaceful unification of the entire country on a democratic basis. *again, containment or rollback*

14. It can be assumed that under present circumstances the communists have the capability of dominating China. Communist domination of China is significant to the USSR primarily because it enhances USSR capabilities for obtaining Soviet objectives in Asia. Soviet ability to capitalize on the situation in China will depend on the degree of control that the Kremlin can exert over Chinese communist leaders, and on the control that the Chinese communists can exert over all elements of Chinese society. Development of these two varieties of control will not necessarily proceed in parallel. The formidable problems of overpopulation, limited and undeveloped natural resources, technical backwardness, and social and political lag which confront the Chinese communists have contributed to the downfall of every Chinese regime in recent history. Chinese communist success in surmounting their internal difficulties might well be accompanied by a lessening rather than an intensification of their subservience to the Kremlin. Similarly Chinese communist failure to achieve an effective solution of China's problems might drive the Chinese communists to depend more rather than less on the USSR. For the very immediate future it may be assumed that both Kremlin influence on the Chinese communists and Chinese communist control over China will grow more firm and that China will represent a political asset to the USSR in accomplishment of its global objectives. But longer range development of Kremlin influence over the Chinese communists will

8. At Cairo in November 1943, President Franklin D. Roosevelt met with Winston Churchill and Chiang Kai-shek before proceeding to Teheran for a summit with Marshal Josef Stalin. On December 1, 1943, the Cairo conferees issued a statement saying that they, "mindful of the enslavement of the people of Korea [by Japan], are determined that in due course Korea shall become free and independent." (*Foreign Relations of the United States: Conferences at Cairo and Teheran, 1943*, p. 403). [Ed. note]

9. "The Position of the US with Respect to Korea" (printed in *Foreign Relations of the United States: 1949*, VII (part 2), 969–78). [Ed. note]

be subject to the interplay of such presently unpredictable factors as Chinese communist effectiveness, USSR policy toward the Chinese communists, and the relations between the Chinese communists and the non-communist world. If the Kremlin should attempt to extend to China the pattern of political and economic control and exploitation that has characterized its relations with its European satellites, it is quite possible that serious frictions would develop between the Chinese communist regime and Moscow. Moreover, an attempt by the USSR to mobilize directly all Chinese resources in pursuance of its strategic objectives might well result in China's becoming more of a liability than an asset to the Soviet Union. The actions of the United States or of other Western powers cannot be expected greatly to weaken Chinese communist control of China in the foreseeable future, but may have influence on the relations between the Chinese communists and the USSR. In fact, any attempt on the part of the United States openly to deny Chinese territory such as Formosa to the communists would probably react to the benefit of the communists by rallying all the anti-foreign sentiment in China to their side.

15. Furthermore, action by the U.S. to occupy Formosa would inevitably expose the U.S. to charges of "imperialism" and seriously affect the moral position of the U.S. before the bar of world opinion, particularly in the Far East, at a time when the U.S. is seeking to expose Soviet imperialist designs on other nations. Such action would provide the Chinese communists with an irredentist issue for their propaganda against the U.S. and a cause which would rally almost unanimous public sentiment behind them in China.

16. It is not believed that denial of Formosa to the Chinese communists can be achieved by any method short of actual U.S. military occupation. As a CIA intelligence estimate of October 19, 1949 (ORE 76–49, concurred in by the intelligence organizations of the Departments of State, Army, Navy and Air Force) states:

Without major armed intervention, U.S. political, economic, and logistic support of the present Nationalist island regime cannot insure its indefinite survival as a non-communist base. Communist capabilities are such that only extended U.S. military occupation and control of Taiwan can prevent its eventual capture and subjugation by Chinese communist forces. Failing U.S. military occupation and control, a non-communist regime on Taiwan probably will succumb to the Chinese communists by the end of 1950.

17. In the light of the foregoing, and in view of the estimate of the JCS, reaffirmed in NSC 37/7[10] of August 22, 1949, that "the strategic impor-

10. "The Position of the US with Respect to Formosa" (printed in *Foreign Relations of the United States: 1949*, IX, 376–78). [Ed. note]

tance of Formosa does not justify overt military action . . . '', it is believed that U.S. military occupation of Formosa, which would require concurrent responsibility for the administration of the Island, would not be in the U.S. national interest.

18. On December 23, 1949, the Joint Chiefs of Staff stated that events which have taken place in China have not changed their above views (NSC 37/7, dated August 22, 1949). However, within these limitations, the Joint Chiefs of Staff believe that a modest, well-directed and closely supervised program of military advice and assistance to the anti-Communist government in Formosa would be in the security interest of the United States, and should be integrated with a stepped-up political, economic and psychological program pursued energetically in extension of present United States programs there.

19. In south Asia we are favored by the fact that communist groups and leaders played a minor part in the nationalist movements of the area, which attained independence through a peaceful transfer of power by the British. The present south Asian governments are non-communist and, except in Burma, are maintaining law and order and have good prospects of remaining in power for the next few years. Soviet and Chinese communist hostility and internal communist opposition, on the one hand, and friendliness and circumspection on the part of the United States, the United Kingdom and the other Western powers, on the other, have during the past two years strengthened the Western orientation of the south Asian governments.

20. India and Pakistan, the pivotal nations of the area, inherited from the British well trained armies, a corps of experienced civil administrators, transport and communications facilities well developed by Asian standards, important agricultural and extractive industries, and a few large-scale processing and manufacturing industries. They, and Ceylon, remain within the Commonwealth and have significant military, economic and cultural ties with the United Kingdom—as does Burma which chose to leave the Commonwealth.

21. There are, unfortunately, adverse factors which threaten the continued relative stability of south Asia. Active disputes between India and Pakistan and between Pakistan and Afghanistan, and suspicion of India in varying degree among its smaller neighbors at the minimum impede essential regional cooperation. At the unlikely maximum, they could embroil the area in war. Internally, all the governments of south Asia are faced with the necessity of bringing to their peoples within the next few years at least some hope of improved economic and social conditions. Failing this, they may lose control to extreme groups of the right or the left.

22. Consideration of the foregoing unfavorable aspects of the south Asian situation together with the current reluctance of the area to align itself overtly with any "power bloc" leads to the conclusion that it would be unwise for us to regard south Asia, more particularly India, as the sole bulwark against the extension of communist control in Asia. We should, however, recognize that the non-communist governments of the area already constitute a bulwark against communist expansion. We should accordingly exploit every opportunity to increase the present Western orientation of south Asia and to assist, within our capabilities, its non-communist governments in their efforts to meet the minimum aspirations of their people and to maintain (in the case of Burma to restore) internal security.

23. The current conflict between colonialism and native independence is the most important political factor in southeast Asia. This conflict results not only from the decay of European imperial power in the area but also from a widening political consciousness and the rise of militant nationalism among the subject peoples. With the exception of Thailand and the Philippines, the southeast Asia countries do not possess leaders practiced in the exercise of responsible power. The question of whether a colonial country is fit to govern itself, however, is not always relevant in practical politics. The real issue would seem to be whether the colonial country is able and determined to make continued foreign rule an overall losing proposition for the metropolitan power. If it is, independence for the colonial country is the only practical solution, even though misgovernment eventuates. A solution of the consequent problem of instability, if it arises, must be sought on a non-imperialist plane. In any event, colonial-nationalist conflict provides a fertile field for subversive communist activities, and it is now clear that southeast Asia is the target of a coordinated offensive directed by the Kremlin. In seeking to gain control of southeast Asia, the Kremlin is motivated in part by a desire to acquire southeast Asia's resources and communication lines, and to deny them to us. But the political gains which would accrue to the USSR from communist capture of southeast Asia are equally significant. The extension of communist authority in China represents a grievous political defeat for us; if southeast Asia also is swept by communism we shall have suffered a major political rout the repercussions of which will be felt throughout the rest of the world, especially in the Middle East and in a then critically exposed Australia. The United States should continue to use its influence looking toward resolving the colonial-nationalist conflict in such a way as to satisfy the fundamental demands of the nationalist-colonial conflict, lay the basis for political stability and resistance to communism, and avoid weakening the colonial powers who are our western allies. However,

it must be remembered that the long colonial tradition in Asia has left the peoples of that area suspicious of Western influence. We must approach the problem from the Asiatic point of view in so far as possible and should refrain from taking the lead in movements which must of necessity be of Asian origin. It will therefore be to our interests wherever possible to encourage the peoples of India, Pakistan, the Philippines and other Asian states to take the leadership in meeting the common problems of the area.

24. Although European influence has certainly declined throughout Asia and European powers are no longer able fully to shape the course of events in that part of the world, nevertheless the influence of such powers is by no means negligible. This is particularly true of the United Kingdom because of the advanced policies followed in Asia by that nation since the end of the war. With the successful conclusion of the Round Table talks at the Hague[11] (for which this Government can claim preeminent credit) the Dutch will undoubtedly regain much of their lost popularity. It would be to the interest of the United States to make use of the skills, knowledge and long experience of our European friends and, to whatever extent may be possible, enlist their cooperation in measures designed to check the spread of USSR influence in Asia. If members of the British Commonwealth, particularly India, Pakistan, Australia and New Zealand, can be persuaded to join with the United Kingdom and the United States in carrying out constructive measures of economic, political and cultural cooperation, the results will certainly be in our interest. Not only will the United States be able thus to relieve itself of part of the burden, but the cooperation of the white nations of the Commonwealth will arrest any potential dangers of the growth of a white-colored polarization.

25. With the rise of new nations and the decline of colonialism, a consciousness of common interests and a demand for regional collaboration is beginning to take form among the countries of Asia. However, the wide diversity of political organization and development, the lack of a tradition of cooperation and a sound economic basis for large-scale mutual trade, and the suspicions with which the weaker nations of Asia view the stronger, have all operated to delay the formation of any regional organization up to the present. But efforts continue and will probably increase in tempo as the

---

11. In "round table" meetings from August 23, 1949 to November 2, 1949, the United States took a leading role in convincing the Netherlands to grant Indonesian independence. (See documentation in *Foreign Relations of the United States: 1949*, VII (part 1),119-590). [Ed. note]

advance of Soviet influence becomes more and more a direct threat. As stated above the peoples of Asia are suspicious of the West and in any cooperation the United States may extend to a developing regionalism it will be necessary to do nothing which would excite further suspicion of our motives. Asian leaders have already taken the initiatve in this matter and it should continue to rest in their hands. There are many indications for example that India aspires to draw Ceylon, Burma and southeast Asia into a regional association. These aspirations are aided by the considerable moral influence which India enjoys throughout this area, derived from the great prestige of its revolutionary leaders and its position as the largest of the Asian dependencies to become independent of colonial rule. India has gained additional goodwill by its strong support of the Indonesian independence movement. Prime Minister Nehru is, however, aware of the difficulties of creating an effective regional organization in south and southeast Asia, and is moving slowly and cautiously. He and other Indian leaders prefer that such an association develop from indigenous desires and would not look with favor upon attempts by outside powers to impose, or even too actively to foster, a regional organization of the area. United States interests would appear to demand that our sympathetic support be given to Asiatic leaders to the end that any regional association which may develop be one with which we could cooperate on equal terms and which would be in harmony with the UN Charter.

26. Asia is only one of several fronts on which the United States directly or indirectly confronts the USSR. Pressures, or lack of them, on any front affect all the others. The fortunate circumstance of occupying a favorable geographic position both in Europe and in Asia allows the USSR great flexibility in the pressures it may apply. Operating from the center of the Eurasian continent, it may advance or retreat in the east or in the west as the occasion demands. Because there is no longer a force either in Europe or Asia which can withstand without full United States assistance the power of the USSR if it should be unleashed, determination of the effective use of United States power, in its total sense, on any or all of its fronts with the USSR—European, Near Eastern, or Asiatic—requires decisions based upon a constant and skillful reevaluation of the costs involved and the probable results to be obtained in each case, both in the event of war and its probable aftermath, and in the event of continued peace. The United States for its part must be able to apply pressure on fronts at times of its own choosing rather than spreading itself thin in reacting to every threat posed by the Soviets if it is not to lose the advantages of the initiative in the struggle between the So-

viet world and the free world. Mobilization of our cold war potential and implementation by effective techniques is essential.

27. United States ability to exert counter influence against the Kremlin in Asia rests on U.S. ability to provide economic assistance and cooperation to Asiatic countries; on preservation and development of the U.S. traditional reputation as a non-imperialistic champion of freedom and independence for all nations; on the frictions which will arise between Asiatic nationalisms and USSR imperialism; on U.S. cultural and philanthropic contacts in Asia; on U.S. ability to exert constructive influence on the European Far Eastern colonial powers and to gain assistance from these powers in the Far East; on U.S. military power, and on the U.S. strategic position in the Pacific. Appropriate development and utilization of these U.S. assets in Asia through effective diplomacy and propaganda will naturally increase the influence which the United States can now bring to bear to check the USSR in that area.

28. It must be remembered, however, that helping Asiatic countries to resist USSR pressure is not something we can do by our own policy alone. We will depend for success on interaction between our policy and what already exists in the way of will and ability to resist on the part of the Asiatic countries themselves. It must also be borne in mind that the sweeping changes which have been taking place in Asia since the war have been stimulated in very considerable part by the determination of the peoples of Asia to control their own destinies and to redress the grievances of the past which they associate with foreign rule and foreign influence. Intervention in their affairs, particularly by the Western powers, however well-intentioned, will of itself be suspect and be likely to result in the undoing of the very interests which prompted the intervention. In the conflict between the U.S. and the USSR, the advantage in the long run in Asia is likely to rest with the side which succeeds in identifying its own cause with that of the Asian peoples and which succeeds in working in harmony with the dominant motivating forces in Asia today and in influencing these forces rather than attempting by direct or impatient methods to control them.

STRATEGIC CONSIDERATIONS

29. The potential power of Asia is strategically significant both to the United States and to the USSR because of its capacity in the long run to affect the relative military strength of these two countries and hence the character of military operations in the event of war between them. Translation of the Asian power potential into military strength would require development

of each of its elements—organization and training of manpower, exploitation of natural resources, development of sea transportation, improvement of communications and further industrialization—as well as their integration toward coordinated objectives. Even given the most favorable atmosphere for development, including the power to consolidate as necessary, the authority to divert channels of trade, and the military force required to protect long sea routes and other lines of communication—the full development of Asia's potential power is a long-term affair. In the power potential of Asia, Japan plays the most important part by reason of its industrious, aggressive population, providing a large pool of trained manpower, its integrated internal communications system with a demonstrated potential for an efficient merchant marine, its already developed industrial base and its strategic position. Because of Japan's economic importance in Asia, of the extreme vulnerability of Japan to blockade, of the long period required under the best of circumstances for the development of significant strategic potential in Asia, and of the hazards involved in attempts to harness Chinese potential to Soviet ends, there exists no serious danger that the USSR will in the near future be able to undertake military aggression based on Asia's strategic potential.

30. The location of Asia, contiguous to the USSR and separated from the United States, presents different strategic implications, both offensive and defensive, to the United States and to the USSR. The Asian power potential is more valuable to Russia than to the United States, since American industrial power is so much greater than Russian. The industrial plant of Japan would be the richest strategic prize in the Far East for the USSR. For Japan and major Asian raw-material producing areas, together with the necessary transportation lines, to be controlled by the Soviet Union would add measurably to the war-making potential of the USSR. Russia could not, however, quickly build up a powerful self-sufficient war-making complex in Asia without access to and control over Japan and could not effectively mobilize Japan in war without a larger merchant fleet in the Pacific than the USSR and Japan are likely to have for years to come. Other Asiatic assets of potential value to Russia include soybeans, tin, rubber, and South China's tungsten. Petroleum, coming from Indonesia including Boreno, while not essential to meet Russian domestic requirements, is one of the most important strategic materials in the region.

31. The strategic value of Asia to the United States rests on three considerations: In the first place denial of USSR control over Asia might prevent the acquisition by the Soviets of elements of power which might in time add

significantly to the Russian war-making potential. Secondly, to the degree that Asian indigenous forces develop opposition to the expansion of USSR influence, they would assist the U.S. in containing Soviet control and influence in the area, possibly reducing the drain on the United States economy. The indigenous forces of Asia, including manpower reserves, would also be a valuable asset, if available for the support of the United States in the event of war. Thirdly, Asia is a source of numerous raw materials, principally tin and natural rubber, which are of strategic importance to the United States, although the United States could, as in World War II, rely on other sources if necessary.

32. Since, from the military point of view, the primary strategic interests and war objectives of the United States consistent with the aim of destruction of the enemy's means to wage war are not now in Asia, the current basic concept of strategy in the event of war with the USSR is to conduct a strategic offense in the "West" and a strategic defense in the "East." In keeping with this basic concept and in light of the strategic interests of the United States and the USSR as developed above, certain principles may be stated. As a primary matter in the event of war, it is essential that a successful strategic defense in the "East" be assured with a minimum expenditure of military manpower and material in order that the major effort may be expended in the "West". In order to gain freedom of access to the Asian continent within these limitations, the United States must now concentrate its efforts on bringing to bear such power as can be made available, short of the commitment of United States military forces, in those areas which will show the most results in return for the United States effort expended. In addition the United States must maintain a strategic position which will facilitate control of coastal and overseas lines of communication in Asia.

33. From the military point of view, the United States must maintain a minimum position in Asia if a successful defense is to be achieved against future Soviet aggression. This minimum position is considered to consist of at least our present military position in the Asian offshore island chain, and in the event of war its denial to the Communists. The chain represents our first line of defense and in addition, our first line of offense from which we may seek to reduce the area of Communist control, using whatever means we can develop, without, however, using sizable United States armed forces. The first line of strategic defense should include Japan, the Ryukyus, and the Philippines. This minimum position will permit control of the main lines of communication necessary to United States strategic development of the important sections of the Asian area.

[handwritten margin notes: "same today (1979)"; "the defense perimeter on the cheap"; "the 'minimum position' in context of general world war"]

ECONOMIC CONSIDERATIONS

34. Except for industrialization in Japan and to a lesser extent in India, Asia is basically an agricultural region. Pressure of population on the land has depressed living standards to the margin of subsistence. Communications and transportation facilities are poor and productivity is low. However, Asia is the source of important raw and semi-processed materials, many of them of strategic value. Moreover, in the past, Asia has been a market for the processed goods of industrialized states, and has also been for the western colonial powers a rich source of revenue from investments and other invisible earnings.

35. The United States has an interest in the attainment by the free peoples of Asia of that degree of economic recovery and development needed as a foundation for social and political stability. This interest stems from the priniciple that a viable economy is essential to the survival of independent states. In the two major non-Communist countries of this area, India and Japan, U.S. aid (direct in the case of Japan, and via convertible sterling releases in the case of India) is averting a deterioration in economic conditions that would otherwise threaten political stability. While scrupulously avoiding assumption of responsibility for raising Asiatic living standards, it is to the U.S. interest to promote the ability of these countries to maintain, on a self-supporting basis, the economic conditions prerequisite to political stability. Japan can only maintain its present living standard on a self-supporting basis if it is able to secure a greater proportion of its needed food and raw material (principally cotton) imports from the Asiatic area, in which its natural markets lie, rather than from the U.S., in which its export market is small. In view of the desirability of avoiding preponderant dependence on Chinese sources, and the limited availability of supplies from pre-war sources in Korea and Formosa, this will require a considerable increase in Southern Asiatic food and raw material exports.

36. The Indian problem is somewhat analogous: The sizeable post-war Indian dollar deficit may be traced largely to this country's unprecedented dollar food imports. These imports have been necessitated by the failure of Indian food production to keep pace with population growth and to the reduced post-war availability of food exports from India's soft currency suppliers in Southern Asia. Even with these significant dollar food imports, Indian food consumption has fallen below pre-war levels. A further decline would almost certainly produce serious political instability in the major cities of India. A serious problem would thus result if the U.K. were no longer

able to bear the burden of the convertible sterling releases that have so far met the Indian dollar deficit.

37. It is thus difficult to foresee a time at which Japan and India will be self-supporting in the absence of greatly increased food production and some increased cotton production and Southern and Southeast Asia. One major prerequisite to such an increase is the restoration of political stability in the food exporting countries of Burma and Indo China. Given such a restoration, perhaps as much as 2.5 million more tons of rice exports could be secured from these countries with only minimal loans for rehabilitation of damaged facilities, e.g., transportation. Another major prerequisite is expanded agricultural development in the stable Southern Asiatic countries in which such development would be economic: India, Pakistan—which exports wheat and cotton, Thailand—which exports rice, and Ceylon—whose sizable rice imports reduce the availability of Asiatic foodstuffs to India and Japan. Japanese and Indian food requirements, and Japanese cotton requirements, could be met if certain projected irrigation, reclamation, and transportation projects were executed in the above countries.

38. These projects will probably require: (i) a more effective mobilization of local resources by the governments concerned, (ii) some external technical aid, (iii) some limited external financial aid. Most of the countries in question are now taking steps to mobilize local resources more effectively in the agricultural field, and they should be encouraged along those lines. External technical aid should be made available under the Point IV program.[12] The external financial aid required is of such a limited character that it can probably be adequately provided by the International Bank and the Export-Import Bank. We should, therefore, continue to urge these institutions to give serious consideration to requests for loans to finance sound development projects that would increase agricultural production in India, Thailand, Pakistan and Ceylon. This encouragement should, of course, be without prejudice to other additional loans these institutions may wish to make for non-agricultural purposes to these countries.

39. Expanded agricultural development in Southern and Southeast Asia would make a contribution to the political stability and the welfare of the exporting, as well as the importing countries. Through increased sales of rice, wheat, and cotton, Thailand and Pakistan could most economically secure the imports of capital and consumer goods to develop and diversify their economies. A comparable effect would be felt in India and Ceylon, if in-

12. Point IV was a program of scientific and economic aid for underdeveloped countries announced as the fourth point in Harry S. Truman's inaugural address on January 20, 1949. [Ed. note]

creased food production enabled these countries to reduce the disproportionate amount of foreign exchange that they presently devote to the purchase of food imports.

40. Our interest in a viable economy in the non-Communist countries of Asia would be advanced by increased trade among such countries. Japanese and Indian industrial revival and development can contribute to enlarged intra-regional trade relations which suffered a set-back because of the economic vacuum resulting from the defeat of Japan, the devastation caused by the war in other areas and the interference and restrictions arising from extensive governmental controls. Given a favorable and secure atmosphere—plus adequate freedom to individual traders, readily available working capital, suitable commercial agreements establishing conditions favorable to commerce and navigation and general assistance in the promotion of trade—it is expected that a substantial increase in intra-Asia trade can occur. The patterns of such trade, however, may differ from those existing before the war. In any event, a strong trading area among the free countries of Asia would add to general economic development and strengthen social and political stability. Some kind of regional association, facilitating interchange of information, among the non-Communist countries of Asia might become an important means of developing a favorable atmosphere for such trade among themselves and with other parts of the world.

41. Asia, particularly South and Southeast Asia, are among the principal sources of United States imports of several basic commodities which could contribute greatly to United States security for stockpiling purposes and would be of great assistance in time of war if they remained available to us. Exports to Asia from the United States are of less importance than are imports, but are not now insignificant and could grow in importance to the stability of our own domestic economy. In brief, the economic advantage derived by the United States from our trade with non-Communist Asia is considerable and there is little doubt of the wisdom of its development.

42. One effective means available to the United States for assisting in economic development, particularly in Southeast Asia, is to enlarge, consistent with security considerations, and despite possible objections of U.S. competitors, the orderly and sustained procurement, both by private and public agencies, of strategic and other basic commodities, such as tin, hard fibers and particularly natural rubber. United States purchases of strategic materials on current account would represent an important source of dollars for use by Asian countries in and outside the sterling area in meeting their current and capital needs.

43. The USSR is the primary target of those U.S. economic policies

designed to contain or turn back Soviet-Communist imperialism, and not China or any of the Soviet satellites considered as individual countries. It would, therefore, be inappropriate to apply to the willing or unwilling partners of the USSR punitive or restrictive economic measures which are not being applied to the USSR itself. This guiding principle should be the point of departure in application of procedures for conduct of our economic relations with Communist China. It should be our objective to take steps to prevent the Soviets and their satellites from obtaining, via trans-shipment in the Far East, strategic goods now denied them through direct channels. It should also be our objective to prevent Chinese Communists from obtaining supplies of goods of direct military utility which might be used to threaten directly the security interests of the western powers in Asia. It is not, however, either necessary or advisable to restrict trade with China in goods which are destined for normal civilian uses within China provided safe-guards are established to accomplish the two objectives mentioned above. Three reasons exist for this position: (1) Japan's economy cannot possibly be restored to a self-sustaining basis without a considerable volume of trade with China, the burden of Japan on the United States economy cannot be moved unless Japan's economy is restored to a self-sustaining basis and U.S. interference with natural Japanese trade relations with China would produce profound Japanese hostility; (2) permitting trade with Communist China in goods destined for normal civilian end uses within China will enable us to obtain quantities of important commodities needed by the U.S. (e.g., tung oil, bristles, tungsten, antimony, etc.) and might contribute to internal economic and political tensions between the urban and rural sectors of the Chinese economy, and permit China to choose between a Soviet and a Western orientation in their foreign economic relations; and (3) restriction of trade for any purpose other than those indicated by the objectives outlined above would be ineffective and impractical in view of the existence of alternative sources of supply in other countries which will not cooperate in export controls affecting normal trade with China. The U.S. should seek the cooperation of friendly countries in exercising export controls to achieve the objectives indicated, and request SCAP to conform to our general policy in this respect. While SCAP should be requested to avoid preponderant dependence on Chinese markets and sources of supply he should not be expected to apply controls upon Japan's trade with China more restrictive than those applied by Western European countries in their trade with China. At the same time SCAP should encourage development of alternative Japanese markets elsewhere in the world, including Southern and Southeast Asia, on an economic basis. Notwithstanding the advantages of the permissive trade policy outlined above, there would be no advantage for the United States to extend governmental economic assistance to or encourage private investment in Communist China.

---

34   **T O P   S E C R E T**

The Position of the United States with Respect to Asia

NSC 48/2   December 30, 1949

[Source: *United States-Vietnam Relations, 1945–1967* (Washington, 1971), VIII, 265–72]

Conclusions

1. Our basic security objectives with respect to Asia are:
   a. Development of the nations and peoples of Asia on a stable and self-sustaining basis in conformity with the purposes and principles of the United Nations Charter.
   b. Development of sufficient military power in selected non-Communist nations of Asia to maintain internal security and to prevent further encroachment by communism.
   c. Gradual reduction and eventual elimination of the preponderant power and influence of the USSR in Asia to such a degree that the Soviet Union will not be capable of threatening from that area the security of the United States or its friends and that the Soviet Union would encounter serious obstacles should it attempt to threaten the peace, national independence and stability of the Asiatic nations.
   d. Prevention of power relationships in Asia which would enable any other nation or alliance to threaten the security of the United States from that area, or the peace, national independence and stability of the Asiatic nations.
2. In pursuit of these objectives, the United States should act to:
   a. Support non-Communist forces in taking the initiative in Asia;
   b. Exert an influence to advance its own national interests; and
   c. Initiate action in such a manner as will appeal to the Asiatic nations as being compatible with their national interests and worthy of their support.

3. As the basis for realization of its objectives, the United States should pursue a policy toward Asia containing the following components:

    a. The United States should make known its sympathy with the efforts of Asian leaders to form regional associations of non-Communist states of the various Asian areas, and if in due course associations eventuate, the United States should be prepared, if invited, to assist such associations to fulfill their purposes under conditions which would be to our interest. The following principles should guide our actions in this respect:

        (1) Any association formed must be the result of a genuine desire on the part of the participating nations to cooperate for mutual benefit in solving the political economic, social and cultural problems of the area.

        (2) The United States must not take such an active part in the early stages of the formation of such an association that it will be subject to the charge of using the Asiatic nations to further United States ambitions.

        (3) The association, if it is to be a constructive force, must operate on the basis of mutual aid and self-help in all fields so that a true partnership may exist based on equal rights and equal obligations.

        (4) United States participation in any stage of the development of such an association should be with a view to accomplishing our basic objectives in Asia and to assuring that any association formed will be in accord with Chapter VII of the Charter of the United Nations[13] dealing with regional arrangements.

    b. The United States should act to develop and strengthen the security of the area from Communist external aggression or internal subversion. These steps should take into account any benefits to the security of Asia which may flow from the development of one or more regional groupings. The United States on its own initiative should now:

        (1) Improve the United States position with respect to Japan, the Ryukyus and the Philippines.

---

13. Chapter VIII of the Charter of the United Nations comprised Articles 52, 53, and 54. These articles recognized that regional arrangements were not precluded by the UN as long as they were consistent with the "purposes and principles" of that body; envisioned the use of regional orgnizations by the UN itself; and required that the Security Council be kept fully informed of the activities or plans of such organizations in maintaining international peace and security. [Ed. note]

(2) Scrutinize closely the development of threats from Communist aggression, direct or indirect, and be prepared to help within our means to meet such threats by providing political, economic, and military assistance and advice where clearly needed to supplement the resistance of the other governments in and out of the area which are more directly concerned.

(3) Develop cooperative measures through multilateral or bilateral arrangements to combat Communist internal subversion.

(4) Appraise the desirability and the means of developing in Asia some form of collective security arrangements, bearing in mind the following considerations:

(a) The reluctance of India at this time to join in any anti-Communist security pact and the influence this will have among the other nations of Asia.

(b) The necessity of assuming that any collective security arrangements which might be developed be based on the principle of mutual aid and on a demonstrated desire and ability to share in the burden by all the participating states.

(c) The necessity of assuring that any such security arrangements would be consonant with the purposes of any regional association which may be formed in accordance with paragraph 3a above.

(d) The necessity of assuring that any such security arrangement would be in conformity with the provisions of Article 51 of the Charter relating to individual and collective self-defense.

c. The United States should encourage the creation of an atmosphere favorable to economic recovery and development in non-Communist Asia, and to the revival of trade along multilateral, non-discriminatory lines. The economic policies of the United States should be adapted to promote, where possible, economic conditions that will contribute to political stability in friendly countries of Asia, but the United States should carefully avoid assuming responsibility for the economic welfare and development of that continent. Such policies might be projected along the following lines:

(1) Vigorous prosecution of the Point IV program in friendly countries of Asia, in an endeavor to assist them, by providing technical assistance, to make a start toward the solution of some of their long-range economic problems.

(2) Maintenance of a liberal United States trade policy with Asia and stimulation of imports from Asia. The special problems concerning trade with China are treated in paragraph 3f (4) below.

(3) Execution of a stockpiling program for strategic materials, based upon United States needs for strategic reserves and upon immediate and long-range economic effects in the supplying countries.

(4) Negotiation of treaties of friendship, commerce and navigation with non-Communist countries of Asia to define and establish conditions facilitating capital movements, trade and other economic relations between them and the United States.

(5) Encouragement of private United States investment in non-Communist countries and support of the early extension of credits by the International Bank and the Export-Import Bank for specific key economic projects of a self-liquidating nature, especially those directed towards increasing production of food in this area.

(6) Efforts to obtain the adherence of Asiatic countries to the principles of multilateral, non-discriminatory trade as embodied in the General Agreements on Tariffs and Trade, as a means of reducing trade barriers and expanding the international and intra-regional trade of the region on an economic basis. This would include, for example, further efforts to secure the benefits of most-favored-nation treatment for Japan.

d. The question of a peace settlement with Japan, now receiving separate consideration, will be presented for the consideration of the National Security Council at a later date and policies with respect to Japan will be re-evaluated after the decision regarding a peace treaty has been made.

e. (1) The United States should continue to provide for the extension of political support and economic, technical, military and other assistance to the democratically-elected Government of the Republic of Korea.[14]

(2) The United States should therefore press forward with the implementation of the ECA, MDAP, USIE, and related programs for Korea, and should continue to accord political sup-

---

14. NSC 8/2, approved March 23, 1949. [Note in source text]

port to the Republic of Korea, both within and without the framework of the United Nations.

f. (1) The United States should continue to recognize the National Government of China until the situation is further clarified.[15] The United States should avoid recognizing the Chinese Communist regime until it is clearly in the United States interest to do so. The United States should continue to express to friendly governments its own views concerning the dangers of hasty recognition of the Chinese Communist regime but should not take a stand which would engage the prestige of the United States in an attempt to prevent such recognition. In general, however, it should be realized that it would be inappropriate for the United States to adopt a posture more hostile or policies more harsh towards a Communist China than towards the USSR itself. It should also be realized that the according of recognition by other friendly countries would affect the bargaining position of the United States in the absence of United States recognition and would affect United States private and national interests in China. In the event that recognition of the Chinese Communists is anticipated, appropriate steps should be taken to make it clear that recognition should not be construed as approval of the Chinese Communist regime, or abatement of our hostility to Soviet efforts to exercise control in China.

(2) The United States should continue the policies of avoiding military and political support of any non-Communist elements in China unless such elements are willing actively to resist Communism with or without United States aid and unless such support would mean reasonable resistance to the Communists and contribute to the over-all national interests of the United States. In determining whether or in what manner any such assistance or encouragement should be given, consideration would have to be given to the protection which Chinese Communist authorities, as they become generally recognized by other governments, would be able to claim under international law and the Charter of the United Nations. The United States should maintain so far as feasible active contact with all ele-

Korea clearly different than China here

15. NSC 34/2. [Note in source text]

ments in China and maintain our cultural and informational program at the most active feasible level.

(3) The United States should exploit, through appropriate political, psychological, and economic means, any rifts between the Chinese Communists and the USSR and between the Stalinists and other elements in China, while scrupulously avoiding the appearance of intervention. Where appropriate, covert as well as overt means should be utilized to achieve these objectives.[16]

(4) The United States should, as a security measure, seek to prevent the USSR, its European satellites, and North Korea from obtaining from abroad through China supplies of strategic materials and equipment which are currently denied them by the United States and its European allies through direct channels. The United States should also use every effort to prevent the Chinese Communists from obtaining from non-Soviet sources supplies of materials and equipment of direct military utility (1A items).[17] The United States should, on the other hand, permit exports to China of 1B items within quantitative limits of normal civilian use and under controls which can be applied restrictively if it becomes necessary to do so in the national interest, and should place no obstacle in the way of trade with China in non-strategic commodities. The United States should seek the support and concurrence of its principal European allies in these policies. The United States should not extend governmental economic assistance to Communist China or encourage private investment in Communist China.

g. (1) The United States should continue the policy set forth in NSC 37/2 and 37/5[18] of attempting to deny Formosa and the Pescadores to the Chinese Communists through diplomatic and economic means within the limitations imposed by the fact that successful achievement of this objective will primarily

[handwritten marginalia: Formosa also different]

16. NSC 34/2. [Note in the source text]

17. Strategic commodities were divided into two categories: ''1A'' items were of direct military utility; ''1B'' items were of indirect use in war effort. The former were more tightly controlled. [Ed. note]

18. NSC 37/2, ''The Current Position of the US with Respect to Formosa,'' February 3, 1949 (printed in *Foreign Relations of the United States: 1949,* IX, 281–82); NSC 37/5, ''Supplementary Measures with Respect to Formosa,'' March 1, 1949 (*ibid.,* pp. 290–92). [Ed. note]

depend on prompt initiation and faithful implementation of essential measures of self-help by the non-Communist administration of the islands, and by the fact that freedom of U.S. diplomatic and economic action will be influenced, necessarily, by action taken by other countries.

(2) Since the United States may not be able to achieve its objectives through political and economic means, and in view of the opinion of the Joint Chiefs of Staff (reaffirmed in NSC 37/7 of August 22, 1949) that, while Formosa is strategically important to the United States, ''the strategic importance of Formosa does not justify overt military action . . . so long as the present disparity between our military strength and our global obligations exists'', the United States should make every effort to strengthen the over-all U.S. position with respect to the Philippines, the Ryukyus, and Japan. The United States should, for example, proceed apace with implementation of the policy set forth in regard to the Ryukyus in paragraph 5 of NSC 13/3.[19]

don't say this about Korea

h. The United States should continue to use its influence in Asia toward resolving the colonial-nationalist conflict in such a way as to satisfy the fundamental demands of the nationalist movement while at the same time minimizing the strain on the colonial powers who are our Western allies. Particular attention should be given to the problem of French Indo-China and action should be taken to bring home to the French the urgency of removing the barriers to the obtaining by Bao Dai or other non-Communist nationalist leaders of the support of a substantial proportion of the Vietnamese. With the successful conclusion of the Round Table Conference at The Hague the United States should give immediate consideration to the problems confronting the new Republic of United Indonesia and how best it can be aided in maintaining its freedom in the face of internal and external Communist pressures.

i. Active consideration should be given to means by which all members of the British Commonwealth may be induced to play a more active role in collaboration with the United States in Asia.

19. NSC 13/3, ''Recommendations with Respect to US Policy Toward Japan,'' May 6, 1949, in paragraph five noted the decision to retain and develop Okinawa as a military base and to cease exacting payments in support of occupation costs from islands of the Ryukyu chain south of latitude 29°. (*Foreign Relations of the United States: 1949*, VII (part 2), 731). [Ed. note]

Similar collaboration should be obtained to the extent possible from other non-Communist nations having interests in Asia.

j. Recognizing that the non-Communist governments of South Asia already constitute a bulwark against Communist expansion in Asia, the United States should exploit every opportunity to increase the present Western orientation of the area and to assist, within our capabilities, its governments in their efforts to meet the minimum aspirations of their people and to maintain internal security.

k. The United States should undertake an information program, both foreign and domestic, and publish United States policies and programs vis-a-vis Asia designed to gain maximum support both at home and abroad.

l. Nothing in this paper shall be construed as amending approved NSC papers unless a specific statement to that effect has been made on each point.

m. The sum of $75,000,000 for assistance to the general area of China, which was made available under Section 303 of the Mutual Defense Assistance Act of 1949, should be programmed as a matter of urgency.[20]

20. Section 303 of the Mutual Defense Assistance Act, passed on October 6, 1949, authorized the President to spend up to $75 million to cope with the rapidly changing situation "in the general area of China." The President was not required to account for expenditures, only to certify them. (Public Law 329, 63 Stat. 714) [Ed. note]

❧ 6 ❧

IMPLEMENTATION: MILITARY PLANNING, 1947–50

ONE OF THE MOST STRIKING NOVELTIES of the Cold War was the fact that for the first time in its history the United States possessed a powerful and perhaps permanent enemy in peacetime. This adversary relationship with the Soviet Union gave new importance to American defense planning, and, as the documents in this chapter show, led Washington officials to seek a military posture appropriate to the new conditions of world politics.

This chapter is divided into three parts. The documents in Part I reflect attempts by American planners to identify the nature and characteristics of the postwar strategic environment. JCS 1731/22 and PPS 7 (Documents 35 and 36) represent evaluations by the Joint Chiefs of Staff and the Policy Planning Staff of prospects for reaching agreement with the Soviet Union on arms control. JSPC 814/3 (Document 37) is an early attempt by the Joint Strategic Plans Committee to anticipate the political context in which foreign and military policy would have to be conducted over the next decade. NSC 20/2 (Document 38) provides the Policy Planning Staff's view of the role of military force in implementing the strategy of containment.

The documents in Part II of this chapter consist of a representative group of contingency plans for war with the Soviet Union. Three categories of war plans had evolved by 1947: emergency plans covering the first year of war and capable of immediate implementation on the basis of forces available during the current fiscal year; intermediate plans, intended to serve as the basis for budget and industrial mobilization planning during the next two years; and long-range plans, designed to forecast trends and events eight to ten years into the future, and thus to guide long-term research and development.[1] JCS 1725/1 (Document 39), though not a comprehensive war plan in the sense indicated above, nonetheless represents one of the earliest attempts

---

1. Robert D. Little, "Organizing for Strategic Planning, 1945–1950; The National System and the Air Force" (Washington, 1964), p. 15. Declassified with deletions as of December 1, 1975.

by Pentagon planners to forecast the course and characteristics of a future war with the Soviet Union. JCS 626/3 (Document 40), addressed itself to the problems of logistics and access to strategic materials which might arise in such a war. JCS 1844/13 (Document 41), code-named HALFMOON, was the first emergency war plan actually approved by the Joint Chiefs of Staff as a guide for detailed operational planning. It in turn was succeeded by OFFTACKLE, JSPC 877/59 (Document 42), the plan for fiscal 1950, which showed significant political and military changes from its predecessor. The final document in the group, DC 6/1 (Document 43), is a strategic concept for the North Atlantic Treaty Organization. Drawn up in the NATO Defense Committee, it illustrates the extension of American strategic planning into the field of alliance relationships.

The documents in Part III of this chapter reflect the efforts of American planners to come to grips with the strategic implications of the atomic bomb, a problem not fully worked out in the emergency war plans. NSC 30 (Document 44) was the first formal National Security Council paper on the subject; not surprisingly in view of the novel nature of the weapon, it argued against making prior commitments regarding the use or non-use of the bomb in combat. The Army General Staff study, "Brief on the Pattern of War in the Atomic Warfare Age" (Document 45), is a tentative effort to evaluate the extent to which the advent of atomic weapons had changed the nature of war. JCS 1952/1 (Document 46) summarizes plans for using atomic weapons in connection with the JCS 1844/13 (HALFMOON) emergency war plan (Document 41). The assumptions behind this plan were challenged by a review committee headed by Air Force Lieutenant General H. R. Harmon, which wrote a report (Document 47) questioning the efficacy of atomic weapons in a general war with the Soviet Union. PPS 58 (Document 48) is an attempt by the Policy Planning Staff to anticipate the effects on American and world opinion of a demonstrated Soviet atomic bomb capability—a capability that became fact late in the summer of 1949. Secretary of the Air Force W. Stuart Symington assessed the impact of that development for American security in a letter to Secretary of Defense Louis Johnson in November, 1949 (Document 49). There ensued an intense debate within the government over how the United States should respond to this development. The last two documents in this chapter reflect this debate, with the Joint Chiefs of Staff advocating construction of a thermonuclear, or super-bomb (Document 50) and Kennan arguing, unsuccessfully as it turned out, against depending at all on weapons of mass destruction (Document 51).

It should be noted that, of the war plans printed in this chapter, only four—JCS 1844/13, JSPC 877/59, JCS 1952/1, and DC 6/1—had been approved, even for planning purposes, by the beginning of 1950. The elaborate apparatus erected to formulate United States national security policy still had produced no approved intermediate or long-range war plan, and even the approved short-range plans depended on levels of budgeting, forces, and logistic support beyond what was available at the time. It was with these deficiencies in mind that President Truman authorized the sweeping review of national security policy which, in the spring of 1950, produced NSC-68 (Document 52).

<><><><><><><><><><><><><><><><><><><><><><><><><><><><><><><><>

PART I: THE STRATEGIC ENVIRONMENT

35   **S E C R E T**

Guidance for Discussions on the Military Aspects of Regulation of Armaments

JCS 1731/22   June 5, 1947

[Source: *Foreign Relations of the United States: 1947,* I, 485–86]

JCS 1731/22, the conclusions of which are printed below, set forth in general terms the Pentagon's views on the subject of arms control. Not surprisingly, the document reflected a certain skepticism regarding prospects for effective regulation of armaments as long as international tensions remained high. It also stressed the importance of safeguards in any control plan, and cautioned in particular against relinquishing prematurely the high-technology weapons on which postwar U.S. military strength largely rested. The latter argument closely resembles that set forth the previous year in Clark Clifford's September 24, 1946, memorandum for President Truman (see Document 4).

Conclusions

12. The following preamble and principles regarding the military aspects of the problem of regulation and reduction of armaments are basic to the security interests of the United States:

PREAMBLE

Armaments do not cause war. They result, rather, from the causes of war. Disarmament in itself will neither remove the causes of war nor prevent war. War and armaments can only be eliminated when the ideological, political, economic and other causes of war are exorcised. Concurrently with all disarmament negotiations, supreme effort must be continued to eliminate these causes. A highly important feature of this effort is the codification and establishment of a complete body of international law as envisaged by Article 13 of the Charter of the United Nations.

PRINCIPLES

a. There should be no unilateral disarmament by the United States by international agreement, nor should there be a unilateral reduction of armaments, by any means, which jeopardized the military security of the United States.

b. In any program, commitment or schedule for abolition or regulation and reduction of armaments, the establishment of effective safeguards, including international inspections and punishments, against violation and evasion of agreements is an essential prelude to the implementation of each step in the agreed program.

c. Once agreements on safeguards are reached, evasion will still be feasible unless the veto is eliminated in so far as these specific agreements are concerned. It follows that this possibility must be obviated to satisfy our military security interests.

d. Commitments or agreements regarding abolition or regulation and reduction of any armaments should neither become effective nor be rigidly cast until after the peace treaties have been consummated and the collective security forces contemplated by Article 43 of the United Nations Charter have been effectively established to perserve international security.

e. The first step to be accomplished in the control of armaments is the establishment of an effective system for the international control of atomic energy (U.S. [Baruch] Proposal).[2]

f. The next step is the establishment of an effective system for the international control of other major weapons adaptable to mass destruction.

g. Until the above principles are established and implemented the

2. Brackets in source text. On June 14, 1946, the United States government presented to the United Nations a plan for internationalizing control of atomic energy in phases which would protect the United States from the risks involved. The proposal became known as the Baruch Plan after Bernard Baruch, United States representative on the United Nations Atomic Energy Commission. [Ed. note]

United States cannot determine its military needs for self-preservation as recognized by Article 51 of the United Nations Charter.

h. Pending establishment and implementation of the principles enumerated above, discussions regarding regulation and reduction of conventional armaments should be directed toward solution of the questions of how and when rather than what elements of armaments should be regulated and reduced.

i. Undue reduction of the mechanical weapons in which we excel, such as long-range bombers, naval forces and mechanized ground forces, would jeopardize the power of self-preservation of the United States.

j. All moves toward regulation and reduction of armaments which accomplish merely the abolition or limitation of destructive and complicated weapons operate to the advantage of nations primarily superior in manpower and to the disadvantage of nations superior in technology and industrial capacity.

k. The armament requirements for self-preservation of the United States will increase greatly if we fail to retain and to acquire by negotiation the advanced bases needed for our own use and if we neglect to deny them to potential enemies.

l. Until an effective system of international security is established, our own requirements in armaments for security will be greater than those of an aggressor nation.

m. The extensive and general reduction that we have already made since V–J Day in our own armaments should be an important consideration in arriving at the terms of any future program for regulation or reduction of armaments.

n. Any attempt again to resolve the problem of regulation and reduction of conventional armaments on the basis of a differentiation between offensive and defensive weapons, or other comparative formulae, will be impractical, unrealistic and contrary to the interests of the United States.

<><><><><><><><><><><><><><><><><><><><><><><><><><><><><><><><><><>

36   **T O P   S E C R E T**

*General United States Policy with respect to International Control of
Atomic Energy (Through and after the Submission of the Second Report
of the United Nations Atomic Energy Commission to the Security
Council)*

PPS 7   August 21, 1947

[Source: *Foreign Relations of the United States: 1947,* I, 604–8]

After more than a year of unsuccessful negotiation with the Soviet Union in the
United Nations on the international control of atomic energy, American policymakers
had to face up to the implications of an impasse. PPS 7 marked a turning-point in
such considerations, raising the possibility that international control might not be attainable on terms consistent with American security requirements. The document
called for continued discussions with the Russians, but in a context that would make
clear American willingness to live with military competition if no agreement proved
possible. In anticipation of what political scientists would later call "inducement,"
PPS 7 advocated improving American civil-defense capabilities as a means of encouraging the Russians to negotiate.

Excerpts from PPS 7 are reprinted below.

I. The Situation to Date

After fourteen months of negotiations in the United Nations Atomic Energy Commission (UNAEC) the impasse continues. . . .

  •   •   •   •   •   •   •

Several basic differences divide the Soviet Union and Poland from the
other ten members of the AEC. While these differences include, of course,
the mechanics of inspection and the relation of the veto to the use of sanctions, there are two points of disagreement which are basic and which have
become even more significant:

First, the majority believes that outlawry of atomic weapons should be accomplished only as part of an international agreement providing for the development, by stages, of an adequate system of control, with safeguards
necessary to protect complying states against the hazards of violations and
evasions. The Soviet Union, on the other hand, evidently does not intend to
abandon its insistence on the destruction of atomic bomb stocks before adoption of an international control convention, or at least before it can become
reasonably effective.

Second, the United States and most other UNAEC countries believe that an international control plan would afford no security unless it envisaged an atomic development authority endowed with broad powers over practically all operations connected with the production of atomic energy. Its powers would be those which, in Western nomenclature at least, are usually subsumed in the term ownership. The Soviet Union has repeatedly rejected the idea of such an authority, claiming to see in it an instrument for interference with the internal affairs of sovereign states.

Without a settlement on these two points it appears impossible for the United States, even though it continues to seek a solution, to agree with the USSR on a plan for the international control of atomic energy.

．　　．　　．　　．　　．　　．　　．

II. Basic Requirements of Future U.S. Policy

In the face of these fundamental differences the United States must begin to develop a policy which does not appear to place all our eggs in the UN Atomic Energy Commission basket.

The best estimates indicate that the Soviet Union will have effective use of the atomic bomb within —— years.[3]

A due regard for United States security does not permit us to stand idly by while the Soviet Union continues its filibuster in the UNAEC. The Russians are using delaying tactics in the Commission while they pursue specific objectives outside the meeting hall. These include:

a. Hastening their own development of atomic bombs;

b. Dividing opinion in other United Nations, particularly those having atomic energy resources or skills;

c. Infiltration of research and control programs in any or all other countries;

d. Breaking down existing secret US arrangements for procurement of raw materials outside the United States;

e. Extension of their area of effective political domination by infiltration or direct pressure.

This enumeration demonstrates that we cannot consider the debate in the AEC as taking place in a vacuum. The extent to which Soviet strategic and diplomatic objectives are furthered by delay in the Commission is obvious, and too pat for mere coincidence. We must consider Soviet tactics in the

3. To be supplied. [Note in source text]

AEC as part of the Kremlin's general strategy; and we able to recognize the end of the line when we come to it.

We are now faced with the basic fact that under present circumstances the effort to achieve international control affords less hope for protecting our national security than other means. We must begin, therefore, to take alternative measures which, while they would not provide as high a degree of security as effective international control, would at least materially improve the United States position in a world in which others possess atomic weapons.

This means that we turn a corner in our thinking and this turning-point must soon be made unmistakable to the peoples of the United States, the Soviet Union and the rest of the world.

This does not mean, however, that there is any necessity for terminating the work of the Commission at this point. On the contrary it is desirable that the door be left open to further negotiation with the Russians *subsequent* to the taking of these alternative measures. For although the measures would be taken primarily in the interests of our own security, they might just possibly have some effect in inclining the Russians toward the plan of the other UNAEC nations. This is so for the following reasons:

The Russians are trained to reason dialectically. Their diplomatic history shows that they seldom approach an objective along one course without at the same time having in reserve an alternative and sometimes entirely dissimilar course. In pressing their own demands, they are quick to take into account the extent to which their opponent has alternatives to the acceptance of their demands. If they think he has no acceptable alternative, they are insistent and intractable.

Thus far, we have not demonstrated to the Russians that we have any alternative to the present course of basing our future atomic security on general international agreement. On the contrary, we have tended to labor the point that there is no effective means of defense against atomic weapons. The Russians have probably concluded from this that we see no alternative to international agreement. This has put them in a position where they feel at liberty to stall the negotiations indefinitely, believing that as long as they refuse to reach agreement with us their basic security position will not deteriorate, because little will be done here to reduce our vulnerability and to increase our retaliatory power in the face of atomic attack.

The Russians are probably negotiating under the impression that this country has not taken, nor even seriously contemplated, any serious measures of civilian defense. This being the case, the possibility of being able, in the event of a military conflict, to cause great damage and panic by a surprise attack must be an appealing one to them. It must put a premium, in their minds, on the possibility that they may some day be able to use the weapon against us.

There is no intention here to make light of the damage which can be done by the atomic weapon or the difficulties of defense against it. Nor is there any disposition to minimize the importance of the planning for atomic warfare and defense which has already been done in the military establishments. But there must be degrees in vulnerability to atomic attack; and there are certainly degrees in determination and effectiveness of retaliatory force.

If it were clearly established in the Russian mind that there was no possibility of this country's being a push-over in the face of surprise atomic attack—that there existed in this country mechanisms which would enable us to recuperate with relative promptness and to impose swift retribution, even in the face of the heaviest blow; and that we were ready to depart from traditional American policy in the direction of effective international understandings which increase our retaliatory power—then there could be no doubt that the prospect of the atomic age would take on a somewhat different color to Russian eyes.

It cannot be said with any assurance that the effect thus achieved would be strong enough to overcome the inhibitions on the Russian side which stand in the way of Soviet acceptance of our atomic energy proposals. Indeed, the odds are probably rather on the other side. But the possibility that their attitude might be affected to some extent by such a state of affairs is a strong one; and unless that possibility had been explored before the work of the Atomic Energy Commission was permitted to come to a final end, it would not be possible for us to say that we had exhausted every possibility of bringing the Russians near to our point of view.

<><><><><><><><><><><><><><><><><><><><><><><><><><><><>

37   **T O P S E C R E T**  *not approved*

Estimate of Probable Developments in the World Political Situation up to 1957

JSPC 814/3   December 11, 1947

[Source: Records of the Joint Chiefs of Staff on deposit in the Modern Military Records Branch, National Archives, Washington, D.C.]

JSPC 814/3 is an early estimate by the Joint Strategic Plans Committee of the Joint Chiefs of Staff of what course world political developments would take in the next ten years, written to facilitate planning for the future configuration of American military forces. Especially noteworthy in what is otherwise a generally accurate prediction is the report's failure to anticipate the victory of communism in China, its pessimism concerning Korea's chances for remaining free of Soviet control, its speculation that Russian acquisition of atomic weapons might produce "world hysteria", and its expectation of a crisis point in Soviet-American relations sometime after 1957 at which the Russians would have to choose between war and revolution on the one hand, and a decline in world influence and reversion to "Russian nationalism" on the other.

Printed here is the Appendix, which elaborates on the conclusions set out in the initial sections of the document.

The Problem

1. To estimate probable developments in the world political situation up to 1957.

.   .   .   .

1. The past decade has been one of extraordinary political activity. Up to 1937, only two overt moves (Japanese intervention in Manchuria and Italian intervention in Ethiopia) had occurred in the political interplay which has produced the greatly altered world situation of today. The political factors evident in 1937, which led to this result, were perhaps neither so dynamic nor so numerous as those which are evident in 1947 to influence future events. There are current indications that further sharp and extensive political change is likely to occur after, rather than before, 1957.

2. Among fundamental long-term trends to which consideration must be give in gauging the course of world politics are the following:

   a. The continuing effective shrinkage of the world resulting from the accelerated pace of technological progress.
   b. Population changes which affect national potentialities and which create grave dislocations among backward and dependent peoples.
   c. The growth of nationalism and the desire for an improved lot among backward and dependent peoples.

3. The major dynamic factors which must be envisaged as affecting world political developments during the coming decade include, at the minimum:

   a. The conflict in ideology and objectives between the Soviet bloc and the western democratic powers.
   b. The development of atomic energy.

    c. Chaotic political, economic and social conditions in continental Europe, particularly in Germany.

    d. The absence of indigenous power, except for that of the USSR in Asia.

    e. The United Nations concept.

4. Among these various factors, any of which might normally effect major political changes, one in particular produces the framework within which the remainder must operate. This is in the conflict in ideology and objectives between the Soviet Communist bloc and the western democratic powers, which in the short term appears likely to exercise a compelling influence upon world affairs. The United Nations can be regarded only as an arena in this conflict, a dynamic factor principally in providing a focal point for world opinion.

5. Soviet policy is founded on the concept of a basic conflict between "Communism" and "Capitalism", resolvable only by the eventual destruction of one or the other. Despite their occasional tactic of denying this concept, Soviet leaders as frequently reaffirm it, and Soviet actions remain consistent with underlying belief in its validity. The western democracies do not accept the thesis, on ideological grounds, that Soviet Communism must be destroyed by war as a necessary condition to their own survival. They must, however, accept the central fact in the situation as it exists: that while the present Soviet policy and attitude of hostility persists, the Soviet and non-Soviet worlds are and will be, at the minimum, in a state of political belligerency. It is a situation in which force is now being used and will continue to be used, although open and declared warfare may never eventuate.

6. The basic objective of the U.S.S.R appears to be a limitless expansion of Soviet Communism accompanied by a considerable territorial expansion of Russian imperialism. She will pursue this objective with persistence and flexibility, recognizing no neutral ground, and hence no neutrals, and using any means which fit her purpose. In the face of this Soviet objective and these Soviet tactics, and in the light of enormous Soviet military and political power, in being, in Europe and in Asia, the western democracies will be forced to mobilize their political and military resources to support what is to them an equally fundamental objective which clashes directly with Soviet aims. This objective might be stated as the preservation at all costs of democratic economic and political processes, emphasizing individual and national freedom, which are favorable to the prospect of international change by evolution, rather than by force. Such preservation will depend primarily on the leadership and strength of the U.S. and the British Commonwealth, and

the effectiveness with which the anti-Communist nations cooperate in the rehabilitation and strengthening of their economy.

7. A period without open war would appear to be desirable to the Soviet planners if the U.S.S.R. is: (a) to recuperate from World War II; (b) to overcome a probable Soviet disadvantage in atomic weapons; (c) to create, in alien areas under Soviet domination conditions giving reasonable guarantees against dangerous subversion in the event of war; (d) to gain some opportunity of exploiting the war potential of such areas prior to and during a war; (e) to achieve, if possible, a barrier of distance around the political and industrial heart of the Soviet Union proper to assist in holding beyond range those weapons which might be used decisively against her; and (f) to create and perfect adequate Communist fifth columns in countries not adhering to the Soviet cause. It should follow that the most profitable short-term lines of Soviet political action would include: (a) consolidation of control within the Soviet perimeter, expanding that perimeter by continuing opportunist pressure at all soft spots wherever they develop or may be created; and (b) continuation and acceleration of Communist international activities in order to weaken opposition to Soviet policy and to prepare subversive forces for possible employment in war. Theoretically the U.S.S.R. should not, in the short term, commence any planned war. Considering the internal industrial and scientific tasks confronting the Soviet Union in her program of war preparation, and her politico-economic problems in recently subjugated territories, this short term should be at least five, and probably ten, years. During this period, "accidental" war, resulting perhaps from Soviet miscalculation as to how far one or more of the western countries can be pushed without striking back, must be considered a continuing possibility. In the longer term, five to ten years or more, unless basic Soviet policy changes, it must at present be concluded that the likelihood of war will increase in direct proportion to: (a) difficulties encountered by the Soviets at attaining their objectives by means short of war; (b) their success in overcoming deficiencies in the Soviet war potential, and (c) failure of the western powers to maintain adequate military and economic strength.

8. The U.S. and the British Commonwealth, in company to a greater or lesser degree with the remaining western powers, have elected to oppose the expansionist course of Soviet Communism. The position assumed in accordance with this decision is currently one of "thus far and no farther". A geographic advance of Soviet influence, either direct or by Soviet satellites, is resisted within the framework of the status quo and of existing international agreements, as in Iran, Greece or Turkey, both diplomatically and by

the threat of force. Expansion of Communist influence beyond the Soviet periphery is opposed by direct support to Communist-threatened governments, and by the indirect means of mutual cooperation to reestablish or reinforce the economic stability and independence of the anti-communist nations.

9. The course of action which the western democracies are now following possesses the merit of flexibility. It permits of increases or decreases in the degree of counter-pressure they exert against the Soviets, depending upon the Soviet and world reaction. It permits a continuing adaptation of their tools of power, whether the threat of force, moral suasion, or economic pressure, to a political conflict the end of which is not now in sight. If their course of action is to succeed, however:

    a. Readiness for military action by the western democracies must be sustained on a basis calculated to present the Soviets at all times with a genuine prospect of decisive defeat in war precipitated by Soviet aggression.

    b. The valid possibility must exist that political action by the western powers can find a peaceful solution to the basic conflict between the U.S.S.R. and the non-Soviet world. The task will obviously be one of extreme difficulty. If realistic and fully adequate preparation for war by the western democracies can assure purchase of time, only inspired political and economic action on their part, including positive and effective propaganda counters to the appeal of Communism, can exploit this time effectively. The general international situation ten years hence, unless war has intervened, will be favorable or unfavorable to an ultimate peaceful solution largely in terms of the vigor and effectiveness of United States and British policies and actions during the interim. The future attitude of the United States is a principal factor in attempting an estimate of probable world political developments during the next ten years.

10. A principal factor arises in considering the possible development of British policy during the coming decade. In general, the aims and objectives of the British Commonwealth of Nations would be obtained, as would those of the United States, by complete success for the stated aims of the United Nations charter under less stress than is likely to develop from Soviet pressure, there can be little doubt that Anglo-American cooperation would accomplish the peaceful concerted solution of world problems on a basis favorable to the fundamental western democratic objectives. [sic] Even under conditions of severe Soviet pressure, it appears likely that the British Commonwealth will remain steadfast in opposing Soviet-Communist expansion.

However, the United Kingdom itself is faced by three fundamental considerations of major importance:

    a. The necessity for a period of peace and economic opportunity to permit recuperation from the effects of the supreme effort she made in World War II, which places the United Kingdom in poor position to contemplate the prospect of another war in the near future.

    b. United Kingdom vulnerability to a type of attack, from cross-Channel positions, by weapons similar to those developed by the Germans at the end of World War II and the possibility of severence of "lifeline" communications.

    c. The implications of adopting a position which might develop into irrevocable alignment with the United States, whose ideals though fixed may be susceptible to variations in emphasis which could affect U.S. foreign policy, thereby conceivably placing British security in some jeopardy.

These considerations might lead the British to consider a variation of their traditional "balance-of-power" role in Europe, this time as mediators on a global scale between the United States and the U.S.S.R. Strong United States and Dominion support, together with the reasonable prospect of being able to prevent or survive Soviet missile and rocket attack, would permit Britain to remain resolute in opposition to Soviet pressure.

11. Another principal factor in the development of the world political situation is implicit in the diminishing likelihood of achieving international control of atomic energy. Such control must depend upon effective safeguards including international inspection for atomic activities; these, it now appears certain the U.S.S.R. will not accept. Genuine acceptance and implementation by the Soviet Union of effective arrangements for the control of atomic energy are so unlikely that an atomic armanents race must be anticipated during the next ten years and beyond. The increasing probability that at least two opposed nations will possess atomic weapons by the middle of the period, will probably result in a tense and excitable state of world public opinion—possibly in a species of world hysteria—wherein minor political incidents are exaggerated into political crises.

12. A major prize in the continuing conflict throughout the coming decade will be the adherence of wavering peoples to the Soviet or to the western democratic cause. The Soviets can be expected to exploit their favorable opportunity of championing the causes of colonial peoples, to whom nationalism and Communism may temporarily be made to appear synonymous.

The general good will felt for the U.S., if not for the colonial powers, among backward and dependent peoples, should make it unlikely, however, that any large segments will be completely won over to Soviet views in the short term, unless: (a) the United States, the British Commonwealth and potential allies display great political ineptitude; or (b) the United States and British economic systems suffer a severe recession, with attendant serious economic and political world repercussions and a consequent turn to Soviet economic (and political) methods by peoples who have seen all other methods discredited. This effect would not be restricted to backward and colonial areas, but would equally—and with more far-reaching results—extend to continental European nations struggling to regain economic stability, many of whom might then be impelled by disillusionment toward Communism. A breakdown in the Soviet economy, should it occur, would be less harmful to Soviet international aims, since it would be capable of effective concealment and since the Soviet system interlocks little with other major economic systems. There are few indications that the Communist hold on Russia might be broken in the short term: it must be anticipated, on the contrary, that the Soviet Union will continue to present a front of solid unity to the outside world. On the other hand, effective western democratic action may increasingly induce a decline in international Communist strength and effectiveness, and may turn Soviet Communism more and more into the fold of Russian nationalism.

13. The possibilities for the general short term trend of world politics are (a) an approximate maintenance of the status quo; (b) an improving western democratic position, and (c) an improving Soviet bloc and Communist position. The possibility exists, of course, that unpredictable events might occur at any time to alter or reverse an apparent trend; such as, for example, in case the Soviets demonstrated that they had obtained quantity production of atomic weapons.

14. The probability that the status quo will maintain throughout the period cannot be considered great. While the western democracies possess little urge to rapid change, authoritarian Soviet and Communist elements must continue an aggressive political momentum or face a deteriorating position.

15. A trend toward improvement of the Soviet political and power position would perhaps result less from positive Soviet and Communist action, especially in view of the political ineptitude frequently displayed by these elements, than from inadequacies in western democratic policy and action. Should the western democracies, particularly the U.S. and Britain, fall in

firm, cooperative and imaginative opposition to Soviet expansionism, should their lack of war preparedness invite Soviet aggression, or should their economic systems (especially that of the U.S.) suffer serious failure, it might be anticipated that the Soviet bloc would encounter increasing success in world politics. By 1957, the western democracies could in such case find themselves confronted with overwhelming Soviet political and military power, weakened domestic positions, and the prospect of probable defeat in any war which might then eventuate. A deterioration of this type in the western democratic position would be evidenced by an increasing rapprochement of the German peoples, France, Italy and the smaller western European powers with the Soviet Union; by an extension of direct or indirect Soviet control in the Near and Middle East; by complete political chaos or Communist gains in India, Malaya and Indonesia; by a consolidation of Soviet control over peripheral Chinese provinces and Communist infiltration into the Chinese Government; and by diminished U.S. prestige in Latin America. Even in such case, it appears unlikely that a Soviet planned war would occur until after 1957, especially as Soviet objectives under such conditions could more readily be obtained by means short of war.

16. It appears more likely that the western democracies will continue to recognize the necessity of protecting their essential national interests. The U.S. and Britain have in World War II evidenced the cost in lives, material, wealth and economic stability of tardy and inadequately forceful action to forestall aggression. The U.S. has twice within the last generation considered its fundamental interests menaced by a threatening European situation to an extent requiring U.S. participation in overseas warfare. The current state of world political conflict is now recognized as possessing elements of menace to the U.S. at least as great as any others during the past generation. So long as the U.S. elects to take those steps required to safeguard its national security, it may be anticipated that Britain and the remaining western powers will be sufficiently reassured to remain joined with the U.S. in a firm policy counter to that of the Soviets. In this event, the most probable short-term trend in world politics should be one of an improving western democratic political and power position. Improvement in the western democratic position will of necessity and in the best of circumstances be less rapid than would an improvement of the Soviet bloc position in the less likely event that the political trend should take a reverse direction: in certain areas of conflict the Soviet bloc position possesses current strength sufficient to make further Communist success likely despite any measures short of war which can be taken by the western powers. However, in the longer term, as

western democratic successes achieve an inevitable propaganda impact upon restive aliens under Soviet control, it may be anticipated that a trend favorable to the western democracies would meet with continuing and increasing success.

17. The ten-year trend in world politics, in the event that the western powers take positive steps to safeguard their national interests, might be gauged on a geographic basis somewhat as follows:

    a. *Within the Soviet bloc area,* Communist totalitarian control will probably be extended and intensified. Additional emphasis will be placed on nationalism and Pan-Slavism. There can be anticipated little change in Soviet political objectives, which represent, for the most part, the objectives of Russian imperialism and Pan-Slavism as well as Soviet Communism. Soviet Communism, presented as the sole bulwark against capitalistic imperialism, will continue to be utilized as the principal vehicle for the expansion of direct and indirect Soviet influence. It might be anticipated that some of such diverse peoples as Poles, Finns, Hungarians, Bulgars, Yugoslavs, Albanians and Rumanians, will remain restive under Soviet domination, but with diminishing vigor as Communist control liquidates or converts all opposition.

    b. *Outside the Soviet bloc area,* the community of political and economic interest should be extended by further effective world shrinkage resulting from technological progress, as well as by the common interest in building for an enduring peace in terms of their common political evolution.

    c. *Within western Europe,* France and Italy, having suffered from serious Communist-inspired civil disturbance and, possibly, insurrection, will finally reduce the effectiveness of Soviet influence and national communists and adhere to the western democratic group. The smaller democratic powers will follow the lead of the U.S. and Britain, except that Switzerland, because of its traditions, and Scandinavia, because of its vulnerability to Soviet force, will attempt to pursue a course of neutrality. Spain and Portugal, whose governments fear nothing so much as Communism and which are unlikely to forget the power demonstrated by the Allies during World War II, will adhere to the western democratic side in countering Soviet and Communist expansion. It appears likely that Spain may gradually come to adopt more democratic principles of government, although the process will probably not have been completed by 1957. Germany (and, with less likelihood, Austria) will probably remain divided substantially as at present, the Soviets continuing to hold and occupy eastern Germany. While German nationalism will impel German unity, the dividing force resulting from sharply differing political ideologies in the two main divisions of Germany will operate equally to force reluctant German acceptance of an unsatisfactory situation. It can scarcely be doubted that both the Soviets and the western democracies will be forced to make partners, to the extent possible in terms of existing international agreements, public opinion, and the inherent danger in such a course, of the German peoples under their surveillance. At the same time, the interdependence of the European economy is likely to force a series of trade agreements between eastern and western Europe, scope of which will be determined for the most part by the minimum requirements of eastern Europe. European economic recovery, upon which ultimately the peace of the world may turn, is likely to be slow. Diplomatic crises will be frequent and recurring, especially in areas of marginal friction.

d. *In the Near and Middle East* political conflict and tension is likely to increase throughout the period. Greece, aided by U.S. economic support and military advice and protected from Soviet-inspired insurrection to the extent that United Nations surveillance will succeed, should be able to regain her political and economic independence and remain in the anti-Communist bloc. Turkey, backed by the western democracies, will resist Soviet pressure and will retain its independence of action, although the Montreux Convention[4] will probably be revised on terms more favorable to the Soviet Union. (It may be anticipated that the Mediterranean will remain under western democratic control, though not without challenge from Soviet bloc bases on Balkan coastlines.) Despite its rough handling by the U.S. and, to a lesser extent, Britain on the Palestine question, the Arab League is fundmentally distrustful of Russia and Communism, and it is not likely that this area will come under Soviet domination, however acute may be the continued friction in Palestine. It may be anticipated that the general political situation in the Middle East will undergo no sharp

4. The Montreux Convention of July 1936 granted Turkey the authority to fortify the Dardanelles and to regulate passage of military vessels through it. [Ed. note]

change, although increased Soviet pressure on Iran must be expected as their expansionism is resisted in other areas. The pressure of Soviet expansionism in the Middle East, both as a threat to British Empire communications and because of estimated serious oil deficiencies best remediable through access to Middle Eastern oil reserves, will continue and may mount.

e. *In the Far East* it cannot be anticipated that China will have emerged as an important factor, regardless of the political trend during the coming decade. It appears likely that peripheral Chinese provinces, including Inner Mongolia and Sinkiang, will have come under Soviet control to the same extent now obtaining in Outer Mongolia. Manchuria, key to the Chinese power position, may remain under Chinese Government control, but will probably be rendered unexploitable by Soviet pressure and the Soviet threat of force in the area. The Chinese Government, hampered by continuing internal conflict, will remain friendly to the western democracies, particularly the U.S., to such effect as may be determined by an unpredictable future course of U.S. action. Korea is likely to come entirely under indirect Soviet domination; a probable withdrawal of occupation forces before 1957 will leave Korea's politically immature people open to control through highly-organized Communist minorities. It is difficult to visualize how the surveillance of the United Nations Commission can do more than bring the machinations of Soviet-Communist infiltration to the attention of world public opinion. Japan, however, will in all likelihood be increasingly oriented toward the U.S. both economically and politically. In the face of a predominantly American occupation, Communist propaganda and infiltration methods will probably meet with little success. It must be anticipated that the Soviets, confronted with an extension of American power throughout the Pacific and in Japan, will be seriously perturbed over their security position in Asiatic Russia, and will make repeated attempts both to speed the departure of U.S. troops from Japan and to substitute Soviet for U.S. influence in Japan.

f. *The Latin American states* will continue to offer difficult diplomatic problems for solution principally by the U.S. In the final analysis, and despite strong Leftist and divisive tendencies in many areas, Latin America will adhere to the principal of western hemispheric solidarity. Its predominance of such institutions as large landholding, private capital and the Catholic Church, though susceptible to long-term deterioration, will in the short-term impel, singly or in combination, a profound distrust of the Soviets and Communism regardless of the degree of friendliness felt by the various states for the U.S. It is profoundly in the national interest of Latin American states to avoid any irrevocable break with those hemispheric and Atlantic neighbors whose power can readily be brought to bear in South America. These neighbors are the U.S. and Britain. Significant Soviet power can scarcely, in the short-term, be projected to the Western Hemisphere.

g. *Within colonial and backward areas,* the ends of a rising nationalism will combine temporarily with population pressures and the superficial appeal of Communism to create political, social and economic dislocations, none of which in the short-term should produce either complete chaos or cause for war. India and Pakistan will not soon compose their ancient religious and racial differences, but should achieve a state of reasonable stability, in the international political sense, during the short-term and should remain no more subject to Communist propaganda influence than at present. It appears likely that by the end of the decade they will have rendered themselves even less capable of assisting the western powers in the event of war than was India during World War II. In this sense, the Indian political situation will have improved from a Soviet point of view, and deteriorated in the eyes of the western democracies. [In] Indonesia and Malaya, where, as in India, population pressures combine with nationalistic ideas to favor the prospect of sharp political changes, the ten-year prospect points to continuing local disturbance but with small likelihood of its assuming international proportions. While the Soviets will champion the cause of dependent peoples within the United Nations, they will be incapable of extending them active military or economic assistance. The western democracies, already meeting the Soviet and Communist ideological threat by increasing concessions to dependent peoples, will be in a position to take effective political, military and economic action in satisfying economic wants on the one hand while suppressing disturbance on the other. Africa will supply cause for international friction principally in the Italian colonies and Egypt, but will probably offer no, or few, international problems of a nature threatening war. The Italian colonies will probably come under a form of United Nations trusteeship. Incipient African nationalisms farther south offer only minor short-term cause for international political friction. The French North African colonies, despite a nationalistic trend toward separation from France, are unlikely in the short-term to achieve a goal of this type in view of the powerful resistance which would be encountered in a France whose national esteem has too recently and too strongly been wounded by the events of World War II.

18. The United Nations will remain for the most part a forum both for Soviet propaganda and for the similar expression of western democratic views. It appears most unlikely that use will be made of United Nations Security Forces. The possibility exists that the Soviet Union and its satellites, if consistently defeated by parliamentary methods, might withdraw from active participation in the United Nations, but it appears more likely that they will continue to remain one of the "permanent members" because of the prestige value and, also, because of the power for obstruction inherent in their veto right.

---

38   **T O P S E C R E T**

Factors Affecting the Nature of the U.S. Defense Arrangements in the Light of Soviet Policies

NSC 20/2   August 25, 1948

[Source: *Foreign Relations of the United States, 1948:* I (part 2), 615–24]

Like NSC 20/1 (see Document 22) this document originated with the Policy Planning Staff in response to Secretary Forrestal's July 10, 1948, letter. It was significant as an expression of the State Department's concept of the role of military force in implementing containment and for its discussion of a problem that preoccupied American military planners for the next half-decade: whether to prepare for a peak period of military danger from the Soviet Union, or whether to configure forces on the assumption that long-term preparedness would be required.

Excerpts from NSC 20/2 are printed below.

The following report is designed to clarify the factors bearing on the question as to the nature which the U.S. defense effort should assume in the light of Soviet policies and attitudes (with particular relation to the question whether U.S. defense preparations should be pointed to meet an expected conflict at a given probable time or whether they should be planned on a basis which could and would be permanently maintained).

.   .   .   .

. . . The evidence points to the conclusion that the Soviet Government is not now planning any deliberate armed action of this nature and is still seeking to achieve its aims predominantly by political means, accompanied—of course—by the factor of military intimidation. The tactics which it is employing, however, themelves heighten the danger that military complications may arise from fortuitous causes or from miscalculation. War must therefore be regarded, if not as a probability, at least as a possibility, and one serious enough to be taken account of fully in our military and political planning.

.   .   .   .

It is not probable that the pattern of Soviet intentions as outlined above would be appreciably altered in the direction of greater aggressiveness by the development of the atomic weapon in Russia.

.   .   .   .

The following are the requirements, arising from the attitudes and policies of the Soviet Government, for which it is necessary that this Government maintain armed strength.

1. As an indispensable background of our own political attitude with respect to the U.S.S.R.

In dealing with a government so highly centralized, so incorrigibly conspiratorial in its methods, so hostile traditionally towards its world environment, so despotic at home, and so unpredictable in foreign affairs, it is necessary that we keep ourselves in a state of unvacillating mental preparedness. Without military preparedness, this would be a sham.

2. As a deterrent.

This is of outstanding importance. There is no question but that if the opposing strength is estimated to be so great that there would be little possibility of final victory, the Russians will not deliberately resort to the use of armed force. On the other hand, excessive military weakness here and in western Europe might indeed create a factor which would operate to overcome the other reasons why the Soviet Government would not be inclined to use armed force, and might thus constitute a compelling invitation to aggression.

There is no evidence that anything likely to occur in Russia within the foreseeable future will in any way alter this situation. We must reckon that the necessity for the maintenance of armed forces as a deterrent will continue undiminished as long as the Soviet power, as we know it today, continues to be dominant in Russia, and probably even longer.

3. As a source of encouragement to nations endeavoring to resist Soviet political aggression.

The peoples who consider themselves as lying between the U.S.S.R. and the U.S. and who are endeavoring to resist Soviet political pressures are strongly influenced by what may be called the shadows of the armed strength maintained by the two great powers. If the shadow of the Soviet armed strength remains too formidable, in comparison with ours, this may well have a paralyzing effect on the will to resist in western Europe and may become an important factor in enabling the Russians to achieve their aims by political rather than military means. It is therefore necessary for this country to maintain the outward evidences of firm armed strength and resolution as a means of stiffening the attitude of those peoples who would like to resist Soviet political pressures.

Like the requirement of armed force as a deterrent, this requirement may be expected to endure at least as long as the communist party remains the dominant power in Russia. There is no reason to expect the achievement of any political understanding with the Soviet leaders which could appreciably offset the need for strong U.S. forces as a factor of encouragement to the peoples in western Europe. This necessity is not likely to pass even with the termination of the present Soviet regime.

4. As a means of waging war successfully in case war should develop as a result of an accident or miscalculation or any other cause.

It is impossible to state at this time how long the relatively high degree of danger implicit in the present dispositions of Soviet and western forces in Europe will endure or what will be the general development of the probability of planned Soviet military aggression. It is possible, but by no means certain, that within two or three years the danger of military complications arising from accidental causes may be reduced by changes in the dispositions of armed forces in Europe. However, there is no likelihood of any reduction in the general power of Soviet armed forces; on the contrary, this may be expected to increase steadily in the next few years. In view of the long time-lags involved in any basic alterations of a major military establishment, our defense policy cannot take into account minor fluctuations in the degree of danger. From the political standpoint, therefore, the only safe deduction would be that for at least the next five or ten years we will require

such an establishment as would make it possible for us to wage war successfully if it should be forced upon us. What would constitute waging war
"successfully" is a question which can be answered only in the light of
U.S. national objectives.

5. Conclusions:

None of the purposes for which we must maintain armed forces, in the
light of Soviet attitudes and policies, are ones which may be expected to undergo any material alteration at any specific predictable time in the future,
and they must all be considered as being of an enduring nature.

D. Probable Effects of the Respective Courses under Consideration

1. A U.S. defense effort founded on the principle of a long-term state of
readiness.

    a. This type of effort would have the greatest effect as a deterrent,
since it would be evident to the Soviet leaders that they were
dealing with a permanent factor on their political horizon and not
with a temporary one which they could expect to disappear again
within a relatively short time.

    b. This type of effort would have the greatest effect in encouraging
countries endeavoring to resist Soviet political pressures. The anxieties of people in western Europe and elsewhere as to the U.S. ability and will to defend them in the event they should become militarily involved with the U.S.S.R. relate in large measure to their
doubts as to the stability and long-term consistency of U.S. policy.
A U.S. defense effort laid out on long-term lines will be much
more apt to reassure them than one aimed at a given peak of probable likelihood of war but subject to later downward fluctuations.

    c. From the standpoint of the possibility of an actual waging of war
with Russia, a defense effort laid out on a permanent basis would
lack the advantages of being able to meet a particular peak danger
by a peak effort in military preparedness; but it would have distinct
advantages if military complications were to occur at a time other
than that which we had calculated to be the most likely one.

2. A U.S. defense effort founded on the idea of meeting a peak of war
danger by a peak of military preparedness.

    a. As a deterrent to the Soviet Union, this type of effort would be ef-
fective only for the period toward which it was directed; for the

subsequent period it would have the reverse effect. If the Soviet leaders knew that we were undertaking a defense effort of this nature (and it is certain that they would know it), they would be able to plan for maximum military and political pressure at a date when our own military effort might be expected to have subsided.

b. From the standpoint of encouragement to peoples resisting Soviet pressures, this type of defense effort would have only a limited value. To the extent that it gave the impression that U.S. plans were sporadic and undependable, it might do more harm than good.

c. From the standpoint of actual waging of war, such a defense effort could conceivably have advantages only in the event that our calculations as to the likely timing of Soviet military aggression were correct. At present, we have no adequate means of arriving at a correct calculation of such a factor. But in any case we must always bear in mind that the defense effort itself would undoubtedly alter the situation on which our expectancy had been based; for it would probably act as an effective deterrent for that particular period and we would probably not be called upon actually to use our forces at the time for which we had planned their maximum strength. This means that there would be relatively little likelihood of our forces being used for waging of a war against Russia at the moment of their maximum efficiency if they were shaped to meet an anticipated danger peak. We must always bear in mind here the extreme flexibility and patience of Soviet policy.

3. Conclusions:

In general, the factors cited above indicate that a U.S. defense policy based on the maintenance of a permanent state of adequate military preparation meets better the requirements of the situation, insofar as these arise out of Soviet policies and attitudes, than a defense effort pointed toward a given estimated peak of war danger.

<<><><><><><><><><><><><><><><><><><><><><><><><><><><><><><><>>

PART II: WAR PLANS

39   **T O P   S E C R E T**

Strategic Guidance for Industrial Mobilization Planning

JCS 1725/1   May 1, 1947

[Source: Records of the Joint Chiefs of Staff on deposit in the Modern Military Records Branch, National Archives, Washington, D.C.]

JCS 1725/1 originated as an effort by the Joint Staff Planners to provide guidance for industrial mobilization planning in case of war with the Soviet Union within the next three years. It was not, strictly speaking, a war plan. Nonetheless, the document constituted an extensive early statement of how American military planners evaluated Soviet capabilities and intentions in the event of war, and of how they thought the United States and its allies might fight such a war to a successful conclusion.

Two features of this statement stand out with particular emphasis: (1) the assumption that the Soviet Union would be capable of overrunning Western Europe, and that the United States and its allies would find the eastern Mediterranean and the Middle East to be the most feasible location from which to launch a counteroffensive; and (2) its failure to take into account the possible use of the atomic bomb, which the United States alone possessed. A prefatory note attached to this document observed that "it appears almost certain that these [weapons] could be made available in considerable quantities initially and an additional number produced over the three-year period covered by this guidance. Should these weapons be employed, the initial effort would be approximately as outlined in the plan, but after the initial phases, a considerable decrease in the requirements for very heavy bombers and accompanying fighters would exist."

Reprinted here is Appendix A to JCS 1725/1, setting forth the Joint Staff Planners' "appreciation" of what a war between the Soviet Union and the West would be like.

•   •   •   •   •   •   •

1. In a war between the U.S.S.R. and a combination of powers including Great Britain and the U.S., irrespective of the manner in which it began, certain governing considerations would influence the development of the general strategic pattern of the war. These considerations are outlined in the paragraphs below.

Probable Soviet Strategy During the Next Three Years

2. Soviet Russia possesses ground and tactical air forces greatly superior in numbers to those which any combination of probable opponents could

hope to bring to bear against her in the early stages of the war. Her airborne capabilities within limited range are considerable. Her submarines represent a considerable and increasing threat; her other naval forces have not been sufficiently developed to present a serious threat. Her strategic air arm has not yet been developed into an effective long-range striking force. It is probable that the Soviets would plan to take full advantage of their superiority in land forces to occupy key areas and neutralize others, which might be used by the Allies as bases for operations against the U.S.S.R., and thus create a strategic situation in which her opponents would find themselves stalemated.

3. a. The Soviet land armies and air forces are capable of overrunning most, if not all, of western Europe in a short time. The initial objective would probably include the destruction of the Allied forces of occupation in Germany, and seizure of the ports and the Channel coast of France and the lowlands, with the subsequent objective of neutralizing Great Britain. After the main effort had overrun France, it might be continued through Spain, in order to seize the western entrance to the Mediterranean.

b. In conjunction with this effort in western Europe, it is probable that the Soviets would launch operations designed to overrun Turkey and the Middle East in order to gain control of the eastern Mediterranean and the Middle East oil reserves.

c. Yugoslav forces, with Soviet support as necessary, would probably be utilized to overrun Greece and at least a portion of Italy.

d. In the Far East the U.S.S.R. probably would so limit operations that they would not interfere with her operations in western Europe and the Middle East. Once these latter efforts had been successfully concluded, the U.S.S.R. could attain her objectives in the Far East at leisure. Coincident with the foregoing offensive efforts, however, she would be capable of quickly overrunning Manchuria, Korea, parts of North China, and, perhaps, Hokkaido.

4. The rapidity with which Soviet operations attained their objectives would depend in considerable degree upon the careful selection of objectives, the relative timing of the several campaigns, and upon the extent to which the Soviets had been successful in molding to their advantage the political situation, both local and world-wide. As for Soviet operations envisaged for Europe and the Middle East, their support over long, and in many cases difficult, lines of communication would require a considerable logistic effort. In their wake there would probably be considerable requirements for occupation forces. Under certain circumstances these considerations might appreciably retard Soviet operational capabilities.

5. In view of the various ways in which the war might start and the numerous operations which would ultimately comprise the general Russian offensive, it is not possible to predict with any certainty the exact sequence or the relative timing of the major or even the minor phases of Soviet operations.

Allied Strategy

6. During the initial stages, the Allies would be on the strategic defensive and their initial operations would of necessity be limited to strategic moves to counter enemy offensives. The ability of the Allies to meet and retard the Soviet efforts would depend to a very large degree upon the length of the period of warning they received and the use they made of it. This period of warning would be a critical factor. A related factor of great, though lesser, importance is that of the amount of prior support given potential Allies of limited capabilities but great strategic significance, such as Turkey and Spain and also Greece and Italy. The necessity for flexibility in Allied plans is emphasized.

7. If the period of warning were insufficient to permit expansion of war-making industry and training, U.S. and Allied forces (particularly air forces) would be inadequate for accomplishment of minimum initial objectives; moreover, political agitation on a world-wide scale might tend to disperse such forces as are available. If warning were short, the Allies would experience great difficulties in concentrating their forces with sufficient rapidity to meet the enemy's threats. Only the vital first priority tasks could be undertaken. Such a situation would require that the Allies make full use of any warning received, guard against any dispersion of effort and keep lines of communication as short as possible. It would be of the greatest importance that the United States recognize early that a war is practically at hand, that the war will involve vital American interests, that early U.S. entry will yield important military advantages, and may in fact be essential to the prevention of military domination of the world by the U.S.S.R.

8. The Allies must delay a Soviet advance in the Middle East and the build-up of a Soviet offensive against the United Kingdom. They must shake the conviction of the Soviet people in their leaders and the conviction of the leaders in an early victory, meanwhile sustaining Allied morale by all measures possible. During this early critical phase, while on the strategic defensive, it would be necessary to blunt the enemy's offensive capabilities before the climax was reached.

9. There are certain basic undertakings which must be successfully discharged if the war is not to be lost, at least by stalemate. These include, the security and the maintenance of the industrial capacity of North America, the security of the British Isles, the security of certain key areas and bases and the security of minimum essential communications lines. Simultaneously with the prosecution of these undertakings, the strategic air effort against Russia would be initiated. To these basic undertakings must logically be added all practical measures to evacuate the occupation forces in Europe and Korea and to protect others in the Far East. These basic undertakings are a first charge against our resources.

10. As envisaged above, the end of the first few months of hostilities would find Soviet forces so located as to provide a cushion of conquered territory around the greater portion of the periphery of the U.S.S.R. The Allies do not have the capability of mobilizing or transporting, in the early stages of the war, ground and tactical air forces of sufficient strength to destroy the Soviet armed forces which would have to be encountered in depth along any of the avenues of approach which lead to the heart of Russia. Such an approach would require overland operations against the strongest elements of Soviet military strength; an element which could afford and would take tremendous losses in manpower. Initial Allied operations must be confined to vital areas. Harassment or destruction of Soviet forces in periphery areas would not achieve a decision. Furthermore, such harassment, particularly by air operations, against Soviet forces in areas occupied by them must be qualified by the political considerations inolved.

11. On the other hand, provided adequate base areas are secured and held and the lines of communications maintained, the United States has a capability of undertaking soon after the beginning of the war an offensive strategic air effort against vital Russian industrial complexes and against Russian population centers. If this effort, adequately expanded, did not achieve victory, it would destroy elements of Soviet industrial and military power to such an extent that the application of this and other forms of military force should accomplish the desired end.

12. After provision for the basic undertakings, the next charge against Allied resources must be the provision of forces and equipment for the development of a sustained strategic air offensive against the industrial heart of Russia.

13. In addition to the requirements for forces for the basic undertakings and for support of the sustained strategic air offensive, there must be provided ground, naval and air forces to retake key areas which will promote

the effectiveness of the strategic air effort and facilitate the initiation of a major land campaign if required.

14. Vital areas of the U.S.S.R. . . .

a. Recent preliminary examinations of possible target systems in the U.S.S.R. indicate that the destruction of the petroleum industry could be accomplished with less effort and would be reflected in reduction of the Russian military potential earlier than any other industry. The most effective means of attacking this industry would be by the destruction of refineries, bomb tonnage requirements for which are within our early capability. Approximately 84 per cent of Soviet refining capacity is believed to be located in the Caucasus, although information indicates that new developments are being located in the ''Second Baku'' area of the Urals; 15 per cent of the total Soviet oil production is obtained from the Ploesti oil fields of Rumania. Approximately 80 per cent of the entire industry is within the radius of B-29's operating from bases in the British Isles and the Cairo-Suez area.

b. Further detailed analyses will be necessary to establish the relative importance of various areas of the U.S.S.R. to the war-making capability of that nation. Certain areas are of obvious importance; the Ukraine for its grain; the Donbas mining and industrial area; Moscow, the seat of government, a communications and nerve center and an important production center for end products; the Ural industrial centers and the ''Second Baku'' oil producing area; and the Kuzbass mining and industrial area.

c. Many areas which are of strategic importance to the Soviets lie outside of their borders. In order to establish a defensive barrier around the vital Caucasus area, the U.S.S.R. must extend her sphere of influence to include Turkey, the eastern Mediterreanean, Iran and Iraq. The extremely large oil reserves of Mesopotamia are doubtless a tempting prize. Soviet acquisition of the Middle East oil reserves would eventually increase materially Soviet military capabilities and would immediately reduce those of Great Britain.

Possible Allied Base Areas Within Reach of Vital Areas of the U.S.S.R.

15. . . . It will be noted that the Caucasus and Ploesti areas, where so much of the Soviet oil industry is located, can be subjected to air bombardment most effectively from bases along the eastern shore of the Mediterranean or from the Cairo-Suez area. The Moscow area, where bombing would produce the most widespread morale effect, is within B-29 range of bases in the British Isles or the Cairo-Suez area. The vital Ural and Kuzbass areas

could be reached from bases in India. For the most effective prosecution of a strategic air campaign, therefore, base areas should be secured in the Near East, the British Isles and India. Base areas selected for the support of strategic air operations should, in so far as practicable, serve also for the support of surface operations.

16. The extent of surface offensives as well as the nature and degree of opposition to their continued progress, cannot be accurately estimated. The destructive and disruptive effects of the strategic air offensive, together with political and psychological considerations both in the U.S.S.R. and in Soviet-occupied countries, would influence the nature of the conflict in the closing phase of the war. Peace might come through capitulation, through negotiation, or only after the defeat and subjection of those Soviet forces which continued to offer significant resistance. The Allies might find it sufficient to progress only to some strategic natural barrier, there to establish a front from behind which the destruction of Soviet military potential could be maintained by air action until the resultant chaos convinced the Soviet people that further resistance was futile. The eventual control of the U.S.S.R. could probably be effected by occupying relatively limited areas, but the areas and distances involved and the number of people, military and civilian, to be controlled would probably require considerable Allied forces. When to the requirements for the U.S.S.R. proper are added those for certain liberated areas, it is evident that there may be a very large requirement for Allied forces of occupation. Although these requirements cannot be accurately estimated, it is considered that the forces required for this purpose would not be in excess of those which had been created to bring about the Soviet defeat. Some conversion of elements of these forces might be required.

17. The "industrial heart" of the U.S.S.R. lies in that area west of the Urals and north of the Caspian and Black Seas. In general, there are two broad avenues of approach by air and surface from the west toward this "heartland":

    a. One through the Central Europe—Scandinavian area (Northern Approach), and

    b. One through the Mediterranean—Near Eastern area (Southern Approach).

18. If a major surface advance were undertaken, it would probably not take place prior to the third year of war because of the time required for sufficient deterioration of enemy capabilities and the time required to mobilize, train, and support the required forces. During such a period of time, it might

be that political, psychological and underground factors of the great mass of people involved in Europe and Asia, combined with development and/or employment of new weapons on both sides, would result in the appearance of decisive strategic factors not now known which would influence the eventual decision as to the exact course of subsequent action.

19. If the southern approach were to be utilized, or if Cairo-Suez were used as a base area, control of the eastern Mediterranean would be essential from the outset of the war. This control could best be retained by preventing the U.S.S.R. from overrunning Turkey. Turkey could thereafter be used either as an allied base area or as cover for a base area from which the Allies could not only attack Soviet vital areas, but could also sever Soviet overland lines of communications leading to the oil resources of the Middle East and to the Cairo-Suez area.

20. Due to the comparatively small number of Allied ground and air forces that will be available initially, their ability to retard and finally check a Soviet advance through Turkey and the Middle East aimed at the Cairo-Suez area, will depend in large measure upon the period of forewarning, and the amount of prior material assistance that had been given to Turkey. In view of the poor lines of cummunication (LOC) though this area, it is considered that, with forces presently available in the general area and with the reinforcements that could be brought in in time the Soviet advance could be delayed and probably halted indefinitely in Palestine, if not further to the north. In the event that Soviet forces had not overrun Turkey by the time substantial Allied air forces could arrive in the eastern Mediterranean area, Cyprus would probably be of great strategic advantage to the Allies as a base from which Allied air forces could support Turkish ground forces. While a detailed examination of Cyprus has not yet been made, it appears that its use might contribute materially to the general defense against a Soviet advance into the Middle East and toward the Suez area. During later stages of the war, if the air defense of Cyprus proved feasible, the island, which has sites for approximately 10 VHB fields, might prove a highly important base for operations of planes of that type.

21. A detailed analysis based upon integrated operational plans would be required to determine probable petroleum needs. The use of jets, heavier bombers and larger transport aircraft, as well as higher aircraft utilization figures may result in a requirement for aviation fuel substantially greater than at the peak of World War II. Estimates of these requirements, combined with those of other forces, indicate that the United States may not have sufficient production capacity to satisfy her petrol, oil and lubricants

(POL) needs. With the loss of oil production from Iraq and Iran, the British Empire would be deprived of approximately 46 per cent of her peace-time requirements. Should the Allies require additional production of petroleum for the successful prosecution of the war as now seems probable, operations might be required in the Near East directed specifically toward obtaining POL.

Strategic Considerations Relating to the Mediterranean LOC

22. During the early stages of the war, naval forces, including carriers, tactical air forces, and ground combat forces need to be moved at once to the Mediterranean to blunt and finally to stall the enemy's advances. The importance of maintaining the Mediterranean Sea LOC to support these Allied forces in the eastern Mediterranean is emphasized by the vulnerability of the Suez Canal to mining and blocking. The control depth of the Canal is 37 feet and it can be blocked at almost any point along its 87 mile length by sinking a medium sized ship. It is susceptible to closure by ground mines at both entrances and throughout its length. The Canal cannot be depended upon as an *uninterrupted* sea route to the Eastern Mediterranean if enemy air bases are established within range.

23. The Mediterranean LOC assumes even greater importance when the added requirement of shipping to any eastern Mediterranean base area by any other route is considered. From New York to Cairo via the Mediterranean is 5,313 miles; the alternate route around South Africa is 12,085 miles. Furthermore, unless the Suez Canal can be kept open, it would be necessary to establish port facilities in the Red Sea and trans-ship supplies overland to the Cairo-Sinai base area.

24. The most serious threat that the Soviets could present to the Mediterranean route would be to overrun Spain and establish sufficient forces there to interdict the route in the vicinity of the Straits of Gibraltar. It would be highly essential for the allies to prevent such action or, if it occurred, to re-establish effective control of the route. Otherwise a drastic change in the concept of operations might be required. The Straits of Gibraltar are not suitable for effective mining and it is probable that Allied submarines could continue to utilize this route throughout the war.

25. Should the Allies have a sufficient warning period, the chances of maintaining the Mediterranean route should be favorable. Should the Soviets undertake a campaign against Spain after overrunnning France, it is possible that the Soviets would delay their advance at the Pyrenees in order to con-

centrate forces and resources. By this time they would be operating over extremely long lines of communication. The Spanish army, now showing some improvement but still inadequately equipped, might be able, with some Allied assistance particularly Allied air, to retard the Soviet advance to a considerable degree. As regards Italy, it might be possible to withdraw some Italian forces which, with Allied assistance, would have a good chance of holding Sicily. Similarly, Greek forces withdrawn from Greece might be able to garrison and hold Crete.

Other Operations

26. In the Far East, no good purpose would be served by engaging the enemy with U.S. forces on the ground on the Asiatic mainland. The enemy naval forces in this area with the exception of submarines, could be destroyed or immobilized with comparatively small effort. Enemy submarines, however, would present a serious hazard to Allied LOC in the northern and western Pacific. It appears that U.S. naval and air power operating from bases in Japan, Alaska, and the Pacific should be able to harass Russian coastal areas to such an extent that any danger of a major invasion of our positions by the Soviets could be eliminated. However, some threat to Hokkaido would continue.

27. As for the periphery of western Europe, there would exist a capability on our part for limited raids. The over-all value of these raids is doubtful, but they might have political and psychological values. It is not at all unlikely that in France, perhaps also in Italy and other countries, the Soviets would set up a government which was superficially autonomous, thereby placing our forces in the position of attacking a state which had not formally declared war on us. Hence, there is doubt that in western Europe there will be targets for remunerative action short of our generating a capability to seize and "liberate" these areas. An exception would be planes, guided missiles, submarine bases and concentrations, other military concentrations, other facilities which the Soviets might set up to attack Britain or interdict Allied LOC, and perhaps key industrial installations.

28. Except for long-range air operations, the enemy will initially possess the strategic initiative everywhere in Eurasia. In view of this fact inflexibility in mobilization planning must be avoided. Such planning should be designed to support operations along any of several axes. For reasons set forth earlier *it appears at the present time that initial establishment of Allied forces in the Middle East is the most promising course of action,* although its feasibility is directly dependent upon the extent that the route through the

Mediterranean can be utilized. While detailed studies of other axes of operation have not been made, it is believed that requirement for alternative operations would be such that the industrial program planned to support an initial effort in the Middle East could be adjusted without major loss of time or effort to support alternatives which might be selected as a result of later studies or which might be forced upon us by enemy action.

29. From the above analysis it appears that the Middle East area should be selected subject to further examination, for the purpose of estimating force requirements, as a major theater for operations against the U.S.S.R. In summary, advantages include the following:

   a. As a base area for strategic air operations, it is within closest operating range of the greatest percentage of those industrial complexes vital to the Soviet war effort.
   b. It constitutes a satisfactory base of operations for a surface advance toward vital Soviet areas, should such an advance prove necessary.
   c. In this area the U.S. and Britain would have an Allied people, the Turks, whose cooperation would be of great strategic value.
   d. Retention of a base area in the Middle East would facilitate Allied recovery of Middle East oil resources should these resources prove essential to Allied effort as the war progresses.
   e. Retention of a base area in the Middle East would facilitate denial of Middle East oil resources to the Soviets.
   f. Rentention of the Middle East would deny the Soviets access to North Africa via the Suez area.

30. The retention and use of the Cairo-Suez area represents initially the minimum Allied requirement in the Middle East. The Soviet efforts directed against this area should therefore be halted at an adequate distance from this key area, and in any event before they progress south of Palestine.

---

40   **S E C R E T**

Formula for the Determination of a National Stockpile

JCS 626/3   February 3, 1948

[Source: Records of the Joint Chiefs of Staff on deposit in the Modern Military Records Branch, National Archives, Washington D.C.]

Prompted by a request from the Munitions Board on December 30, 1947, the Joint Chiefs of Staff instructed the Joint Strategic Survey Committe to reexamine the premises underlying American policy concerning strategic stockpiling. The Joint

Chiefs of Staff received the Committee's evaluations on January 22, 1948, and approved them with slight revisions on February 2, 1948. Printed here are the premises regarding access to strategic raw materials upon which the committee based its assessment. They suggest that, despite the American atomic monopoly, war with the Soviet Union within "the next few years" was expected to resemble World War II in both character and duration.

    ·   ·   ·   ·   ·   ·   ·

1. The following definitions have been adopted for the purposes of this paper:

Major losses —more than 10% less in transit over the period the route is used.

Serious losses—5% to 10% less in transit over the period the route is used.

Minor losses —less than 5% loss in transit over the period the route is is used. . . .

    ·   ·   ·   ·   ·   ·   ·

. . . In future war losses will probably follow the pattern of World War II and be very high initially, tapering off as available enemy submarines are depleted and convoying becomes more effective. Press comment to the contrary, information this committee has received from competent U.S. Naval officers and from the minutes of Submarine Conferences held periodically in the U.S. Navy Department tend to indicate that in future war *average* losses in transit should not be substantially larger than those sustained in World War II.

2. It is considered that strategic premises or assumptions concerning when war will occur, the nature and duration of the war, the accessibility of sources of strategic and critical materials at the beginning and during the course of the war, and probable losses in transit should be considered when calculating national stockpile objectives.

3. When war will occur is important for the following reasons:

a. Refinements of present, and development of new, weapons of war is progressing daily. The results which have been achieved when war occurs will have a major effect on our ability to maintain communications between the United States and the sources of essential strategic and critical materials.

b. The outcome of the present political and ideological struggle between the democracies of the West and the totalitarian states of the East will determine whether many sources of strategic and critical materials will be available to the United States at the beginning and during the war. The Joint Strategic Survey Committee cannot predict the outcome of the present political and ideological struggle nor the national realignments and objectives which will exist as a result of this struggle. Hence, at present and until realignments have been stabilized, only rather vague assumptions can be made concerning access to many sources of important strategic and critical materials. For this reason it is felt that in case there is only one source of a strategic or critical material and this source is located outside the Western Hemisphere, the strategic considerations in this paper should be disregarded and the material stockpiled to a level permitting five years' industrial operation without imports.

4. It seems reasonable to assume that planned premeditated major warfare will not occur until our most probable opponent has developed and attained a stockpile of atomic or other weapons capable of comparable effect if used against the war making capacity of the United States, and until he has developed an industrial capacity capable of supporting a long major war without industrial assistance from outside Eurasia. However, the possibility of spontaneous unplanned war cannot be eliminated so long as the present explosive international political situation exists.

5. It seems probable that if the United States is involved in war, the war will be global and total and will last not less than five years. On the other hand, the possibility exists that the refinement of present, and the development of new, weapons of warfare may give to one side the ability to compel quick capitulation by its opponent at any time later than five years hence.

6. For all of the foregoing reasons the strategic premises for calculating national stockpile objectives should be reviewed periodically, preferably annually.

7. In view of the Treaty of Reciprocal Assistance of Rio de Janeiro,[5] it can be assumed as a premise for calculating stockpile objectives that the Western Hemisphere will be accessible in war as a source of raw materials, due allowance being made for estimated losses in transit. Such losses due to enemy action may be serious.

5. The "Rio Pact," as this treaty became known, was signed September 2, 1947. Eventually all twenty-one American republics adhered to the treaty, which provided that under Article 51 of the United Nations Charter, the signatories would exercise their collective right of self-defense. In any dangerous situation short of armed attack they would consult; in armed attack, every state had a duty to other signatories to help meet the attack until the United Nations Security Council should have taken effective action. In accord with traditional American concerns in such matters, no state could be required to use armed force in violation of its internal laws or processes. [Ed. note]

8. The Joint Chiefs of Staff have approved as a basis for planning the premise that the English-speaking nations of the British Commonwealth will ally with the United States if war occurs prior to 1 January 1956. Hence, for the purpose of this paper it is assumed that strategic and critical raw materials presently obtained from Australia, New Zealand, South Africa and Great Britain, will be accessible at the beginning and for the duration of war, due allowance being made for estimated losses in transit. Such losses due to enemy action should be very small in the case of Australia and New Zealand. During the same period considerably higher losses could be expected in transit between the United States and Great Britain and South Africa.

9. Though many European countries would endeavor to remain strictly neutral in the case of war in the next few years, it would be both unrealistic and dangerous to assume that any European country, with the possible exception of Spain, will be available as a source of strategic and critical materials. Losses due to enemy action during transit between Spain and the United States would be on the order of losses in transit between the United States and Great Britain.

10. The Near and Middle East will most probably be inaccessible as a source of strategic and critical materials unless the United States moves adequate forces into the areas prior to the outbreak of war and unless the present ill will on the part of the Arab states toward the United States is eliminated. Pakistan, India, Burma, Malaya, Siam, French Indo-China, China (south of the Yellow River), Japan, the Philippines and the islands lying between the Philippines and Australia will probably be available as sources of critical and strategic materials in the case of war within the next few years. However, varying conditions of internal unrest in these areas might conceivably curtail production or even in some cases, notably Pakistan, Malaya, Siam, French Indo-China and the Dutch East Indies, deny to the United States procurement from these areas. It is not believed that extensive interruption or complete stoppage of seaborne commerce between the United States and the Philippines and the islands lying between the Philippines and Australia, is a capability of any probable enemy of the United States at present, or within the next few years. However, serious losses could be expected between the United States and Japan. Serious losses would probably occur in transit between the United States and Pakistan, India and China. Minor losses should probably be expected between the United States and Burma, Malaya, Siam, French Indo-China and the Philippines. Enemy military occupation of these areas, with the possible exception of Pakistan, is not considered likely during a major war occurring during this period.

11. The accessibility of northwest Africa at the beginning of warfare will to a very large extent depend upon the status of France. If France is neutral or occupied, armed forces will be required to render this area accessible. The same is true of the Belgian Congo. Resistance in both areas would probably be weak. The remainder of Africa will most probably be accessible, although there will probably be internal unrest in Libya, Egypt, the Sudan, Eritrea, Abyssinia and Italian Somaliland. Madagascar will probably be accessible throughout the war. The same is true for Iceland and Greenland, although losses due to enemy action in transit between the United States and Iceland and Greenland can be expected to be on the order of losses in transit between the United States and Great Britain.

---

41   **T O P   S E C R E T**

Brief of Short Range Emergency War Plan (HALFMOON)

JCS 1844/13   July 21, 1948

[Source: Records of the Joint Chiefs of Staff on deposit in the Modern Military Records Branch, National Archives, Washington, D.C.]

By early 1948, approximately a year after the Joint Chiefs of Staff had defined the three principal categories of strategic planning (emergency, intermediate, and long range), no joint strategic plans had shown enough merit and sophistication to receive approval. But the events of February, March, and April 1948—including the war scare emanating from the reporting of General Lucius D. Clay in Berlin—stimulated renewed planning effort. One result was a Joint Outline Emergency War Plan named HALFMOON, approved for planning on May 19, 1948, and, under the name FLEETWOOD, distributed to commands on September 1, 1948, as a guide in preparing detailed operational plans (later still the plan was renamed DOUBLESTAR).

HALFMOON assumed that war with the Soviet Union was a distinct possibility; that in the first phase of war the Soviet Union would be capable of wide-ranging, concurrent, and effective offensives in virtually every major region of the globe; and that the United States would use atomic weapons in counteroffensive operations against the Soviets in Europe.

I. Estimate

1. There is a possibility that war will occur at any time as a result of miscalculation by the USSR as to the extent that the United States or other Western Powers would or could resist their present expansion policy. It is also possible that the active opposition of the Western Powers to Soviet expansion policy may induce the Soviets to believe that it would be advan-

tageous or even mandatory for them to anticipate any increase in this opposition by starting a war themselves. Such war would come with little or no warning.

2. *Operations by the Soviets*. Should war eventuate within the period covered by this plan, the Soviets can be expected to launch offensives concurrently or successively into western and northern Europe, southern Europe, the Middle East and the Far East. It is estimated that the first objectives of the Soviets would be:

    a. Seizure of Middle East and its oil resources.

    b. Destruction or neutralization of all forces of the Allies on the Eurasian land mass.

    c. Simultaneously to accomplish seizure or neutralization of those areas from which the Western Powers might swiftly and effectively strike at the USSR.

    d. Neutralization or seizure of the United Kingdom.

    e. Expansion and consolidation of positions in China, Manchuria and Korea.

    f. Disruption of the Allied war-making capacity by subversion and sabotage.

    g. Disruption of vital Allied lines of communication by aggressive submarine warfare, mining and air operations.

3. The following brief of emergency plan of action is based on maximum utilization of U.S. forces and estimated Allied forces initially available and estimated build-up during the first year of war. It is aimed at the early initiation and sustaining of an air offensive against vital elements of the Soviet war-making capacity and the regaining of Middle East oil to assure availability of these resources to the Allies during later phases. The shortcomings of this plan are recognized in that it does not provide adequate assistance to the countries of Western Europe, nor does it provide for the initial retention by the Allies of the Middle East oil resources.

II. United States Plan of Action
First Period

4. Under the concept of the present plan, in the event of hostilities in the immediate future, United States armed forces would immediately mobilize and accomplish the undertakings listed below.

5. Defend the Western Hemisphere. This would be accomplished by:

a. Provision for the security of Canada, Newfoundland, and the United States to the extent permitted by available forces and facilities which would include:

(1) Activation of limited air warning net.

(2) Provision by Canada of forces (estimated at approximately one infantry brigade group, six transport squadrons and two light bomb squadrons at reduced strength) for the defense of northeast Canada, Newfoundland and Labrador.

(3) Provision by the United States of six fighter groups (day) and one squadron all-weather fighters for defense of critical industrial areas in the United States and southern Canada. In addition it is anticipated that Canada will augment this defense with the equivalent of two and one-half day fighter squadrons.

(4) Maintenance of a reserve in the United States of two-thirds airborne division and two troop carrier groups.

(5) Sending one-third infantry division to Alaska for the defense of the Fairbanks-Anchorage area, and employing air forces presently deployed less MB group.

(6) Defense of atomic installations and stockpiles of atomic weapons—special ground units equivalent of two-thirds division with antiaircraft support, and two fighter groups, one squadron all-weather fighters, all of which are included in the forces specified in paragraph 5a (3) above. Antiaircraft units will consist primarily of federalized National Guard.

(7) Defense of Saulte Ste. Marie Canal—special units equivalent of one-third division.

(8) Defense against sabotage and subversion in U.S.—initially by special units equivalent to three divisions.

(9) Local defense of ports and harbors.

(10) Defense of coastal lines of communication.

(11) Requisition of U.S. merchant shipping essential to military purposes and induction of merchant marine personnel into the naval service as necessary.

b. Defense of Panama Canal and Caribbean bases—equivalent of two infantry regiments now deployed, Air Force elements reduced to one fighter squadron (day), one fighter squadron (AW), one reconnaissance squadron, one cargo squadron, rescue and liaison units.

c. Invoking the provisions of the Inter-American Treaty of Reciprocal Assistance and implementing the Inter-American Military Cooperation Act,[6] thereby insuring the cooperation and assistance of a maximum of the Latin American countries in the conduct of war. This cooperation and assistance should include: Contribution of manpower, resources, or bases; maintenance of internal security and local defense against clandestine action; maintenance of bases; and assistance in providing security for air, sea and land lines of communication by the conduct of antisubmarine and escort of convoy operations and by other means, thereby minimizing requirements for United States forces for hemisphere defense. (Note: Forces allocated to defense of the Western Hemisphere will be continuously reviewed and progressively adjusted in consonance with the evaluation of the threat.)

6. *Evacuation.*

  a. *Europe.* It is contemplated that the initial withdrawal of Allied forces will be to the Rhine. Further withdrawal in the face of Soviet pressure must take maximum advantage of all opportunities to delay Soviet advances and to stimulate resistance to the Soviets in friendly countries. Withdrawal of U.S. forces from Germany will take place in accordance with Commander in Chief, European Command (CINCEUR) plan. The timing, direction and extent of withdrawal must depend on the tactical situation but it is probable that U.S. forces will withdraw through France either to French coastal ports or to the Pyrenees. U.S. forces in Austria will join forces in Germany to the extent possible. Those unable to join forces in Germany may withdraw through Italy, the Belfort Gap or may enter Switzerland. British forces in Austria, if unable to withdraw to Germany, will withdraw through Italy to Genoa. Coordination between the local commanders concerned is required to implement the above concepts.

  b. *Mediterranean.* U.S. forces in Trieste will be withdrawn in accordance with TRUST force plan.[7] U.S. military missions in Turkey

6. The Inter-American Treaty was the Rio Pact of September 2, 1947. See the note to JCS 626/3, Document 38. The Inter-American Military Cooperation Act, proposed by the Truman Administration in 1946, was intended to standardize the military equipment of the Latin American republics by transferring quantities of surplus American military equipment. In two successive sessions Congress failed to pass the bill. By mid-1948, the United States exhausted its surplus of World War II equipment. Thereafter the problem of military equipment for Latin America became one more facet of the developing military assistance program legislated in 1949. [Ed. note]

7. TRUST was the code name of the headquarters of the United States Army in Trieste established September 16, 1947. The reference is to that headquarters' local plan for operations in case war should occur. [Ed. note]

and Greece will initially assist indigenous forces. Plans for evacuation by sea of these military missions and U.S. nationals from areas in the Mediterranean will be prepared for implementation by the Commander in Chief, U.S. Naval Forces, Eastern Atlantic and Mediterranean (CINCNELM). Naval support will be furnished CINCNELM in accordance with Commander in Chief, Atlantic (CINCLANT) plan. British forces in Trieste and Greece will similarly be withdrawn in accordance with plans made by Commanders in Chief, Middle East. Coordination between CINCNELM and the Commanders in Chief, Middle East, is required.

    c. Occupation forces being withdrawn can expect no reenforcements.

7. *Secure the United Kingdom.* This task must be performed initially by British forces. It is considered that over the first six months, British forces will have the capability of defending the United Kingdom to the extent that it can be used initially as an operating base area. Thereafter, if the U.K. base is to continue to be available to the Allies, there will be an additional requirement for fighter aircraft and AA defenses, unless in the meantime our air offensive has reduced the scale of Soviet attack.

8. *Secure the Cairo-Suez Base Area.*

    a. This area will be secured and supported through the Mediterranean, at least initially. . . .

    b. The LOC throughout the Mediterranean will be operated as long as possible. The following weaknesses will be accepted:

        (1) Defense of Spain will be left to Spanish forces.

        (2) Defense of Sicily will be left to Italian forces.

        (3) Air Defense and security forces of naval bases in French North African will be provided by French Colonial forces.

        (4) Malta will not be reenforced.

    It is recognized that closure of the Mediterranean may occur about D+6[8] in which event a LOC via the Cape of Good Hope-Red Sea route will be established.

    c. British and U.S. light carrier forces will be used on defensive missions in protection of shipping through the Mediterranean. Heavy U.S. carrier task forces in the Mediterranean will be used primarily for offensive missions in securing and maintaining air superiority over the LOC's and in interdiction of enemy LOC's. CVE trans-

---

8. D + 6, that is, the sixth month of military operations in the projected war. [Ed. note]

port[9] will be provided for movement of Air Force fighters, carrier replacement aircraft and crews from the U.S. . . .

    d. Antiaircraft defense of Egyptian ports will be provided mainly by Egyptian forces.

9. *Secure the Bering Sea-Japan Sea-Yellow Sea Line*

    a. Operations required for this task are provided for in existing plans of Commander in Chief, Far East (CINCFE), Commander in Chief, Pacific (CINCPAC), and Commander in Chief, Alaska (CINCAL). These include:

      (1) Withdrawal of United States forces from Korea.

      (2) Maintenance of United States forces in China in their present location, their redeployment to tenable locations in China, or their withdrawal from China if necessary.

      (3) Defense of Japan and the Ryukyus Islands.

      (4) Destruction by air and naval forces of enemy ports, air bases, industrial installations, stockpiles and naval forces; blockading of that portion of East Asia under Soviet control.

      (5) Provision of some aid to China if feasible.

    b. Forces available are those presently assigned, less certain of CINCPAC forces which are redeployed elsewhere. Filler replacements will be shipped to CINCFE to arrive between D plus sixty and D plus ninety days.

    c. It is anticipated that British forces will provide for the internal security of Malay.

10. *Air Offensive.* Initiate as early as practicable an air offensive against vital elements of the Soviet war-making capacity. (Note: Assumption is made that authority to employ atomic bombs has been obtained.)

    a. Deploy available units of the Strategic Air Command to bases in England (alternatively to Iceland), and to the Khartoum-Cairo-Suez area and conduct operations from these bases and Okinawa utilizing available atomic bombs against selected targets. Initial deployments will be accomplished by air movements of some elements of the Strategic Air Command in unit aircraft and by air transport.

    b. Operations would begin and be sustained from:

    England   —D + 15 days

9. CVEs were small, straight-decked carriers of World War II vintage originally used in antisubmarine hunter-killer groups, and converted to aircraft transport ships after the war. These later were designated CVTs. [Ed. note]

Okinawa   —D-day (D + 15 days with atomic
                                bombs)
Khartoum-Cairo-Suez area—D + 15 days. . . .

.   .   .   .

d. In conjunction with the atomic campaign, units of the Strategic
   Air Command, as available, would operate against remaining elements of the Soviet petroleum industry and submarine operating
   facilities and conduct extensive mining operations in Soviet ports
   and waterways.
e. Carrier task groups will supplement and support the air offensive
   to the extent practical consistent with their primary task.

11. Air and Naval bases will be established in Iceland and the Azores.
Advanced combat elements of the Marine security force for Iceland base
will be air lifted on D-day or as soon thereafter as possible. The balance of
the Iceland force and the Azores forces, making the total of one Marine
Brigade with Marine tactical air units for each base, will be moved amphibi-
ously to each base immediately after D-day. A U.S. escort fighter group, to
be eventually deployed to the U.K., will proceed so as to arrive in Iceland in
time to cover landing of advance elements of Marine force. Elements of this
group will remain there until Marine air tactical units arrive.

12. A Marine reenforced battalion will be deployed from Mediterranean
to the Bahrein area to assist in evacuation of United States nationals and for
possible neutralization of oil installations. This movement is to be made as
soon as possible after D-day by Naval air lift and by utilization of service
and commercial aircraft available in the Mediterrean area. It is considered
that a similar responsibility for the neutralization of oil installations in Iraq
and at the head of the Persian Gulf and destruction of rail LOC's to Persian
Gulf will be assumed by the British.

13. In order to establish control of sea areas necessary for the execution
of the concept, naval forces will be deployed to contain or destroy Soviet
naval forces and shipping.

14. To secure essential sea and air LOC's control and routing of shipping
will be instituted as necessary. Essential air and naval bases will be established as rapidly as possible. Only limited fighter defense and air early
warning for LOC's within range of enemy air attack can be provided. Surface escort, local sea defense forces, advanced base units, and naval and air
force squadrons will be deployed to assigned areas.

Second Period

15. *Tasks*. Tasks to which forces have been committed in the first period will be a continuing charge against available forces. Forces required for these tasks are assumed to be the same as for the first period with the following exceptions:

a. *The Air Offensive*. The air offensive against vital elements of Soviet war-making capacity must be intensified and sustained, base areas and operating facilities improved and expanded, and defense of bases and base areas strengthened.

b. *Security of the Cairo-Suez Base Area*. (See paragraph 16 below.)

c. *Defense of the United Kingdom*. In the event that the Soviets achieve a large build-up of air forces in Western Europe, it is anticipated that a Soviet air offensive would by $D + 6$ materially reduce the RAF. Under such circumstances the United Kingdom might be rendered unusable as an air base and would be subject to airborne and seaborne invasion by the Soviets. In order to forestall the conquest of the United Kingdom, reenforcement in the form of fighter aircraft and AA defenses would be required. Redeployment of the heavy carrier task groups from the Mediterranean to the United Kingdom would render brief reenforcement but would not meet the requirement of air reenforcements. The scale and timing of reenforcement to be provided for the defense of the United Kingdom is dependent on the effects of the Allied air offensive on the maintenance of Soviet air forces deployed in Western Europe and the decisions relative to the use of the U.K. bases.

d. *Security of Lines of Communication*. Dependent upon the effectiveness of the air offensive, mining campaign, and ASW operations, additional forces may be required in the second period for defense of essential LOC's and possibly including the longer sea-route around the Cape of Good Hope.

e. *Defense of Western Hemisphere*. It may be possible by the beginning of or during the second period to redeploy some forces allocated to the defense of the Western Hemisphere to other tasks, depending upon a continuous evaluation of the threat.

f. *Security of Far East*. It may be possible to withdraw some air force units from the Far East for redeployment to other tasks during the later part of the second period.

16. During this period a build-up of forces will be required to insure the retention of the Khartoum-Cairo-Suez area as an operating base area. As

soon as practicable this base area will be expanded to the north and east in order to increase the security of the Cairo-Suez area. . . .

17. *Further Operations*

a. By D + 12 the Allies can provide, in addition to those already enumerated, approximately twenty-three divisions together with air groups totalling approximately 1,400 aircraft which would be available for the execution of those tasks considered most essential at that time. Such tasks might include:

(1) Reopening of the Mediterranean.

(2) Regaining of Middle East oil.

b. *Reopening of the Mediterranean.* By D + 6 the Soviets have the capability of occupying and consolidating the entire northern littoral of the Mediterranean from the Pyrenees to Syria, and of bringing the Mediterranean LOC under heavy air attack. In addition they have the capability of occupying Spain by approximately D + 6 and bringing the line of communication under artillery fire. These might have the result of closing the Mediterranean LOC. If the air offensive is effective, however, the operational capabilities of the Soviet forces, deployed to cover the Mediterranean, should be seriously impaired. In this event it may be feasible to force the opening of the Mediterranean, particularly if Spain is unoccupied. These operations may initially involve the regaining of Sicily, the establishment of strong air forces along the North African littoral, and the reopening of French ports in Algeria and Tunisia. Reopening of the Mediterranean would be a most important factor in support of offensive action in and from the Middle East.

c. *Regaining of Middle East Oil.* Present estimates indicate that it will be necessary for the Allies to regain a substantial portion of Middle East oil resources by the end of the second year. The Allied offensive to regain these resources might be directed toward Kirkuk or the Persian Gulf, or both. The Kirkuk operation would involve an overland offensive in unfavorable terrain; the Persian Gulf offensive would impose difficult amphibious or triphibious operations.

.   .   .   .

[The plan concludes with a brief list of Army, Navy, Air Force, and British Commonwealth forces available for carrying out the tasks listed in paragraph 17.]

42   **T O P   S E C R E T**

Brief of Joint Outline Emergency War Plan (OFFTACKLE)

JSPC 877/59   May 26, 1949

[Source: Records of the Joint Chiefs of Staff on deposit in the Modern Military Records Branch, National Archives, Washington, D.C.]

Because emergency, or short-range, war plans were keyed to available forces in any given fiscal year, they required at least annual revision. Perhaps the rapidly changing political and military circumstances of the latter 1940s would have necessitated frequent revision in any case. Because of the approach of the new fiscal year, and to take into account such developments as the signing of the North Atlantic Treaty and the worsening situation of Chinese Nationalist forces, the Joint Chiefs of Staff in April 1949 directed the Joint Strategic Plans Committee to prepare a new emergency war plan for the first two years of a war beginning on July 1, 1949, based on forces available in fiscal year 1950. The strategic concept: "In collaboration with our allies, to impose the war objectives of the United States upon the USSR by destroying the Soviet will and capacity to resist, by conducting a strategic offensive in Western Eurasia and a strategic defensive in the Far East."

   The resulting Joint Outline Emergency War Plan, named OFFTACKLE, differed from its predecessor HALFMOON-FLEETWOOD-DOUBLESTAR (Document 41) in several respects. Foremost in importance, OFFTACKLE was the first postwar plan to have the advantage of proceeding from statements of national interest devised in the State Department and in the National Security Council, notably NSC 20/4 (see Document 23). The Joint Chiefs of Staff had long resented the absence of such guidance, and immediately incorporated it into formulations of national objectives and strategic concepts in war planning. In other important differences from earlier plans, OFFTACKLE evinced less exaggerated views of Soviet capabilities, stressed coordination with new allies, and downgraded the importance of retaining or retaking Middle East oil.

   Like earlier plans and papers, OFFTACKLE stressed the American reliance on atomic counteroffensives to blunt Soviet operations and to deprive the Soviet Union of warmaking capability. Interestingly, the plan also noted that "intelligence estimates indicate that the USSR will not have atomic bombs available in fiscal year 1950."

   OFFTACKLE was approved by the Joint Chiefs of Staff on December 8, 1949. Subsequently its name was changed to SHAKEDOWN, and later still to CROSSPIECE.

I. The Problem

1. To prepare a joint outline emergency war plan for the first two years of a war beginning on 1 July 1949 based on forces available under the FY 1950 budget.

II. Basic Assumption

2. On 1 July 1949, war has been forced upon the United States by acts of aggression by the USSR and/or her satellites.

III. Assumptions

3. a. The following countries will be allied with the Soviet Union: Bulgaria, Roumania, Hungary, Poland, Albania, Czechoslovakia, and North and Central China (including Manchuria, Mongolia and Sinkiang). *North Korea?*

   b. Although the following countries would desire to ally with the Anglo-American powers their political or strategic situation would be so precarious that they could not be relied upon and would be likely to be rapidly overrun by the Soviet Union: Austria, Greece, Iran, Finland, West Germany, South China, and South Korea.[10]

   c. Yugoslavia's objective will be to avoid active participation and especially to forestall occupation by Soviet troops. Yugoslavia will attempt to attain these objectives, probably by professing neutrality, possibly by professing adherence to the USSR. A profession of neutrality would probably be accompanied by sub-rosa assistance to the USSR. In either case, Yugoslavia will resist general occupation by Soviet troops, but might permit the passage of Soviet troops across Yugoslavia. Whenever Yugoslavia becomes sufficiently important strategically to the USSR, the latter will overrun and occupy it.

   d. The following countries will be allied against the Soviet Union: United States, United Kingdom, Canada, Australia, New Zealand, Union of South Africa, Ceylon, the British Colonial Empire, France, the Benelux Countries, Norway, Denmark, Portugal, Italy, Iceland, and the Philippine Islands, together with their overseas possessions.

   e. The following countries will attempt to remain neutral but will be friendly disposed towards the Anglo-American Powers and will join them if attacked by the Soviet Union: Turkey and Spain.

   f. The following countries will remain neutral if permitted to do so: Ireland, Switzerland, Sweden, and Afghanistan. Ireland and Switzerland will resist attack by either side but will ally with the

10. East Germany and North Korea have already been occupied by the Soviet Union. [Note in source text]

Anglo-American Powers if attacked by the Soviets. Sweden and Afghanistan may submit to occupation by the Soviets.

g. The Arab States deeply distrust the USSR and, if they were unable to remain neutral, would prefer to support the Anglo-American Powers, in spite of great disillusionment over U.S. and U.K. policy toward Palestine. However, because political turmoil in the Arab States will probably continue, the Arab governments, although unlikely to oppose the use by Western Powers of territories and resources in Arab control, will be unable (even though willing) to afford any significant cooperation, at least initially. Israel, although unlikely to offer effective opposition to the Western Powers, would be reluctant to afford them any cooperation.

h. Other Asiatic countries, including India and Pakistan, but excluding Soviet satellites, can be expected to remain neutral but might be prepared, under pressure, to make their economic resources, and possibly their territories, available to the Anglo-American Powers.

i. While the countries which have signed the Atlantic Pact will have improved economically and militarily, they will be unable, with the exception of the United Kingdom, to effectively resist being overrun and occupied by Soviet forces.

j. Other countries of Central and South America will be Allied with the United States in accordance with the Inter-American Treaty of Reciprocal Assistance.[11]

k. High governmental approval will be obtained and atomic weapons will be used by the United States. Atomic weapons will be used by the USSR if available. (Intelligence estimates indicate that the USSR will have no atomic bombs available in fiscal year 1950.)

l. Biological and chemical warfare may be used by either side subject to considerations of retaliation. The Soviets will have biological weapons sufficiently advanced to use on a limited scale, but the Allies will not have sufficient quantities to permit offensive employment in the period under consideration. Both the United States and the USSR have chemical warfare weapons developed for employment on a major scale.

m. At best, war will be preceded by a period of political negotiations and increasing tension. Under these conditions the Allies may have a few months warning that war is likely. The decision to start the

---

11. The Rio Pact of September 2, 1947. [Ed. note]

main attack might be taken by the Allied governments in which case the Allies should be able to take certain preparatory measures. On the other hand, war may break out without warning.

n. Present estimates indicate that the regaining of Middle East oil is not vital[12] but will be highly desirable. Regaining these resources by the end of the second year of the war will provide insurance against the adverse effect of presently unforeseeable factors (JCS 1741/15).[13]

IV. National War Objectives

4. The national objectives of the United States with respect to the USSR are set forth in NSC 20/4 (JCS 1903/3).[14] Pertinent extracts are:

U.S. Objectives and Aims Vis-à-Vis the USSR

19. To counter the threats to our national security and well-being posed by the USSR, our general objectives with respect to Russia, in time of peace as well as in time of war, should be:

a. To reduce the power and influence of the USSR to limits which no longer constitute a threat to the peace, national independence and stability of the world family of nations.

b. To bring about a basic change in the conduct of international relations by the government in power in Russia to conform with the purposes and principles set forth in the United Nations charter.

In pursuing these objectives due care must be taken to avoid permanently impairing our economy and the fundamental values and institutions inherent in our way of life.

22. In the event of war with the USSR we should endeavor by successful military and other operations to create conditions which would permit satisfactory accomplishment of U.S. objectives without a predetermined requirement for unconditional surrender. War aims supplemental to our peacetime aims should include:

a. Eliminating Soviet Russian domination in areas outside the borders of any Russian state allowed to exist after the war.

b. Destroying the structure of relationships by which the leaders of the All-Union Communist Party have been able to exert moral and disciplinary authority over individual citizens, or groups of citizens, in countries not under communist control.

c. Assuring that any regime or regimes which may exist on traditional Russian territory in the aftermath of war:

(1) Do not have sufficient military power to wage aggressive war.

(2) Impose nothing resembling the present iron curtain over contacts with the outside world.

12. Subject to confirmation by responsible government agencies. [Note in source text]
13. Not printed. [Ed. note]
14. See Document 23. [Ed. note]

d. In addition, if any Bolshevik regime is left in any part of the Soviet Union, insuring that it does not control enough of the military-industrial potential of the Soviet Union to enable it to wage war on comparable terms with any other regime or regimes which may exist on traditional Russian territory.

e. Seeking to create postwar conditions which will:

(1) Prevent the development of power relationships dangerous to the security of the United States and international peace.

(2) Be conducive to the successful development of an effective world organization based upon the purposes and principles of the United Nations.

(3) Permit the earliest practicable discontinuance within the United States of wartime controls.

V. Mission

5. To accomplish the military defeat of the USSR and her satellites to a degree that will bring about a political and military situation which will permit the United States to accomplish the national objectives outlined in NSC 20/4 (JCS 1903/3).

VI. Over-all Strategic Concept

6. In collaboration with our Allies, to impose the war objectives of the United States upon the USSR by destroying the Soviet will and capacity to resist, by conducting a strategic offensive in Western Eurasia and a strategic defensive in the Far East.

VII. Basic Undertakings

7. In collaboration with our allies:

a. To insure the integrity of the Western Hemisphere and to promote and develop its war-making capacity.

b. To secure, maintain, and defend such bases, land and sea areas, and lines of communication as are required for the execution of the concept.

VIEW "A" [15]	VIEW "B"
c. To conduct, at the earliest practicable date, a strategic	c. To conduct, at the earliest practicable date, a strategic

15. While plans were under discussion, divergent views among the military services were presented in this fashion for consideration at higher levels of the Joint Staff Organization. The

| air offensive against the vital elements of the Soviet war-making capacity. | air offensive against the vital elements of the Soviet war-making capacity, and against other elements of the Soviet offensive military power. |

d. To stabilize the Soviet offensive as early as practicable by means of air, sea, land, and special operations.

e. To initiate development of the offensive power of the armed forces for such later operations as may be necessary for achievement of the national war objectives.

f. To provide essential aid to our Allies in support of efforts contributing directly to the over-all strategic concept.

g. Exploit at the earliest practicable date the psychological weaknesses of the USSR and its satellites by information activities and other special operations.

VIII. Estimate

8. *Outbreak of War.* There is a possibility that war will occur at any time as a result of miscalculation by the USSR or a satellite as to the extent that the United States or other Western Powers would or could resist their present policy of expansion. It is also possible that the active opposition of the Allies to Soviet expansion policy may induce the Soviets to believe that it would be advantageous or even mandatory for them to anticipate any increase in this opposition by starting a war themselves. Such war would come with little or no warning.

9. *Operations by the Soviets.* Should war eventuate within the period covered by this plan, the Soviets can be expected to launch offensives into western and northern Europe, southern Europe, the Middle East and the Far East. It is doubtful, however, whether the Russians have the command ability and resources to undertake all these campaigns concurrently. It is estimated that the early objectives of the Soviets, not in order of priority, would be:

a. Seizure of the Middle East and its oil resources.

---

moderate differences in language between Views A and B reflect the Navy's opposition (View A) to an enlarging strategic air war, which would imply a greater role and a greater share of resources for the Air Force (View B). In later versions of this plan, View A won out. [Ed. note]

  b. Destruction or neutralization of all forces of the Allies on the Eurasian land mass.

  c. Seizure or neutralization of those areas from which the Western Powers might swiftly and effectively strike at the USSR.

  d. Neutralization or seizure of the United Kingdom.

  e. Expansion and consolidation of positions in the satellites, China, and Korea.

  f. Disruption of the Allied war-making capacity by subversion and sabotage.

  g. Disruption of vital Allied lines of communication by aggressive submarine warfare, mining and air operations.

  h. Accomplishment of diversionary attacks on Allied-held territory for the purpose of causing mal-deployment of Allied forces.

IX. Brief of Allied Plan of Action

10. *General.* The Allied plan of action is based on three distinct but interrelated series of operations:

  a. Essential defensive tasks.

  b. A strategic air offensive.

  c. Operations in Western Eurasia which have as their immediate aim the securing of as much of Western Europe as is possible from Soviet military control, and as their ultimate aim the military defeat of forces of the USSR.

11. *Defensive Tasks.* The following defensive tasks must be accomplished on an austerity basis, regardless of the direction of any offensive:

  a. Insure the security of the Western Hemisphere to include:

    (1) Defense of the contintental United States.

    (2) Defense of the Fairbanks-Anchorage-Kodiak area of Alaska.

    (3) Defense of the Venezuelan oil area.

    (4) Defense of the Panama Canal.

  b. Insure the security of Iceland, Greenland, and the Azores.

  c. Insure the continued availability of Okinawa as a base for military operations. Defend Japan with forces initially available on D-day plus such minor augmentations as can be made available during the first few months of the war.

  d. Secure the lines of communication from the United States and Canada to the United Kingdom, Straits of Gibraltar, Central Africa, South America, Alaska, Okinawa, and Japan.

12. *Strategic Air Offensive*. This operation requires immediate utilization of the forces available as of D-day for a maximum exploitation of the atomic bomb.

VIEW ''A'' [16]	VIEW ''B''
It is recognized that the degree of success of the initial atomic offensive will largely determine the speed with which the war will be brought to a successful conclusion and the subsequent course of Allied action. Therefore, operational and logistic support priorities must be established to permit the early initiation of a concentrated strategic air offensive to destroy the war-making capacity of the USSR. This air offensive will be sustained until decisive results are attained or until Soviet capabilities are so reduced as to permit the accomplishment of this end by employment of forces on a scale which would not jeopardize the national economy.	It is recognized that the degree of success of the initial atomic offensive will largely influence subsequent Allied action. Therefore, operational and logistic support priorities must be established to permit the early initiation of this effort. This air offensive will be continued until Soviet military capabilities are so reduced as to permit the commitment to action of Allied military forces on a scale which would not jeopardize the national economy.

13. *Operations in Western Eurasia.*

   a. The security of the United States requires, with respect to continental Europe, the pursuance of a continuing policy to develop at the earliest possible moment, with the Nations of Western Europe, the capability of holding a line covering the Western Europe complex preferably no farther to the west than the Rhine. The logical extension of this line involves the United Kingdom on the left flank and the Cairo-Suez area on the right flank. Realizing that the accomplishment of this purpose is infeasible with the forces which will be available in FY 1950, this plan envisages the holding of a substantial bridgehead in Western Europe. Or, if this proves in-

16. Here, View A is that of the Air Force; View B is that of its competitors in the contest for strategic missions and resources. Subsequently, this passage read: ''A strategic air offensive with atomic and conventional bombs will be initiated at the earliest possible date subsequent to the outbreak of hostilities. This offensive will be aimed at vital elements of the Soviet warmaking capacity and at the retardation of Soviet advances in western Eurasia. Operational and logistic support priorities will be established to permit the earliest initiation of this effort.'' See JCS 1844/46, 8 November 1949, p. 353, National Archives, Modern Military Records Branch (not printed). [Ed. note]

feasible, the earliest practicable return to Western Europe in order to prevent the exploitation and Communization of that area with long-term disastrous effects on U.S. national interests.

   b. Accordingly, the concept of operations for this plan includes the following basic tasks in the following order of priority:

     (1) Secure the United Kingdom against invasion, and defend it against air attack to the degree necessary to insure its availability as a major base for all types of military operations.

     (2) Maintain Allied control of the Western Mediterranean-North African area (to include Tunisia) to the extent necessary to ensure continued capability of carrying on effectively military operations in that area. This will involve holding on the Pyrenees line if possible, and at a minimum, that area of the Iberian Peninsula which is necessary to secure the western entrance to the Mediterranean.

     (3) Maintain Allied control of the Cairo-Suez area to facilitate support of the Turks and other friendly forces in the general vicinity, to enable Allied air forces, both land- and sea-based, to support friendly forces in the Eastern Mediterranean littoral, to permit the launching of strategic air bombing attacks against remunerative targets from bases in that area, and to exploit natural resources and any enemy weaknesses in the Middle East.

   c. Secure air and sea lines of communication to Allied forces deployed to accomplish the tasks outlined in subparagraph b above.

14. *Phasing.* It is recognized that the following phases are only approximate and that they will inevitably overlap to a varying degree with each individual operation or campaign, and that they may be materially changed as Soviet intentions are transmitted into actual operations. This plan of action for the first two years of war is developed in three time phases with subsequent operations shown under a fourth phase.

   a. *First Phase.* The first phase (estimated from D to D + 3 months) covers the period during which the initial atomic offensive of the war will have been largely completed and its effects evaluated; from this evaluation will stem the next phase of the war. During this period allied forces will be deployed to undertake those tasks listed in paragraphs 11 to 13 inclusive above and operations to impede Soviet offensives.

   b. *Second Phase.* The second phase (estimated from D + 3 to

D + 12) is one of continuing the air offensive; of applying all
other available forces to stagnate Soviet advances initially, and
later, to enhance the Allied military position in Western Eurasia;
and at the same time, generating the forces required to permit the
realization of allied military objectives in Western Europe.

c. *Third Phase.* The third phase (estimated from D + 12 to D + 24
months) is a period during which the allied forces will continue
the operations set forth for the first and second phases and will undertake the exploitation of allied efforts of earlier phases to defeat
the Soviet forces in Western Europe by invasion if necessary.

d. *Fourth Phase.* The fourth phase (estimated from D + 24 to the end
of the war) is covered in this plan only in general terms. A broad
estimate of the possible scheme of operations which might be followed should the war continue for more than two years is set
forth.

X. *General Tasks*
(All Phases)

15. *Introduction*

a. In this section, and those which follow, the specific tasks which
must be undertaken to implement the concept and carry out the
Allied plan of action are defined. Insofar, as practicable, the tasks
are discussed under the respective phases. In the case of continuing tasks, the change in nature of these tasks for each of the time
phases is indicated. Where no appreciable change is expected in a
continuing task, or in the cases of tasks which should be completed within a certain time phase, it is dropped from further discussion.

b. In the case of the more important tasks, the deployment of forces
for each specific task is contained in the discussion thereof. A
restatement of such deployments, and a recapitulation for each
service are contained in the annexes to this plan. Deployments to
specific tasks must not be considered as inviolate. There are areas
of activity in which specific forces will have to be employed in the
execution of more than one task.

c. This plan is not written with any particular command organization
in mind, although it is inevitable that certain tasks will fall naturally into the existing structure. Implementation of this plan, in

which tasks will be specifically assigned to present or prospective commands, will be accomplished by implementation directives.

16. *Cooperation*
   a. This plan is not the result of combined planning. However, information on the plans of our allies and their capabilities was used to the extent it was available. It was assumed that the United Kingdom, our principal ally, would deploy the forces essentially as indicated in the latest combined plan. Redeployment of U.K. forces might result in a material strengthening of the tasks listed under Priorities 1 and 2 to such an extent that a more substantial base area could be assured.
   b. General consideration is given to the assistance which the United States may expect from its allies in waging the war envisaged by this plan. One of the most important U.S. tasks will be the effective utilization of this assistance. This will require both political and military consultations to insure that plans for the implementation of this concept be effectively coordinated among all the Allies in order to make maximum use of Allied assistance as it becomes available.

17. *Aid to Allies.* A separate plan will be prepared to provide feasible aid to those nations whose contribution to the Allied war effort will assist in the implementation of the overall strategic concept, including the minimum necessary to those nations vital to the execution of this plan. Initially the amount of this aid will be modest and must be allocated only to the most vital tasks.

18. *Unconventional Warfare.* Guidance for the conduct of military psychological warfare and other means of unconventional warfare in the support of current joint emergency war plans is being prepared. When approved, this guidance will be furnished to commanders operating directly under the Joint Chiefs of Staff.

.   .   .   .

[Paragraphs 19 through 48 constituted a detailed discussion of the tasks, forces available, and operations in the anticipated phases of the war as outlined above. Ed. note]

<><><><><><><><><><><><><><><><><><><><><><><><><><><><><><><>

43   **T O P S E C R E T**

Strategic Concept for the Defense of the North Atlantic Area

DC 6/1   December 1, 1949

[Source: *Foreign Relations of the United States: 1949,* IV, 352–56]

The signing of the North Atlantic Treaty in April 1949 opened a new era militarily as well as politically for the United States. One of the first necessities for America and its new allies was to state objectives and agree on a general approach to the problems of mutual defense. In essence, the signatories of the NATO treaty, through their representatives to the Defense Committee of the organization, pledged cooperation in peace and combination in war. They called for planning, preparation, standardization, and joint exercise in peace in the conviction that these would lead to strength in war if they did not in fact deter the Soviet Union from ever attacking at all. The United States received primary responsibility for strategic atomic bombing in war; the United Kingdom assumed a leading role in defending the ocean lines of communication; and NATO's other nations recognized their obligation to provide ground forces and tactical aircraft in Europe at least in the initial phases of any future war.

I
Preamble

1. The attainment of the objectives of the North Atlantic Treaty requires the integration by the parties to the Treaty of those political, economic, and psychological, as well as purely military means, which are essential to the defense of the North Atlantic area. Of particular significance is the requirement that the objectives of the North Atlantic Treaty be accomplished in accordance with the purposes and principles of the Charter of the United Nations. The parties to the Atlantic Treaty have declared:

They are determined to safeguard the freedom, common heritage, and civilization of their peoples, founded on the principles of democracy, individual liberty, and the rule of law.

They seek to promote stability and well-being in the North Atlantic Area.

They are resolved to unite their efforts for collective defense and for the preservation of peace and security.

2. For the purpose of, first, preventing war, and, second, insuring in the event of war the effective application of the military and industrial strength of the Treaty nations in a common defense, the military means available to the nations of the North Atlantic Treaty must be effectively coordinated. As a basis for such coordination a common strategic concept for the defense of

the North Atlantic area must serve as the keystone for the plans of the Military Committee and the Regional Planning Groups. It is the purpose of this document to outline a broad concept for the over-all defense of the North Atlantic area.

3. This broad concept is built on considerations of geographic position, industrial capacity, and financial resources of the population, the military capabilities of the Treaty nations, and recognizing that each nation's contributions should be in proportion to these considerations. The objective is adequate military strength accompanied by economy of effort, resources and manpower. It is desirable that each nation develop its military strength to the maximum extent consistent with over-all strategic plans in order to provide for its own defense and to participate in the common defense.

4. This concept is the initial step in the initiation of realistic, vital and productive defense planning aimed at securing peace and lessening the possibility of aggression. It is aimed at providing the basic strategic guidance needed by the regional planning groups in order to assure coordinated planning in consonance with the principles set forth in Title II below. The measures required to implement this concept will require constant review.

II
North Atlantic Treaty Defense Principles

5. Certain general principles are recognized as underlying the North Atlantic Treaty defensive organizations. These principles are accepted as fundamental to the successful functioning of the organization and the development of a common defense program. As such, those applicable to defense planning are set out in the following paragraphs as an integral part of the basic guidance for regional planning groups.

    a. The main principle is common action in defense against armed attack through self-help and mutual aid. The immediate objective is the achievement of arrangements for collective self-defense among the Atlantic Treaty nations.

    b. In accordance with the general objective of Article 3 of the North Atlantic Treaty, each nation will contribute in the most effective form, consistent with its situation, responsibilities and resources, such aid as can reasonably be expected of it.

    c. In developing their military strength consistent with over-all strategic plans the participating nations should bear in mind that economic recovery and the attainment of economic stability constitute important elements of their security.

d. The armed forces of those nations so located as to permit mutual support in the event of aggression should be developed on a coordinated basis in order that they can operate most economically and efficiently in accordance with a common strategic plan.

e. A successful defense of the North Atlantic Treaty nations through maximum efficiency of their armed forces, with the minimum necessary expenditures of manpower, money and materials, is the goal of defense planning.

f. A basic principle of North Atlantic Treaty planning should be that each nation should undertake the task, or tasks, for which it is best suited. Certain nations, because of the geographic location or because of their capabilities, will be prepared to undertake appropriate specific missions.

III

Objectives of the North Atlantic Treaty Defensive Concept

6. The purpose of the North Atlantic Treaty defensive organization is to unite the strength of the North Atlantic Treaty nations in order to promote the preservation of peace and to provide for the security of the North Atlantic area. The general objectives of the defensive concept are:

a. To coordinate, in time of peace, our military and economic strength with a view to creating a powerful deterrent to any nation or group of nations threatening the peace, independence and stability of the North Atlantic family of nations.

b. To develop plans, for use in the event of war, which will provide for the combined employment of military forces available to the North Atlantic nations to counter enemy threats, to defend and maintain the peoples and home territories of the North Atlantic Treaty nations and the security of the North Atlantic Treaty area.

IV

Military Measures to Implement Defense Concept

BASIC UNDERTAKINGS

7. Over-all defense plans must provide in advance of war emergency, specifically for the following basic undertakings in furtherance of the common objective to defend the North Atlantic area. The successful conduct of these undertakings should be assured by close coordination of military action as set forth in over-all plans.

a. Insure the ability to carry out strategic bombing promptly by all means possible with all types of weapons, without exception. This is primarily a U.S. responsibility assisted as practicable by other nations.

b. Arrest and counter as soon as practicable the enemy offensives against North Atlantic Treaty powers by all means available, including air, naval, land and psychological operations. Initially, the hard core of ground forces will come from the European nations. Other nations will give aid with the least possible delay and in accordance with over-all plans.

c. Neutralize as soon as practicable enemy air operations against North Atlantic Treaty powers. In this undertaking the European nations should initially provide the bulk of the tactical air support and air defense, other nations aiding with the least possible delay in accordance with over-all plans.

d. Secure and control sea and air lines of communication, and ports and harbors, essential to the implementation of common defense plans. The defense and control of sea and air LOC's will be performed through common cooperation in accordance with each nation's capabilities and agreed responsibilities. In this regard it is recognized that the United States and United Kingdom will be primarily responsible for the organization and control of ocean lines of communication. Other nations will secure and maintain their own harbor defenses and coastal LOC's and participate in the organization and control of vital LOC's to their territories as may be indicated in over-all plans.

e. Secure, maintain and defend such main support areas, air bases, naval bases and other facilities as are essential to the successful accomplishment of the basic undertaking. These undertakings will be a responsibility of the nations having sovereignty over these essential bases, areas and facilities, aided as necessary and to the extent set forth in collective defense plans.

f. Mobilize and expand the over-all power of the Treaty nations in accordance with their planned contribution to later offensive operations designed to maintain security of the North Atlantic Treaty area.

COOPERATIVE MEASURES

8. The essence of our over-all concept is to develop a maximum of strength through collective defense planning. As a prerequisite to the suc-

cessful implementation of common plans, it is recognized that certain cooperative measures must be undertaken in advance. These measures are:

    a. Standardization, insofar as practicable, of military doctrines and procedures.

    b. Conduct of combined training exercises, when deemed desirable.

    c. Compilation and exchange of intelligence information and data peculiar to the conduct of contemplated Atlantic Treaty organization defense planning and operations resulting therefrom.

    d. Cooperation in the construction, maintenance, and operation of military installations of mutual concern, in conformity with the agreements between the interested countries.

    e. Standardization of maintenance, repair, and service facilities which will be of mutual concern in the event contemplated defense plans have to be implemented.

    f. Standardization, insofar as practicable, of military material and equipment for use in operations as developed by common defense plans.

    g. Collective cooperation in arranging for military operating arrangements mutually agreed between countries in peacetime, in furtherance of common defense requirements.

    h. Cooperation, within the legal limitations and administrative restrictions of each country, in research and development of new weapons and in the development of new methods of warfare.

    i. Cooperation, insofar as is practicable, in planning for the conduct of psychological and other special operations.

PART III: THE ATOMIC BOMB

44   **T O P   S E C R E T**

United States Policy on Atomic Weapons

NSC 30   September 10, 1948

[Source: *Foreign Relations of the United States: 1948,* I (part 2), 624–28]

Following the Czechoslovakian crisis and the beginning of the Berlin blockade, the National Security Council in May 1948 inaugurated discussion of a policy statement on the use of atomic weapons. The result was NSC 30, prepared in consultation with the Departments of State, Army, Navy, Air Force, the National Security Resources Board, and the Central Intelligence Agency. After considering whether to establish a public policy regarding the use or nonuse of atomic weapons in any future conflict, the Council decided, with the concurrence of the Joint Chiefs of Staff, that even to discuss the possibility of not using such weapons posed unacceptable dangers, both in terms of encouraging the Russians and discouraging American allies in Western Europe.

On September 16, 1948, the National Security Council approved paragraphs 12 and 13 of NSC 30, which included language indicating that the National Military Establishment should plan for the use of atomic weapons. In the opinion of W. Walton Butterworth, Director of the Office of Far Eastern Affairs in the State Department, this recommendation in effect decided the question in favor of the use of atomic weapons, for planning on the assumption of their use would leave no alternative in crisis. The real questions, he wrote in a memorandum of September 15, 1948, were "when and how such weapons should be used. Should we, for example, in the event of war, begin by bombing major centers of population in enemy territory or start with smaller centers important for transportation or specific industries? This question should be answered not so much on the basis of humanitarian principles as from a practical weighing of the long-run advantage to this country." [17]

The Problem

1. To determine the advisability of formulating, at this time, policies regarding the use of atomic weapons.

Analysis

2. The decision to employ atomic weapons is a decision of highest policy. The circumstances prevailing when war is joined cannot be wholly forecast with any greater certainty than can the arrival of war. It appears imprudent either to prescribe or to prohibit beforehand the use of any particular weapons when the character of future conflict is subject only to imperfect prediction. In this circumstance, a prescription preceding diagnosis could invite disaster.

3. If war itself cannot be prevented, it appears futile to hope or to suggest that the imposition of limitations on the use of certain military weapons can prevent their use in war.

4. The United States has nothing presently to gain, commensurable with the risk of raising the question, in either a well-defined or an equivocal decision that atomic weapons would be used in the event of war. An advance decision that atomic weapons will be used, if necessary, would presumably be of some use to the military planners. Such a decision does not appear essential, however, since the military can and will, in its absence,

17. *Foreign Relations of the United States: 1948,* I (part 2), 630–31.

plan to exploit every capability in the form of men, materials, resources and science this country has to offer.

5. In this matter, public opinion must be recognized as a factor of considerable importance. Deliberation or decision on a subject of this significance, even if clearly affirmative, might have the effect of placing before the American people a moral question of vital security significance at a time when the full security impact of the question had not become apparent. If this decision is to be made by the American people, it should be made in the circumstances of an actual emergency when the principal factors involved are in the forefront of public consideration.

6. Foreign opinion likewise demands consideration. Official discussion respecting the use of atomic weapons would reach the Soviets, who should in fact never be given the slightest reason to believe that the U.S. would even consider not to use atomic weapons against them if necessary. It might take no more than a suggestion of such consideration, perhaps magnified into a doubt, were it planted in the minds of responsible Soviet officials, to provoke exactly that Soviet aggression which it is fundamentally U.S. policy to avert.

7. If Western Europe is to enjoy any feeling of security at the present time, without which there can be no European economic recovery and little hope for a future peaceful and stable world, it is in large degree because the atomic bomb, under American trusteeship, offers the present major counterbalance to the ever-present threat of the Soviet military power. This was recognized by the then Secretary of State, James F. Byrnes, who, in an address before the United Nations General Assembly on December 13, 1946, acknowledged, with the applause of the Assembly, that: "In the recent past, the concern of peace-loving nations has not been that America maintained excessive armaments. The concern has been that America failed to maintain adequate armaments to guard the peace. . . . It was our military weakness, not our military strength, that encouraged Axis aggression." [18] Were the United States to decide against, or publicly debate the issue of the use of the atomic bomb on moral grounds, this country might gain the praise of the world's radical fringe and would certainly receive the applause of the Soviet bloc, but the United States would be thoroughly condemned by every sound citizen in Western Europe, whose enfeebled security this country would obviously be threatening.

8. Furthermore, consideration must be given to whether any public uni-

18. Document AEC/31. [Not printed; note in source text]

lateral decision respecting the use of atomic weapons should be made when the international control of atomic energy is subject to debate within the United Nations. In the "General Conclusions and Recommendations" of the *Third Report of the Atomic Energy Commission to the Security Council,* dated 17 May 1948, it is stated:

> The new pattern of international cooperation and the new standards of openness in the dealings of one country with another that are indispensable in the field of atomic energy might, in practice, pave the way for international cooperation in broader fields, for the control of other weapons of mass destruction, and even for the elimination of war itself as an instrument of national policy.
>
> However, in the field of atomic energy, the majority of the Commission has been unable to secure the agreement of the Soviet Union to even those elements of effective control considered essential from the technical point of view, let alone their acceptance of the nature and extent of participation in the world community required of all nations in this field by the first and second reports of the Atomic Energy Commission. As a result, the Commission has been forced to recognize that agreement on effective measures for the control of atomic energy is itself dependent on *cooperation in broader* fields of policy.[19] (The Commission concluded that no useful purpose can be served by carrying on negotiations at the Commission level.)

9. International cooperation in "broader fields of policy" has been woefully and dangerously lacking on the part of the Soviet Union and its satellites. Any attempt now or in the future under these circumstances, to prohibit or negatively to qualify the employment of atomic bombs could result catastrophically. The measure of success achieved by the United States in collaboration with other nations in the establishment of an effective system of international control of atomic energy should directly determine the measure of control the United States will impose upon itself in the employment of atomic weapons. Until international agreement can be reached on an acceptable plan to control atomic energy (only the Soviet Union, Poland and the Ukrainian S.S.R. have blocked the attainment of this goal)[20] it is dangerously delusive to consider the self-imposition of any unilateral qualifications of the use of atomic weapons.

10. The United States has offered, along with all other nations, to eliminate atomic weapons from national armaments if and when a fully effective, enforceable system of international control is put into effect. In the meantime United States policy should ensure that no commitment be made in the absence of an established and acceptable system of international control of

---

19. Underlining [italics] supplied for emphasis. [Note in source text]
20. This reference is to the votes of the Soviet Union, Poland, and the Ukraine against the Baruch Plan in the United Nations Atomic Energy Commission. [Ed. note]

atomic energy which would deny this country the right to employ such weapons in the event of actual hostilities. The actual decision to employ weapons should be made by the Chief Executive and in the light of prevailing circumstances.

11. The time and circumstances under which atomic weapons might be employed are incapable of accurate determination prior to the evident imminence of hostilities. The type and character of targets against which atomic weapons might be used is primarily a function of military selection in the preparation and planning of grand strategy. In this case, however, there is the additional requirement for blending a political with a military responsibility in order to assure that the conduct of war, to the maximum extent practicable, advances the fundamental and lasting aims of U.S. policy.

Conclusions

12. It is recognized that, in the event of hostilities, the National Military Establishment must be ready to utilize promptly and effectively all appropriate means available, including atomic weapons, in the interest of national security and must therefore plan accordingly.

13. The decision as to the employment of atomic weapons in the event of war is to be made by the Chief Executive when he considers such decision to be required.

14. In the light of the foregoing, no action should be taken at the present time:

    a. To obtain a decision either to use or not to use atomic weapons in any possible future conflict;

    b. To obtain a decision as to the time and circumstances under which atomic weapons might or might not be employed.

---

45   SECRET

Brief on the Pattern of War in the Atomic Warfare Age

December 16, 1948

[Source: Dwight D. Eisenhower Papers, Dwight D. Eisenhower Library, Abilene, Kansas]

Although military planners expected future wars to resemble World War II more than they would differ from it, they also anticipated many changes in underlying considerations relating to the nature and course of warfare, especially after the Soviet Union had acquired atomic weapons. The Advanced Study Branch Plans Group of the United States Army General Staff therefore prepared an extensive study on the subject to guide war planning. This study was especially interesting for its reading of trends in civilian control of warfare, the effects of alliance relationships on freedom of action and the rational use of force, the probable war aims of the Soviet Union and a United States-led coalition, and an analysis of stages through which an atomic war might progress. It also emphasized the new importance of immediate strategic counteroffensives to reduce the offensive power of adversaries, and gave much attention to the heightened significance of psychological operations.

The document is published here as amended on March 28, 1949.

1. The study is not a war plan. It is set forth only in order to influence, in light of long range implications, the formulation of current policies and programs.

2. National policy on national security, which is now lacking, is vitally needed.

3. For purposes of this study, national policy on national security is assumed to be that set forth in "Concepts on Objectives," Appendix "A" hereto.[21]

4. War, as suggested herein, is not predicted; but because the U.S. must ride two horses, one heading towards peace and progress and the other headed toward war preparation, an idea of the pattern of atomic warfare is needed in order to provide guidance for the appropriate military posture.

5. The time period used herein is the atomic warfare age which is defined as arriving when two or more nations have available to them a significant quantity of atomic weapons, together with suitable means of delivery.

6. An enemy would probably need 100 to 200 or more atomic weapons to have a significant quantity as defined above. Intelligence indicates this might take 10 to 20 years, and, hence, 1964 has been selected as the year in which it is assumed a war would start.

Significant Major Trends Which Will Affect Materially the Character of a Future War

7. Significant major trends which would have material affect on the pattern of war should be analyzed.

8. The expansion of democracy in every aspect of control of human life will result in more emphasis on human relations in war.

9. There is a trend towards a formal supra-national community accom-

21. Not printed. [Ed. note]

panied by an extension of regional alliances; all of which is restricting more and more the freedom of nations for independent action and is making for a more rational approach to war.

10. Neutrality will be more attractive to minor nations.

11. The war objectives of antagonists will tend to become more limited than in past wars with more emphasis being given to a military posture which might allow long-range political objectives to be obtained gradually by non-military means.

12. Civilian control, at the expense of military control, will become more dominant in the conduct of war by the U.S. Government.

13. The potency of military offensive power that can be stockpiled before a war will tend to place greater emphasis than in past wars on a counter-offensive against the offensive power in being of an enemy.

14. Logistic support means will become more vulnerable and will be higher priority targets than in past wars.

Assumptions with Regard to a War in 1964

15. The USSR is assumed to be the enemy.

16. A war between the U.S. and Allies (ALLIES) and the USSR and her Allies (SOVIET BLOC) is assumed to start in 1964 after the international conflict over extension of communism has reached an impasse.

17. The war is assumed to start after the ALLIES, bonded together under the provisions of Article 51 of the UN Charter after failure of the Security Council to agree, issued an ultimatum that the USSR get out of Iran.

18. There would be no strategic surprise in the initiation of such a war as warning indications could be noted six to twelve months or longer in advance.

19. Tactical surprise on the initiation of war, comparable to that achieved at Pearl Harbor, will be striven for by the enemy and is apt to be successful to some extent.

20. Appendix "B"[22] includes more detailed assumptions.

War Objectives of the Opposing Powers

21. Allied objectives would be to force acceptance of these armistice terms:

22. Not printed. [Ed. note]

a. Cessation of hostilities.
b. Acceptance, without Soviet veto, of peace settlement to be determined by the UN.
c. Enemy withdrawal from territory occupied after war started.
d. Destruction of all atomic, biological and chemical weapons, strategic bombers and submarines, together with safe access for Allied inspectors to observe compliance with terms.

22. Soviet Bloc minimum war objectives would be to:
a. Force Western European nations, less UK, to adopt communistic governments which would support the Soviet Bloc.
b. Eliminate Allied domination of the Near East.
c. After the above have been achieved, create militarily, at least, a war stalemate and cause UN recognition of the new communistic governments.
d. Create conditions, without forcing communism on the U.S. or the UK, which would allow the USSR to exploit in her interests Western Europe, Africa and the Near East and thus probably cause the U.S. and UK to conform ultimately to the Soviet concept of world order.
e. Cessation of hostilities.

23. Assumed objectives differ radically from World War II in that:
a. Allies would attempt only to reduce enemy military power and prevent material gains from occupation which would be materially less than unconditional surrender.
b. The Soviet Bloc would have less extensive territorial demands than did Hitler and they would be playing up to social unrest.

Conditions Which Would Probably Cause Acceptance of Terms

24. It is difficult but necessary to forecast the military, political and economic conditions which would probably cause acceptance of armistice terms.

25. *Conditions for Allied victory.* It would be necessary to:
a. Reduce enemy's offensive capabilities so that only insignificant destructive attacks could be launched against Allied home territory.
b. Reduce enemy's defensive capabilities so that Allied strategic air forces could penetrate successfully, without undue losses to all critical areas of enemy territory.

  c. Prevent enemy from obtaining popular support for governments in captured territory or support from neutral nations.

  d. Reduce enemy's war economy to a point where he could not regain initiative or air supremacy.

  e. Prevent enemy from obtaining war support from captured territory.

26. *Conditions for Soviet Bloc victory.* The Soviet Bloc might expect Allied surrender on their terms when:

  a. No Allied forces would remain in the European continent, in the Near East or in Asia.

  b. The UK had been neutralized as an effective Allied military base and reduced to a starvation economy.

  c. Relatively strong governments with at least moderate popular support had been established in captured territory and these nations were contributing substantial war support to the Soviet Bloc.

  d. Neutral nations were imploring Allies to accept.

  e. U.S. war potential had been so reduced that it would take Allies at least two years free of destructive air attack to regain the military initiative and Soviet aerial supremacy was on the increase.

27. Conditions somewhere between those forecast for Allied or Soviet Bloc victory might induce a war stalemate lasting for years.

The General Pattern of War

28. The Soviet Bloc would attempt to extend throughout Europe and the Near East, to neutralize the ABC air potential of the Allies, and to undermine the support of the Allies.

29. The Allies would probably decide on the following basic undertakings in the war:

  a. *First undertaking*—Neutralize the enemy's offensive capabilities against the Allies.

  b. *Second undertaking*—A political, social and economic warfare campaign, coordinated with military strategy in order to convince the enemy to accept the Allied terms.

  c. *Third undertaking*—Prevent any successful exploitation of enemy territorial gains.

  d. *Fourth undertaking*—An aerial offensive to gain the military posture and the degree of aerial supremacy which would probably cause the enemy to accept the Allied terms.

e. *Fifth undertaking*—If the enemy should not accept the armistice terms after the above four undertakings have been achieved, maintain ever-increasing military, political, social and economic pressure on the enemy until he accepts the terms.

30. The purpose of military force in war is *not* to destroy the will of the enemy to resist. Rather, *the purpose is to create in the mind of the enemy the idea that he will accept the terms that the Allies propose.*

31. Military intelligence would probably not give adequate warning of the character of the initial enemy attack although political intelligence as to intentions would be available.

32. The major undertakings were listed in order of importance and also in chronological order, except for the second, the political, etc. campaigns, which would be the primary undertaking of the war and would precede the war as well as be carried on after the war.

First Undertaking—Neutralization of the Enemy Offensive

33. The enemy would attempt, and probably achieve, tactical surprise in an all-out effort to neutralize the Allied ABC air power in being.

34. The enemy would attempt an initial knockout blow against Allied air power in being, employing such tactics as A-bombs against concentration of bombers or missiles on above ground bases, ABC anti-personnel weapons to destroy bomber crews and assembly personnel, vertical envelopment, sabotage and destruction of critical underground facilities, missile or torpedo attack against aircraft carriers, etc. without regard as to conventional ideas of military costs.

35. The enemy potential would probably not support an initial attack against the industry as a whole or the population of the Allies in addition to the blows against Allied ABC air power in being, although psychological and political means combined with sabotage and subversion would be employed to undermine support of the Allies.

36. The initial Allied strategy must provide a counter to the forecast initial enemy attack.

37. The Allies would launch a counter-offensive against the enemy ABC air offensive forces in being, utilizing Allied ABC air power against aircraft and missile bases, storage areas, logistic bottlenecks, etc.

38. Allied airborne raids of a suicide character would be required against enemy targets relatively invulnerable to bombardment.

39. The Allied counter-offensive *must* succeed, regardless of cost. It would be an air battle, greater than any battle of history.

40. Defensive measures should include as near to 100 percent protection as may be possible for a portion of the economy and counter-offensive forces in being, combined with a degree of active defense to the remainder with effective utilization of passive defense.

41. A "Military Offensive Complex" (MOC), completely separate from the normal economy and having military forces set aside for the sole purposes of its defense, may be needed in order to provide as near to 100 percent protection as possible to the Allied counter-offensive means.

42. Active defense should be sufficient to limit materially an enemy attack against industry as a whole or the population. Passive defense should include civil defense and dispersion of critical industries.

43. The first Allied undertaking, if successful, would take from three months to a year or longer.

Second Undertaking—The Political, Social and Economic Campaigns of the War

44. This would be the major undertaking of the war, and would be a continuation of a peacetime campaign modified and intensified for war purposes.

45. The campaigns themselves will be the accommodation of words to acts and vice versa with the objective of convincing the enemy to accept the armistice terms; these terms would have been previously set forth to the world.

46. The Allied political, social and economic campaigns designed to achieve acceptance of the Allied terms would emphasize the spirit rather than the form of democracy and would promote universal adherence to democratic principles in government.

47. Efforts would be made to keep the UN active during the war with all enemy and neutral nations participating in order to provide a forum in which armistice terms and peace settlements may be approached rationally by the antagonists.

48. The campaigns would not oppose communism per se but would foster the idea that the Allied democracies can co-exist progressively with governments or any type of ideology including communism provided that international conflicts would be solved peacefully and that nations would not exploit other nations.

49. The Allies should develop and demonstrate the themes that the Soviet Bloc cannot win militarily and that Allied weapons will be used humanely against vital targets of a military character.

50. Neutrals should be encouraged to exert their influence on the enemy to convince him to trust the Allies and to accept the Allied terms.

51. The peoples in areas occupied by the enemy should be encouraged and prepared to make the necessary sacrifices and to support the military and subversive operations that would be designed to make the enemy expend more of his own resources in occupation than he gains from indigenous sources and to cause the enemy strategic position in occupied areas to deteriorate continuously.

52. Allied agreement should be sought to a policy of equality in the sharing of war costs to the end that the Allies less affected by the war will grant aid during and after the war to the more affected Allies until a condition is reached after the war when the *relative* standards of living and economic conditions amongst the Allies are comparable to the relative pre-war status of the Allies in these respects. Allied campaigns would emphasize this policy in sustaining resistance to occupation and in gaining support of neutrals.

53. The Allies should endeavor to cause the enemy masses to bring pressure to bear on their leaders in order to cause acceptance of the Allied terms.

54. Covert and overt operations would be directed so as to convince the enemy elites to accept the terms, or to weaken their leadership and their opposition to the Allies, or to bring into power covertly from indigenous sources leaders amenable to acceptance of Allied terms. The Allies should design subversive "hardware" for these purposes.

55. A major share of these campaigns would be in direct support of Allied military operations with the objective ultimately of convincing the enemy leaders, military as well as civil, and the enemy masses of the ultimate overwhelming superiority of Allied air power and the futility of land or other military operations in face of the increasing Allied air superiority.

56. Campaigns in the Allied homefronts would be necessary in order to develop and secure popular support to counter enemy campaigns and to condition the peoples for the expected enemy attacks.

57. Success of the Allies in establishing popularly supported indigenous governments in territories that the Allies occupied for military operations would be a material factor in gaining the trust and confidence of the rest of the world, including the enemy, in the Allied intentions.

58. The character and tempo of the political, social and economic campaigns would change with Allied military progress and the demonstrated military prowess backing up threats of inevitable greater military hurt would be utilized to convince the enemy to surrender.

59. *The major problem,* after Allied air superiority had been achieved,

would be to convince the enemy leaders to trust the Allies to carry out only the terms that the Allies had proposed.

60. When enemy acceptance of Allied terms appears likely, emphasis would have to be given to convincing the enemy leaders and masses to acceptance of Allied inspectors and their safe conduct in enemy territory under penalty of immediate, retaliatory, and destructive air blows if the terms are violated or the inspectors are attacked.

61. Concepts with regard to political, psychological, economic, subversive and other similar methods of warfare should be studied in order to devise techniques that might accomplish the purposes outlined above for this undertaking.

Third Undertaking—Prevent Exploitation of Enemy Territorial Gains

62. It is vital to the Allied cause to prevent the enemy from maintaining control of Western Europe and the Near East and from increasing his war potential by occupation and to cause the enemy strategic position in occupied areas to deteriorate continuously, because otherwise the enemy would be in position to achieve his limited objectives and thus victory in the war.

63. The Allies could prevent exploitation of enemy territorial gains by the obvious method of preventing the enemy from occupying such areas and, when that method fails, by conducting internal and external operations against the enemy in occupied areas which would deny gain to the enemy and cause his strategic position to deteriorate.

64. In defending Western Europe, the Allies would probably have to face an initial military superiority of the Soviet Bloc.

65. It is to be hoped that the expected enemy campaign to overthrow internally the French, German and Italian governments would fail; and, thus, the enemy would be forced to launch a land and air campaign across Germany with the objective of eliminating Allied military forces on the continent.

66. The Allies initial move would probably be to defend the Rhine-Alps-French and Italian border line—which would have to be done in face of initial enemy superiority on land and in the air based in part on ABC weapons.

67. While the initial primary role of Allied long-range strategic bombardment forces would be to launch the counter-offensive described in the first

undertaking, the second mission of these forces would be to check enemy progress of the land battle of Western Europe.

68. The Allies would initiate immediately an air battle with the objective of eliminating the initial enemy air superiority over the land battle area of Western Europe. Short-range trans-sonic or super-sonic Allied aircraft would attack all air bases utilized by the enemy to support the land battle. A-weapons capable of destroying all aircraft on the ground and denying enemy use of the base for protracted periods would be used in lightning attacks. The Allies should be able to eliminate enemy air superiority in this area.

69. The above air battle would be a major contribution to the battle for overall air superiority (fourth Allied undertaking), because the battle for Western Europe would provide the Allies with a great opportunity to defeat, under conditions favorable to the Allies, a great portion of the enemy air power in being which would have to be accomplished before Allied victory could be achieved.

70. In spite of the prospect of early elimination of initial enemy air superiority, Allied land forces may be forced to withdraw from the Rhine, but they should be able to stabilize a position before being driven back to the Atlantic.

71. If Allied withdrawal from the Rhine is forced, an extensive base on the Atlantic and Channel Coasts, with previously prepared positions, should be held by the Allies in order to provide a base for Allied operations into occupied areas, to contribute to the air defense of the UK, and to reduce the enemy Atlantic submarine threat, and to provide Allied air bases for the continuing reduction of enemy air power.

72. The U.S. should provide an expeditionary force, immediately upon the initiation of war if not prior to the war, to participate in the ground defense of Western Europe in order to sustain Allied resistance and morale.

73. Resistance movements should be well organized by the Allies before any withdrawal.

74. If withdrawal is necessary, instead of a "scorched earth" policy, the Allies should use ABC weapons which can deny areas and interfere with communications, with a very minimum of destruction, in order to prevent the enemy from benefiting from the resources of captured areas. Internal attacks by resistance forces should be supported by selective air attack and airborne raids.

75. A threat of a "breakout" from the Allied continental base should be maintained continuously in order to strain the enemy and to attract enemy air forces into close range of Allied air power.

76. The peoples of occupied countries should be made fully aware of Allied operations on their behalf, of the general Allied strategy, and of the Allied intentions to liberate them ultimately.

77. Allied areas occupied by the enemy would be liberated ultimately by over-running types of land campaigns, more similar to the liberation of Brittany than to the assault of the Siegfried line in World War II, shortly prior to surrender of the enemy.

78. In the Near East, the enemy would probably occupy readily the oil areas near the Arabian Gulf, perhaps by-passing Turkey if the latter remains neutral, and then would attempt to occupy or neutralize bases for Allied air power in Egypt.

79. The Allies would probably not be able to defend any Near East areas, except Egypt in the event that moderate ground and substantial air and naval forces were in that area prior to enemy attack.

80. The Allies could neutralize enemy oil production in the Near East by air attack, airborne raids, and sabotage utilizing selective ABC type weapons.

81. Until overwhelming Allied air superiority could be achieved late in the war, the Allies probably could not exploit Near East oil resources even if they succeeded in capturing the areas.

82. In the Far East, air attacks on transportation, key heavy industries, and enemy air and sub bases should neutralize enemy exploitation of this area. The enemy would probably not attempt to occupy Japan.

Fourth Undertaking—Aerial Supremacy Over the Enemy

83. Because Allied success in their first three undertakings would have stopped the enemy and wrested the initiative from him, the Allies should next attain aerial superiority over the Soviet Bloc territory to such an extent that the enemy's air defense would deteriorate continuously, and the enemy could not produce the air power necessary to regain the initiative on any substantial front.

84. The objective would be Soviet air power; the forces in being, the defense, the bases and storage areas, and the vital communications in direct support of Soviet air power and the weapons used.

85. Allied success would depend on having bases within 2,500 miles of critical targets and success in the first three undertakings should provide such bases in the UK, on the continent and possibly in the Near East.

86. Water or ice bases, used for launching and landing aircraft, would be relatively invulnerable to atomic attack.

87. Advanced bases would be less vulnerable to ABC attack if they were

used only as a stage base for aircraft which were permanently based in rear, well protected areas.

88. When a base must be seized in enemy defended territory, local Allied air superiority over the selected area should be achieved by atomic attack against all enemy air bases outside of the target area which the enemy would use for air support, and the target area should be softened up by a lethal ABC attack which would cripple the defense but would not destroy the essential facilities.

90. A lightning vertical envelopment followed up immediately by air transported forces or amphibious attack would be employed in order to seize the area. Fighter, AA, ground and tactical air-defense units would be prepared for counter attack with defense against surface attack relying heavily on the denial effects of ABC weapons.

91. Because of enemy capability for ABC air attack against extended air and ground LOC in support of major combat forces, advanced bases should not be located more than 150 to 200 miles from a sea LOC base, except for limited periods of two to three weeks.

92. If seaplane bombers, fighters and tactical aircraft become available, a mobile base could be established in protected waters with air, naval and land units combined to seize, defend and operate a staging base.

93. Allied air attacks would fan out from advanced bases in ever-deepening penetration attacks against the enemy air force, defensive bases, logistic support means, and the industrial complex in support of the enemy air force. When the climax is reached, the enemy air defense should deteriorate rapidly as did that of Germany following the climax of the air battle in the spring of 1944.

94. Allied air bases should be located so as to maintain an attack from all quarters of the compass.

95. Small Army airborne raid forces would be utilized to destroy or neutralize vital enemy targets which would be relatively invulnerable to air attack.

96. It might take the Allies four to five years or longer to achieve the desired air supremacy over enemy territory.

Fifth Undertaking—Pressure After Air Supremacy is Won

97. Although successful prosecution of the above four undertakings by the Allies should cause the enemy to surrender, the Allies would have to be prepared to carry on if the enemy does not accept.

98. In selection of a course of action to be followed in this undertaking, the Allies should give great weight to convincing the enemy leaders to trust the Allies to enforce *only* the proposed terms. Other factors which should be considered are: conditions in the affected nations which would foster post-war supra-national security; military capabilities; and costs in men and resources.

99. The first course of action available to the Allies, that of maintaining the military status quo while increasing the political, social and economic pressures, would: be most apt to convince the enemy leaders to trust the Allies; leave the affected nations in a condition best suited for post-war supra-national security; be relatively easy to accomplish militarily without prohibitive cost.

100. The second alternative, to intensify the air battle in order to reduce the enemy's economy below the minimum needed to sustain his civil economy, and at the same time, to increase the political and social pressures would be less apt to cause great destruction which would run counter to post-war Allied aims; although, the Allies should be able to accomplish this military campaign without prohibitive cost.

101. The third alternative, great land campaigns to occupy strategic enemy areas accompanied by increased political, social and economic pressures, would be least apt to cause the enemy leaders to trust the Allies, would result in extensive destruction and dislocation of economies both in enemy and Allied nations, and would be the most expensive and difficult military campaign to undertake; and such campaigns might not be successful.

102. The first alternative, maintenance of a military status quo while increasing the political, social and economic pressures on the enemy, would be the best available Allied course of action.

103. If some Allied territory should remain to be liberated, air and resistance attacks against the enemy occupation forces and their support means would be intensified until "over-running" types of liberation campaigns could be undertaken by relatively small mobile Army forces, as contrasted to the great Allied armies of World War II that were engaged in the "Overlord"[23] campaign against determined and sustained enemy resistance.

104. Adoption of these strategies should lead to enemy acceptance of the proposed Allied terms.

23. The code name for the Allied cross-channel invasion of Europe in June 1944. [Ed. note]

Post Surrender Operations

105. Small military forces, for inspection of enemy compliance with the terms, would be all that the Allies would need, as there would be no military government of enemy territory or other such provision which would require great occupation forces capable of dominating the enemy areas.

106. Allied inspection forces would be located on enemy air bases which would be provided with defensive forces adequate to permit immediate air evacuation in emergencies, and with small, highly mobile forces which could furnish individual protection to inspectors or missions away from the air base.

107. Allied air bases in enemy territory should be located in the vicinity of: centers of government, industries capable of producing aircraft, submarines and ABC agents; principal air and naval headquarters; and land commanders controlling major forces.

108. Success of post-surrender operations would depend on the immediate availability of overwhelming Allied air forces, located on external and protected bases, who would maintain frequent surveillance flights over the enemy areas, and would be capable of launching devastating retailiatory attacks in the event of resistance to terms or of attack on Allied inspectors.

109. Rehabilitation of Allied areas in Europe would involve considerable post-war commitments by the Western Hemisphere Allies.

General Considerations

110. When considered fully and tested adquately, the political, social and economic concepts upon which this study was based, may be rejected in part or in full by the responsible authorities.

111. If, contrary to the concepts of this study, national policy should require Allied imposition of an armistice involving a non-indigenous change of the enemy government, separation of large areas from enemy territory or military government of the enemy territory, then great and very difficult land campaigns would probably be required in order to occupy large areas of enemy territory before the enemy could be defeated.

112. If the political, social and economic forces of the world were mobilized, in line with the philosophy of this study, to repudiate the use of military force as an instrument of national policy, such a war as depicted herein could probably be avoided.

113. Studies on war should be made in a reverse chronological order,

first taking up objectives, then postwar conditions, then armistice terms, then the military campaigns in reverse order, and finally preparations for possible war.

114. The nature of a future war should be made a continuing study, which, it is predicted, will tend to confirm the concepts set forth herein.

◇◇◇◇◇◇◇◇◇◇◇◇◇◇◇◇◇◇◇◇◇◇◇◇◇◇◇◇◇◇◇◇◇◇◇◇◇◇

46   **T O P S E C R E T**

Evaluation of Current Strategic Air Offensive Plans

JCS 1952/1   December 21, 1948

[Source: Records of the Joint Chiefs of Staff on deposit in the Modern Military Records Branch, National Archives, Washington, D.C.]

The importance of strategic air operations in early postwar American war plans made the Berlin crisis of 1948–49, with the famous airlift, a particularly worrisome proposition. The question arose whether the United States could meet Berlin's needs and still carry out strategic air offensives concurrently, should the requirement arise. In answering this question, the Chief of Staff of the Air Force explicated the assumptions and principal features of Strategic Air Command Emergency War Plan 1–49, the culmination of a series of attempts to devise an emergency, or quick-reaction, war plan that could receive approval all the way to the top of the policy pyramid. Despite objections of the Chief of Naval Operations, SAC EWP 1–49 became the first atomic annex to an emergency war plan to receive approval at the Joint Chiefs of Staff level.

The Problem

1. To evaluate the chances of success in delivering a powerful strategic air offensive against vital elements of the Soviet war-making capacity as contemplated in current war plans; to consider the risks involved in the planned strategic air operations; and to appraise any adverse effect on this offensive of the continuation of the Berlin air lift at its contemplated level until war occurs.

Assumptions

2. War will occur prior to 1 April 1949.
3. Atomic bombs will be used to the extent determined to be practicable and desirable.

4. The Berlin air lift will be continued at the contemplated level until the outbreak of hostilities.

5. The strategic air offensive will be implemented on a first-priority basis.

. . . .

VI. Evaluation

32. The factors affecting our chances of success in delivering a powerful strategic air offensive against the vital elements of the Soviet warmaking capacity as affected by the Berlin air lift operations and as compared with the risk involved in such an air offensive can be summarized as follows:

   a. After due consideration of the number of atomic bombs available, the radii of action of Allied air forces, the estimated bombing accuracy, the available weight of attack and the time required for realization of effects, the highest priority target system is that system constituted by the major Soviet urban-industrial concentrations. Destruction of this system should so cripple the Soviet industrial and control centers as to reduce drastically the offensive and defensive power of their armed forces.

   b. Target folders and navigation charts will be available by 1 February 1949 for operations against the first seventy cities. Currently available aeronautical charts (scale 1:1,000,000) are sufficiently accurate to permit aerial navigation to any desired point in the USSR.

   c. An effective program of attack against petroleum refining targets in the USSR and Soviet occupied areas, would, after depletion of inventories, practically destroy the offensive capabilities of the USSR and seriously cripple its defensive capabilities.

   d. Major attacks against the Soviet hydro-electric system can be undertaken at about $D + 8$ months and completed by approximately $D + 14$ months.

   e. Attacks on the inland transportation system as a major objective can be undertaken by approximately $D + 14$ to $D + 16$ months with the effect of disrupting the entire system within two months. The transportation offensive would seriously disrupt the entire Soviet economy.

   f. The Soviet early warning system is composed primarily of World War II lend-lease or captured equipment. It is doubtful that the Soviets have overcome the previous lag in electronic development which was detrimental to their antiaircraft artillery and fighter control system.

g. Soviet antiaircraft can not maintain effective fire at 30,000 feet, the operational altitude of attacking bombers. The proximity fuze, even if available to the Soviets would be relatively ineffective due to Soviet radar deficiency and allied jamming operation. Consideration of these facts leads to the conclusion that the total effectiveness of Soviet ground defenses will be below that encountered and overcome by the Allies in World War II.

h. It is not believed that the Soviets have developed a fighter suitable for night and all-weather operations, or that they possess an effective system of fighter control. The large areas to be defended as compared to the number of aircraft operationally available and the inherent difficulties, time-wise, of effectively intercepting high altitude, high-speed bombers operating at night or in bad weather reduce appreciably the hazards to the delivery of the air offensive.

i. Soviet jamming of U.S. Air Force radar bombing sets, if attempted, would be ineffective.

j. Soviet counter air operations against Allied base areas will be limited initially by the range of bombing aircraft. It can be stated, in addition, that all available intelligence and operational data make it difficult to foresee development of a Russian capability for making United Kingdom bases untenable before D + 45 to 60 days at the earliest, and of making Cairo-Suez bases untenable before D + 4 to 6 months. These estimates are based on intelligence data regarding Soviet capabilities only and do not reflect the effects of Allied opposition. Losses due to the Soviet air offensive against Allied bases are not expected to be of such severe nature as to preclude conducting the strategic air offensive.

k. The missions as planned to implement the atomic offensive and the tactics and techniques to be used give maximum chances of successful penetration, successful attack on selected targets, and minimum risk to Allied aircraft. Where necessary or operationally desirable, daylight attacks can and would be conducted. However, night and weather operations, jamming capabilities, speed and altitude of the bombers would all be used in reducing the risks involved.

l. For the initial atomic attacks a possible 25 per cent attrition loss has been accepted for planning purposes, which still leaves ample capability for delivery of the entire stockpile of atomic bombs. As the effects of the atomic offensive are reflected in the Soviet air defense system, aircraft losses should be reduced.

m. The Berlin air lift operations have reduced considerably the strategic air lift available to the National Military Establishment. However, preliminary studies indicate that air lift requirements to implement the strategic air offensive, if accorded first priority, are within our remaining capabilities, even though the Berlin air lift is continued at its contemplated level.

33. The following conclusions may be drawn from an evaluation of the foregoing:

a. A powerful strategic air offensive against vital elements of the Soviet war-making capacity could be delivered as planned.

b. Certain risks, such as tenability of base areas and attrition of personnel and materiel during operations, do exist, but these risks are not unreasonable and can be taken without unduly jeopardizing the successful execution of the strategic air offensive.

c. The risks existing during the early phases of the campaign should decrease appreciably within a relatively short time due to the cumulative effects of the strategic air offensive.

d. Preliminary studies of the strategic air lift requirements to implement the short-range emergency war plans and the effects of continuation of the Berlin air lift on U.S. Air Force capabilities indicate that the strategic air offensive, if accorded first priority, could be delivered as planned even though the Berlin air lift is continued at its contemplated level.

---

47   **TOP SECRET**

Evaluation of Effect on Soviet War Effort Resulting from the Strategic Air Offensive

May 11, 1949

[Source: Records of the Organizational Research and Policy Division of the Office of the Chief of Naval Operations (Op-23), Naval Historical Center, Washington, D.C.]

Most American war plans in the 1940s relied substantially on American ability to halt Soviet offensive operations by means of air-delivered atomic counteroffensives. In 1949, a review committee composed of senior Army, Navy, and Air Force officers headed by Air Force Lieutenant General H. R. Harmon assessed the likely results of strategic air operations in a war with the Soviet Union for the Joint Chiefs of Staff and the Secretary of Defense. Because the Harmon Committee was critical of the idea that such operations would destroy Soviet warmaking capability—and this at a time when the Air Force was demanding a vast increase in its size and budget—the committee's report became a highly controversial and closely held document. The conclusions emphasized in particular some of the psychological disadvantages that the United States should anticipate in any use of the atomic bomb against the Soviet Union and warned that it was not to be considered a decisive weapon.

.   .   .   .

The Problem

1. To evaluate the effect on the war effort of the U.S.S.R. of the Strategic Air Offensive contemplated in current war plans, including an appraisal of the psychological effects of atomic bombing on the Soviet will to wage war. . . .

Facts Bearing on the Problem

.   .   .   .

3. The plan for the strategic air offensive . . . contemplates two distinct phases:
  a. An initial phase, consisting of a series of attacks primarily with atomic bombs on 70 target areas (presently planned by the Strategic Air Command to be accomplished in approximately 30 days).
  b. A second phase, consisting of a continuation of the initial attacks with both atomic and conventional weapons.

.   .   .   .

Conclusions

8. It is concluded that complete and successful execution of the initial atomic offensive against the U.S.S.R., as planned, would probably affect the war effort, and produce psychological effects upon the Soviet will to wage war as set forth below. . . .

Effect on Industrial Capacity

9. Physical damage to installations, peronnel casualties concentrated in industrial communities, and other direct or indirect cumulative effects would result in a 30 to 40 percent reduction of Soviet industrial capacity. This loss

would not be permanent and could either be alleviated by Soviet recuperative action or augmented depending upon the weight and effectiveness of follow-up attacks.

10. Of outstanding importance is the prospect that the petroleum industry in the U.S.S.R. would suffer severe damage especially in refining capacity. The supply of high-test aviation gasoline would become rapidly critical.

Personnel Casualties

11. The initial atomic offensive could produce as many as 2,700,000 mortalities, and 4,000,000 additional casualties, depending upon the effectiveness of Soviet passive defense measures. A large number of homes would be destroyed and the problems of living for the remainder of the 28,000,000 people in the 70 target cities would be vastly complicated.

Psychological Effects

12. The atomic offensive would not, per se, bring about capitulation, destroy the roots of Communism or critically weaken the power of Soviet leadership to dominate the people.

13. For the majority of Soviet people, atomic bombing would validate Soviet propaganda against foreign powers, stimulate resentment against the United States, unify these people and increase their will to fight. Among an indeterminate minority, atomic bombing might stimulate dissidence and the hope of relief from oppression. Unless and until vastly more favorable opportunities develop for them, the influence of these elements will not appreciably affect the Soviet war effort.

14. A psychological crisis will be created within the U.S.S.R. which could be turned to advantage by the Allies through early and effective exploitation by armed forces and psychological warfare. Failing prompt and effective exploitation, the opportunity would be lost and subsequent Soviet psychological reactions would adversely affect the accomplishment of Allied objectives.

Effects on the Soviet Armed Forces

15. The capability of Soviet armed forces to advance rapidly into selected areas of Western Europe, the Middle East and Far East, would not be seriously impaired, but capabilities thereafter would progressively diminish due to the following factors:

a. The supply of petroleum products of all types will rapidly become critical to all branches of Soviet armed forces, resulting in:
   (1) Greatly reducing the mobility of the Army.
   (2) Reducing the scale of operations by the Soviet Navy and merchant shipping, although submarine warfare would probably be unaffected.
   (3) Seriously reducing air operations involving training, transport, support of ground and naval forces, and independent offensive action, although proper allocation of fuel would allow continued operations by air defense forces. *Note:* The point at which capabilities of Soviet armed forces would diminish to a critical degree would depend upon many variable or unpredictable factors most important of which is the level of stockpiles prevailing at the initiation of hostilities.
b. After consumption of initial stocks of basic equipment and consumable supplies, progressive shortages of a wide variety of items, particularly aircraft, would handicap operations and affect morale of the armed forces.
c. Logistic support would be handicapped due to disruption of planning, impairment of controls, damage to industry and interference with transportation.

16. The Soviet High Command would be forced quickly to re-estimate their strategic position and make important decisions regarding operational plans under difficult circumstances. They would probably limit, postpone, or abandon certain campaigns, but it is impossible to predict what specific decisions would be made.

17. Atomic bombing would open the field and set the pattern for all adversaries to use any weapons of mass destruction and result in maximum retaliatory measures within Soviet capabilities.

General

18. Atomic bombing will produce certain psychological and retaliatory reactions detrimental to the achievement of Allied war objectives and its destructive effects will complicate post-hostilities problems. However, the atomic bomb would be a major element of Allied military strength in any war with the U.S.S.R., and would constitute the only means of rapidly inflicting shock and serious damage to vital elements of the Soviet war-making capacity. In particular, an early atomic offensive will facilitate greatly the application of other Allied military power with prospect of greatly low-

ered casualties. Full exploitation of the advantages to be obtained is dependent upon the adequacy and promptness of associated military and psychological operations. From the standpoint of our national security, the advantages of its early use would be transcending. Every reasonable effort should be devoted to providing the means to be prepared for prompt and effective delivery of the maximum numbers of atomic bombs to appropriate target systems.

.   .   .   .

48   S E C R E T

Political Implications of Detonation of Atomic Bomb by the U.S.S.R.

PPS 58   August 16, 1949

[Source: *Foreign Relations of the United States: 1949,* I, 514–16]

There was irony in the Policy Planning Staff's consideration of the implications of a Russian atomic detonation in August 1949, for in that very month the Soviet Union exploded its first test device, a fact not known, or even suspected, by American officials at the time. The American government had certain knowledge of the explosion early in September 1949, and President Truman announced the fact on September 22. Doubtless the Staff's reflections on the possible effects on public opinion of such a development aided in preparing an official announcement.

The Problem

To determine the political implications if this Government could know with certainty when the U.S.S.R. detonates an atomic bomb.

Analysis and Conclusions

The Department of State obviously cannot pass on the question whether scientific techniques or equipment can be developed to detect the explosion by the U.S.S.R. of an atomic bomb, and it cannot express judgment as between competing demands for research and development funds. It is clear, however, that *only if a high degree of certainty can be placed on systems of detection, would this Government be warranted in basing policy decisions on intelligence derived from them.*

Definite knowledge by this Government of the explosion by the USSR of its first bomb is considered by the Department to be important for the following reasons:

1. It would have a steadying effect on the American people and give them a sense of security if this Government could give assurance that the U.S.S.R. probably could not, without our knowledge, have a bomb or bombs for any length of time. With this knowledge, the Government would be able to combat intelligently defeatist or irrational attitudes arising from uncertainty as to whether the U.S.S.R. was capable of using atomic bombs, and would be in a position to refute with conviction false claims or rumors.

2. It would be of the utmost importance for us to know when the U.S.S.R. has successfully tested a bomb in order to anticipate and counter possible changes in Soviet foreign policy which might result therefrom, and to know whether a shift in its foreign policy was the result of the possession of atomic bombs. We cannot know whether the U.S.S.R. would make the knowledge public if it did possess the atomic bomb; however, we would be in a position to know the truth of what the U.S.S.R. said publicly.

3. The Soviet possession of a bomb or bombs may require a reevaluation of U.S. policy in the United Nations in our efforts to obtain effective international control.

4. Most of the free nations of the world are inclined at present to cooperate with the United States in view of the threat of Soviet aggression. A belief that we are now the sole possessor of atomic bombs and that the U.S.S.R. has none probably tends to increase their desire to collaborate with us and also their sense of safety in doing so. This tendency would probably be reinforced even further by certain knowledge that the U.S.S.R. does not possess the bomb and that we would have means of knowing if and when it did come into possession of the bomb. However, it is realized that knowledge that the U.S.S.R. did in fact possess the bomb also might tend to incline third countries toward a position of neutrality between the United States and the U.S.S.R.

5. If at some later time we should learn with certainty that the U.S.S.R. did possess the atomic bomb, this knowledge would be of importance in reevaluating the necessity for precautionary measures to reduce U.S. vulnerability to atomic attack. However, this is a matter of primary concern to the NME.

Knowledge of the rate at which the U.S.S.R. produces bomb fuel would be of even greater importance than knowing when a bomb has been exploded, but whether it is possible by scientific methods to obtain such information is entirely outside the competence of the Department of State.

49   **S E C R E T**

Memorandum for Secretary Johnson

November 8, 1949

[Source: Dwight D. Eisenhower Papers, Dwight D. Eisenhower Library, Abilene, Kansas]

With the Soviet explosion of an atomic device in August 1949, comfortable American assumptions of invulnerability to attack and of long preparation time for any potential war with the Soviet Union gave way. In a memorandum for Secretary of Defense Louis Johnson, immediately passed on to President Truman, Secretary of the Air Force W. Stuart Symington discussed some of the military implications of the Soviet bomb test. Anxious to procure more resources for the Air Force, which at that time had principal responsibility for delivering atomic weapons, Symington pointed to the danger of underreaction to the Soviet atomic capability and emphasized that only a strengthened retaliatory capability could deter a Soviet attack in coming years.

At the time of the President's announcement of the atomic explosion in Russia, the Air Force subscribed completely to the policy that exploitation of that event might develop a dangerous snowball of fear. I believe it was the judgment of everyone in the Government that a reconsideration of military plans and programs should be the result of sober reflection rather than reaction to a single dramatic event. There may be equal danger, however, that we may become inured to crisis and assume a "business as usual" course of inaction when there is a critical need for action.

After almost two months of careful consideration of the significance of the Russian atomic explosion, the Air Force realizes that that incident compels us to focus on requirements of the immediate future in fields where heretofore we could look at the indefinite future. With all reasonable effort to avoid exaggeration or over-statement, we must conclude that the question of the survival of the United States may be involved.

With this in mind we respectfully present some of the factors bearing on this problem.

Emergency war plans of the United States have been based upon an assumption as to the date upon which the USSR would obtain the atomic bomb in operational quantity.

There was considerable difference of opinion about that date. Sir Henry Tizard, formerly scientific advisor to Mr. Churchill and now head of the British Atomic Energy outfit, placed the date at 1957 or 1958.

Privately there were responsible people who expressed the view that it might be even later; and there were some who thought the Russians might never be able to solve the technical and industrial problems. There were, of course, some who anticipated the date with considerable accuracy.

With considered caution, both the President's Air Policy Commission and the Joint Congressional Aviation Policy Board adopted the date of 1952 or 1953, on the theory that American planning should be based on a most pessimistic hypothesis.

It now appears that even this gloomy hypothesis was too optimistic; and by a substantial period.

The recent atomic explosion in Russia indicates that the Soviets can have a militarily significant number of atomic bombs by a date two or three years earlier than was expected from original estimates.

In addition, should Russia use the relatively simple and completely proven process of refueling in flight, she would now have the capacity to deliver the bomb against this country without resorting to suicide missions.

Therefore the planned build-up of the Air Force—which comprises two elements: (a) Increase in group strength, and (b) modernization of equipment, now proves to be inadequate in the light of demonstrated Soviet technical and industrial capabilities.

.   .   .   .

Within the confines of the military system, from the Commander-in-Chief down through all levels of policy planning, we must consider military realities which could not be placed before the public.

If the Soviet Union should decide upon war, we must assume that they would adopt the most effective plan for conducting it. Their political objective would be the expansion of Soviet power to the whole of Eurasia, principally Western Europe and the United Kingdom. Their best strategic plan, however, would be an immediate atomic attack upon the United States.

Only the power of the United States is preserving the integrity of Western Europe. If the military power of the United States were destroyed or seriously damaged, Western Europe would fall almost without a struggle.

If the Soviet Union were able to drop any considerable number of atomic bombs upon key American targets, substantial damage to American military power would have taken place.

The only consideration which could keep the Soviet Union from making this attempt is the fear of a retaliatory atomic attack by the Air Force against the Soviet Union. The only force which could prevent the attack from being successful, if attempted, is an adequate air defense of the United States. Both the retaliatory force and the defense force must be in a state of instant readiness to have any effect.

It is a psychological tendency of normal healthy human beings to become accustomed to danger. So far as this tendency reduces the paralyzing effects of fear, it is a good thing. So far as it leads to discounting the danger and failing to provide against it, it can lead to disaster.

.   .   .   .

When the history of this period comes to be written it will be recognized that at this time the United States is in the most favored position that any nation has ever enjoyed—a political system based upon the freedom of the individual, patiently developed over nearly two centuries, plus the blessings of a standard of living unequalled in the history of the world.

It is hard to be faced with the decision to make some reduction in this living standard in order to protect the entire favored position. Reluctance to do so is understandable; but the consequences of inadequate provision are unthinkable.

It was Admiral Mahan who said: "It behooves countries whose people, like all free peoples, object to paying for large military establishments, to see to it that they are at least strong enough to gain the time to turn the spirit and capacity of their subjects into the new activities which war calls for."

Today, however, in this air-atomic age, there is no "time" to buy; and therefore how can we stay free unless we stay strong?

In conclusion, it seems to us that at least two requirements have been brought into sharper focus by the recent atomic explosion in Russia. First, we must provide *now* the defenses to permit us to survive an initial atomic attack. Second, we must have *now* the means of carrying the attack back to the enemy. Our actions to meet these requirements must be based on sound and calm judgments—but let us not mistake inaction for calmness.

<><><><><><><><><><><><><><><><><><><><><><><><><><><><><><><><>

50   **TOP SECRET**

Request for Comments on Military View of Members of General Advisory Committee

January 13, 1950

[Source: Harry S. Truman Papers, Harry S. Truman Library, Independence, Missouri]

In response to a request from the Secretary of Defense, the Joint Chiefs of Staff early in 1950 prepared comments on a report by the General Advisory Committee to the

Atomic Energy Commission concerning the possible development of a nuclear fusion weapon, popularly known as a "super" or "hydrogen" bomb. Their reply to the Secretary of Defense, cast in the form of a catechism, unequivocally supported development of such a device, in part because the JCS hoped that the fusion bomb would prove to be a "decisive" weapon, as the atomic fission bomb had not. Their response also contained a number of important statements on military, political, psychological, and moral implications of that course of action, including a strong assertion that nuclear weapons should not be categorized only as retaliatory weapons but should be available for "first use."

Excerpts from the JCS reply are printed below.

·   ·   ·   ·   ·   ·   ·

B. MILITARY VALUE.

1. QUESTION: What would be the effect upon a possible enemy of the United States if it became known that the United States had undertaken the development of a super bomb?

COMMENT: Just as the known development of the atomic bomb is considered to have been a deterrent to aggression on the part of a possible enemy so would it be the case with the super bomb as well. However, the Joint Chiefs of Staff are convinced that the United States is not the only nation interested in the development of a super weapon. They are aware of the possibility that even the secret development of the super bomb in the United States may, by devious means, assist a possible enemy in the development of a similar weapon. However, they are constantly reminded, because of their responsibility for the military security of the United States, of the fact that failure on the part of the United States to proceed along normal lines of development of nuclear physics to the goal of a super bomb would not deter a possible enemy from such development but, on the other hand, United States success, if known, might have a sobering effect in favor of peace.

2. QUESTION: What effect would possession of the super bomb have upon the defensive power of the United States?

COMMENT: The Joint Chiefs of Staff realize that a balance between the defensive and the offensive aspects of warfare is essential if the United States is so to mobilize its strategic resources that it can develop its full capabilities against an enemy. The nature of modern war is such that defense alone cannot bring about a favorable decision. They believe that the truism, "the best defense is a good offense", is still valid. Hence, they are convinced that it is necessary to have within the arsenal of the United States a weapon of the greatest capability, in this case the super bomb. Such a weapon would improve our defense in its broadest sense, as a potential offensive weapon, a possible deterrent to war, a potential retaliatory weapon, as well as a defensive weapon against enemy forces.

. . . .

4. QUESTION: Would possession of the super bomb increase the United States retaliatory power and strength to the extent that it would be decisive?

COMMENT: Possession of the super bomb would most certainly increase the United States retaliatory power and total military strength. Whether the increase would be sufficient to produce of itself a decision, the Joint Chiefs of Staff are not certain. They believe, however, that there is a possibility that such a weapon might be a decisive factor if properly used and prefer that such a possibility be at the will and control of the United States rather than of an enemy.

5. QUESTION: If the value of the super bomb is regarded as only that of retaliation, would the atomic bomb also be relegated to that category?

COMMENT: If any type of atomic weapon is to be used for retaliation only, then it must be assumed that all types of atomic weapons will be relegated to this category. However, the Joint Chiefs of Staff cannot accept as a premise that either the super bomb or the atomic bomb is valuable only as a weapon of retaliation.

. . . .

13. QUESTION: If the super bomb is developed, should its effect be demonstrated as an example?

COMMENT: No. The Joint Chiefs of Staff believe that any possible moral and psychological advantages of a demonstration are outweighed by its many well-known military disadvantages.

14. QUESTION: Would the super bomb be in a class outside that of a "military" weapon because it would be directed at the destruction of large cities or rendering large areas uninhabitable for long periods?

COMMENT: The Joint Chiefs of Staff believe not. They are responsible for the proper and efficient use of any weapon available to them. Further, they do not subscribe to the belief that the super bomb can be used only as implied in the question. They do not intend to destroy large cities per se; rather, only to attack such targets as are necessary in war in order to impose the national objectives of the United States upon an enemy.

C. DIPLOMATIC VALUE.

Although this is a field in which the Joint Chiefs of Staff do not have primary cognizance, they believe that the following questions have military connotations and as such are within their purview: . . .

.   .   .   .

2. QUESTION: What effect would renunciation of the super bomb by the United States have upon the world?

COMMENT: In the present world, where peace and security rests so completely on the military capability of the United States vis-a-vis Communist aggression, it would be foolhardy altruism for the United States voluntarily to weaken its capability by such a renunciation. Public renunciation by the United States of super bomb development might be interpreted as the first step in unilateral renunciation of the use of all atomic weapons, a course which would inevitably be followed by major international realignments to the disadvantage of the United States. Thus, the peace of the world generally and, specifically, the security of the entire Western Hemisphere would be jeopardized.

3. QUESTION: Would introduction of United States renunciation of the super bomb into armament negotiations change the course of these discussions?

COMMENT: The Joint Chiefs of Staff, having been closely associated with the armament negotiations in the United Nations, believe that the record of such negotiations indicates the impossibility of a change in the course of future negotiations until the USSR alters its uncompromising attitude. It is likely that known possession of the super bomb on the part of the United States and the lack of such a bomb on the part of the USSR could well affect future armament negotiations.

.   .   .   .

D. PSYCHOLOGICAL VALUE.

4. QUESTION: Would known possession of the super bomb grossly alter the psychological balance between the United States and the USSR?

COMMENT: They believe it would, and, further, that the balance would be grossly in favor of the United States until such time as the USSR had developed a stock pile of super bombs.

5. QUESTION: What effect did announcement of the Russian explosion have upon the feeling of security of the American public?

COMMENT: The Joint Chiefs of Staff are informed that this is a question now under highest priority study by the Central Intelligence Agency. So far as the responsibilities of the Department of Defense are concerned, the Joint Chiefs of Staff are of the opinion that the American public now feels less secure than prior to their knowledge of Russian possession of atomic capability and that the public expects the Department of Defense to take action necessary to regain the favorable balance previously held.

·   ·   ·   ·   ·   ·   ·

E. MORAL VALUE.

1. QUESTION: Would the moral position of the United States in the eyes of Americans and the people of the world be changed by knowledge of United States development of the super bomb to such an extent that the United States position of leadership would be altered?

COMMENT: There are people of the world who believe in the integrity and the rectitude of the United States in its position as a world leader. Further, there are people who malign that leadership at every opportunity. The Joint Chiefs of Staff believe that the former will look to the United States to retain its moral and physical leadership position and will expect the United States to take whatever action is necessary in order to do so. Friendly peoples undoubtedly would accept the development of a super bomb as a requirement for maintaining the world power position. They know that the United States would never use such power for aggrandizement but would use it in order to protect the security interests of those people who, too, seek the achievement of international peace and security. Those who malign the position of the United States will believe that which they are told to believe.

The Joint Chiefs of Staff hold themselves responsible for the recommendation of such action as they see necessary to achieve a military position for the United States that will, in the first instance, deter a possible enemy from undertaking war and, in the last instance, win that war should an enemy undertake it. They believe that it is imperative to determine conclusively the feasibility of a thermonuclear explosion and its characteristics. Such determination is essential for U.S. defense planning, preparations for retaliation, and direction for our research and development programs. There are undoubtedly a number of moral objections which may be considered to argue against research and development by the United States leading to the development and test of a thermonuclear weapon. The above military considerations outweigh such possible objections. In addition, it is difficult to escape the conviction that in war it is folly to argue whether one weapon is more immoral than another. For, in the larger sense, it is war itself which is immoral, and the stigma of such immorality must rest upon the nation which initiates hostilities.

◇◇

51   **T O P   S E C R E T**

International Control of Atomic Energy

January 20, 1950

[Source: *Foreign Relations of the United States: 1950,* I, 22, 28–30, 35–50, 43–44]

Within the government the Joint Chiefs of Staff's position on the hydrogen bomb was not unanimously shared, as the following document makes apparent. Begun as a Policy Planning Staff study in the fall of 1949, the essay was submitted by Kennan to Acheson as a personal paper on January 20, 1950. In the excerpts from this 79-page document printed below, Kennan noted the contradiction involved in relying on nuclear weapons to implement United States strategy on the one hand while simultaneously seeking the international control of atomic energy on the other. The United States need not in fact depend on weapons of mass destruction to achieve its strategic objectives, Kennan argued; indeed such devices (Kennan clearly had the proposed hydrogen bomb in mind) risked endangering the very interests containment had been designed to secure. "I consider it to have been in its implications one of the most important, if not the most important, of all the documents I ever wrote in government," he later observed.[24] Kennan's arguments elicited little support within the government, however, and on January 31, 1950, President Truman announced that the Atomic Energy Commission would "continue its work on all forms of atomic weapons, including the so-called hydrogen or super-bomb."[25]

The Policy Planning Staff has been asked to re-examine the present position of the United States with respect to the international control of atomic energy, and to assess the adequacy of this position in the light of present circumstances, particularly the demonstrated Soviet atomic capability. The following paper is intended to contribute to this re-examination.

•   •   •   •   •   •   •

24. Kennan, *Memoirs: 1925–1950,* p. 472.
25. *Public Papers of the Presidents: Harry S. Truman, 1950* (Washington: 1965), p. 138.

III

The problem whether it is desirable for this Government to move now as far as possible and as rapidly as possible toward international control is only part of a deeper problem, involving certain very far-reaching judgments and decisions of national policy, both foreign and domestic. It is not the purpose of this paper to deal exhaustively with this deeper problem or to make recommendations for its solution. But it is important, in any consideration of the international control problem, to identify the larger problem of which it is a part, to see what other things are logically involved in it, and to note certain factors bearing upon it which have particular importance from the standpoint of international control.

The real problem at issue, in determining what we should do at this juncture with respect to international control, is the problem of our attitude toward weapons of mass destruction in general, and the role which we allot to these weapons in our own military planning. Here, the crucial question is: Are we to rely upon weapons of mass destruction as an integral and vitally important component of our military strength, which we would expect to employ deliberately, immediately, and unhesitatingly in the event that we become involved in a military conflict with the Soviet Union? Or are we to retain such weapons in our national arsenal only as a deterrent to the use of similar weapons against ourselves or our allies and as a possible means of retaliation in case they are used? According to the way this question is answered, a whole series of decisions are influenced, of which the decision as to what to do about the international control of atomic energy and the prohibition of the weapon is only one.

We must note, by way of clarification of this question, that barring some system of international control and prohibition of atomic weapons, it is not questioned that *some* weapons of mass destruction must be retained in the national arsenal for purposes of deterrence and retaliation. The problem is: for what purpose, and against the background of what subjective attitude, are we to develop such weapons and to train our forces in their use?

We may regard them as something vital to our conduct of a future war—as something without which our war plans would be emasculated and ineffective—as something which we have resolved, in the face of all the moral and other factors concerned, to employ forthwith and unhesitatingly at the outset of any great military conflict. In this case, we should take the consequences of that decision now, and we should obviously keep away from any program of international dealings which would bring us closer to the possibility of agreement on international control and prohibition of the atomic weapon.

Or we may regard them as something superfluous to our basic military posture—as something which we are compelled to hold against the possibility that they might be used by our opponents. In this case, of course, we take care not to build up a reliance upon them in our military planning. Since they then represent only a burdensome expenditure of funds and effort, we hold only the minimum required for the deterrent-retaliatory purpose. And we are at liberty, if we so desire, to make it our objective to divest ourselves of this minimum at the earliest moment by achieving a scheme of international control.

We should remember that more depends on this basic decision than simply our stance toward the problems of international control. It must also have an important effect on our domestic atomic energy program, and particularly on what we do about the superbomb. If we decide to hold weapons of mass destruction only for deterrent-retaliatory purposes then the limit on the number and power of the weapons we should hold is governed by our estimate as to what it would take to make attack on this country or its allies by weapons of mass destruction a risky, probably unprofitable, and therefore irrational undertaking for any adversary. In these circumstances, the problem of whether to develop the superbomb and other weapons of mass destruction becomes only a question of the extent to which they would be needed to achieve this purpose. It might be, for example, that the present and prospective stockpile of conventional bombs, combined with present and prospective possibilities for delivery, would be found adequate to this purpose and that anything further in the way of mass destruction weapons would be redundant, or would fall into an area of diminishing returns.[26]

If, on the other hand, we are resolved to use weapons of mass destruction deliberately and prior to their use against us or our allies, in a future war, then our purpose is presumably to inflict maximum destruction on the forces, population and territory of the enemy, with the least expenditure of effort, in full acceptance of the attendant risk of retaliation against us, and in the face of all moral and political considerations. In this case, the only limitations on the number and power of mass destruction weapons which we

26. Note that the Soviets claim that their aim in developing the bomb is only to have "enough" for purposes of retaliation. Vyshinski, in his speech before the U.N. Assembly on November 10, 1949, said: "We in the Soviet Union are utilizing atomic energy, but not in order to stockpile atomic bombs—although I am convinced that if, unfortunately and to our great regret, this were necessary, we should have as many of these as we need—no more and no less." [Note in source text]

would wish to develop would presumably be those of ordinary military economy, such as cost, efficiency, and ease of delivery.

Depending, therefore, on which of these courses is selected, our decision on the superbomb might be one of two diametrically opposite ones.

.   .   .   .

VII

It flows from the above discussion that if, as I understand to be the case at the present moment, we are not prepared to reorient our military planning and to envisage the renunciation, either now or with time, of our reliance on "first use" of weapons of mass destruction in a future war, then we should not move closer than we are today to international control. To do so would be doubly invidious; for not only would we be moving toward a situation which we had already found unacceptable, but we would meanwhile be making that situation even more unacceptable by increasing our reliance on plans incompatible with it.

If our military plans are to remain unchanged in this respect, then it is probably best for us to rest on the present U.N. majority proposals,[27] not pressing them with any particular vigor, but taking care not to undermine them by any statements which would suggest a lack of readiness on our part to accept them should they find acceptance in the Soviet camp. It is true that this position is somewhat disingenuous, since if the Russians should accept what we are ostensibly urging them to accept, we might be acutely embarrassed. But the danger of their accepting it is not serious. And in the present circumstances any new departure, involving even the suggestion of a withdrawal from the U.N. proposals or of a willingness to consider other ones, would result in much confusion, as between ourselves and our friends, which would be both difficult to dispel and unnecessary.

Unless, therefore, we are prepared to alter our military concepts as indicated above, thereby placing ourselves in a position where we could afford to take these weapons or leave them as the fortunes of international negotiation might determine, I urge that we consider the question of the desirability of some new international approach to have been studied and answered in the negative, and that we bury the subject of international control as best we can for the present.

The remaining discussion in this paper accordingly relates only to what

27. On the international control of atomic energy. [Ed. note]

we might do if we *had* reviewed our military concepts, if we *had* come to the conclusion that we would no longer rely on mass destruction weapons in our planning for a future war, and if we *had* resolved to work ourselves out of our present dependence on those weapons as rapidly as possible.

The first thing we would obviously have to do would be to discuss this new state of mind with our allies in the Atlantic Pact group, with a view to obtaining their understanding for our background thinking and their agreement to the modifications of military planning which it implies. If it proved impossible to come to any meeting of the minds with our allies on these points a new situation would be created, which would have to be examined on its merits. The other members of the Atlantic Pact have no formal right, of course, to compel us to plan to wage war with weapons which we had concluded to be unacceptable to our people as weapons of "first use". On the other hand, we would have to calculate the political and psychological damage which might be done by overriding their objections too brutally. If this damage seemed exorbitant, in terms of the cold war, then we would presumably have no choice but to carry on with the present position both as respects military plans and international control. However, in this case we should be careful to bring home to the Europeans the full consciousness of the responsibility they were undertaking in asking us to defer to them on this point.

Assuming, however, that our new position with relation to the use of mass destruction weapons was finally to commend itself to the other members of the Atlantic Pact group, we would then be able to take a public position with regard to mass destruction weapons similar to that taken by the Soviet Government: namely that we deplore the existence and abhor the use of these weapons; that we have no intention of initiating their use against anyone; that we would use them only with the greatest of reluctance and only if this were forced upon us by methods of warfare used against us or our allies; and that in the absence of international agreement on the abolition of such weapons under suitable safeguards we would hold only enough to assure that it would be suicidal folly for anyone else to use them against ourselves or our allies. The President being charged with the supreme responsibility for the operations of our armed forces, including advance planning activities, this position should be taken as a matter of executive policy. To the extent that Congressional opinion might associate itself with such a position, this would be all to the good; but I see no reason why Congressional support need be a prerequisite.

Having taken such a public attitude, we would then have, for the first time since we began to amass stockpiles of atomic bombs, a clear and suitable position from which to address ourselves to the problem of international control. Our first decision would then have to be whether, even in these circumstances, we would be prepared to accept international control on terms which would yield less security against violation than the present U.N. proposals or whether we would prefer to rest our security on the maintenance of stockpiles of mass destruction weapons for such deterrent-retaliatory value as they might have. This is of course the central question in the whole international control problem; and impressive arguments can be advanced on both sides.

It is my own view that arrangements based on any or all of the suggestions contained in the second section of this report, above, while quite possibly inferior to the present U.N. proposals from the strict standpoint of theoretical atomic security, would still be preferable to a situation in which both sides would be retaining atomic weapons, and presumably other weapons of mass destruction, for purposes of retaliation, with no agreement existing concerning their control or prohibition. I base this conclusion on my conviction that it would be difficult for us, if we are to hold and develop such weapons at all, to keep them in their proper place as an instrument of national policy and to arrive at the delicate judgments which would have to be made currently about the money and effort which should be devoted to their cultivation and the role which should be allotted to them in our military planning. I believe that the peculiar psychological overtones by which these weapons will always be accompanied will tend to give them a certain top-heaviness as instruments of our national policy, and that this top-heaviness, in turn, will inevitably impart a certain eccentricity to our military planning, where there should be equilibrium.

I fear, moreover, that this tendency to eccentricity may not be limited to our military planning but may tend to affect our concept of what it is that we could achieve by the conduct of war against the Soviet Union. Whether or not war on the grand scale can achieve positive aims for an aggressive totalitarian power, it is my belief that it cannot achieve such aims for a democracy. It would be useful, in my opinion, if we were to recognize that the real purposes of the democratic society cannot be achieved by large-scale violence and destruction; that even in the most favorable circumstances war between great powers spells a dismal deterioration of world conditions from the standpoint of the liberal-democratic tradition; and that the only positive function it can fulfill for us—a function, the necessity and legitimacy of which I do not dispute—is to assure that we survive physically as an independent nation when our existence and independence might otherwise be jeopardized and that the catastrophe which we and our friends suffer, if cataclysm is unavoidable, is at least less than that suffered by our enemies. For such positive purposes as we wish to pursue, we must look to other things than war: above all, to bearing, to example, to persuasion, and to the judicious exploitation of our strength as a deterrent to world conflict. The best that war can do is to keep our nation intact, in order that we may have an opportunity to continue to function as a unified and effective society and to employ these other instruments of national policy on which real progress must rest. I feel that the absence of international agreement outlawing the weapons of mass destruction, and the retention in the national arsenals of this country and of the Soviet Union of such weapons, will have a tendency to confuse our people with regard to the realities to which I have just referred and to encourage the belief that somehow or other results decisive for the purposes of democracy can be expected to flow from the question of who obtains the ultimate superiority in the atomic weapons race. We cannot have a clear and sound national policy unless it is based on a correct appreciation by our people of the role and possibilities of the various weapons of war, and of warfare itself, as instruments of national policy. I fear that the atomic weapon, with its vague and highly dangerous promise of "decisive" results, of people "signing on dotted lines", of easy solutions to profound human problems, will impede understanding of the things that are important to a clean, clear policy and will carry us toward the misuse and dissipation of our national strength.

While both dangers are great, I would hold this latter danger to be a more serious one than that which would reside in an imperfect system of international prohibition and control, and I would therefore favor the latter.

It may be said that all weapons are cruel and destructive, if they are to serve their purpose; that many of the conventional weapons also bring death and hardship to civilian populations; that the destructive horror of the atomic weapon is only a matter of degree; and that the above concept is therefore an unsound one which, if carried to its ultimate conclusions, would lead to a Ghandian policy of unilateral demilitarization, non-resistance and appeasement.

As to the assertion that this is only a matter of degree, I think that the following words of Shakespeare are entirely relevant and applicable:

"Take but degree away—untune that string
And hark what discord follows: . . .

> Then everything includes in power—
> Power into will, will into appetite,
> And appetite, a universal wolf,
> So doubly seconded with will and power,
> Must make perforce a universal prey
> And last eat up himself.''[28]

These words would have a prophetic applicability even if there were no distinction of substance between the weapons which we know as the weapons of mass destruction and the others. But I believe that there is such a distinction. It may be an inexact and imperfect one; but if we were to reject all distinctions in life on the basis of inexactness and imperfection, no civilization would be possible. The distinction lies in the way in which a weapon can be applied. By and large, the conventional weapons of warfare have admitted and recognized the possibility of surrender and submission. For that reason, they have traditionally been designed to spare the unarmed and helpless non-combatant, who was assumed already to be in a state of submission when confronted with military force, as well as the combatant prepared to lay down his arms. This general quality of the conventional weapons of warfare implied a still more profound and vital recognition: namely that warfare should be a means to an end other than warfare, an end connected with the beliefs and the feelings and the attitudes of people, an end marked by submission to a new political will and perhaps to a new regime of life, but an end which at least did not negate the principle of life itself.

The weapons of mass destruction do not have this quality. They reach backward beyond the frontiers of western civilization, to the concepts of warfare which were once familiar to the Asiatic hordes. They cannot really be reconciled with a political purpose directed to shaping, rather than de-stroying, the lives of the adversary. They fail to take account of the ultimate responsibility of men for one another, and even for each other's errors and mistakes. They imply the admission that man not only can be but is his own worst and most terrible enemy.

It is entirely possible that war may be waged against us again, as it has been waged against us and other nations within our time, under these con-cepts and by these weapons. If so, we shall doubtless have to reply in kind, for that may be the price of survival. I still think it vital to our own under-

---

28. From ''Troilus and Cressida''. [Note in source text]

standing of what it is we are about that we not fall into the error of initiating, or planning to initiate, the employment of these weapons and concepts, thus hypnotizing ourselves into the belief that they may ultimately serve some positive national purpose. I doubt our ability to hold the respective weapons in our national arsenal, to fit them into our military and political plans, to agree with our allies on the circumstances of their use, and to entertain the prospect of their continued cultivation by our adversaries, without backsliding repeatedly into this dangerous, and possibly mortal, error. In other words, even if we were to conclude today that "first use" would not be advantageous, I would not trust the steadfastness of this outlook in a situation where the shadow of uncontrolled mass destruction weapons continues to lie across the peoples of the world. Measured against this alternative, an imperfect system of international control seems to me less dangerous, and more considerate of those things in international life which are still hopeful.

· · · · · · ·

IX

It may be adduced, with regard to the above discussion, that it charts out a course replete with a whole series of difficulties and obstacles and that there is extremely little likelihood, judged by present circumstances, that we would ever successfully make our way to the end of it, which would be an agreement on international control. From this, it may be argued that it could hardly be worthwhile for us to embark upon it.

This is a respectable argument; and if the progress of world events in our time were slower, simpler, and easier to foresee, it might be unanswerable. But St. Paul's observation that, "We know in part and we prophesy in part", was never truer than it is of the time ahead of us, particularly in respect to the development of the international situation, the meaning of war and the function of weapons. In such a time there is only one thing a nation can do which can have any really solid and dependable value: and that is to see that the initial lines of its policy are as close as possible to the principles dictated by its traditions and its nature, and that where it is necessary to depart from these lines, people are aware that this *is* a departure and understand why it is necessary. For this reason, there is value in a clean and straight beginning, even though the road ahead may be torturous and perhaps impassable.

GEORGE F. KENNAN

≫ 7 ≪

NSC 68: THE STRATEGIC REASSESSMENT OF 1950

NSC 68 constitutes the most elaborate effort made by United States officials during the early Cold War years to integrate political, economic, and military considerations into a comprehensive statement of national security policy. In response to a presidential directive to analyze the combined implications of the Communist victory in China, the Soviet atomic bomb, and the American decision to construct a thermonuclear weapon, a special State and Defense Department study group headed by Paul Nitze (who in January 1950 had replaced Kennan as head of the Policy Planning Staff) drafted NSC 68 in February and March 1950. The completed study, comprising some seventy single-spaced, legal-sized typed pages, was forwarded to President Truman on April 7, 1950.[1]

NSC 68 was intended as a successor to, and, to some extent, an elaboration of the analysis contained in NSC 20/4 (Document 23). Like that earlier document, NSC 68 associated American interests in the world with diversity, not uniformity; it viewed Soviet expansionism as stemming more from internal insecurities than from ideological compulsions; it recommended dealing with that threat by mobilizing the moral and material strength of the West while working to alter the Soviet concept of international relations as a prerequisite for negotiations.

Prior assessments of the Soviet threat, however, had rested on the assumption that the Russians would not start a war, except by miscalculation. The Kremlin's unexpectedly early attainment of an atomic bomb capability caused Washington planners increasingly to doubt the validity of that proposition. Projections indicated that if existing trends continued unchanged, the Soviet Union by 1954 might be in a position to initiate war against the United States with a reasonable prospect of winning. NSC 68 can be viewed

---

1. The best account of the drafting of NSC 68 is Paul Y. Hammond, "NSC-68: Prologue to Rearmament," in Warner R. Schilling, Paul Y. Hammond, and Glenn H. Snyder, *Strategy, Politics, and Defense Budgets* (New York: Columbia University Press, 1962), pp. 267–378.

as a "call to arms" to stave off that prospect by significantly upgrading Western defense capabilities. It can also be seen as an argument in favor of what later came to be known as "flexible response"—the ability to respond to aggression at varying levels of violence corresponding to the extent of the offense, thereby avoiding the unpalatable alternatives of surrender or all-out war.

Until 1950 the primary constraint that had prevented an increase in military spending had been the concern, widely shared throughout the government, that such expenditures might cause unacceptable inflation. NSC 68 pointedly challenged that argument by harking back to the World War II experience, when government spending had increased vastly without producing damaging inflation; the implication was that in 1950 the United States could tolerate at least a tripling of defense expenditures without significantly impairing current standards of living. Paradoxically this argument in favor of higher military budgets emanated largely from Secretary of State Dean Acheson and his advisers in the Department of State; its most vociferous opponent was Secretary of Defense Louis Johnson, a fiscal conservative.

Another critic of NSC 68 was Kennan, though on grounds different from Secretary Johnson's. In part, Kennan's skeptical attitude reflected his habitual distrust of comprehensive written policy statements as guides to action; in part it grew out of what he considered to be the document's excessive preoccupation with Soviet capabilities, and its corresponding neglect of probable Soviet intentions. But there was yet a deeper conflict between the intellectual assumptions of NSC 68 and Kennan's earlier formulations of containment strategy: NSC 68 assumed a view of the world in which gains for communism anywhere constituted, to an equivalent degree, losses for the United States and its allies. Kennan had never endorsed such a "zero sum game" view of the world; moreover, he had stressed the need to differentiate between international communism and Soviet expansionism, seeing in the former a possible instrument to be used in attempting to contain the latter. Kennan had also emphasized the need to define interests in terms of limited capabilities; NSC 68 took the approach that, because capabilities were not as limited as had been thought, interests need not be either.

NSC 68 was not formally approved by President Truman until September 30, 1950 (as NSC 68/2); by this time events appeared to have confirmed the validity of its analysis and conclusions. The outbreak of fighting in Korea two months after that document was submitted to the White House could not have been better calculated to ensure its approval, given NSC 68's prediction of greater Soviet aggressiveness, its anticipation of limited war, and its rationale for increased defense expenditures. By the summer of 1950, NSC 68 had become the definitive statement of American national security policy. It also marked an important stage in the process by which the strategy of containment evolved, over the years, into something very different from what its founder had intended.

◇◇◇

52   **T O P   S E C R E T**

United States Objectives and Programs for National Security

NSC 68   April 14, 1950

[Source: *Foreign Relations of the United States: 1950*, I, 237–292] [2]

Analysis

I. BACKGROUNDS OF THE PRESENT WORLD CRISIS

Within the past thirty-five years the world has experienced two global wars of tremendous violence. It has witnessed two revolutions—the Russian and the Chinese—or extreme scope and intensity. It has also seen the collapse of five empires—the Ottoman, the Austro-Hungarian, German, Italian and Japanese—and the drastic decline of two major imperial systems, the British and the French. During the span of one generation, the international distribution of power has been fundamentally altered. For several centuries it had proved impossible for any one nation to gain such preponderant strength that a coalition of other nations could not in time face it with greater strength. The international scene was marked by recurring periods of violence and war, but a system of sovereign and independent states was maintained, over which no state was able to achieve hegemony.

Two complex sets of factors have now basically altered this historical distribution of power. First, the defeat of Germany and Japan and the decline of the British and French Empires have interacted with the development of the United States and the Soviet Union in such a way that power has increasingly gravitated to these two centers. Second, the Soviet Union, unlike previous aspirants to hegemony, is animated by a new fanatic faith, antithetical to our own, and seeks to impose its absolute authority over the rest of the world. Conflict has, therefore, become endemic and is waged, on the part of the Soviet Union, by violent or non-violent methods in accordance

2. The full text of NSC 68 was first published in the *Naval War College Review*, XXVII, No. 6/ Sequence No. 255 (May/June 1975), pp. 51–108.

with the dictates of expediency. With the development of increasingly terrifying weapons of mass destruction, every individual faces the ever-present
possibility of annihilation should the conflict enter the phase of total war.

On the one hand, the people of the world yearn for relief from the anxiety
arising from the risk of atomic war. On the other hand, any substantial further extension of the area under the domination of the Kremlin would raise
the possibility that no coalition adequate to confront the Kremlin with
greater strength could be assembled. It is in this context that this Republic
and its citizens in the ascendancy of their strength stand in their deepest
peril.

The issues that face us are momentous, involving the fulfillment or destruction not only of this Republic but of civilization itself. They are issues
which will not await our deliberations. With conscience and resolution this
Government and the people it represents must now take new and fateful
decisions.

II. FUNDAMENTAL PURPOSE OF THE UNITED STATES

The fundamental purpose of the United States is laid down in the Preamble to the Constitution: ". . . to form a more perfect Union, establish Justice, insure domestic Tranquility, provide for the common defence, promote
the general Welfare, and secure the Blessings of Liberty to ourselves and to
our Posterity." In essence, the fundamental purpose is to assure the integrity
and vitality of our free society, which is founded upon the dignity and worth
of the individual.

Three realities emerge as a consequence of this purpose: Our determination to maintain the essential elements of individual freedom, as set forth in
the Constitution and Bill of Rights; our determination to create conditions
under which our free and democratic system can live and prosper; and our
determination to fight if necessary to defend our way of life, for which as in
the Declaration of Independence, "with a firm reliance on the protection of
Divine Providence, we mutually pledge to each other our lives, our Fortunes and our sacred Honor."

III. FUNDAMENTAL DESIGN OF THE KREMLIN

The fundamental design of those who control the Soviet Union and the international communist movement is to retain and solidify their absolute
power, first in the Soviet Union and second in the areas now under their
control. In the mind of the Soviet leaders, however, achievement of this

design requires the dynamic extension of their authority and the ultimate elimination of any effective opposition to their authority.

The design, therefore, calls for the complete subversion or forcible destruction of the machinery of government and structure of society in the countries of the non-Soviet world and their replacement by an apparatus and structure subservient to and controlled from the Kremlin. To that end Soviet efforts are now directed toward the domination of the Eurasian land mass. The United States, as the principal center of power in the non-Soviet world and the bulwark of opposition to Soviet expansion, is the principal enemy whose integrity and vitality must be subverted or destroyed by one means or another if the Kremlin is to achieve its fundamental design.

IV. THE UNDERLYING CONFLICT IN THE REALM OF IDEAS AND VALUES BETWEEN THE U.S. PURPOSE AND THE KREMLIN DESIGN

A. *Nature of conflict*

The Kremlin regards the United States as the only major threat to the achievement of its fundamental design. There is a basic conflict between the idea of freedom under a government of laws, and the idea of slavery under the grim oligarchy of the Kremlin, which has come to a crisis with the polarization of power described in Section I, and the exclusive possession of atomic weapons by the two protagonists. The idea of freedom, moreover, is peculiarly and intolerably subversive of the idea of slavery. But the converse is not true. The implaccable purpose of the slave state to eliminate the challenge of freedom has placed the two great powers at opposite poles. It is this fact which gives the present polarization of power the quality of crisis.

The free society values the individual as an end in himself, requiring of him only that measure of self discipline and self restraint which make the rights of each individual compatible with the rights of every other individual. The freedom of the individual has as its counterpart, therefore, the negative responsibility of the individual not to exercise his freedom in ways inconsistent with the freedom of other individuals and the positive responsibility to make constructive use of his freedom in the building of a just society.

From this idea of freedom with responsibility derives the marvelous diversity, the deep tolerance, the lawfulness of the free society. This is the explanation of the strength of free men. It constitutes the integrity and the vitality of a free and democratic system. The free society attempts to create and maintain an environment in which every individual has the opportunity to realize his creative powers. It also explains why the free society tolerates those within it who would use their freedom to destroy it. By the same token, in relations between nations, the prime reliance of the free society is on the strength and appeal of its idea, and it feels no compulsion sooner or later to bring all societies into conformity with it.

For the free society does not fear, it welcomes, diversity. It derives its strength from its hospitality even to antipathetic ideas. It is a market for free trade in ideas, secure in its faith that free men will take the best wares, and grow to a fuller and better realization of their powers in exercising their choice.

The idea of freedom is the most contagious idea in history, more contagious than the idea of submission to authority. For the breath of freedom cannot be tolerated in a society which has come under the domination of an individual or group of individuals with a will to absolute power. Where the despot holds absolute power—the absolute power of the absolutely powerful will—all other wills must be subjugated in an act of willing submission, a degradation willed by the individual upon himself under the compulsion of a perverted faith. It is the first article of this faith that he finds and can only find the meaning of his existence in serving the ends of the system. The system becomes God, and submission to the will of God becomes submission to the will of the system. It is not enough to yield outwardly to the system— even Ghandian non-violence is not acceptable—for the spirit of resistance and the devotion to a higher authority might then remain, and the individual would not be wholly submissive.

The same compulsion which demands total power over all men within the Soviet state without a single exception, demands total power over all Communist Parties and all states under Soviet domination. Thus Stalin has said that the theory and tactics of Leninism as expounded by the Bolshevik party are mandatory for the proletarian parties of all countries. A true internationalist is defined as one who unhesitatingly upholds the position of the Soviet Union and in the satellite states true patriotism is love of the Soviet Union. By the same token the "peace policy" of the Soviet Union, described at a Party Congress as "a more advantageous form of fighting capitalism," is a device to divide and immobilize the non-Communist world, and the peace the Soviet Union seeks is the peace of total conformity to Soviet policy.

The antipathy of slavery to freedom explains the iron curtain, the isolation, the autarchy of the society whose end is absolute power. The existence and persistence of the idea of freedom is a permanent and continuous threat to the foundation of the slave society; and it therefore regards as intolerable the long continued existence of freedom in the world. What is new, what makes the continuing crisis, is the polarization of power which now inescapably confronts the slave society with the free.

The assault on free institutions is world-wide now, and in the context of the present polarization of power a defeat of free institutions anywhere is a defeat everywhere. The shock we sustained in the destruction of Czechoslovakia was not in the measure of Czechoslovakia's material importance to us. In a material sense, her capabilities were already at Soviet disposal. But when the integrity of Czechoslovak institutions was destroyed, it was in the intangible scale of values that we registered a loss more damaging than the material loss we had already suffered.

Thus unwillingly our free society finds itself mortally challenged by the Soviet system. No other value system is so wholly irreconcilable with ours, so implacable in its purpose to destroy ours, so capable of turning to its own uses the most dangerous and divisive trends in our own society, no other so skillfully and powerfully evokes the elements of irrationality in human nature everywhere, and no other has the support of a great and growing center of military power.

B. *Objectives*

The objectives of a free society are determined by its fundamental values and by the necessity for maintaining the material environment in which they flourish. Logically and in fact, therefore, the Kremlin's challenge to the United States is directed not only to our values but to our physical capacity to protect their environment. It is a challenge which encompasses both peace and war and our objectives in peace and war must take account of it.

1. Thus we must make ourselves strong, both in the way in which we affirm our values in the conduct of our national life, and in the development of our military and economic strength.

2. We must lead in building a successfully functioning political and economic system in the free world. It is only by practical affirmation, abroad as well as at home, of our essential values, that we can preserve our own integrity, in which lies the real frustration of the Kremlin design.

3. But beyond thus affirming our values our policy and actions must be such as to foster a fundamental change in the nature of the Soviet system, a change toward which the frustration of the design is the first and perhaps the most important step. Clearly it will not only be less costly but more effective if this change occurs to a maximum extent as a result of internal forces in Soviet society.

In a shrinking world, which now faces the threat of atomic warfare, it is not an adquate objective merely to seek to check the Kremlin design, for the absence of order among nations is becoming less and less tolerable. This fact imposes on us, in our own interests, the responsibility of world leadership. It demands that we make the attempt, and accept the risks inherent in it, to bring about order and justice by means consistent with the principles of freedom and democracy. We should limit our requirement of the Soviet Union to its participation with other nations on the basis of equality and respect for the rights of others. Subject to this requirement, we must with our allies and the former subject peoples seek to create a world society based on the principle of consent. Its framework cannot be inflexible. It will consist of many national communities of great and varying abilities and resources, and hence of war potential. The seeds of conficts will inevitably exist or will come into being. To acknowledge this is only to acknowledge the impossibility of a final solution. Not to acknowledge it can be fatally dangerous in a world in which there are no final solutions.

All these objectives of a free society are equally valid and necessary in peace and war. But every consideration of devotion to our fundamental values and to our national security demands that we seek to achieve them by the strategy of the cold war. It is only by developing the moral and material strength of the free world that the Soviet regime will become convinced of the falsity of its assumptions and that the pre-conditions for workable agreements can be created. By practically demonstrating the integrity and vitality of our system the free world widens the area of possible agreement and thus can hope gradually to bring about a Soviet acknowledgement of realities which in sum will eventually constitute a frustration of the Soviet design. Short of this, however, it might be possible to create a situation which will induce the Soviet Union to accommodate itself, with or without the conscious abandonment of its design, to coexistence on tolerable terms with the non-Soviet world. Such a development would be a triumph for the idea of freedom and democracy. It must be an immediate objective of United States policy.

There is no reason, in the event of war, for us to alter our over-all objectives. They do not include unconditional surrender, the subjugation of the Russian peoples or a Russia shorn of its economic potential. Such a course would irrevocably unite the Russian people behind the regime which enslaves them. Rather these objectives contemplate Soviet acceptance of the specific and limited conditions requisite to an international environment in which free institutions can flourish, and in which the Russian peoples will have a new chance to work out their own destiny. If we can make the Russian people our allies in this enterprise we will obviously have made our task easier and victory more certain.

The objectives outlined in NSC 20/4 (November 23, 1948) and quoted in Chapter X, are fully consistent with the objectives stated in this paper and they remain valid. The growing intensity of the conflict which has been imposed upon us, however, requires the changes of emphasis and the additions that are apparent. Coupled with the probable fission bomb capability and possible thermonuclear bomb capability of the Soviet Union, the intensifying struggle requires us to face the fact that we can expect no lasting abatement of the crisis unless and until a change occurs in the nature of the Soviet system.

C. *Means*

The free society is limited in its choice of means to achieve its ends.

Compulsion is the negation of freedom, except when it is used to enforce the rights common to all. The resort to force, internally or externally, is therefore a last resort for a free society. The act is permissible only when one individual or groups of individuals within it threaten the basic rights of other individuals or when another society seeks to impose its will upon it. The free society cherishes and protects as fundamental the rights of the minority against the will of a majority, because these rights are the inalienable rights of each and every individual.

The resort to force, to compulsion, to the imposition of its will is therefore a difficult and dangerous act for a free society, which is warranted only in the face of even greater dangers. The necessity of the act must be clear and compelling; the act must commend itself to the overwhelming majority as an inescapable exception to the basic idea of freedom; or the regenerative capacity of free men after the act has been performed will be endangered.

The Kremlin is able to select whatever means are expedient in seeking to carry out its fundamental design. Thus it can make the best of several possible worlds, conducting the struggle on those levels where it considers it profitable and enjoying the benefits of a pseudo-peace on those levels where it is not ready for a contest. At the ideological or psychological level, in the struggle for men's minds, the conflict is world-wide. At the political and economic level, within states and in the relations between states, the struggle for power is being intensified. And at the military level, the Kremlin has thus far been careful not to commit a technical breach of the peace, although using its vast forces to intimidate its neighbors, and to support an aggressive foreign policy, and not hesitating through its agents to resort to arms in favorable circumstances. The attempt to carry out its fundamental design is being pressed, therefore, with all means which are believed expedient in the present situation, and the Kremlin has inextricably engaged us in the conflict between its design and our purpose.

We have no such freedom of choice, and least of all in the use of force. Resort to war is not only a last resort for a free society, but it is also an act which cannot definitively end the fundamental conflict in the realm of ideas. The idea of slavery can only be overcome by the timely and persistent demonstration of the superiority of the idea of freedom. Military victory alone would only partially and perhaps only temporarily affect the fundamental conflict, for although the ability of the Kremlin to threaten our security might be for a time destroyed, the resurgence of totalitarian forces and the re-establishment of the Soviet system or its equivalent would not be long delayed unless great progress were made in the fundamental conflict.

Practical and ideological considerations therefore both impel us to the conclusion that we have no choice but to demonstrate the superiority of the idea of freedom by its constructive application, and to attempt to change the world situation by means short of war in such a way as to frustrate the Kremlin design and hasten the decay of the Soviet system.

For us the role of military power is to serve the national purpose by deterring an attack upon us while we seek by other means to create an environment in which our free society can flourish, and by fighting, if necessary, to defend the integrity and vitality of our free society and to defeat any aggressor. The Kremlin uses Soviet military power to back up and serve the Kremlin design. It does not hesitate to use military force aggressively if that course is expedient in the achievement of its design. The differences between our fundamental purpose and the Kremlin design, therefore, are reflected in our respective attitudes toward and use of military force.

Our free society, confronted by a threat to its basic values, naturally will take such action, including the use of military force, as may be required to protect those values. The integrity of our system will not be jeopardized by any measures, covert or overt, violent or non-violent, which serve the purposes of frustrating the Kremlin design, nor does the necessity for conducting ourselves so as to affirm our values in actions as well as words forbid such measures, provided only they are appropriately calculated to that end and are not so excessive or misdirected as to make us enemies of the people instead of the evil men who have enslaved them.

But if war comes, what is the role of force? Unless we so use it that the

Russian people can perceive that our effort is directed against the regime and
its power for aggression, and not against their own interests, we will unite
the regime and the people in the kind of last ditch fight in which no underlying problems are solved, new ones are created, and where our basic principles are obscured and compromised. If we do not in the application of force
demonstrate the nature of our objectives we will, in fact, have compromised
from the outset our fundamental purpose. In the words of the Federalist (No.
28) "The means to be employed must be proportioned to the extent of the
mischief." The mischief may be a global war or it may be a Soviet campaign for limited objectives. In either case we should take no avoidable initiative which would cause it to become a war of annihilation, and if we have
the forces to defeat a Soviet drive for limited objectives it may well be to
our interest not to let it become a global war. Our aim in applying force
must be to compel the acceptance of terms consistent with our objectives,
and our capabilities for the application of force should, therefore, within the
limits of what we can sustain over the long pull, be congruent to the range
of tasks which we may encounter.

V. SOVIET INTENTIONS AND CAPABILITIES

A. *Political and psychological*

   The Kremlin's design for world domination begins at home. The first concern of a despotic oligarchy is that the local base of its power and authority
be secure. The massive fact of the iron curtain isolating the Soviet peoples
from the outside world, the repeated political purges within the U.S.S.R.,
and the institutionalized crimes of the MVD are evidence that the Kremlin
does not feel secure at home and that "the entire coercive force of the socialist state" is more than ever one of seeking to impose its absolute authority over "the economy, manner of life, and consciousness of people" (Vyshinski, "The Law of the Soviet State," pp. 74).[3] Similar evidence in the
satellite states of Eastern Europe leads to the conclusion that this same policy, in less advanced phases, is being applied to the Kremlin's colonial
areas.

   Being a totalitarian dictatorship, the Kremlin's objectives in these policies
is the total subjective submission of the peoples now under its control. The
concentration camp is the prototype of the society which these policies are
designed to achieve, a society in which the personality of the individual is so

   3. Andrei Y. Vyshinski, ed., *The Law of the Soviet State,* trans. Hugh W. Babb (New York:
Macmillan, 1948). [Ed. note]

broken and perverted that he participates affirmatively in his own degradation.

The Kremlin's policy toward areas not under its control is the elimination of resistance to its will and the extension of its influence and control. It is driven to follow this policy because it cannot, for the reasons set forth in Chapter IV, tolerate the existence of free societies; to the Kremlin the most mild and inoffensive free society is an affront, a challenge and a subversive influence. Given the nature of the Kremlin, and the evidence at hand, it seems clear that the ends toward which this policy is directed are the same as those where its control has already been established.

The means employed by the Kremlin in pursuit of this policy are limited only by considerations of expediency. Doctrine is not a limiting factor; rather it dictates the employment of violence, subversion and deceit, and rejects moral considerations. In any event, the Kremlin's conviction of its own infallibility has made its devotion to theory so subjective that past or present pronouncements as to doctrine offer no reliable guide to future actions. The only apparent restraints on resort to war are, therefore, calculations of practicality.

With particular reference to the United States, the Kremlin's strategic and tactical policy is affected by its estimate that we are not only the greatest immediate obstacle which stands between it and world domination, we are also the only power which could release forces in the free and Soviet worlds which could destroy it. The Kremlin's policy toward us is consequently animated by a peculiarly virulent blend of hatred and fear. Its strategy has been one of attempting to undermine the complex of forces, in this country and in the rest of the free world, on which our power is based. In this it has both adhered to doctrine and followed the sound principle of seeking maximum results with minimum risks and commitments. The present application of this strategy is a new form of expression for traditional Russian caution. However, there is no justification in Soviet theory or practice for predicting that, should the Kremlin become convinced that it could cause our downfall by one conclusive blow, it would not seek that solution.

In considering the capabilities of the Soviet world, it is of prime importance to remember that, in contrast to ours, they are being drawn upon close to the maximum possible extent. Also in contrast to us, the Soviet world can do more with less—it has a lower standard of living, its economy requires less to keep it functioning and its military machine operates effectively with less elaborate equipment and organization.

The capabilities of the Soviet world are being exploited to the full because the Kremlin is inescapably militant. It is inescapably militant because it possesses and is possessed by a world-wide revolutionary movement, because it is the inheritor of Russian imperialism and because it is a totalitarian dictatorship. Persistent crisis, conflict and expansion are the essence of the Kremlin's militancy. This dynamism serves to intensify all Soviet capabilities.

Two enormous organizations, the Communist Party and the secret police, are an outstanding source of strength to the Kremlin. In the Party, it has an apparatus designed to impose at home an ideological uniformity among its people and to act abroad as an instrument of propaganda, subversion and espionage. In its police apparatus, it has a domestic repressive instrument guaranteeing under present circumstances the continued security of the Kremlin. The demonstrated capabilities of these two basic organizations, operating openly or in disguise, in mass or through single agents, is unparalleled in history. The party, the police and the conspicuous might of the Soviet military machine together tend to create an overall impression of irresistible Soviet power among many peoples of the free world.

The ideological pretensions of the Kremlin are another great source of strength. Its identification of the Soviet system with communism, its peace campaigns and its championing of colonial peoples may be viewed with apathy, if not cynicism, by the oppressed totalitariat of the Soviet world, but in the free world these ideas find favorable responses in vulnerable segments of society. They have found a particularly receptive audience in Asia, especially as the Asiatics have been impressed by what has been plausibly portrayed to them as the rapid advance of the U.S.S.R. from a backward society to a position of great world power. Thus, in its pretensions to being (a) the source of a new universal faith and (b) the model "scientific" society, the Kremlin cynically identifies itself with the genuine aspirations of large numbers of people, and places itself at the head of an international crusade with all of the benefits which derive therefrom.

Finally, there is a category of capabilities, strictly speaking neither institutional nor ideological, which should be taken into consideration. The extraordinary flexibility of Soviet tactics is certainly a strength. It derives from the utterly amoral and opportunistic conduct of Soviet policy. Combining this quality with the elements of secrecy, the Kremlin possesses a formidable capacity to act with the widest tactical latitude, with stealth and with speed.

The greatest vulnerability of the Kremlin lies in the basic nature of its relations with the Soviet people.

That relationship is characterized by universal suspicion, fear and denunciation. It is a relationship in which the Kremlin relies, not only for its power but its very survival, on intricately devised mechanisms of coercion. The Soviet monolith is held together by the iron curtain around it and the iron bars within it, not by any force of natural cohesion. These artificial mechanisms of unity have never been intelligently challenged by a strong outside force. The full measure of their vulnerability is therefore not yet evident.

The Kremlin's relations with its satellites and their peoples is likewise a vulnerability. Nationalism still remains the most potent emotional-political force. The well-known ills of colonialism are compounded, however, by the excessive demands of the Kremlin that its satellites accept not only the imperial authority of Moscow but that they believe in and proclaim the ideological primacy and infallibility of the Kremlin. These excessive requirements can be made good only through extreme coercion. The result is that if a satellite feels able to effect its independence of the Kremlin, as Tito was able to do, it is likely to break away.

In short, Soviet ideas and practices run counter to the best and potentially the strongest instincts of men, and deny their most fundamental aspirations. Against an adversary which effectively affirmed the constructive and hopeful instincts of men and was capable of fulfilling their fundamental aspirations, the Soviet system might prove to be fatally weak.

The problem of succession to Stalin is also a Kremlin vulnerability. In a system where supreme power is acquired and held through violence and intimidation, the transfer of that power may well produce a period of instability.

In a very real sense, the Kremlin is a victim of its own dynamism. This dynamism can become a weakness if it is frustrated, if in its forward thrusts it encounters a superior force which halts the expansion and exerts a superior counterpressure. Yet the Kremlin cannot relax the condition of crisis and mobilization, for to do so would be to lose its dynamism, whereas the seeds of decay within the Soviet system would begin to flourish and fructify.

The Kremlin is, of course, aware of these weaknesses. It must know that in the present world situation they are of secondary significance. So long as the Kremlin retains the initiative, so long as it can keep on the offensive unchallenged by clearly superior counter-force—spiritual as well as material—its vulnerabilities are largely inoperative and even concealed by its successes. The Kremlin has not yet been given real reason to fear and be diverted by the rot within its system.

B. *Economic*

The Kremlin has no economic intentions unrelated to its overall policies. Economics in the Soviet world is not an end in itself. The Kremlin's policy, in so far as it has to do with economics, is to utilize economic processes to contribute to the overall strength, particularly the war-making capacity of the Soviet system. The material welfare of the totalitariat is severely subordinated to the interests of the system.

As for capabilities, even granting optimistic Soviet reports of production, the total economic strength of the U.S.S.R. compares with that of the U.S. as roughly one to four. This is reflected not only in gross national product (1949: U.S.S.R. $65 billion; U.S. $250 billion), but in production of key commodities in 1949:

	U.S.	U.S.S.R.	U.S.S.R. and European Orbit Combined
Ingot steel (Million met. tons)	80.4	21.5	28.0
Primary aluminum (Thousands met. tons)	617.6	130–135	140–145
Electric power (Billion kwh.)	410	72	112
Crude oil (Million met. tons)	276.5	33.0	38.9

Assuming the maintenance of present policies, while a large U.S. advantage is likely to remain, the Soviet Union will be steadily reducing the discrepancy between its overall economic strength and that of the U.S. by continuing to devote proportionately more to capital investment than the U.S.

But a full-scale effort by the U.S. would be capable of precipitately altering this trend. The U.S.S.R. today is on a near maximum production basis. No matter what efforts Moscow might make, only a relatively slight change in the rate of increase in overall production could be brought about. In the U.S., on the other hand, a very rapid absolute expansion could be realized. The fact remains, however, that so long as the Soviet Union is virtually mobilized, and the United States has scarcely begun to summon up its forces, the greater capabilities of the U.S. are to that extent inoperative in the struggle for power. Moreover, as the Soviet attainment of an atomic capability has demonstrated, the totalitarian state, at least in time of peace, can focus its efforts on any given project far more readily than the democratic state.

In other fields—general technological competence, skilled labor resources, productivity of labor force, etc.—the gap between the U.S.S.R. and the U.S. roughly corresponds to the gap in production. In the field of scientific research, however, the margin of United States superiority is unclear, especially if the Kremlin can utilize European talents.

C. *Military*

The Soviet Union is developing the military capacity to support its design for world domination. The Soviet Union actually possesses armed forces far in excess of those necessary to defend its national territory. These armed forces are probably not yet considered by the Soviet Union to be sufficient to initiate a war which would involve the United States. This excessive strength, coupled now with an atomic capability, provides the Soviet Union with great coercive power for use in time of peace in furtherance of its objectives and serves as a deterrent to the victims of its aggression from taking any action in opposition to its tactics which would risk war.

Should a major war occur in 1950 the Soviet Union and its satellites are considered by the Joint Chiefs of Staff to be in a sufficiently advanced state of preparation immediately to undertake and carry out the following campaigns.

  a. To overrun Western Europe, with the possible exception of the Iberian and Scandinavian Peninsulas; to drive toward the oil-bearing areas of the Near and Middle East; and to consolidate Communist gains in the Far East;

  b. To launch air attacks against the British Isles and air and sea attacks against the lines of communications of the Western Powers in the Atlantic and the Pacific;

  c. To attack selected targets with atomic weapons, now including the likelihood of such attacks against targets in Alaska, Canada, and the United States. Alternatively, this capability, coupled with other actions open to the Soviet Union, might deny the United Kingdom as an effective base of operations for allied forces. It also should be possible for the Soviet Union to prevent any allied "Normandy" type amphibious operations intended to force a re-entry into the continent of Europe.

After the Soviet Union completed its initial campaigns and consolidated its positions in the Western European area, it could simultaneously conduct:

  a. Full-scale air and limited sea operations against the British Isles;

  b. Invasions of the Iberian and Scandinavian Peninsulas;

  c. Further operations in the Near and Middle East, continued air operations against the North American continent, and air and sea operations against Atlantic and Pacific lines of communication; and

d. Diversionary attacks in other areas.

During the course of the offensive operations listed in the second and third paragraphs above, the Soviet Union will have an air defense capability with respect to the vital areas of its own and its satellites' territories which can oppose but cannot prevent allied air operations against these areas.

It is not known whether the Soviet Union possesses war reserves and arsenal capabilities sufficient to supply its satellite armies or even its own forces throughout a long war. It might not be in the interest of the Soviet Union to equip fully its satellite armies, since the possibility of defections would exist.

It is not possible at this time to assess accurately the finite disadvantages to the Soviet Union which may accrue through the implementation of the Economic Cooperation Act of 1948, as amended, and the Mutual Defense Assistance Act of 1949. It should be expected that, as this implementation progresses, the internal security situation of the recipient nations should improve concurrently. In addition, a strong United States military position, plus increases in the armaments of the nations of Western Europe, should strengthen the determination of the recipient nations to counter Soviet moves and in event of war could be considered as likely to delay operations and increase the time required for the Soviet Union to overrun Western Europe. In all probability, although United States backing will stiffen their determination, the armaments increase under the present aid programs will not be of any major consequence prior to 1952. Unless the military strength of the Western European nations is increased on a much larger scale than the current programs and at an accelerated rate, it is more likely that those nations will not be able to oppose even by 1960 the Soviet armed forces in war with any degree of effectiveness. Considering the Soviet Union military capability, the long-range allied military objective in Western Europe must envisage an increased military strength in that area sufficient possibly to deter the Soviet Union from a major war, or, in any event, to delay materially the overrunning of Western Europe and, if feasible, to hold a bridgehead on the continent against Soviet Union offensives.

We do not know accurately what the Soviet atomic capability is but the Central Intelligence Agency intelligence estimates, concurred in by State, Army, Navy, Air Force, and Atomic Energy Commission, assign to the Soviet Union a production capability giving it a fission bomb stockpile within the following ranges:

By mid-1950	10– 20
By mid-1951	25– 45
By mid-1952	45– 90
By mid-1953	70–135
By mid-1954	200

This estimate is admittedly based on incomplete coverage of Soviet activities and represents the production capabilities of known or deducible Soviet plants. If others exist, as is possible, this estimate could lead us into a feeling of superiority in our atomic stockpile that might be dangerously misleading, particularly with regard to the timing of a possible Soviet offensive. On the other hand, if the Soviet Union experiences operating difficulties, this estimate would be reduced. There is some evidence that the Soviet Union is acquiring certain materials essential to research on and development of thermonuclear weapons.

The Soviet Union now has aircraft able to deliver the atomic bomb. Our intelligence estimates assign to the Soviet Union an atomic bomber capability already in excess of that needed to deliver available bombs. We have at present no evaluated estimate regarding the Soviet accuracy of delivery on target. It is believed that the Soviets cannot deliver their bombs on target with a degree of accuracy comparable to ours, but a planning estimate might well place it at 40–60 percent of bombs sortied. For planning purposes, therefore, the date the Soviets possess an atomic stockpile of 200 bombs would be a critical date for the United States for the delivery of 100 atomic bombs on targets in the United States would seriously damage this country.

At the time the Soviet Union has a substantial atomic stockpile and if it is assumed that it will strike a strong surprise blow and if it is assumed further that its atomic attacks will be met with no more effective defense opposition than the United States and its allies have programmed, results of those attacks could include:

a. Laying waste to the British Isles and thus depriving the Western Powers of their use as a base;

b. Destruction of the vital centers and of the communications of Western Europe, thus precluding effective defense by the Western Powers; and

c. Delivering devastating attacks on certain vital centers of the United States and Canada.

The possession by the Soviet Union of a thermonuclear capability in addition to this substantial atomic stockpile would result in tremendously increased damage.

During this decade, the defensive capabilities of the Soviet Union will probably be strengthened particularly by the development and use of modern aircraft, aircraft warning and communications devices, and defensive guided missiles.

VI. U.S. INTENTIONS AND CAPABILITIES—ACTUAL AND POTENTIAL

A. *Political and psychological*

Our overall policy at the present time may be described as one designed to foster a world environment in which the American system can survive and flourish. It therefore rejects the concept of isolation and affirms the necessity of our positive participation in the world community.

This broad intention embraces two subsidiary policies. One is a policy which we would probably pursue even if there were no Soviet threat. It is a policy of attempting to develop a healthy international community. The other is the policy of "containing" the Soviet system. These two policies are closely interrelated and interact on one another. Nevertheless, the distinction between them is basically valid and contributes to a clearer understanding of what we are trying to do.

The policy of striving to develop a healthy international community is the long-term constructive effort which we are engaged in. It was this policy which gave rise to our vigorous sponsorship of the United Nations. It is of course the principal reason for our long continuing endeavors to create and now develop the Inter-American system. It, as much as containment, underlay our efforts to rehabilitate Western Europe. Most of our international economic activities can likewise be explained in terms of this policy.

In a world of polarized power, the policies designed to develop a healthy international community are more than ever necessary to our own strength.

As for the policy of "containment", it is one which seeks by all means short of war to (1) block further expansion of Soviet power, (2) expose the falsities of Soviet pretensions, (3) induce a retraction of the Kremlin's control and influence and (4) in general, so foster the seeds of destruction within the Soviet system that the Kremlin is brought at least to the point of modifying its behavior to conform to generally accepted international standards.

It was and continues to be cardinal in this policy that we possess superior overall power in ourselves or in dependable combination with other like-minded nations. One of the most important ingredients of power is military strength. In the concept of "containment", the maintenance of a strong military posture is deemed to be essential for two reasons: (1) as an ultimate guarantee of our national security and (2) as an indispensable backdrop to the conduct of the policy of "containment". Without superior aggregate military strength, in being and readily mobilizable, a policy of "containment"—which is in effect a policy of calculated and gradual coercion—is no more than a policy of bluff.

At the same time, it is essential to the successful conduct of a policy of "containment" that we always leave open the possibility of negotiation with the U.S.S.R. A diplomatic freeze—and we are in one now—tends to defeat the very purposes of "containment" because it raises tensions at the same time that it makes Soviet retractions and adjustments in the direction of moderated behavior more difficult. It also tends to inhibit our initiative and deprives us of opportunities for maintaining a moral ascendency in our struggle with the Soviet system.

In "containment" it is desirable to exert pressure in a fashion which will avoid so far as possible directly challenging Soviet prestige, to keep open the possibility for the U.S.S.R. to retreat before pressure with a minimum loss of face and to secure political advantage from the failure of the Kremlin to yield or take advantage of the openings we leave it.

We have failed to implement adequately these two fundamental aspects of "containment". In the face of obviously mounting Soviet military strength ours has declined relatively. Partly as a by-product of this, but also for other reasons, we now find ourselves at a diplomatic impasse with the Soviet Union, with the Kremlin growing bolder, with both of us holding on grimly to what we have and with ourselves facing difficult decisions.

In examining our capabilities it is relevant to ask at the outset—capabilities for what? The answer cannot be stated solely in the negative terms of resisting the Kremlin design. It includes also our capabilities to attain the fundamental purpose of the United States, and to foster a world environment in which our free society can survive and flourish.

Potentially we have these capabilities. We know we have them in the economic and military fields. Potentially we also have them in the political and psychological fields. The vast majority of Americans are confident that the system of values which animates our society—the principles of freedom, tolerance, the importance of the individual and the supremacy of reason over will—are valid and more vital than the ideology which is the fuel of Soviet dynamism. Translated into terms relevant to the lives of other peoples—our system of values can become perhaps a powerful appeal to millions who now seek or find in authoritarianism a refuge from anxieties, bafflement and insecurity.

Essentially, our democracy also possesses a unique degree of unity. Our society is fundamentally more cohesive than the Soviet system, the solidarity of which is artificially created through force, fear and favor. This means that expressions of national consensus in our society are soundly and solidly based. It means that the possibility of revolution in this country is fundamentally less than that in the Soviet system.

These capabilities within us constitute a great potential force in our international relations. The potential within us of bearing witness to the values by which we live holds promise for a dynamic manifestation to the rest of the world of the vitality of our system. The essential tolerance of our world outlook, our generous and constructive impulses, and the absence of covetousness in our international relations are assets of potentially enormous influence.

These then are our potential capabilities. Between them and our capabilities currently being utilized is a wide gap of unactualized power. In sharp contrast is the situation of the Soviet world. Its capabilites are inferior to those of our Allies and to our own. But they are mobilized close to the maximum possible extent.

The full power which resides within the American people will be evoked only through the traditional democratic process: This process requires, firstly, that sufficient information regarding the basic political, economic and military elements of the present situation be made publicly available so that an intelligent popular opinion may be formed. Having achieved a comprehension of the issues now confronting this Republic, it will then be possible for the American people and the American Government to arrive at a consensus. Out of this common view will develop a determination of the national will and a solid resolute expression of that will. The initiative in this process lies with the Government.

The democratic way is harder than the authoritarian way because, in seeking to protect and fulfill the individual, it demands of him understanding, judgment and positive participation in the increasingly complex and exacting problems of the modern world. It demands that he exercise discrimination: that while pursuing through free inquiry the search for truth he knows when he should commit an act of faith; that he distinguish between the necessity for tolerance and the necessity for just suppression. A free society is vulnerable in that it is easy for people to lapse into excesses—the excesses of a permanently open mind wishfully waiting for evidence that evil design may become noble purpose, the excess of faith becoming prejudice, the excess of tolerance degenerating into indulgence of conspiracy and the excess of resorting to suppression when more moderate measures are not only more appropriate but more effective.

In coping with dictatorial governments acting in secrecy and with speed, we are also vulnerable in that the democratic process necessarily operates in the open and at a deliberate tempo. Weaknesses in our situation are readily apparent and subject to immediate exploitation. This Government therefore cannot afford in the face of the totalitarian challenge to operate on a narrow margin of strength. A democracy can compensate for its natural vulnerability only if it maintains clearly superior overall power in its most inclusive sense.

The very virtues of our system likewise handicap us in certain respects in our relations with our allies. While it is a general source of strength to us that our relations with our allies are conducted on a basis of persuasion and consent rather than compulsion and capitulation, it is also evident that dissent among us can become a vulnerability. Sometimes the dissent has its principal roots abroad in situations about which we can do nothing. Sometimes it arises largely out of certain weaknesses within ourselves, about which we can do something—our native impetuosity and a tendency to expect too much from people widely divergent from us.

The full capabilities of the rest of the free world are a potential increment to our own capabilities. It may even be said that the capabilities of the Soviet world, specifically the capabilities of the masses who have nothing to lose but their Soviet chains, are a potential which can be enlisted on our side.

Like our own capabilities, those of the rest of the free world exceed the capabilities of the Soviet system. Like our own they are far from being effectively mobilized and employed in the struggle against the Kremlin design. This is so because the rest of the free world lacks a sense of unity, confidence and common purpose. This is true in even the most homogeneous and advanced segment of the free world—Western Europe.

As we ourselves demonstrate power, confidence and a sense of moral and political direction, so those same qualities will be evoked in Western Europe. In such a situation, we may also anticipate a general improvement in the political tone in Latin America, Asia and Africa and the real beginnings of awakening among the Soviet totalitariat.

In the absence of affirmative decision on our part, the rest of the free world is almost certain to become demoralized. Our friends will become more than a liability to us; they can eventually become a positive increment to Soviet power.

In sum, the capabilities of our allies are in an important sense, a function of our own. An affirmative decision to summon up the potential within ourselves would evoke the potential strength within others and add it to our own.

B. *Economic*

1. Capabilities. In contrast to the war economy of the Soviet world (cf. Ch. V-B), the American economy (and the economy of the free world as a whole) is at present directed to the provision of rising standards of living. The military budget of the United States represents 6 to 7 percent of its gross national product (as against 13.8 percent for the Soviet Union). Our North Atlantic Treaty allies devoted 4.8 percent of their national product to military purposes in 1949.

This difference in emphasis between the two economies means that the readiness of the free world to support a war effort is tending to decline relative to that of the Soviet Union. There is little direct investment in production facilities for military end-products and in dispersal. There are relatively few men receiving military training and a relatively low rate of production of weapons. However, given time to convert to a war effort, the capabilities of the United States economy and also of the Western European economy would be tremendous. In the light of Soviet military capabilities, a question which may be of decisive importance in the event of war is the question whether there will be time to mobilize our superior human and material resources for a war effort (cf. Chs. VIII and IX).

The capability of the American economy to support a build-up of economic and military strength at home and to assist a build-up abroad is limited not, as in the case of the Soviet Union, so much by the ability to produce as by the decision on the proper allocation of resources to this and other purposes. Even Western Europe could afford to assign a substantially larger proportion of its resources to defense, if the necessary foundation in public understanding and will could be laid, and if the assistance needed to meet its dollar deficit were provided.

A few statistics will help to clarify this point.

*Percentage of Gross Available Resources
Allocated to Investment, National Defense,
and Consumption in East and West, 1949*

(in percent of total)

Country	Gross Investment	Defense	Consumption
U.S.S.R.	25.4	13.8	60.8
Soviet Orbit	22.0[4]	4.0[5]	74.0[4]
U.S.	13.6	6.5	79.9
European NAP[6] countries	20.4	4.8	74.8

4. Crude estimate. [Note in source text]
5. Includes Soviet zone of Germany; otherwise 5 percent. [Note in source text]
6. North Atlantic Pact. [Ed. note]

The Soviet Union is now allocating nearly 40 percent of its gross available resources to military purposes and investment, much of which is in war-supporting industries. It is estimated that even in an emergency the Soviet Union could not increase this proportion to much more than 50 percent, or by one-fourth. The United States, on the other hand, is allocating only about 20 percent of its resources to defense and investment (or 22 percent including foreign assistance), and little of its investment outlays are directed to war-supporting industries. In an emergency the United States could allocate more than 50 percent of its resources to military purposes and foreign assistance, or five to six times as much as at present.

The same point can be brought out by statistics on the use of important products. The Soviet Union is using 14 percent of its ingot steel, 47 percent of its military aluminum, and 18.5 percent of its crude oil for military purposes, while the corresponding percentages for the United States are 1.7, 8.6, and 5.6. Despite the tremendously larger production of these goods in the United States than the Soviet Union, the latter is actually using, for military purposes, nearly twice as much steel as the United States and 8 to 26 percent more aluminum.

Perhaps the most impressive indication of the economic superiority of the free world over the Soviet world which can be made on the basis of available data is provided in the following comparisons (based mainly on the *Economic Survey of Europe, 1948*): [7]

It should be noted that these comparisons understate the relative position of the NAT countries for several reasons: (1) Canada is excluded because comparable data were not available; (2) the data for the U.S.S.R. are the 1950 targets (as stated in the fourth five-year plan) rather than actual rates of production and are believed to exceed in many cases the production actually achieved; (3) the data for the European NAT counties are actual data for 1948, and production has generally increased since that time.

Furthermore, the United States could achieve a substantial absolute increase in output and could thereby increase the allocation of resources to a build-up of the economic and military strength of itself and its allies without suffering a decline in its real standard of living. Industrial production declined by 10 percent between the first quarter of 1948 and the last quarter of 1949, and by approximately one-fourth between 1944 and 1949. In March 1950 there were approximately 4,750,000 unemployed, as compared to 1,070,000 in 1943 and 670,000 in 1944. The gross national product de-

7. United Nations, Economic Commission for Europe, *Economic Survey of Europe in 1948* (Geneva, 1949). [Ed. note]

Comparative Statistics on Economic
Capabilities of East and West

	U.S. 1948–9	European NAT Countries 1948–9	Total	U.S.S.R. (1950 Plan)	Satellites 1948–9	Total
Population (millions)	149	173	322	198[8]	75	273
Employment in nonagricultural establishments (millions)	45	—	—	31[8]	—	—
Gross national production (billion dollars)	250	84	334	65[8]	21	86
National income per capita (current dollars)	1,700	480	1,040	330	280	315
Production data—[9] coal (million tons)	582	306	888	250	88	338
Electric power (billion kwh)	356	124	480	82	15	97
Crude petroleum (million tons)	277	1	278	35	5	40
Pig iron (million tons)	55	24	79	19.5	3.2	22.7
Steel (million tons)	80	32	112	25	6	31
Cement (million tons)	35	21	56	10.5	2.1	12.6
Motor vehicles (thousands)	5,273	580	5,853	500	25	525

8. 1949 data. [Note in source text]
9. For the European NAT countries and for the satellites, the data include only output by major producers. [Note in source text]

clined slowly in 1949 from the peak reached in 1948 ($262 billion in 1948 to an annual rate of $256 billion in the last six months of 1949), and in terms of constant prices declined by about 20 percent between 1944 and 1948.

With a high level of economic activity, the United States could soon attain a gross national product of $300 billion per year, as was pointed out in the President's Economic Report (January 1950). Progress in this direction would permit, and might itself be aided by, a build-up of the economic and military strength of the United States and the free world; furthermore, if a dynamic expansion of the economy were achieved, the necessary build-up could be accomplished without a decrease in the national standard of living because the required resources could be obtained by siphoning off a part of the annual increment in the gross national product. These are facts of fundamental importance in considering the courses of action open to the United States (cf. Ch. IX).

2. *Intentions.* Foreign economic policy is a major instrument in the conduct of United States foreign relations. It is an instrument which can powerfully influence the world environment in ways favorable to the security and welfare of this country. It is also an instrument which, if unwisely formulated and employed, can do actual harm to our national interests. It is an instrument uniquely suited to our capabilities, provided we have the tenacity of purpose and the understanding requisite to a realization of its potentials. Finally, it is an instrument peculiarly appropriate to the cold war.

The preceding analysis has indicated that an essential element in a program to frustrate the Kremlin design is the development of a successfully functioning system among the free nations. It is clear that economic conditions are among the fundamental determinants of the will and the strength to resist subversion and aggression.

United States foreign economic policy has been designed to assist in the building of such a system and such conditions in the free world. The principal features of this policy can be summarized as follows:

(1) assistance to Western Europe in recovery and the creation of a viable economy (the European Recovery Program);

(2) assistance to other countries because of their special needs arising out of the war or the cold war and our special interests in or responsibility for meeting them (grant assistance to Japan, the Philippines, and Korea, loans and credits by the Export-Import Bank, the International Monetary Fund, and the International Bank to Indonesia, Yugoslavia, Iran, etc.);

(3) assistance in the development of under-developed areas (the Point IV program and loans and credits to various countries, overlapping to some extent with those mentioned under 2);

(4) military assistance to the North Atlantic Treaty countries, Greece, Turkey, etc.;

(5) restriction of East-West trade in items of military importance to the East;

(6) purchase and stockpiling of strategic materials; and

(7) efforts to re-establish an international economy based on multilateral trade, declining trade barriers, and convertible currencies (the

GATT-ITO program, the Reciprocal Trade Agreements program, the IMF-IBRD program, and the program now being developed to solve the problem of the United States balance of payments).

In both short and long term aspects, these policies and programs are directed to the strengthening of the free world and therefore to the frustration of the Kremlin design. Despite certain inadequacies and inconsistencies, which are now being studied in connection with the problem of the United States balance of payments, the United States has generally pursued a foreign economic policy which has powerfully supported its overall objectives. The question must nevertheless be asked whether current and currently projected programs will adequately support this policy in the future, in terms both of need and urgency.

The last year has been indecisive in the economic field. The Soviet Union has made considerable progress in integrating the satellite economies of Eastern Europe into the Soviet economy, but still faces very large problems, especially with China. The free nations have important accomplishments to record, but also have tremendous problems still ahead. On balance, neither side can claim any great advantage in this field over its relative position a year ago. The important question therefore becomes: what are the trends?

Several conclusions seem to emerge. First, the Soviet Union is widening the gap between its preparedness for war and the unpreparedness of the free world for war. It is devoting a far greater *proportion* of its resources to military purposes than are the free nations and, in significant components of military power, a greater *absolute* quantity of resources. Second, the Communist success in China, taken with the politico-economic situation in the rest of South and South-East Asia, provides a springboard for a further incursion in this troubled area. Although Communist China faces serious economic problems which may impose some strains on the Soviet economy, it is probable that the social and economic problems faced by the free nations in this area present more than offsetting opportunities for Communist expansion. Third, the Soviet Union holds positions in Europe which, if it maneuvers skillfully, could be used to do great damage to the Western European economy and to the maintenance of the Western orientation of certain countries, particularly Germany and Austria. Fourth, despite (and in part because of) the Titoist defection, the Soviet Union has accelerated its efforts to integrate satellite economy with its own and to increase the degree of autarchy within the areas under its control.

Fifth, meanwhile, Western Europe, with American (and Canadian) assistance, has achieved a record level of production. However, it faces the prospect of a rapid tapering off of American assistance without the possibility of achieving, by its own efforts, a satisfactory equilibrium with the dollar area. It has also made very little progress toward "economic integration", which would in the long run tend to improve its productivity and to provide an economic environment conducive to political stability. In particular, the movement towards economic integration does not appear to be rapid enough to provide Western Germany with adequate economic opportunities in the West. The United Kingdom still faces economic problems which may require a moderate but politically difficult decline in the British standard of living or more American assistance than is contemplated. At the same time, a strengthening of the British position is needed if the stability of the Commonwealth is not to be impaired and if it is to be a focus of resistance to Communist expansion in South and South-East Asia. Improvement of the British position is also vital in building up the defensive capabilities of Western Europe.

Sixth, throughout Asia the stability of the present moderate governments, which are more in sympathy with our purposes than any probable successor regimes would be, is doubtful. The problem is only in part an economic one. Assistance in economic development is important as a means of holding out to the peoples of Asia some prospect of improvement in standards of living under their present governments. But probably more important are a strengthening of central institutions, an improvement in administration, and generally a development of an economic and social structure within which the peoples of Asia can make more effective use of their great human and material resources.

Seventh, and perhaps most important, there are indications of a let-down of United States efforts under the pressure of the domestic budgetary situation, disillusion resulting from excessively optimistic expectations about the duration and results of our assistance programs, and doubts about the wisdom of continuing to strengthen the free nations as against preparedness measures in light of the intensity of the cold war.

Eighth, there are grounds for predicting that the United States and other free nations will within a period of a few years at most experience a decline in economic activity of serious proportions unless more positive governmental programs are developed than are now available.

In short, as we look into the future, the programs now planned will not meet the requirements of the free nations. The difficulty does not lie so much in the inadequacy or misdirection of policy as in the inadequacy of planned programs, in terms of timing or impact, to achieve our objectives.

The risks inherent in this situation are set forth in the following chapter and a course of action designed to reinvigorate our efforts in order to reverse the present trends and to achieve our fundamental purpose is outlined in Chapter IX.

C. *Military*

The United States now possesses the greatest military potential of any single nation in the world. The military weaknesses of the United States vis-à-vis the Soviet Union, however, include its numerical inferiority in forces in being and in total manpower. Coupled with the inferiority of forces in being, the United States also lacks tenable positions from which to employ its forces in event of war and munitions power in being and readily available.

It is true that the United States armed forces are now stronger than ever before in other times of apparent peace; it is also true that there exists a sharp disparity between our actual military strength and our commitments. The relationship of our strength to our present commitments, however, is not alone the governing factor. The world situation, as well as commitments, should govern; hence, our military strength more properly should be related to the world situation confronting us. When our military strength is related to the world situation and balanced against the likely exigencies of such a situation, it is clear that our military strength is becoming dangerously inadequate.

If war should begin in 1950, the United States and its allies will have the military capability of conducting defensive operations to provide a reasonable measure of protection to the Western Hemisphere, bases in the Western Pacific, and essential military lines of communication; and an inadequate measure of protection to vital military bases in the United Kingdom and in the Near and Middle East. We will have the capability of conducting powerful offensive air operations against vital elements of the Soviet warmaking capacity.

The scale of the operations listed in the preceding paragraph is limited by the effective forces and material in being of the United States and its allies vis-à-vis the Soviet Union. Consistant with the aggressive threat facing us and in consonance with overall strategic plans, the United States must provide to its allies on a continuing basis as large amounts of military assistance as possible without serious detriment to United States operational requirements.

If the potential military capabilities of the United States and its allies were rapidly and effectively developed, sufficient forces could be produced to deter war, or if the Soviet Union chooses war, to withstand the initial Soviet attacks, to stabilize supporting attacks, and to retaliate in turn with even greater impact on the Soviet capabilities. From the military point of view alone, however, this would require not only the generation of the necessary military forces but also the development and stockpiling of improved weapons of all types.

Under existing peacetime conditions, a period of from two to three years is required to produce a material increase in military power. Such increased power could be provided in a somewhat shorter period in a declared period of emergency or in wartime through a full-out national effort. Any increase in military power in peacetime, however, should be related both to its probable military role in war, to the implementation of immediate and long-term United States foreign policy vis-à-vis the Soviet Union and to the realities of the existing situation. If such a course of increasing our military power is adopted now, the United States would have the capability of eliminating the disparity between its military strength and the exigencies of the situation we face; eventually of gaining the initiative in the "cold" war and of materially delaying if not stopping the Soviet offensives in war itself.

VII. PRESENT RISKS

A. *General*

It is apparent from the preceding sections that the integrity and vitality of our system is in greater jeopardy than ever before in our history. Even if there were no Soviet Union we would face the great problem of the free society, accentuated many fold in this industrial age, of reconciling order, security, the need for participation, with the requirements of freedom. We would face the fact that in a shrinking world the absence of order among nations is becoming less and less tolerable. The Kremlin design seeks to impose order among nations by means which would destroy our free and democratic system. The Kremlin's possession of atomic weapons puts new power behind its design, and increases the jeopardy to our system. It adds new strains to the uneasy equilibrium-without-order which exists in the world and raises new doubts in men's minds whether the world will long tolerate this tension without moving toward some kind of order, on somebody's terms.

The risks we face are of a new order of magnitude, commensurate with the total struggle in which we are engaged. For a free society there is never total victory, since freedom and democracy are never wholly attained, are

always in the process of being attained. But defeat at the hands of the totalitarian is total defeat. These risks crowd in on us, in a shrinking world of polarized power, so as to give us no choice, ultimately, between meeting them effectively or being overcome by them.

B. *Specific*

It is quite clear from Soviet theory and practice that the Kremlin seeks to bring the free world under its dominion by the methods of the cold war. The preferred technique is to subvert by infiltration and intimidation. Every institution of our society is an instrument which it is sought to stultify and turn against our purposes. Those that touch most closely our material and moral strength are obviously the prime targets, labor unions, civic enterprises, schools, churches, and all media for influencing opinion. The effort is not so much to make them serve obvious Soviet ends as to prevent them from serving our ends, and thus to make them sources of confusion in our economy, our culture and our body politic. The doubts and diversities that in terms of our values are part of the merit of a free system, the weaknesses and the problems that are peculiar to it, the rights and privileges that free men enjoy, and the disorganization and destruction left in the wake of the last attack on our freedoms, all are but opportunities for the Kremlin to do its evil work. Every advantage is taken of the fact that our means of prevention and retaliation are limited by these principles and scruples which are precisely the ones that give our freedom and democracy its meaning for us. None of our scruples deter those whose only code is, ''morality is that which serves the revolution''.

Since everything that gives us or others respect for our institutions is a suitable object for attack, it also fits the Kremlin's design that where, with impunity, we can be insulted and made to suffer indignity the opportunity shall not be missed, particularly in any context which can be used to cast dishonor on our country, our system, our motives, or our methods. Thus the means by which we sought to restore our own economic health in the '30's, and now seek to restore that of the free world, come equally under attack. The military aid by which we sought to help the free world was frantically denounced by the Communists in the early days of the last war, and of course our present efforts to develop adequate military strength for ourselves and our allies are equally denounced.

At the same time the Soviet Union is seeking to create overwhelming military force, in order to back up infiltration with intimidation. In the only terms in which it understands strength, it is seeking to demonstrate to the free world that force and the will to use it are on the side of the Kremlin, that those who lack it are decadent and doomed. In local incidents it threatens and encroaches both for the sake of local gains and to increase anxiety and defeatism in all the free world.

The possession of atomic weapons at each of the opposite poles of power, and the inability (for different reasons) of either side to place any trust in the other, puts a premium on a surprise attack against us. It equally puts a premium on a more violent and ruthless prosecution of its design by cold war, especially if the Kremlin is sufficiently objective to realize the improbability of our prosecuting a preventive war. It also puts a premium on piecemeal aggression against others, counting on our unwillingness to engage in atomic war unless we are directly attacked. We run all these risks and the added risk of being confused and immobilized by our inability to weigh and choose, and pursue a firm course based on a rational assessment of each.

The risk that we may thereby be prevented or too long delayed in taking all needful measures to maintain the integrity and vitality of our system is great. The risk that our allies will lose their determination is greater. And the risk that in this manner a descending spiral of too little and too late, of doubt and recrimination, may present us with ever narrower and more desperate alternatives, is the greatest risk of all. For example, it is clear that our present weakness would prevent us from offering effective resistance at any of several vital pressure points. The only deterrent we can present to the Kremlin is the evidence we give that we may make any of the critical points which we cannot hold the occasion for a global war of annihilation.

The risk of having no better choice than to capitulate or precipitate a global war at any of a number of pressure points is bad enough in itself, but it is multiplied by the weakness it imparts to our position in the cold war. Instead of appearing strong and resolute we are continually at the verge of appearing and being alternately irresolute and desperate; yet it is the cold war which we must win, because both the Kremlin design, and our fundamental purpose give it the first priority.

The frustration of the Kremlin design, however, cannot be accomplished by us alone, as will appear from the analysis in Chapter IX, B. Strength at the center, in the United States, is only the first of two essential elements. The second is that our allies and potential allies do not as a result of a sense of frustration or of Soviet intimidation drift into a course of neutrality eventually leading to Soviet domination. If this were to happen in Germany the effect upon Western Europe and eventually upon us might be catastrophic.

But there are risks in making ourselves strong. A large measure of sacrifice and discipline will be demanded of the American people. They will be asked to give up some of the benefits which they have come to associate with their freedoms. Nothing could be more important than that they fully understand the reasons for this. The risks of a superficial understanding or of an inadequate appreciation of the issues are obvious and might lead to the adoption of measures which in themselves would jeopardize the integrity of our system. At any point in the process of demonstrating our will to make good our fundamental purpose, the Kremlin may decide to precipitate a general war, or in testing us, may go too far. These are risks we will invite by making ourselves strong, but they are lesser risks than those we seek to avoid. Our fundamental purpose is more likely to be defeated from lack of the will to maintain it, than from any mistakes we may make or assault we may undergo because of asserting that will. No people in history have preserved their freedom who thought that by not being strong enough to protect themselves they might prove inoffensive to their enemies.

VIII. ATOMIC ARMAMENTS

A. *Military evaluation of U.S. and U.S.S.R. atomic capabilities.*

1. The United States now has an atomic capability, including both numbers and deliverability, estimated to be adequate, if effectively utilized, to deliver a serious blow against the war-making capacity of the U.S.S.R. It is doubted whether such a blow, even if it resulted in the complete destruction of the contemplated target systems, would cause the U.S.S.R. to sue for terms or prevent Soviet forces from occupying Western Europe against such ground resistance as could presently be mobilized. A very serious initial blow could, however, so reduce the capabilities of the U.S.S.R. to supply and equip its military organization and its civilian population as to give the United States the prospect of developing a general military superiority in a war of long duration.

2. As the atomic capability of the U.S.S.R. increases, it will have an increased ability to hit at our atomic bases and installations and thus seriously hamper the ability of the United States to carry out an attack such as that outlined above. It is quite possible that in the near future the U.S.S.R. will have a sufficient number of atomic bombs and a sufficient deliverability to raise a question whether Britain with its present inadequate air defense could be relied upon as an advance base from which a major portion of the U.S. attack could be launched.

It is estimated that, within the next four years, the U.S.S.R. will attain the capability of seriously damaging vital centers of the United States, provided it strikes a surprise blow and provided further that the blow is opposed by no more effective opposition than we now have programmed. Such a blow could so seriously damage the United States as to greatly reduce its superiority in economic potential.

Effective opposition to this Soviet capability will require among other measures greatly increased air warning systems, air defenses, and vigorous development and implementation of a civilian defense program which has been thoroughly integrated with the military defense systems.

In time the atomic capability of the U.S.S.R. can be expected to grow to a point where, given surprise and no more effective opposition than we now have programmed, the possibility of a decisive initial attack cannot be excluded.

3. In the initial phases of an atomic war, the advantages of initiative and surprise would be very great. A police state living behind an iron curtain has an enormous advantage in maintaining the necessary security and centralization of decision required to capitalize on this advantage.

4. For the moment our atomic retaliatory capability is probably adequate to deter the Kremlin from a deliberate direct military attack against ourselves or other free peoples. However, when it calculates that it has a sufficient atomic capability to make a surprise attack on us, nullifying our atomic superiority and creating a military situation decisively in its favor, the Kremlin might be tempted to strike swiftly and with stealth. The existence of two large atomic capabilities in such a relationship might well act, therefore, not as a deterrent, but as an incitement to war.

5. A further increase in the number and power of our atomic weapons is necessary in order to assure the effectiveness of any U.S. retaliatory blow, but would not of itself seem to change the basic logic of the above points. Greatly increased general air, ground and sea strength, and increased air defense and civilian defense programs would also be necessary to provide reasonable assurance that the free world could survive an initial surprise atomic attack of the weight which it is estimated the U.S.S.R. will be capable of delivering by 1954 and still permit the free world to go on to the eventual attainment of its objectives. Furthermore, such a build-up of strength could safeguard and increase our retaliatory power, and thus might put off for some time the date when the Soviet Union could calculate that a surprise blow would be advantageous. This would provide additional time for the effects of our policies to produce a modification of the Soviet system.

6. If the U.S.S.R. develops a thermonuclear weapon ahead of the U.S., the risks of greatly increased Soviet pressure against all the free world, or an attack against the U.S., will be greatly increased.

7. If the U.S. develops a thermonuclear weapon ahead of the U.S.S.R., the U.S. should for the time being be able to bring increased pressure on the U.S.S.R.

B. *Stockpiling and Use of Atomic Weapons*

1. From the foregoing analysis it appears that it would be to the long-term advantage of the United States if atomic weapons were to be effectively eliminated from national peacetime armaments; the additional objectives which must be secured if there is to be a reasonable prospect of such effective elimination of atomic weapons are discussed in Chapter IX. In the absence of such elimination and the securing of these objectives, it would appear that we have no alternative but to increase our atomic capability as rapidly as other considerations make appropriate. In either case, it appears to be imperative to increase as rapidly as possible our general air, ground and sea strength and that of our allies to a point where we are militarily not so heavily dependent on atomic weapons.

2. As is indicated in Chapter IV, it is important that the United States employ military force only if the necessity for its use is clear and compelling and commends itself to the overwhelming majority of our people. The United States cannot therefore engage in war except as a reaction to aggression of so clear and compelling a nature as to bring the overwhelming majority of our people to accept the use of military force. In the event war comes, our use of force must be to compel the acceptance of our objectives and must be congruent to the range of tasks which we may encounter.

In the event of a general war with the U.S.S.R., it must be anticipated that atomic weapons will be used by each side in the manner it deems best suited to accomplish its objectives. In view of our vulnerability to Soviet atomic attack, it has been argued that we might wish to hold our atomic weapons only for retaliation against prior use by the U.S.S.R. To be able to do so and still have hope of achieving our objectives, the non-atomic military capabilities of ourselves and our allies would have to be fully developed and the political weaknesses of the Soviet Union fully exploited. In the event of war, however, we could not be sure that we could move toward the attainment of these objectives without the U.S.S.R.'s resorting sooner or later to the use of its atomic weapons. Only if we had overwhelming atomic superiority and obtained command of the air might the U.S.S.R. be deterred from employing its atomic weapons as we progressed toward the attainment of our objectives.

In the event the U.S.S.R. develops by 1954 the atomic capability which we now anticipate, it is hardly conceivable that, if war comes, the Soviet leaders would refrain from the use of atomic weapons unless they felt fully confident of attaining their objectives by other means.

In the event we use atomic weapons either in retaliation for their prior use by the U.S.S.R. or because there is no alternative method by which we can attain our objectives, it is imperative that the strategic and tactical targets against which they are used be appropriate and the manner in which they are used be consistent with those objectives.

It appears to follow from the above that we should produce and stockpile thermonuclear weapons in the event they prove feasible and would add significantly to our net capability. Not enough is yet known of their potentialities to warrant a judgment at this time regarding their use in war to attain our objectives.

3. It has been suggested that we announce that we will not use atomic weapons except in retaliation against the prior use of such weapons by an aggressor. It has been argued that such a declaration would decrease the danger of an atomic attack against the United States and its allies.

In our present situation of relative unpreparedness in conventional weapons, such a declaration would be interpreted by the U.S.S.R. as an admission of great weakness and by our allies as a clear indication that we intended to abandon them. Furthermore, it is doubtful whether such a declaration would be taken sufficiently seriously by the Kremlin to constitute an important factor in determining whether or not to attack the United States. It is to be anticipated that the Kremlin would weigh the facts of our capability far more heavily than a declaration of what we proposed to do with that capability.

Unless we are prepared to abandon our objectives, we cannot make such a declaration in good faith until we are confident that we will be in a position to attain our objectives without war, or, in the event of war, without recourse to the use of atomic weapons for strategic or tactical purposes.

C. *International Control of Atomic Energy*

1. A discussion of certain of the basic considerations involved in securing effective international control is necessary to make clear why the additional objectives discussed in Chapter IX must be secured.

2. No system of international control could prevent the production and use of atomic weapons in the event of a prolonged war. Even the most effective system of international control could, of itself, only provide (a) assurance that atomic weapons had been eliminated from national peacetime armaments and (b) immediate notice of a violation. In essence, an effective

international control system would be expected to assure a certain amount of time after notice of violation before atomic weapons could be used in war.

3. The time period between notice of violation and possible use of atomic weapons in war which a control system could be expected to assure depends upon a number of factors.

The dismantling of existing stockpiles of bombs and the destruction of casings and firing mechanisms could by themselves give little assurance of securing time. Casings and firing mechanisms are presumably easy to produce, even surreptitiously, and the assembly of weapons does not take much time.

If existing stocks of fissionable materials were in some way eliminated and the future production of fissionable materials effectively controlled, war could not start with a surprise atomic attack.

In order to assure an appreciable time lag between notice of violation and the time when atomic weapons might be available in quantity, it would be necessary to destroy all plants capable of making large amounts of fissionable material. Such action would, however, require a moratorium on those possible peacetime uses which call for large quantities of fissionable materials.

Effective control over the production and stockpiling of raw materials might further extend the time period which effective international control would assure. Now that the Russians have learned the technique of producing atomic weapons, the time between violation of an international control agreement and production of atomic weapons will be shorter than was estimated in 1946, except possibly in the field of thermonuclear or other new types of weapons.

4. The certainty of notice of violation also depends upon a number of factors. In the absence of good faith, it is to be doubted whether any system can be designed which will give certainty of notice of violation. International ownership of raw materials and fissionable materials and international ownership and operation of dangerous facilities, coupled with inspection based on continuous unlimited freedom of access to all parts of the Soviet Union (as well as to all parts of the territory of other signatories to the control agreement) appear to be necessary to give the requisite degree of assurance against secret violations. As the Soviet stockpile of fissionable materials grows, the amount which the U.S.S.R. might secretly withhold and not declare to the inspection agency grows. In this sense, the earlier an agreement is consummated the greater the security it would offer. The possibility of successful secret production operations also increases with developments

which may reduce the size and power consumption of individual reactors. The development of a thermonuclear bomb would increase many fold the damage a given amount of fissionable material could do and would, therefore, vastly increase the danger that a decisive advantage could be gained through secret operations.

5. The relative sacrifices which would be involved in international control need also to be considered. If it were possible to negotiate an effective system of international control the United States would presumably sacrifice a much larger stockpile of atomic weapons and a much larger production capacity than would the U.S.S.R. The opening up of national territory to international inspection involved in an adequate control and inspection system would have a far greater impact on the U.S.S.R. than on the United States. If the control system involves the destruction of all large reactors and thus a moratorium on certain possible peacetime uses, the U.S.S.R. can be expected to argue that it, because of greater need for new sources of energy, would be making a greater sacrifice in this regard than the United States.

6. The United States and the peoples of the world as a whole desire a respite from the dangers of atomic warfare. The chief difficulty lies in the danger that the respite would be short and that we might not have adequate notice of its pending termination. For such an arrangement to be in the interest of the United States, it is essential that the agreement be entered into in good faith by both sides and the probability against its violation high.

7. The most substantial contribution to security of an effective international control system would, of course, be the opening up of the Soviet Union, as required under the U.N. plan. Such opening up is not, however, compatible with the maintenance of the Soviet system in its present rigor. This is a major reason for the Soviet refusal to accept the U.N. plan.

The studies which began with the Acheson-Lilienthal committee[10] and culminated in the present U.N. plan made it clear that inspection of atomic facilities would not alone give the assurance of control; but that ownership and operation by an international authority of the world's atomic energy activities from the mine to the last use of fissionable materials was also essential. The delegation of sovereignty which this implies is necessary for effective control and, therefore, is as necessary for the United States and the rest of the free world as it is presently unacceptable to the Soviet Union.

It is also clear that a control authority not susceptible directly or indirectly

10. Committee chaired by Under-Secretary of State Dean Acheson and David E. Lilienthal, Chairman of the Tennessee Valley Authority, which in early 1946 drafted a preliminary version of the Baruch Plan for the international control of atomic weapons. [Ed. note]

to Soviet domination is equally essential. As the Soviet Union would regard any country not under its domination as under the potential if not the actual domination of the United States, it is clear that what the United States and the non-Soviet world must insist on, the Soviet Union must at present reject.

The principal immediate benefit of international control would be to make a surprise atomic attack impossible, assuming the elimination of large reactors and the effective disposal of stockpiles of fissionable materials. But it is almost certain that the Soviet Union would not agree to the elimination of large reactors, unless the impracticability of producing atomic power for peaceful purposes had been demonstrated beyond a doubt. By the same token, it would not now agree to elimination of its stockpile of fissionable materials.

Finally, the absence of good faith on the part of the U.S.S.R. must be assumed until there is concrete evidence that there has been a decisive change in Soviet policies. It is to be doubted whether such a change can take place without a change in the nature of the Soviet system itself.

The above considerations make it clear that at least a major change in the relative power positions of the United States and the Soviet Union would have to take place before an effective system of international control could be negotiated. The Soviet Union would have had to have moved a substantial distance down the path of accommodation and compromise before such an arrangement would be conceivable. This conclusion is supported by the Third Report of the United Nations Atomic Energy Commission to the Security Council, May 17, 1948, in which it is stated that ". . . the majority of the Commission has been unable to secure . . . their acceptance of the nature and extent of participation in the world community required of all nations in this field. . . . As a result, the Commission has been forced to recognize that agreement on effective measures for the control of atomic energy is itself dependent on cooperation in broader fields of policy."

In short, it is impossible to hope that an effective plan for international control can be negotiated unless and until the Kremlin design has been frustrated to a point at which a genuine and drastic change in Soviet policies has taken place.

IX. POSSIBLE COURSES OF ACTION

Introduction. Four possible courses of action by the United States in the present situation can be distinguished. They are:

    a. Continuation of current policies, with current and currently projected programs for carrying out these policies;

b. Isolation;

c. War; and

d. A more rapid building up of the political, economic, and military strength of the free world than provided under a, with the purpose of reaching, if possible, a tolerable state of order among nations without war and of preparing to defend ourselves in the event that the free world is attacked.

The role of negotiation. Negotiation must be considered in relation to these courses of action. A negotiator always attempts to achieve an agreement which is somewhat better than the realities of his fundamental position would justify and which is, in any case, not worse than his fundamental position requires. This is as true in relations among sovereign states as in relations between individuals. The Soviet Union possesses several advantages over the free world in negotiations on any issue:

a. It can and does enforce secrecy on all significant facts about conditions within the Soviet Union, so that it can be expected to know more about the realities of the free world's position than the free world knows about its position;

b. It does not have to be responsive in any important sense to public opinion;

c. It does not have to consult and agree with any other countries on the terms it will offer and accept; and

d. It can influence public opinion in other countries while insulating the peoples under its control.

These are important advantages. Together with the unfavorable trend of our power position, they militate, as is shown in Section A below, against successful negotiation of a general settlement at this time. For although the United States probably now possesses, principally in atomic weapons, a force adequate to deliver a powerful blow upon the Soviet Union and to open the road to victory in a long war, it is not sufficient by itself to advance the position of the United States in the cold war.

The problem is to create such political and economic conditions in the free world, backed by force sufficient to inhibit Soviet attack, that the Kremlin will accommodate itself to these conditions, gradually withdraw, and eventually change its policies drastically. It has been shown in Chapter VIII that truly effective control of atomic energy would require such an opening up of the Soviet Union and such evidence in other ways of its good faith and its intent to co-exist in peace as to reflect or at least initiate a change in the Soviet system.

Clearly under present circumstances we will not be able to negotiate a settlement which calls for a change in the Soviet system. What, then, is the role of negotiation?

In the first place, the public in the United States and in other free countries will require, as a condition to firm policies and adequate progress directed to the frustration of the Kremlin design, that the free world be continuously prepared to negotiate agreements with the Soviet Union on equitable terms. It is still argued by many people here and abroad that equitable agreements with the Soviet Union are possible, and this view will gain force if the Soviet Union begins to show signs of accommodation, even on unimportant issues.

The free countries must always, therefore, be prepared to negotiate and must be ready to take the initiative at times in seeking negotiation. They must develop a negotiating position which defines the issues and the terms on which they would be prepared—and at what stages—to accept agreements with the Soviet Union. The terms must be fair in the view of popular opinion in the free world. This means that they must be consistent with a positive program for peace—in harmony with the United Nations' Charter and providing, at a minimum, for the effective control of all armaments by the United Nations or a successor organization. The terms must not require more of the Soviet Union than such behavior and such participation in a world organization. The fact that such conduct by the Soviet Union is impossible without such a radical change in Soviet policies as to constitute a change in the Soviet system would then emerge as a result of the Kremlin's unwillingness to accept such terms or of its bad faith in observing them.

A sound negotiating position is, therefore, an essential element in the ideological conflict. For some time after a decision to build up strength, any offer of, or attempt at, negotiation of a general settlement along the lines of the Berkeley speech [11] by the Secretary of State could be only a tactic. [12] Nev-

11. Speech by Dean Acheson at the University of California, Berkeley, March 16, 1950. For text, see the *Department of State Bulletin*, XXII (March 27, 1950), 473–78. [Ed. note]

12. The Secretary of State listed seven areas in which the Soviet Union could modify its behavior in such a way as to permit coexistence in reasonable security. These were:

1. Treaties of peace with Austria, Germany, Japan and relaxation of pressures in the Far East;
2. Withdrawal of Soviet forces and influence from satellite areas;
3. Cooperation in the United Nations;
4. Control of atomic energy and/or conventional armaments;
5. Abandonment of indirect aggression;
6. Proper treatment of official representatives of the United States;
7. Increased access to the Soviet Union of persons and ideas from other countries. [Note in source text]

ertheless, concurrently with a decision and a start on building up the strength of the free world, it may be desirable to pursue this tactic both to gain public support for the program and to minimize the immediate risks of war. It is urgently necessary for the United States to determine its negotiating position and to obtain agreement with its major allies on the purposes and terms of negotiation.

In the second place, assuming that the United States in cooperation with other free countries decides and acts to increase the strength of the free world and assuming that the Kremlin chooses the path of accommodation, it will from time to time be necessary and desirable to negotiate on various specific issues with the Kremlin as the area of possible agreement widens.

The Kremlin will have three major objectives in negotiations with the United States. The first is to eliminate the atomic capabilities of the United States; the second is to prevent the effective mobilization of the superior potential of the free world in human and material resources; and the third is to secure a withdrawal of United States forces from, and commitments to, Europe and Japan. Depending on its evaluation of its own strengths and weaknesses as against the West's (particularly the ability and will of the West to sustain its efforts), it will or will not be prepared to make important concessions to achieve these major objectives. It is unlikely that the Kremlin's evaluation is such that it would now be prepared to make significant concessions.

The objectives of the United States and other free countries in negotiations with the Soviet Union (apart from the ideological objectives discussed above) are to record, in a formal fashion which will facilitate the consolidation and further advance of our position, the process of Soviet accommodation to the new political, psychological, and economic conditions in the world which will result from adoption of the fourth course of action and which will be supported by the increasing military strength developed as an integral part of that course of action. In short, our objectives are to record, where desirable, the gradual withdrawal of the Soviet Union and to facilitate that process by making negotiation, if possible, always more expedient than resort to force.

It must be presumed that for some time the Kremlin will accept agreements only if it is convinced that by acting in bad faith whenever and wherever there is an opportunity to do so with impunity, it can derive greater advantage from the agreements than the free world. For this reason, we must take care that any agreements are enforceable or that they are not susceptible of violation without detection and the possibility of effective countermeasures.

This further suggests that we will have to consider carefully the order in which agreements can be concluded. Agreement on the control of atomic energy would result in a relatively greater disarmament of the United States than of the Soviet Union, even assuming considerable progress in building up the strength of the free world in conventional forces and weapons. It might be accepted by the Soviet Union as part of a deliberate design to move against Western Europe and other areas of strategic importance with conventional forces and weapons. In this event, the United States would find itself at war, having previously disarmed itself in its most important weapon, and would be engaged in a race to redevelop atomic weapons.

This seems to indicate that for the time being the United States and other free countries would have to insist on concurrent agreement on the control of non-atomic forces and weapons and perhaps on the other elements of a general settlement, notably peace treaties with Germany, Austria, and Japan and the withdrawal of Soviet influence from the satellites. If, contrary to our expectations, the Soviet Union should accept agreements promising effective control of atomic energy and conventional armaments, without any other changes in Soviet policies, we would have to consider very carefully whether we could accept such agreements. It is unlikely that this problem will arise.

To the extent that the United States and the rest of the free world succeed in so building up their strength in conventional forces and weapons that a Soviet attack with similar forces could be thwarted or held, we will gain increased flexibility and can seek agreements on the various issues in any order, as they become negotiable.

In the third place, negotiation will play a part in the building up of the strength of the free world, apart from the ideological strength discussed above. This is most evident in the problems of Germany, Austria and Japan. In the process of building up strength, it may be desirable for the free nations, without the Soviet Union, to conclude separate arrangements with Japan, Western Germany, and Austria which would enlist the energies and resources of these countries in support of the free world. This will be difficult unless it has been demonstrated by attempted negotiation with the Soviet Union that the Soviet Union is not prepared to accept treaties of peace which would leave these countries free, under adequate safeguards, to participate in the United Nations and in regional or broader associations of states consistent with the United Nations' Charter and providing security and adequate opportunities for the peaceful development of their political and economic life.

This demonstrates the importance, from the point of view of negotiation as well as for its relationship to the building up of the strength of the free world (see Section D below), of the problem of closer association—on a regional or a broader basis—among the free countries.

In conclusion, negotiation is not a possible separate course of action but rather a means of gaining support for a program of building strength, of recording, where necessary and desirable, progress in the cold war, and of facilitating further progress while helping to minimize the risks of war. Ultimately, it is our objective to negotiate a settlement with the Soviet Union (or a successor state or states) on which the world can place reliance as an enforceable instrument of peace. But it is important to emphasize that such a settlement can only record the progress which the free world will have made in creating a political and economic system in the world so successful that the frustration of the Kremlin's design for world domination will be complete. The analysis in the following sections indicates that the building of such a system requires expanded and accelerated programs for the carrying out of current policies.

A. *The first course—continuation of current policies, with current and currently projected programs for carrying out these policies.*

   1. *Military aspects.* On the basis of current programs, the United States has a large potential military capability but an actual capability which, though improving, is declining relative to the U.S.S.R., particularly in light of its probable fission bomb capability and possible thermonuclear bomb capability. The same holds true for the free world as a whole relative to the Soviet world as a whole. If war breaks out in 1950 or in the next few years, the United States and its allies, apart from a powerful atomic blow, will be compelled to conduct delaying actions, while building up their strength for a general offensive. A frank evaluation of the requirements, to defend the United States and its vital interests and to support a vigorous initiative in the cold war, on the one hand, and of present capabilities, on the other, indicates that there is a sharp and growing disparity between them.

   A review of Soviet policy shows that the military capabilities, actual and potential, of the United States and the rest of the free world, together with the apparent determination of the free world to resist further Soviet expansion, have not induced the Kremlin to relax its pressures generally or to give up the initiative in the cold war. On the contrary, the Soviet Union has consistently pursued a bold foreign policy, modified only when its probing revealed a determination and an ability of the free world to resist encroachment upon it. The relative military capabilities of the free world are declining, with the result that its determination to resist may also decline and that the security of the United States and the free world as a whole will be jeopardized.

From the military point of view, the actual and potential capabilities of the United States, given a continuation of current and projected programs, will become less and less effective as a war deterrent. Improvement of the state of readiness will become more and more important not only to inhibit the launching of war by the Soviet Union but also to support a national policy designed to reverse the present ominous trends in international relations. A building up of the military capabilities of the United States and the free world is a precondition to the achievement of the objectives outlined in this report and to the protection of the United States against disaster.

Fortunately, the United States military establishment has been developed into a unified and effective force as a result of the policies laid down by the Congress and the vigorous carrying out of these policies by the Administration in the fields of both organization and economy. It is, therefore, a base upon which increased strength can be rapidly built with maximum efficiency and economy.

2. *Political aspects.* The Soviet Union is pursuing the initiative in the conflict with the free world. Its atomic capabilities, together with its successes in the Far East, have led to an increasing confidence on its part and to an increasing nervousness in Western Europe and the rest of the free world. We cannot be sure, of course, how vigorously the Soviet Union will pursue its initiative, nor can we be sure of the strength or weakness of the other free countries in reacting to it. There are, however, ominous signs of further deterioration in the Far East. There are also some indications that a decline in morale and confidence in Western Europe may be expected. In particular, the situation in Germany is unsettled. Should the belief or suspicion spread that the free nations are not now able to prevent the Soviet Union from taking, if it chooses, the military actions outlined in Chapter V, the determination of the free countries to resist probably would lessen and there would be an increasing temptation for them to seek a position of neutrality.

Politically, recognition of the military implications of a continuation of present trends will mean that the United States and especially other free countries will tend to shift to the defensive, or to follow a dangerous policy of bluff, because the maintenance of a firm initiative in the cold war is closely related to aggregate strength in being and readily available.

This is largely a problem of the incongruity of the current actual capabilities of the free world and the threat to it, for the free world has an economic and military potential far superior to the potential of the Soviet Union and its satellites. The shadow of Soviet force falls darkly on Western Europe and Asia and supports a policy of encroachment. The free world lacks adequate means—in the form of forces in being—to thwart such expansion locally. The United States will therefore be confronted more frequently with the dilemma of reacting totally to a limited extension of Soviet control or of not reacting at all (except with ineffectual protests and half measures). Continuation of present trends is likely to lead, therefore, to a gradual withdrawal under the direct or indirect pressure of the Soviet Union, until we discover one day that we have sacrificed positions of vital interest. In other words, the United States would have chosen, by lack of the necessary decisions and actions, to fall back to isolation in the Western Hemisphere. This course would at best result in only a relatively brief truce and would be ended either by our capitulation or by a defensive war—on unfavorable terms from unfavorable positions—against a Soviet Empire comprising all or most of Eurasia. (See Section B.)

3. *Economic and social aspects.* As was pointed out in Chapter VI, the present foreign economic policies and programs of the United States will not produce a solution to the problem of international economic equilibrium, notably the problem of the dollar gap, and will not create an economic base conducive to political stability in many important free countries.

The European Recovery Program has been successful in assisting the restoration and expansion of production in Western Europe and has been a major factor in checking the dry rot of Communism in Western Europe. However, little progress has been made toward the resumption by Western Europe of a position of influence in world affairs commensurate with its potential strength. Progress in this direction will require integrated political, economic and military policies and programs, which are supported by the United States and the Western European countries and which will probably require a deeper participation by the United States than has been contemplated.

The Point IV Program and other assistance programs will not adequately supplement, as now projected, the efforts of other important countries to develop effective institutions, to improve the administration of their affairs, and to achieve a sufficient measure of economic development. The moderate regimes now in power in many countries, like India, Indonesia, Pakistan, and the Philippines, will probably be unable to restore or retain their popular support and authority unless they are assisted in bringing about a more rapid improvement of the economic and social structure than present programs will make possible.

The Executive Branch is now undertaking a study of the problem of the United States balance of payments and of the measures which might be taken by the United States to assist in establishing international economic equilibrium. This is a very important project and work on it should have a high priority. However, unless such an economic program is matched and supplemented by an equally far-sighted and vigorous political and military program, we will not be successful in checking and rolling back the Kremlin's drive.

4. *Negotiation*. In short, by continuing along its present course the free world will not succeed in making effective use of its vastly superior political, economic, and military potential to build a tolerable state of order among nations. On the contrary, the political, economic, and military situation of the free world is already unsatisfactory and will become less favorable unless we act to reverse present trends.

This situation is one which militates against successful negotiations with the Kremlin—for the terms of agreements on important pending issues would reflect present realities and would therefore be unacceptable, if not disastrous, to the United States and the rest of the free world. Unless a decision had been made and action undertaken to build up the strength, in the broadest sense, of the United States and the free world, an attempt to negotiate a general settlement on terms acceptable to us would be ineffective and probably long drawn out, and might thereby seriously delay the necessary measures to build up our strength.

This is true despite the fact that the United States now has the capability of delivering a powerful blow against the Soviet Union in the event of war, for one of the present realities is that the United States is not prepared to threaten the use of our present atomic superiority to coerce the Soviet Union into acceptable agreements. In light of present trends, the Soviet Union will not withdraw and the only conceivable basis for a general settlement would be spheres of influence and of no influence—a "settlement" which the Kremlin could readily exploit to its great advantage. The idea that Germany or Japan or other important areas can exist as islands of neutrality in a divided world is unreal, given the Kremlin design for world domination.

B. *The second course—isolation*

Continuation of present trends, it has been shown above, will lead progressively to the withdrawal of the United States from most of its present commitments in Europe and Asia and to our isolation in the Western Hemisphere and its approaches. This would result not from a conscious decision but from a failure to take the actions necessary to bring our capabilities into line with our commitments and thus to a withdrawal under pressure. This pressure might come from our present Allies, who will tend to seek other "solutions" unless they have confidence in our determination to accelerate our efforts to build a successfully functioning political and economic system in the free world.

There are some who advocate a deliberate decision to isolate ourselves. Superficially, this has some attractiveness as a course of action, for it appears to bring our commitments and capabilities into harmony by reducing the former and by concentrating our present, or perhaps even reduced military expenditures on the defense of the United States.

This argument overlooks the relativity of capabilities. With the United States in an isolated position, we would have to face the probability that the Soviet Union would quickly dominate most of Eurasia, probably without meeting armed resistance. It would thus acquire a potential far superior to our own, and would promptly proceed to develop this potential with the purpose of eliminating our power, which would, even in isolation, remain as a challenge to it and as an obstacle to the imposition of its kind of order in the world. There is no way to make ourselves inoffensive to the Kremlin except by complete submission to its will. Therefore isolation would in the end condemn us to capitulate or to fight alone and on the defensive, with drastically limited offensive and retaliatory capabilities in comparison with the Soviet Union. (These are the only possibilities, unless we are prepared to risk the future on the hazard that the Soviet Empire, because of over-extension or other reasons, will spontaneously destroy itself from within.)

The argument also overlooks the imponderable, but nevertheless drastic, effects on our belief in ourselves and in our way of life of a deliberate decision to isolate ourselves. As the Soviet Union came to dominate free countries, it is clear that many Americans would feel a deep sense of responsibility and guilt for having abandoned their former friends and allies. As the Soviet Union mobilized the resources of Eurasia, increased its relative military capabilities, and heightened its threat to our security, some would be tempted to accept "peace" on its terms, while many would seek to defend the United States by creating a regimented system which would permit the assignment of a tremendous part of our resources to defense. Under such a state of affairs our national morale would be corrupted and the integrity and vitality of our system subverted.

Under this course of action, there would be no negotiation, unless on the Kremlin's terms, for we would have given up everything of importance.

It is possible that at some point in the course of isolation, many Americans would come to favor a surprise attack on the Soviet Union and the area under its control, in a desperate attempt to alter decisively the balance of power by an overwhelming blow with modern weapons of mass destruction. It appears unlikely that the Soviet Union would wait for such an attack before launching one of its own. But even if it did and even if our attack were successful, it is clear that the United States would face appalling tasks in establishing a tolerable state of order among nations after such a war and after Soviet occupation of all or most of Eurasia for some years. These tasks appear so enormous and success so unlikely that reason dictates an attempt to achieve our objectives by other means.

C. The third course—war

Some Americans favor a deliberate decision to go to war against the Soviet Union in the near future. It goes without saying that the idea of "preventive" war—in the sense of a military attack not provoked by a military attack upon us or our allies—is generally unacceptable to Americans. Its supporters argue that since the Soviet Union is in fact at war with the free world now and that since the failure of the Soviet Union to use all-out military force is explainable on grounds of expediency, we are at war and should conduct ourselves accordingly. Some further argue that the free world is probably unable, except under the crisis of war, to mobilize and direct its resources to the checking and rolling back of the Kremlin's drive for world dominion. This is a powerful argument in the light of history, but the considerations against war are so compelling that the free world must demonstrate that this argument is wrong. The case for war is premised on the assumption that the United States could launch and sustain an attack of sufficient impact to gain a decisive advantage for the free world in a long war and perhaps to win an early decision.

The ability of the United States to launch effective offensive operations is now limited to attack with atomic weapons. A powerful blow could be delivered upon the Soviet Union, but it is estimated that these operations alone would not force or induce the Kremlin to capitulate and that the Kremlin would still be able to use the forces under its control to dominate most or all of Eurasia. This would probably mean a long and difficult struggle during which the free institutions of Western Europe and many freedom-loving people would be destroyed and the regenerative capacity of Western Europe dealt a crippling blow.

Apart from this, however, a surprise attack upon the Soviet Union, despite the provocativeness of recent Soviet behavior, would be repugnant to many Americans. Although the American people would probably rally in support of the war effort, the shock of responsibility for a surprise attack would be morally corrosive. Many would doubt that it was a "just war" and that all reasonable possibilities for a peaceful settlement had been explored in good faith. Many more, proportionately, would hold such views in other countries, particularly in Western Europe and particularly after Soviet occupation, if only because the Soviet Union would liquidate articulate opponents. It would, therefore, be difficult after such a war to create a satisfactory international order among nations. Victory in such a war would have brought us little if at all closer to victory in the fundamental ideological conflict.

These considerations are no less weighty because they are imponderable, and they rule out an attack unless it is demonstrably in the nature of a counter-attack to a blow which is on its way or about to be delivered. (The military advantages of landing the first blow become increasingly important with modern weapons, and this is a fact which requires us to be on the alert in order to strike with our full weight as soon as we are attacked, and, if possible, before the Soviet blow is actually delivered.) If the argument of Chapter IV is accepted, it follows that there is no "easy" solution and that the only sure victory lies in the frustration of the Kremlin design by the steady development of the moral and material strength of the free world and its projection into the Soviet world in such a way as to bring about an internal change in the Soviet system.

D. *The remaining course of action—a rapid build-up of political,*
   economic, and military strength in the Free World

A more rapid build-up of political, economic, and military strength and thereby of confidence in the free world than is now contemplated is the only course which is consistent with progress toward achieving our fundamental purpose. The frustration of the Kremlin design requires the free world to develop a successfully functioning political and economic system and a vigorous political offensive against the Soviet Union. These, in turn, require an adequate military shield under which they can develop. It is necessary to have the military power to deter, if possible, Soviet expansion, and to defeat, if necessary, aggressive Soviet or Soviet-directed actions of a limited or total character. The potential strength of the free world is great; its ability to develop these military capabilities and its will to resist Soviet expansion will be determined by the wisdom and will with which it undertakes to meet its political and economic problems.

1. *Military aspects*. It has been indicated in Chapter VI that U.S. military capabilities are strategically more defensive in nature than offensive and are more potential than actual. It is evident, from an analysis of the past and of the trend of weapon development, that there is now and will be in the future no absolute defense. The history of war also indicates that a favorable decision can only be achieved through offensive action. Even a defensive strategy, if it is to be successful, calls not only for defensive forces to hold vital positions while mobilizing and preparing for the offensive, but also for offensive forces to attack the enemy and keep him off balance.

The two fundamental requirements which must be met by forces in being or readily available are support of foreign policy and protection against disaster. To meet the second requirement, the forces in being or readily available must be able, at a minimum, to perform certain basic tasks:

a. To defend the Western Hemisphere and essential allied areas in order that their war-making capabilities can be developed;

b. To provide and protect a mobilization base while the offensive forces required for victory are being built up;

c. To conduct offensive operations to destroy vital elements of the Soviet war-making capacity, and to keep the enemy off balance until the full offensive strength of the United States and its allies can be brought to bear;

d. To defend and maintain the lines of communication and base areas necessary to the execution of the above tasks; and

e. To provide such aid to allies as is essential to the execution of their role in the above tasks.

In the broadest terms, the ability to perform these tasks requires a build-up of military strength by the United States and its allies to a point at which the combined strength will be superior for at least these tasks, both initially and throughout a war, to the forces that can be brought to bear by the Soviet Union and its satellites. In specific terms, it is not essential to match item for item with the Soviet Union, but to provide an adequate defense against air attack on the United States and Canada and an adequate defense against air and surface attack on the United Kingdom and Western Europe, Alaska, the Western Pacific, Africa, and the Near and Middle East, and on the long lines of communication to these areas. Furthermore, it is mandatory that in building up our strength, we enlarge upon our technical superiority by an accelerated exploitation of the scientific potential of the United States and our allies.

Forces of this size and character are necessary not only for protection against disaster but also to support our foreign policy. In fact, it can be argued that larger forces in being and readily available are necessary to inhibit a would-be aggressor than to provide the nucleus of strength and the mobilization base on which the tremendous forces required for victory can be built. For example, in both World Wars I and II the ultimate victors had the strength, in the end, to win though they had not had the strength in being or readily available to prevent the outbreak of war. In part, at least, this was because they had not had the military strength on which to base a strong foreign policy. At any rate, it is clear that a substantial and rapid building up of strength in the free world is necessary to support a firm policy intended to check and to roll back the Kremlin's drive for world domination.

Moreover, the United States and the other free countries do not now have the forces in being and readily available to defeat local Soviet moves with local action, but must accept reverses or make these local moves the occasion for war—for which we are not prepared. This situation makes for great uneasiness among our allies, particularly in Western Europe, for whom total war means, initially, Soviet occupation. Thus, unless our combined strength is rapidly increased, our allies will tend to become increasingly reluctant to support a firm foreign policy on our part and increasingly anxious to seek other solutions, even though they are aware that appeasement means defeat. An important advantage in adopting the fourth course of action lies in its psychological impact—the revival of confidence and hope in the future. It is recognized, of course, that any announcement of the recommended course of action could be exploited by the Soviet Union in its peace campaign and would have adverse psychological effects in certain parts of the free world until the necessary increase in strength had been achieved. Therefore, in any announcement of policy and in the character of the measures adopted, emphasis should be given to the essentially defensive character and care should be taken to minimize, so far as possible, unfavorable domestic and foreign reactions.

2. *Political and economic aspects.* The immediate objectives—to the achievement of which such a build-up of strength is a necessary though not a sufficient condition—are a renewed initiative in the cold war and a situation to which the Kremlin would find it expedient to accommodate itself, first by relaxing tensions and pressures and then by gradual withdrawal. The United States cannot alone provide the resources required for such a build-up of strength. The other free countries must carry their part of the burden, but their ability and determination to do it will depend on the action the United States takes to develop its own strength and on the adequacy of its foreign political and economic policies. Improvement in political and economic con-

ditions in the free world, as has been emphasized above, is necessary as a basis for building up the will and the means to resist and for dynamically affirming the integrity and vitality of our free and democratic way of life on which our ultimate victory depends.

At the same time, we should take dynamic steps to reduce the power and influence of the Kremlin inside the Soviet Union and other areas under its control. The objective would be the establishment of friendly regimes not under Kremlin domination. Such action is essential to engage the Kremlin's attention, keep it off balance and force an increased expenditure of Soviet resources in counter-action. In other words, it would be the current Soviet cold war technique used against the Soviet Union.

A program for rapidly building up strength and improving political and economic conditions will place heavy demands on our courage and intelligence; it will be costly; it will be dangerous. But half-measures will be more costly and more dangerous, for they will be inadequate to prevent and may actually invite war. Budgetary considerations will need to be subordinated to the stark fact that our very independence as a nation may be at stake.

A comprehensive and decisive program to win the peace and frustrate the Kremlin design should be so designed that it can be sustained for as long as necessary to achieve our national objectives. It would probably involve:

(1) The development of an adequate political and economic framework for the achievement of our long-range objectives.

(2) A substantial increase in expenditures for military purposes adequate to meet the requirements for the tasks listed in Section D-1.

(3) A substantial increase in military assistance programs, designed to foster cooperative efforts, which will adequately and efficiently meet the requirements of our allies for the tasks referred to in Section D-1-e.

(4) Some increase in economic assistance programs and recognition of the need to continue these programs until their purposes have been accomplished.

(5) A concerted attack on the problem of the United States balance of payments, along the lines already approved by the President.

(6) Development of programs designed to build and maintain confidence among other peoples in our strength and resolution, and to wage overt psychological warfare calculated to encourage mass defections from Soviet allegiance and to frustrate the Kremlin design in other ways.

(7) Intensification of affirmative and timely measures and operations by

covert means in the fields of economic warfare and political and psychological warfare with a view to fomenting and supporting unrest and revolt in selected strategic satellite countries.

(8) Development of internal security and civilian defense programs.

(9) Improvement and intensification of intelligence activities.

(10) Reduction of Federal expenditures for purposes other than defense and foreign assistance, if necessary by the deferment of certain desirable programs.

(11) Increased taxes.

Essential as prerequisites to the success of this program would be (a) consultations with Congressional leaders designed to make the program the object of non-partisan legislative support, and (b) a presentation to the public of a full explanation of the facts and implications of present international trends.

The program will be costly, but it is relevant to recall the disproportion between the potential capabilities of the Soviet and non-Soviet worlds (cf. Chapter V and VI). The Soviet Union is currently devoting about 40 percent of available resources (gross national product plus reparations, equal in 1949 to about $65 billion) to military expenditures (14 percent) and to investment (26 percent), much of which is in war-supporting industries. In an emergency the Soviet Union could increase the allocation of resources to these purposes to about 50 percent, or by one-fourth.

The United States is currently devoting about 22 percent of its gross national product ($225 billion in 1949) to military expenditures (6 percent), foreign assistance (2 percent), and investment (14 percent), little of which is in war-supporting industries. (As was pointed out in Chapter V, the "fighting value" obtained per dollar of expenditure by the Soviet Union considerably exceeds that obtained by the United States, primarily because of the extremely low military and civilian living standards in the Soviet Union.) In an emergency the United States could devote upward of 50 percent of its gross national product to these purposes (as it did during the last war), an increase of several times present expenditures for direct and indirect military purposes and foreign assistance.

From the point of view of the economy as a whole, the program might not result in a real decrease in the standard of living, for the economic effects of the program might be to increase the gross national product by more than the amount being absorbed for additional military and foreign assistance purposes. One of the most significant lessons of our Word War II experience was that the American economy, when it operates at a level approaching full efficiency, can provide enormous resources for purposes other than civilian consumption while simultaneously providing a high standard of living. After allowing for price changes, personal consumption expenditures rose by about one-fifth between 1939 and 1944, even though the economy had in the meantime increased the amount of resources going into Government use by $60–$65 billion (in 1939 prices).

This comparison between the potentials of the Soviet Union and the United States also holds true for the Soviet world and the free world and is of fundamental importance in considering the course of action open to the United States.

The comparison gives renewed emphasis to the fact that the problems faced by the free countries in their efforts to build a successfully functioning system lie not so much in the field of economics as in the field of politics. The building of such a system may require more rapid progress toward the closer association of the free countries in harmony with the concept of the United Nations. It is clear that our long-range objectives require a strengthened United Nations, or a successor organization, to which the world can look for the maintenance of peace and order in a system based on freedom and justice. It also seems clear that a unifying ideal of this kind might awaken and arouse the latent spiritual energies of free men everywhere and obtain their enthusiastic support for a positive program for peace going far beyond the frustration of the Kremlin design and opening vistas to the future that would outweigh short-run sacrifices.

The threat to the free world involved in the development of the Soviet Union's atomic and other capabilities will rise steadily and rather rapidly. For the time being, the United States possesses a marked atomic superiority over the Soviet Union which, together with the potential capabilities of the United States and other free countries in other forces and weapons, inhibits aggressive Soviet action. This provides an opportunity for the United States, in cooperation with other free countries, to launch a build-up of strength which will support a firm policy directed to the frustration of the Kremlin design. The immediate goal of our efforts to build a successfully functioning political and economic system in the free world backed by adequate military strength is to postpone and avert the disastrous situation which, in light of the Soviet Union's probable fission bomb capability and possible thermonuclear bomb capability, might arise in 1954 on a continuation of our present programs. By acting promptly and vigorously in such a way that this date is, so to speak, pushed into the future, we would permit time for the process of accommodation, withdrawal and frustration to produce the necessary changes in the Soviet system. Time is short, however, and the risks of war attendant upon a decision to build up strength will steadily increase the longer we defer it.

Conclusions and Recommendations

CONCLUSIONS

The foregoing analysis indicates that the probable fission bomb capability and possible thermonuclear homb capability of the Soviet Union have greatly intensified the Soviet threat to the security of the United States. This threat is of the same character as that described in NSC 20/4 (approved by the President on November 24, 1948) but is more immediate than had previously been estimated. In particular, the United States now faces the contingency that within the next four or five years the Soviet Union will possess the military capability of delivering a surprise atomic attack of such weight that the United States must have substantially increased general air, ground, and sea strength, atomic capabilities, and air and civilian defenses to deter war and to provide reasonable assurance, in the event of war, that it could survive the initial blow and go on to the eventual attainment of its objectives. In turn, this contingency requires the intensification of our efforts in the fields of intelligence and research and development.

Allowing for the immediacy of the danger, the following statement of Soviet threats, contained in NSC 20/4, remains valid:

14. The gravest threat to the security of the United States within the foreseeable future stems from the hostile designs and formidable power of the U.S.S.R., and from the nature of the Soviet system.

15. The political, economic, and psychological warfare which the U.S.S.R. is now waging has dangerous potentialities for weakening the relative world position of the United States and disrupting its traditional institutions by means short of war, unless sufficient resistance is encountered in the policies of this and other non-communist countries.

16. The risk of war with the U.S.S.R. is sufficient to warrant, in common prudence, timely and adequate preparation by the United States.

    a. Even though present estimates indicate that the Soviet leaders probably do not intend deliberate armed action involving the United States at this time, the possibility of such deliberate resort to war cannot be ruled out.

    b. Now and for the foreseeable future there is a continuing danger that war will arise either through Soviet miscalculation of the determination of the United States to use all the means at its command to safeguard its security, through Soviet misinterpretation of our intentions, or through U.S. miscalculation of Soviet reactions to measures which we might take.

17. Soviet domination of the potential power of Eurasia, whether achieved by

armed aggression or by political and subversive means, would be strategically and politically unacceptable to the United States.

18. The capability of the United States either in peace or in the event of war to cope with threats to its security or to gain its objectives would be severely weakened by internal developments, important among which are:

a. Serious espionage, subversion and sabotage, particularly by concerted and well-directed communist activity.

b. Prolonged or exaggerated economic instability.

c. Internal political and social disunity.

d. Inadequate or excessive armament or foreign aid expenditures.

e. An excessive or wasteful usage of our resources in time of peace.

f. Lessening of U.S. prestige and influence through vacillation or appeasement or lack of skill and imagination in the conduct of its foreign policy or by shirking world responsibilities.

g. Development of a false sense of security through a deceptive change in Soviet tactics.

Although such developments as those indicated in paragraph 18 above would severely weaken the capability of the United States and its allies to cope with the Soviet threat to their security, considerable progress has been made since 1948 in laying the foundation upon which adequate strength can now be rapidly built.

The Analysis also confirms that our objectives with respect to the Soviet Union, in time of peace as well as in time of war, as stated in NSC 20/4 (para. 19), are still valid, as are the aims and measures stated therein (paras. 20 and 21). Our current security programs and strategic plans are based upon these objectives, aims, and measures:

19.

a. To reduce the power and influence of the U.S.S.R. to limits which no longer constitute a threat to the peace, national independence and stability of the world family of nations.

b. To bring about a basic change in the conduct of international relations by the government in power in Russia, to conform with the purposes and principles set forth in the U.N. Charter.

In pursuing these objectives, due care must be taken to avoid permanently impairing our economy and the fundamental values and institutions inherent in our way of life.

20. We should endeavor to achieve our general objectives by methods short of war through the pursuit of the following aims:

a. To encourage and promote the gradual retraction of undue Russian power and influence from the present perimeter areas around traditional Russian boundaries and the emergence of the satellite countries as entities independent of the U.S.S.R.

b. To encourage the development among the Russian peoples of attitudes which may help to modify current Soviet behavior and permit a revival of the national life of groups evidencing the ability and determination to achieve and maintain national independence.

c. To eradicate the myth by which people remote from Soviet military influence are held in a position of subservience to Moscow and to cause the world at large to see and understand the true nature of the U.S.S.R. and the Soviet-directed world communist party, and to adopt a logical and realistic attitude toward them.

d. To create situations which will compel the Soviet Government to recognize the practical undesirability of acting on the basis of its present concepts and the necessity of behaving in accordance with precepts of international conduct, as set forth in the purposes and principles of the U.N. Charter.

21. Attainment of these aims requires that the United States:

a. Develop a level of military readiness which can be maintained as long as necessary as a deterrent to Soviet aggression, as indispensable support to our political attitude toward the U.S.S.R., as a source of encouragement to nations resisting Soviet political aggression, and as an adequate basis for immediate military commitments and for rapid mobilization should war prove unavoidable.

b. Assure the internal security of the United States against dangers of sabotage, subversion, and espionage.

c. Maximize our economic potential, including the strengthening of our peacetime economy and the establishment of essential reserves readily available in the event of war.

d. Strengthen the orientation toward the United States of the non-Soviet nations; and help such of those nations as are able and willing to make an important contribution to U.S. security, to increase their economic and political stability and their military capability.

e. Place the maximum strain on the Soviet structure of power and particularly on the relationships between Moscow and the satellite countries.

f. Keep the U.S. public fully informed and cognizant of the threats to our national security so that it will be prepared to support the measures which we must accordingly adopt.

In the light of present and prospective Soviet atomic capabilities, the action which can be taken under present programs and plans, however, becomes dangerously inadequate, in both timing and scope, to accomplish the rapid progress toward the attainment of the United States political, economic, and military objectives which is now imperative.

A continuation of present trends would result in a serious decline in the strength of the free world relative to the Soviet Union and its satellites. This unfavorable trend arises from the inadequacy of current programs and plans rather than from any error in our objectives and aims. These trends lead in the direction of isolation not by deliberate decision but by lack of the necessary basis for a vigorous initiative in the conflict with the Soviet Union.

Our position as the center of power in the free world places a heavy responsibility upon the United States for leadership. We must organize and enlist the energies and resources of the free world in a positive program for peace which will frustrate the Kremlin design for world domination by creating a situation in the free world to which the Kremlin will be compelled to adjust. Without such a cooperative effort, led by the United States, we will have to make gradual withdrawals under pressure until we discover one day that we have sacrificed positions of vital interest.

It is imperative that this trend be reversed by a much more rapid and concerted build-up of the actual strength of both the United States and the other nations of the free world. The analysis shows that this will be costly and will involve significant domestic financial and economic adjustments.

The execution of such a build-up, however, requires that the United States have an affirmative program beyond the solely defensive one of countering the threat posed by the Soviet Union. This program must light the path to peace and order among nations in a system based on freedom and justice, as contemplated in the Charter of the United Nations. Further, it must envisage the political and economic measures with which and the military shield behind which the free world can work to frustrate the Kremlin design by the strategy of the cold war; for every consideration of devotion to our fundamental values and to our national security demands that we achieve our objectives by the strategy of the cold war, building up our military strength in order that it may not have to be used. The only sure victory lies in the frustration of the Kremlin design by the steady development of the moral and material strength of the free world and its projection into the Soviet world in such a way as to bring about an internal change in the Soviet system. Such a positive program—harmonious with our fundamental national purpose and our objectives—is necessary if we are to regain and retain the initiative and to win and hold the necessary popular support and cooperation in the United States and the rest of the free world.

This program should include a plan for negotiation with the Soviet Union, developed and agreed with our allies and which is consonant with our objectives. The United States and its allies, particularly the United Kingdom and France, should always be ready to negotiate with the Soviet Union on terms consistent with our objectives. The present world situation, however, is one which militates against successful negotiations with the Kremlin—for the terms of agreements on important pending issues would reflect present realities and would therefore be unacceptable, if not disastrous, to the United States and the rest of the free world. After a decision and a start on building up the strength of the free world has been made, it might then be desirable for the United States to take an initiative in seeking negotiations in the hope that it might facilitate the process of accommodation by the Kremlin to the new situation. Failing that, the unwillingness of the Kremlin to accept equitable terms or its bad faith in observing them would assist in consolidating popular opinion in the free world in support of the measures necessary to sustain the build-up.

In summary, we must, by means of a rapid and sustained build-up of the political, economic, and military strength of the free world, and by means of an affirmative program intended to wrest the initiative from the Soviet Union, confront it with convincing evidence of the determination and ability of the free world to frustrate the Kremlin design of a world dominated by its will. Such evidence is the only means short of war which eventually may force the Kremlin to abandon its present course of action and to negotiate acceptable agreements on issues of major importance.

The whole success of the proposed program hangs ultimately on recognition by this Government, the American people, and all free peoples, that the cold war is in fact a real war in which the survival of the free world is at stake. Essential prerequisites to success are consultations with Congressional leaders designed to make the program the object of non-partisan legislative support, and a presentation to the public of a full explanation of the facts and implications of the present international situation. The prosecution of the program will require of us all the ingenuity, sacrifice, and unity demanded by the vital importance of the issue and the tenacity to persevere until our national objectives have been attained.

RECOMMENDATIONS

That the President:

a. Approve the foregoing Conclusions.
b. Direct the National Security Council, under the continuing direction of the President, and with the participation of other Departments and Agencies as appropriate, to coordinate and insure the implementation of the Conclusions herein on an urgent and continuing basis for as long as necessary to achieve our objectives. For this purpose, representatives of the member Departments and Agencies, the Joint Chiefs of Staff or their deputies, and other Departments and Agencies as required should be constituted as a revised and strengthened staff organization under the National Security Council to develop coordinated programs for consideration by the National Security Council.

INDEX

Arthur Rosenberg
Democ & Socialism
1939